Lecture Notes of the Institute for Computer Sciences, Social Informatics and Telecommunications Engineering   505

The LNICST series publishes ICST's conferences, symposia and workshops.

LNICST reports state-of-the-art results in areas related to the scope of the Institute.

The type of material published includes

- Proceedings (published in time for the respective event)
- Other edited monographs (such as project reports or invited volumes)

LNICST topics span the following areas:

- General Computer Science
- E-Economy
- E-Medicine
- Knowledge Management
- Multimedia
- Operations, Management and Policy
- Social Informatics
- Systems

Ao Li · Yao Shi · Liang Xi

Editors

6GN for Future Wireless Networks

5th EAI International Conference, 6GN 2022
Harbin, China, December 17–18, 2022
Proceedings, Part II

Editors
Ao Li
Harbin University of Science and Technology
Harbin, China

Yao Shi
Harbin Institute of Technology
Shenzhen, China

Liang Xi
Harbin University of Science and Technology
Harbin, China

ISSN 1867-8211 ISSN 1867-822X (electronic)
Lecture Notes of the Institute for Computer Sciences, Social Informatics
and Telecommunications Engineering
ISBN 978-3-031-36013-8 ISBN 978-3-031-36014-5 (eBook)
https://doi.org/10.1007/978-3-031-36014-5

This Springer imprint is published by the registered company Springer Nature Switzerland AG
The registered company address is: Gewerbestrasse 11, 6330 Cham, Switzerland

Preface

We are delighted to introduce the proceedings of the 5th EAI International Conference on 6G for Future Wireless Networks (6GN 2022). This conference brought together researchers, developers, and practitioners around the world who are leveraging and developing 6G technology for a smarter cellular network with spectacular speeds and almost non-existent latency, extreme connectivity and sensing, comprehensive and reliable coverage, and unparalleled energy efficiency. The theme of 6GN 2022 was "6G for Future Wireless Networks".

The technical program of 6GN 2022 consisted of 60 full papers which cover multiple technical fields such as wireless communication networks, edge computing, and artificial intelligence. The conference tracks were: Track 1 - Resource Allocation for 6G Networks; Track 2 - Security and Privacy for 6G Networks; Track 3 - Big data mining and pattern analysis techniques for 6G Networks; Track 4 - Artificial intelligent techniques for 6G Networks; Track 5 - Mobile Edge Computing for 6G Networks; and Track 6 - Unmanned Aerial Vehicle Communication for 6G Networks. Aside from the high-quality technical paper presentations, the technical program also featured two keynote speeches. The two keynote speeches were from Xinwang Liu from National University of Defense Technology (NUDT), China and Yong Wang from Harbin Institute of Technology (HIT), China.

Coordination with the Steering Chair, Imrich Chlamtac, was essential for the success of the conference. We sincerely appreciate his constant guidance and all the support from the Steering Committee. It was also a great pleasure to work with the excellent Organizing Committee led by General Chair Deyun Chen, and Co-Chairs Emad Alsusa and Gongliang Liu. In particular, we offer up our thanks to the Technical Program Committee led by Ao Li, Yao Shi, and Liang Xi, who completed the peer-review process of technical papers and made a high-quality technical program. We are also grateful to Conference Manager Ivana Bujdakova for her support and to all the authors who submitted their papers to the 6GN 2022 conference.

We strongly believe that the 6GN 2022 conference provided a good forum for all researchers, developers, and practitioners to discuss all science and technology aspects that are relevant to 6G networks. We also expect that the future 6GN conference will be as successful and stimulating, as indicated by the contributions presented in this volume.

Ao Li
Yao Shi
Liang Xi

Organization

Steering Committee

Imrich Chlamtac   University of Trento, Italy

Organizing Committee

General Chair

Deyun Chen   Harbin University of Science and Technology, China

General Co-chairs

Emad Alsusa   University of Manchester, UK
Gongliang Liu   Harbin Institute of Technology, China

TPC Chair and Co-chairs

Ao Li   Harbin University of Science and Technology, China
Yao Shi   Harbin Institute of Technology, China
Liang Xi   Harbin University of Science and Technology, China
Ruofei Ma   Harbin Institute of Technology, China

Sponsorship and Exhibit Chair

Ao Li   Harbin University of Science and Technology, China

Local Chairs

Yuan Cheng   Harbin University of Science and Technology, China
Shuo Shi   Harbin Institute of Technology, China

Workshops Chair

Qiang Guan   Kent State University, USA

Publicity and Social Media Chair

Xiaomeng Wang   Harbin Institute of Technology, China

Publications Chairs

Emad Alusa   University of Manchester, UK
Shibiao Xu   Beijing University of Posts and
                                       Telecommunications, China

Web Chair

Hailong Jiang   Kent State University, USA

Posters and PhD Track Chairs

Wanlong Zhao   Harbin Institute of Technology, China
Song Li   Harbin University of Science and Technology,
                                       China

Panels Chairs

Mohammed W. Baidas   Kuwait University, Kuwait
Jiguang Zhang   Institute of Automation, Chinese Academy of
                                       Sciences, China

Demos Chairs

Jingchao Li   Shanghai Dianji University, China
Xinlu Li   Huizhou Engineering Vocational College, China

Tutorials Chairs

Hailu Yang   Harbin University of Science and Technology,
                                       China
Jianyue Zhu   Nanjing University of Information Science and
                                       Technology, China

Contents – Part II

Mobile Edge Computing for 6G Networks

Unmanned Aerial Vehicle Communication for 6G Networks

Contents – Part I

Security and Privacy for 6G Networks

Big Data Mining and Pattern Analysis Techniques for 6G Networks

Artificial Intelligent Techniques for 6G Networks

Dual-Point Side-Fed Circularly Polarized Microstrip Antenna Design

Shiyuan Lv and Yao Shi$^{(\boxtimes)}$

Harbin Institute of Technology, Shenzhen 518000, Guangdong, China
22S152074@stu.hit.edu.cn, shiyao@hit.edu.cn

Abstract. With the rapid development of wireless communication technology today, circularly polarized antennas are favored by researchers for their anti-interference and anti-fading properties. However, researchers have not treated circularly polarized microstrip antennae with multiple feed points in much detail. This paper aims to show different ways to design a dual-point side-fed circularly polarized microstrip antenna in HFSS. A novel approach to combining the square patch antenna model and the feeder network is proposed, which uses two vertically bent microstrip lines with 1/4 impedance converters to connect the feeder network and the midpoint of the two adjacent sides of the square patch antenna. The feeder network is a 3 dB directional coupler operating at 2.4 GHz and outputs two resonant modes with equal orthogonal spokes and a phase difference of 90°. The parameters are adjusted by the HFSS simulation to make the model conform to the characteristics of a circularly polarized microstrip antenna. The simulation results demonstrate that the proposed structure of circularly polarized microstrip antenna obtained by double-point side feed is simple and the performance is stable and robust.

Keywords: Circularly Polarized Antenna · Double feed · Directional coupler

1 Introduction

The idea of microstrip antennas dates back to the 1950s, from a scientist named Deschamps. Although the concept was published, there was not much development activity for microstrip antennas for the next 15 years or so due to the lack of good microwave substrates [1]. It was not until the early 1970s that the demand for thin, conformal antennas for missiles and spacecraft contributed to the rapid development of microstrip antennas. With the advent of microwave transistors and other active devices, microstrip lines became popular. Compared with common antennas, microstrip antennas have excellent performance, are more compact and beautiful, and are ideal for commercial applications, while they are

This paper is supported by National Natural Science Foundation of China (NSFC) under grant No. 62201174.

A. Li et al. (Eds.): 6GN 2022, LNICST 505, pp. 3–19, 2023.
https://doi.org/10.1007/978-3-031-36014-5_1

low cost based on printed circuit technology. Moreover, the microstrip structure antenna is also easier to realize multi-band, dual-polarized, and circularly polarized antennas compared with the traditional structure [2]. Therefore, this paper adopts the microstrip antenna to design the circularly polarized antenna.

The polarization of an antenna is the polarization of the electromagnetic radiation produced through the antenna radiation, which is a special property related to the vector of the electric field that will allow its magnitude and direction to follow the change of time. If the endpoints of the electric field intensity depict an elliptical distribution of the trace in space, that is elliptical polarization; when the long axis of the ellipse is equal to the short axis, it is called circular polarization. Different spin directions can be found for the trace pattern of circular polarization: clockwise is right-hand circular polarization and counterclockwise is left-hand circular polarization. The key to generating circularly polarized waves is to generate two orthogonal equal-spoke, line-polarized waves with a phase difference of about 90° through a feeder unit structure [3,4].

Circularly polarized antennas, as a key technology in wireless communication systems, have many advantages compared to wire-polarized antennas. Circularly polarized antennas reflect waves in the opposite direction of rotation when incident on a plane or sphere, which can effectively resist the interference of rain and fog weather. Moreover, any polarization wave can be decomposed into two circularly polarized waves with opposite rotation directions, which has an absolute advantage in electronic reconnaissance and countermeasure fields. At the same time, the orthogonality of the circular polarization antenna makes the left circular polarization antenna and right circular polarization antenna repel each other, and this characteristic is used in radar classification work and electronic countermeasures [5]. Therefore, the design of circularly polarized antennas deserves great attention.

1.1   Related Work

The existing body of research on circular polarization shows that single-feed and multi-feed methods are the most representative ways to achieve circular polarization. The single-fed circularly polarized antenna usually uses tangential or other means of perturbation to achieve circular polarization, while the multi-fed circularly polarized antenna uses a power distribution network to generate two equal-amplitude orthogonal excitations and a 1/4-wavelength delay line to achieve a 90° phase difference between the two modes.

Single Feed Point Circularly Polarized Microstrip Antenna. By introducing a slight perturbation in a patch of a specific shape, two resonant modes can be excited so that a circularly polarized wave can be realized without an external network and with only one feed source [6]. One method is to truncate the diagonal of the two diagonals, like a linearly polarized patch, with the antenna feeding along the center line [7]; the other method is to have one side of the antenna moderately longer than the other, creating a nearly square patch that feeds at the corner of the antenna or along the corresponding diagonal [8]. The feed excites the electric field below the patch, and the signal injected by the feed tends to propagate in one direction guided by the transmission line formed by the patch. Due to the different geometry of the patch, its resonant frequency is slightly shifted. To achieve circular polarization, the amplitudes of the two modes must be equal and the phases must be 90° apart.

The advantage of the single-feed method is simple structure, low cost, and no need to attach a complex feed network, just cutting off or adding a part of the patch can get a circularly polarized wave, easy to miniaturize [9]. Nevertheless, the shortcomings of this method should not be ignored, the antenna designed in this way has a restricted bandwidth and the corresponding polarization performance is poor.

Multi-feed Point Circularly Polarized Microstrip Antenna. The key to the multi-feed point feed approach is to attach a fixed phase value to multiple feed points leading from the microstrip antenna. The feed network must be both reasonably efficient to meet the demand and as cost-effective as possible. Compared with the single-feed method, the advantage of the multi-feed method is that it can significantly enhance the VSWR bandwidth as well as the circularly polarized AR bandwidth, while also overcoming cross-polarization and improving the axis ratio. However, it also has the obvious disadvantages of a complex feeder network that is more costly and comparatively large in size, but not worth mentioning when the budget is sufficient [10]. The multi-feed method is implemented in the form of a 3 dB directional coupler and power divider, which are briefly described below.

3 dB Directional Coupler A four-port device with four terminations. The four quarter-wavelength-long microstrip lines are arranged in a square, and the terminals are all connected to transmission lines with an impedance of 50 Ω [11]. When the system is connected to a matched load on all ports, the signal incident to port 1 is equally distributed to output to port 2 and port 3, and no signal appears on port 4. The signal at port 3 lags the signal at port 2 by 90°. The signal amplitude at ports 2 and 3 depends on the ratio of the shunt and series arm impedances, which usually makes the signals equal. The hybrid interface is completely symmetrical and any port can be used as an input. Assuming the signal is input from port 4, it will again be split between port 2 and port 3, and port 1 is isolated. If port 3 lagged 90° behind port 2 on input 1, port 3 will be 90° ahead on input 4.

T-type Power Dividers. The main component of this feed network is a power divider, with this power divider generates two excitation signals of the same amplitude, between the power divider and the patch with a difference of 1/4 wavelength of two microstrip lines connected to meet the 90° phase difference conditions [12]. Although this construction of the antenna AR bandwidth is wide, in order to achieve circularly polarized waves to a certain degree to limit the relative bandwidth.

Compared with the two ways, the use of a directional coupler allows the microstrip antenna to gain a 90° phase difference over a wider frequency band, and the outputs are isolated from each other, even if the circuit is not symmetrical or the antenna impedance shift will not have an effect, which is difficult with T-type power divider.

Analysis Method. The method of microstrip antenna analysis is to analyze the radiation mechanism of the microstrip antenna by using an equivalent model. In the process of design, the quality and efficiency of the antenna are improved and the cost of research and development is saved. Each analysis method has its own advantages and disadvantages, and there are different analysis methods for microstrip antennas with different structures.

Transmission Line Model. This method treats one radiator unit as a transmission line resonator with unchanged transverse field components so that the microstrip antenna radiation is generated mostly at the open end. The transmission line method is simple and straightforward, and the calculation is small, but there is a requirement for the shape of the patch so there is a limitation in the use [13].

Cavity Model. The main idea of this analysis method is to solve the principal mode of the microstrip antenna, which is regarded as a resonant cavity, according to the boundary conditions, and then utilize the principal mode to calculate various parameters of the antenna. Although compared with the transmission line method, the cavity model method is no longer applicable to a single type of antenna, but there are certain limitations – if the thickness of the antenna's dielectric plate does not satisfy the condition of much smaller than the wavelength, this method will fail [14].

Method of Moment. This method solves the operator equation function by numerical modeling and then uses the solved result to get the current distribution of the antenna. Compared with the first two methods, the method of moments is less restrictive, a variety of antennas can be used to analyze it. The disadvantage is that the matrix operation is computationally intensive, time-consuming, and more expensive [15].

Integral Equation Method. This analysis method is suitable for microstrip antennas with thin dielectric plates, and compared with other methods, the integral equation method has no shape limitation and is more flexible, which is also favored by many researchers. The theoretical basis of the integral equation method is Green's function, and the practical application can select whether to use the exact or approximate Green's function according to the design of the antenna, although there is a certain difference in accuracy, it can successfully decrease the calculation difficulty [16].

The microstrip antenna designed in this paper is utilizing the integral equation method.

1.2 Contribution and Organization

This work studies the performance of the circularly polarized microstrip patch antenna operating at 2.4 GHz and fed by a dual-point side feed in HFSS. To the best of our knowledge, the square patch antenna has not been connected with the four-port directional coupling feed network through microstrip lines of a certain shape. Furthermore, we select the midpoint of two adjacent sides of the square patch as the feed point to ultimately realize the circularly polarized microstrip antenna design.

The rest of this paper is organized as follows. The second section presents the system model. The third section describes the specific structure of the design. The fourth section shows the simulation results using HFSS. The final section concludes the paper.

2 System Model

2.1 Antenna Performance Parameters

Antenna parameters, as a measure of antenna performance, play a vital role in antenna design. Antenna design needs to consider the influence of various parameters and make a balance so that all parameters meet the design specifications as much as possible [17].

Gain. Describe how much power is transmitted to homologous radiation in the direction of the peak radiation.

$$G(\theta, \phi) = \frac{E^2(\theta, \phi)}{E_0^2(\theta, \phi)} \tag{1}$$

$E(\theta, \phi)$ means the field strength in a certain direction. $E_0(\theta, \phi)$ means the field intensity radiated in the same direction by an ideal point source at equal input power [18]. The gain of the antenna is usually the gain in the direction of maximum radiation, so the above equation is also known as:

$$G = \frac{E_{max}^2}{E_0^2} \tag{2}$$

Antenna gain indicates the distribution of radiated energy in all directions, not a simple linear relationship.

Return Loss. The ratio of the reflected power to the incident power at the input of the antenna at the operating frequency.

$$RL = -10lg\frac{P_R}{P_i n} = -20lg|\Gamma_i n| \tag{3}$$

P_R means the reflected power, P_{in} means the incident power, and Γ_{in} means the ratio of the voltage of the incident wave to that of the reflected wave.

The smaller the RL value, the greater the proportion of incident power that is reflected back, and the worse the antenna radiation performance. When $|\Gamma_{in}| = 0$, there is no reflected wave and $RL = \infty$; when $|\Gamma_{in}| = 1$, the incident wave is completely reflected and $RL = 0$. Generally required to meet $RL > 10\,\mathrm{dB}$ in the working band, that is, one-tenth of the incident power is reflected off [19].

Bandwidth. The frequency range in which an antenna can properly radiate or receive energy. Usually, the bandwidth is used to determine what kind of operation the antenna is suitable for, for example, some antennas have very narrow bandwidth and cannot be used for broadband operation. There are relative and absolute bandwidths as follows:

$$Absolute\ Bandwidth = f_{max} - f_{min} \tag{4}$$

$$Relative\ Bandwidth = \frac{f_{max} - f_{min}}{f_0} \tag{5}$$

f_{max} means the high-frequency endpoints of the frequency band, f_{min} means the low, and f_0 means the Center Frequency.

Input Impedance. Ratio between the input voltage and input current.

$$Z_{in} = \frac{U_{in}}{I_{in}} = R_{in} + jX_{in} \tag{6}$$

The input impedance contains both resistance and reactance and varies with frequency. The real part of the impedance represents the power radiated or absorbed; the imaginary part represents the power stored in the nearby field.

VSWR. The degree of matching between the antenna and the transmission line or receiver is called Voltage Standing Wave Ratio (VSWR). VSWR and return loss related as follows:

$$RL = 20lg(10\frac{VSWR+1}{VSWR-1}) \tag{7}$$

VSWR is always greater than or equal to 1. The system is ideally matched when VSWR = 1, but it is difficult to achieve in practical engineering, so VSWR < 2 is typically taken as the criterion for good matching. The power reflected from the antenna on the transmission line interferes with the forward traveling power, hence generating standing voltage waves, which can be evaluated numerically by the value of VSWR [20].

3 Dual-Point Side-Fed Circularly Polarized Microstrip Antenna Design

In this section, the circularly polarized microstrip patch antenna operating at 2.4 GHz and fed by a dual-point side feed is designed. The antenna generates two resonant modes with orthogonal equal spokes and 90° phase difference through a four-port directional coupling feed network, and then connects the square patch antenna and the feed network through a 1/4 impedance converter, and selects the midpoint of two adjacent sides of the square patch as the feed point to ultimately realize the circularly polarized microstrip antenna design. The overall structure is illustrated in Fig. 1.

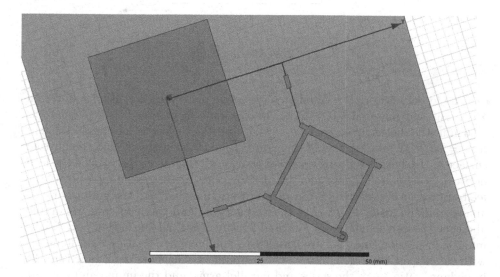

Fig. 1. Overall antenna structure

3.1 Design of the Feeder Network

The feed network structure of the antenna is shown in Fig. 2. This is a four-port directional coupler with port 1 as the input port, port 2 as the pass-through port, port 3 as the coupling port, and port 4 as the isolation port. l_1 is the length of the series arm, l_2 is the length of the shunt arm, w_1 is the width of the series arm, and w_2 is the width of the shunt arm [21].

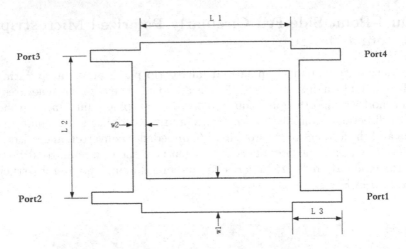

Fig. 2. Feeder network

The feeder network is located on a dielectric plate with dimensions of 87 mm × 87 mm and material FR-4 [22]. The thickness h of the dielectric board is 0.56 mm, the dielectric constant $\varepsilon_r = 4.4$, and the dielectric loss angle tangent $tan\delta = 0.02$. The darker part of the figure is the feeder network, and the bottom surface of the dielectric board is used as the floor by laying copper. When the feed network is simulated independently, all four ports are set as lumped ports, the feed simulation is executed by way of microstrip line feed, and the performance is analyzed individually [23]. Lastly, the feed network and patch antenna are united and then the feed simulation is executed by way of coaxial line feed in port 1. The main transmission lines 1-2 are coupled to the auxiliary transmission lines 4-3 with the help of two branch lines. The coupling coefficient is determined by the impedance ratio $\frac{Z_2}{Z_1}$ of the series and parallel arms, and the inputs and outputs have the same characteristic impedance Z_0. The signal is input from port 1 and output by output port 2 and coupling port 3, and port 4 is the isolated end. In the case of an exact match at input port 1, $S_{11} = 0$, which leads to:

$$\frac{Z_0{}^2}{Z_1} = \frac{Z_0{}^2}{Z_2} - 1 \tag{8}$$

From the scattering matrix of the two-branch line directional coupler, it can be found that:

$$S_{14} = S_{41} = 0 \tag{9}$$

It shows that port 1 and port 4 are isolated from each other. Meanwhile, the phase difference between port 2 and port 3 is fixed at 90°. When the characteristic impedance of the series arm of the coupler $Z_2 = \frac{Z_0}{\sqrt{2}}$ and the characteristic impedance of the parallel arm $Z_1 = Z_0$, the power input to port 1 is output to the square patch antenna by port 2 and port 3 in equal parts, realizing a double-point side feed with orthogonal equal spokes and phase difference of 90°.

The system is fed from the bottom with a coaxial line feed at port 1, and a $50\,\Omega$ grounding resistor is connected at port 4. The coaxial line feed is unrestricted, connecting the outer conductor to the grounding plate, while the inner conductor is connected across the grounding plate to the dielectric substrate and radiating element [24]. The specific parameters of the feeder network design are listed in Table 1.

Table 1. Feeder network parameter values.

Parameters	Values
l_1	17.2 mm
l_2	18.25 mm
l_3	2 mm
w_1	1.775 mm
w_2	1.03 mm
Z_0	$50\,\Omega$
Z_1	$50\,\Omega$
Z_2	$35.35\,\Omega$

3.2   Design of Dual-Point Side-Fed Microstrip Antenna

The patch structure of the antenna is designed as shown in Fig. 3. The midpoint of the two neighboring sides of the square patch with side length l_0 is used as the feed point, and a microstrip line of length $(r_1 + r_2)$ mm, width w_3 microstrip line connected to the feed network. At the same time, there is a 1/4 impedance converter of length lp and width wp in the horizontal direction from the midpoint pp on the microstrip line to achieve the purpose of matching the edge impedance of the patch with the $50\,\Omega$ impedance of the feed network 2 and 3 ports. Let the edge impedance of the antenna be Z_L, the characteristic impedance of 1/4 wavelength impedance converter is Z_T, and the impedance matching condition is $Z_T = \sqrt{Z_0 Z_L}$.

In the design of the microstrip line length and structure, in order to connect the feeder network more accurately, set the distance between the geometric center of the patch and the midpoint of the 2-3 transmission line as d. The geometric relationship between the microstrip line length r_1, r_2 and d can be obtained as follows. And the specific parameters of the chip antenna design are listed in Table 2.

$$r_1 = \frac{\sqrt{2}(d + \frac{l_2}{2}) - l_0}{2} \tag{10}$$

$$r_2 = \frac{\sqrt{2}(d - \frac{l_2}{2})}{2} \tag{11}$$

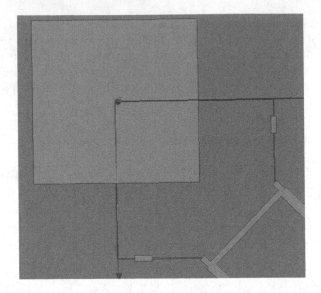

Fig. 3. Patch antenna structure

Table 2. Patch antenna parameter values.

Parameters	Values
l_0	28.4 mm
d	30 mm
r_1	13.16 mm
r_2	14.76 mm
w_3	0.115 mm
pp	3 mm
wp	1 mm
lp	3 mm

4 Simulation Results

The scanning frequency is set to 2.4 GHz with HFSS.

Simulation of Directional Coupler Feeder Network. Firstly the four-port directional coupler feeder network is simulated separately to determine its performance and then the design data is recorded. The design simulation model is shown in Fig. 4. Port 1 in the upper left corner is the input port; port 2 in the upper right corner is the pass-through port; port 4 in the lower left corner is the isolated port; port 3 in the lower right corner is the coupled port. Part of the power input from port 1 is output from the straight-through port, and the other part is coupled to port 3. In the ideal case, there is no power output from the isolated port.

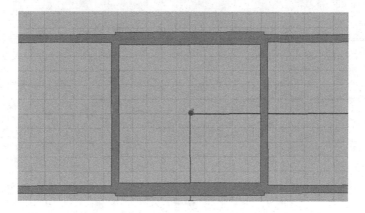

Fig. 4. Feeder network model

The performance of the directional coupler is mainly described by the coupling degree, isolation degree, and input VSWR. The coupling degree reflects the strength of the coupling, ideally, the VSWR is 1 and there is no reflection from the port. When the isolation degree is infinite, it means that there is no power output from the 4-port. The expressions for each performance indicator are as follows.

$$C(coupling\ degree) = 10lg\frac{P_1}{P_3} = 20lg\frac{1}{|S_{31}|}(\text{dB}) \tag{12}$$

P_1 means the input power of port 1, P_2 means the output power of port 2, P_3 means the output power of port 3, P_4 means the input power of port 4. $\frac{P_1}{P_3}$ means Power coupling coefficient, S_31 means transmission coefficient from port 1 to port 3, S_41 means transmission coefficient from port 1 to port 4. S_11 indicates the reflection coefficient of port 1 when the rest of the ports are connected to matching loads.

$$D(isolation\ degree) = 10lg(\frac{P_1}{P_4}) = 20lg\frac{1}{|S_{41}|}(\text{dB}) \tag{13}$$

$$VSWR = \frac{1 + |S_{11}|}{1 - |S_{11}|} \tag{14}$$

It can be seen that the performance parameters of the directional coupler are closely related to the S-parameters, and the S-parameter image should be plotted first to analyze its performance. The following Fig. 5 shows the S-parameter plotting obtained by using HFSS software simulation, and the images of S(1,1), S(2,1), S(3,1), and S(4,1) are obtained by sweeping the frequency setting from 2.2 GHz to 2.7 GHz with a step of 0.01 GHz.

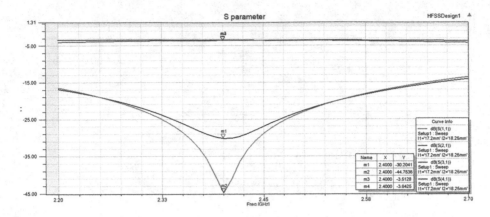

Fig. 5. S-parameter simulation results

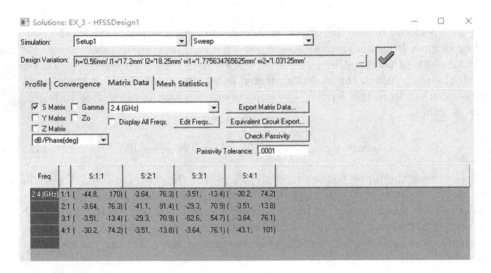

Fig. 6. Phase simulation results

As can be seen from Fig. 6, $S(1,1)$– the resonant frequency of the return loss is 2.4 GHz just identical to the center frequency, meanwhile, $S(2,1)$ and $S(3,1)$ basically coincide, corresponding to the transmission coefficient are about 3 dB, which verify the nature of the output port amplitude equal. The analysis also satisfies that the phase difference between port 2 and port 3 is 90°.

Square Patch Antenna Simulation. In order to get a suitable square patch size and at the same time design a reasonable microstrip line structure to connect the feed network, a separate simulation analysis of the patch antenna is needed. The square patch antenna design model is shown in Fig. 7.

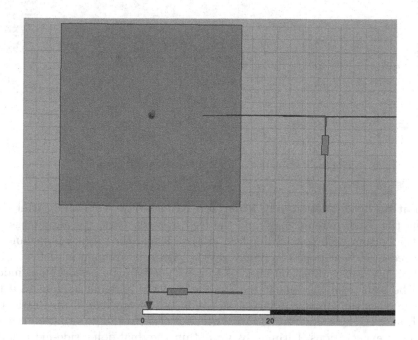

Fig. 7. Patch antenna simulation model

In the design, the microstrip line used for the connection was bent vertically for aesthetic purposes and then docked with the feed network. The size of the square patch is determined by the parametric scan analysis function of HFSS, and multiple scans were performed as shown in Fig. 8. It is found that the larger the value of the patch edge length l_0 is, the lower the resonant frequency is, and finally the best is obtained when $l_0 = 28.4\,\mathrm{mm}$. In order to get better antenna matching performance, utilize the parameter scan again to analyze the impact of impedance transformation of 1/4 wavelength impedance converter on antenna performance. After simulation, it is found that the width wp does not affect the resonant frequency.

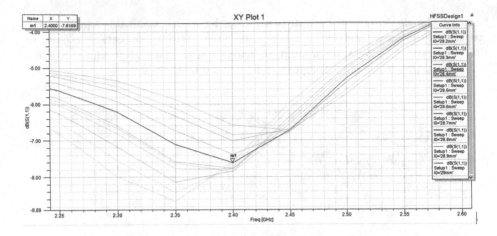

Fig. 8. Parametric scan of the antenna structure

Simulation of the Circularly Polarized Microstrip Antenna. After connecting the patch antenna part and the feed network part, the antenna is fed from the bottom with coaxial line feed at port 1, and the ground impedance is connected to 50 Ω at port 4 to finally get the complete antenna model.

HFSS performs simulation analysis to get the antenna's performance index. It can be seen from Fig. 9 that the axis ratio of the antenna is close to 0 dB, which satisfies the circular polarization condition. Meanwhile, from Fig. 10 the VSWR at 2.4 GHz is equal to 1.143 dB, which is close to 1. The situation is good and meets expectations. Ultimately, we obtain the dual-point side-fed circular polarized microstrip antenna that meets the desired performance indexes.

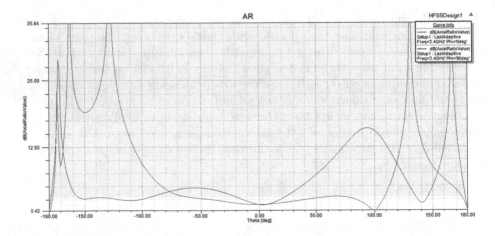

Fig. 9. The axis ratio simulation results

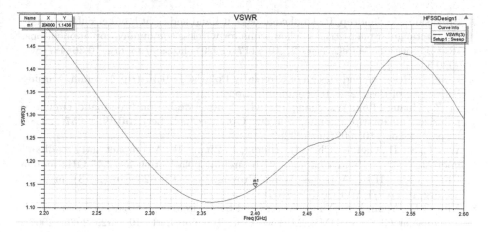

Fig. 10. The VSWR simulation results

5   Conclusion

In this paper, based on the theory of circularly polarized antenna generation, a complete model of dual-point side-fed circularly polarized microstrip antenna is designed, which contains two parts: one is the feeder network, which generates resonant modes with orthogonal equal spokes and 90° phase difference; the other is the square patch antenna with two microstrip antennas connected to the feeder network. In addition, the best model data is obtained by optimizing the structure size with HFSS. The model has good impedance characteristics, a simple structure, and comparatively stable performance, and the system is well matched, whose VSWR is close to 1. These properties make it suitable for a wide range of wireless communication areas.

There are some shortcomings to be improved in the future: on the one hand, although the dual branch line directional coupler feeder network is less affected by the external environment and the performance is more stable, there is still room to improve the relative bandwidth. On the other hand, in response to the requirements of wireless communication development, antennas need to satisfy new performance indicators, such as miniaturization and high integration, and future model improvements can be made to enhance the benefits of reduced patch size.

References

1. Bauer, I.J., Bouhatiya, P.: Microstrip Antennas. Publishing House of Electronics Industry, Beijing (1984)
2. Rathod, J.M.: Comparative study of microstrip patch antenna for wireless communication application. Int. J. Innov. **1**, 4 (2010)
3. Zhong, S.: Microstrip Antenna Theory and Applications. Xidian University Press, Xi'an(1991)

4. Prakasam, V., Sandeep, P.: Dual edge-fed left hand and right hand circularly polarized rectangular microstrip patch antenna for wireless communication applications. IRO J. Sustain. Wirel. Syst. **2**, 107–117 (2020). https://doi.org/10.36548/jsws.2020.3.001
5. Fang, J.: Research and Design of Circularly Polarized Microstrip Antenna. Nanjing University of Posts and Telecommunications (2015)
6. Li, Z., Guang-Ming, W., Xiang-Jun, G.: A novel design on broadband circularly polarized microstrip antenna. Microw. Opt. Technol. Lett. **50**, 954–957 (2008). https://doi.org/10.1002/mop.23257
7. Wu, T., Su, H., Gan, L., Chen, H., Huang, J., Zhang, H.: A compact and broadband microstrip stacked patch antenna with circular polarization for 2.45-GHz mobile RFID reader. IEEE Antennas Wirel. Propag. Lett. **12**, 623–626 (2013). https://doi.org/10.1109/LAWP.2013.2261651
8. Kim, S.M., Yoon, K.S., Yang, W.G.: Dual-band circular polarization square patch antenna for GPS and DMB. Microw. Opt. Technol. Lett. **49**, 2925–2926 (2007). https://doi.org/10.1002/mop.22972
9. Chen, R.-H., Row, J.-S.: Single-fed microstrip patch antenna with switchable polarization. IEEE Trans. Antennas Propag. **56**, 922–926 (2008). https://doi.org/10.1109/TAP.2008.919211
10. Liu, W.: Research on the design and implementation of circularly polarized microstrip antenna. China New Telecommun. **15**(21), 113(2013)
11. Sharma, A.K., Mittal, A.: Diagonal slotted diamond shaped dual circularly polarized microstrip patch antenna with dumbbell aperture coupling. In: The European Conference on Wireless Technology, pp. 463–465 (2005). https://doi.org/10.1109/ECWT.2005.1617757
12. Haro-Baez, R., Burbano-Guerrero, J.P., Benitez, D.S.: On the design of truncated T-type power dividers for x-band with SIW technology. In: 2020 IEEE ANDESCON, pp. 1–6. IEEE, Quito, Ecuador (2020). https://doi.org/10.1109/ANDESCON50619.2020.9271978
13. Meng, H., et al.: A transmission line model for high-frequency power line communication channel. In: Proceedings of the International Conference on Power System Technology, pp. 1290–1295. IEEE, Kunming, China (2002). https://doi.org/10.1109/ICPST.2002.1047610
14. Lo, Y., Solomon, D., Richards, W.: Theory and experiment on microstrip antennas. IEEE Trans. Antennas Propag. **27**, 137–145 (1979). https://doi.org/10.1109/TAP.1979.1142057
15. Farrar, A., Adams, A.T.: Characteristic impedance of microstrip by the method of moments (correspondence). IEEE Trans. Microw. Theor. Tech. **18**, 65–66 (1970). https://doi.org/10.1109/TMTT.1970.1127146
16. Bailey, M., Deshpande, M.: Integral equation formulation of microstrip antennas. IEEE Trans. Antennas Propag. **30**, 651–656 (1982). https://doi.org/10.1109/TAP.1982.1142880
17. Chen, Y.-Y., Wong, K.-L.: Low-profile broadband printed quadrifilar helical antenna for broadcasting satellite application. Microw. Opt. Technol. Lett. **36**, 134–136 (2003). https://doi.org/10.1002/mop.10698
18. Lin, C., Zhang, F.-S., Jiao, Y.-C., Zhang, F., Xue, X.: A three-fed microstrip antenna for wideband circular polarization. IEEE Antennas Wirel. Propag. Lett. **9**, 359–362 (2010). https://doi.org/10.1109/LAWP.2010.2048296
19. Zhang, Z.-Y., Liu, N.-W., Zhao, J.-Y., Fu, G.: Wideband circularly polarized antenna with gain improvement. IEEE Antennas Wirel. Propag. Lett. **12**, 456–459 (2013). https://doi.org/10.1109/LAWP.2013.2253591

20. Lee, C.-H., Chang, Y.-H.: An improved design and implementation of a broadband circularly polarized antenna. IEEE Trans. Antennas Propag. **62**, 3343–3348 (2014). https://doi.org/10.1109/TAP.2014.2309962
21. Prakasam, V., Sandeep, P.: Design and analysis of 2 × 2 circular microstrip patch antenna array for 2.4 GHZ wireless communication application. Int. J. Innov. Eng. Manag. Res. **07**, 9 (2018)
22. Prakasam, V., Anudeep LaxmiKanth, K.R., Srinivasu, P.: Design and simulation of circular microstrip patch antenna with line feed wireless communication application. In: 2020 4th International Conference on Intelligent Computing and Control Systems (ICICCS), pp. 279–284. IEEE, Madurai, India (2020). https://doi.org/10.1109/ICICCS48265.2020.9121162
23. Khraisat, Y.S.H.: Design of 4 elements rectangular microstrip patch antenna with high gain for 2.4 GHz applications. Mod. Appl. Sci. **6**, 68 (2011). https://doi.org/10.5539/mas.v6n1p68
24. Zeng, W.J.: Research and design of miniaturized wideband and dual-band microstrip antennas. Taiyuan University of Technology (2016)

A Semi-supervised Classification Method for 6G Remote Sensing Images Based on Pseudo-label and False Representation Recognition

Xianglong Meng[1], Liang Xi[1(✉)], and Lu Liu[2(✉)]

[1] School of Computer Science and Technology, Harbin University of Science and Technology, Harbin 150080, China
xiliang@hrbust.edu.cn
[2] College of Biomedical Information and Engineering, Hainan Medical University, Haikou 571199, China
liulu@hainmc.edu.cn

Abstract. 6G can connect everything, including aviation equipment. Aviation equipment transmits remote sensing images through 6G network to obtain ground information which can effectively help users analyze geographical types, ground conditions, etc. Recently, deep learning methods have made significant breakthroughs in remote sensing image classification. However, it takes a lot of human resources to add labels to the data. In this article, we design a new semi-supervised image classification framework for remote sensing scenarios. This framework uses pseudo-labels as labels of unlabeled data, so that unlabeled data can also be trained with labels. We provide a hybrid representation learning method for the case that the model may misclassify unlabeled data. Mixing different data to generate pseudo data and taking advantage of all the data can overcome the shortcomings of pseudo labels. We use the NWPU-RESISC45 dataset provided by Northwestern Polytechnical University, from which we randomly select ten-class samples for evaluation. The experimental results show that our proposed method is superior to the comparative methods.

Keywords: 6G network · remote sensing image classification · semi-supervised learning

1 Introduction

Radio communication technology is developing rapidly, and 6G technology will be universal shortly. 6G can interconnect everything, both the ground and the sky. Through the integration of various aviation and satellite systems, 6G can achieve global signal coverage. And through these systems, 6G also can obtain high resolution remote sensing images of the ground at any location in time to help ground users quickly get the geographic information of the relevant position.

We can acquire many high-resolution ground remote sensing images through advanced aviation systems or satellite systems. When the 6G network is widespread,

A. Li et al. (Eds.): 6GN 2022, LNICST 505, pp. 20–31, 2023.
https://doi.org/10.1007/978-3-031-36014-5_2

the ground-sky network framework can timely transmit the current ground image information and apply the knowledge to perform many tasks automatically. Consequently, the demand for fully understanding the semantic information of land scene images and accurate recognition and classification is increasing rapidly [1–3]. Remote Sensing Image Scene Classification (RSISC) is to classify the image into self-defined categories using some methods to obtain the semantic information [4]. Relying on many high-quality labeled datasets, convolutional neural networks have achieved considerable results in object detection [5], semantic segmentation [6], and image recognition [7]. However, the annotation for the dataset consumes a lot of human resources, which makes it unaffordable. As a result, a new method has emerged that can apply a large amount of data with a small number of labels: semi-supervised learning (SSL). SSL is trained with a specific ratio of labeled data and a large amount of unordered and unknown unlabeled data, which reduces the requirement for experimental costs and can achieve more robust results than supervised methods.

In previous studies, some methods [8, 9] align the original and enhanced inputs using consistent regularization. Consistent regularization considers that the classifier can output the same probability distribution for the initial information and improved input. Through this method, the encoder can learn the data disturbing and improve the robustness. Another popular way is to train models to predict unlabeled data and generate artificial labels, such as pseudo-label [10]. However, in this method, because data does not have labels, models may overconfidently assign wrong categories to data, resulting in models that can not comprehensively learn various data representations.

In this article, we propose a new approach that further exploits unlabeled data by using a self-supervised pseudo-label identification strategy for 6G RSISC. We mix two different remote sensing images according to a particular proportion, then combine them with the original dataset to form a new real and fake dataset for the model training. In this way, the encoder can learn more data representations and correct the effects caused by the wrong classification. We evaluated ten classes randomly selected on the NWPU-RESISC45 dataset [11] by Northwestern Polytechnical University, and the results show that our method achieves advanced results.

2   Related Work

2.1   6G Network

Currently, 5G networks are being popularized on a large scale, but it is estimated that there are still more than 80% of areas that cannot be covered by signals. These include deserts, no man's land, oceans, and other sparsely populated areas where no one has built signal base stations. Therefore, 6G will be further upgraded according to 5G technology to truly realize the global domain and Internet of everything.

As mentioned in [12], the 6G network will integrate ground mobile communication, earth-orbiting satellite communication, and short-range wireless communication. Also, 6G will integrate communication, calculation, navigation, conception, and intelligence [13]. Under intelligent management, the 6G network will enable seamless communication coverage in the sky, ground, sea, and space. Ideally, 6G will allow any user and device to access the network at any time and in any area.

Through the 6G network, the satellite system or the aviation system can transmit the collected ground image to any location in the world at the fastest speed, ensuring that the user or the AI intelligent system can obtain the information needed at the fastest speed to take the following action. In this paper, we use remote sensing datasets generated by satellite technology or aviation systems for ground information analysis.

2.2 Semi-supervised

SSL based on deep learning mainly includes pseudo-label and consistent regularization. In this paper, we primarily use pseudo-label to implement our method. In recent years, semi-supervised learning has achieved good results with pseudo-label methods [8, 9, 14, 15]. Pseudo-label learns unlabeled data by training self-generated labels. SSL based on pseudo-label mainly adopts iterative training in the training process:

1) Use raw data and network models to generate self-generated labels, called pseudo-labels,
2) Apply the generated pseudo-labels for training,
3) perform the Step. 1 and 2 repeatedly until the training is complete.

However, the pseudo-label suffers from confirmation bias [16] because it is easy to overfit incorrect predictions during training. [8, 9] both use high confidence prediction to filter noise.

Therefore, to avoid this defect, we apply pseudo-label and self-supervised representation learning to design our method.

2.3 Entropy Regularization

Entropy regularization [17] is a method that benefits from a maximum posteriori estimation framework. Cross-entropy separates classes at low densities by minimizing the conditional entropy of class probabilities predicted from data without building huge models [10].

$$H(y|x) = -\frac{1}{n}\sum_{k=1}^{n}\sum_{j=1}^{c}P\left(y_j^k|x^k\right)logP\left(y_j^k|x^k\right) \tag{1}$$

where n represents the number of samples, C indicates the data class, y_j^k is the actual label or predicted label of the kth labeled/unlabeled data, and x^k is the kth labeled/unlabeled data.

In this paper, we use the cross-entropy loss function as our primary loss function. Cross-entropy loss function can not only better measure the similarity between the predicted and the actual label, but also avoid the problem of learning rate reduction caused by the loss function of mean square error in gradient descent.

2.4 Resnet Network

As the number of layers of neural networks increases, the problem of vanishing/exploding gradients arises [18, 19]. In early studies, this problem was mainly solved by normalization initialization [19–21]. But at the same time, another serious problem has emerged: as the number of layers of the neural network increases, the network accuracy peaks and then drops off at a high-speed rate. Kaiming He [22] proposed the Resnet network framework in 2016 to address these problems. Resnet is mainly composed of multiple identical residual blocks.

In this paper, we use Resnet18 network framework among the five Resnet network frameworks as our encoder, and its specific framework parameters are shown in Tab. 1. There are four residual blocks in Resnet18. Each consists of two basic blocks, each basic block is a basic double block. It consists of two convolutions and a short circuit connection. The specific framework is shown in Fig. 1.

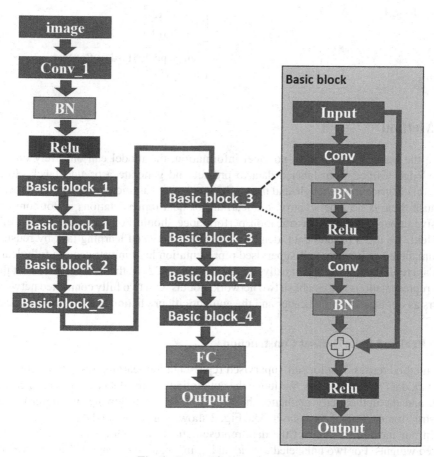

Fig. 1. Resnet18 network model

Table 1. Resnet18 Network framework

Layer name	Output size	18-layer
Conv1	112 × 112	7 × 7,64, stride 2
Basic block_1	56 × 56	3 × 3 max pool, stride 2
		$\begin{bmatrix} 3 \times 3 \ 64 \\ 3 \times 3 \ 64 \end{bmatrix} \times 2$
Basic block_2	28 × 28	$\begin{bmatrix} 3 \times 3 \ 128 \\ 3 \times 3 \ 128 \end{bmatrix} \times 2$
Basic block_3	14 × 14	$\begin{bmatrix} 3 \times 3 \ 256 \\ 3 \times 3 \ 256 \end{bmatrix} \times 2$
Basic block_4	7 × 7	$\begin{bmatrix} 3 \times 3 \ 512 \\ 3 \times 3 \ 512 \end{bmatrix} \times 2$
	1 × 1	Average pool, 512-d fc, SoftMax
FLOPs		1.8×10^9

3 Method

Since the unlabeled data have no label information, the model can only rely on the knowledge learned from labeled data to predict and generate a pseudo label. However, this is inaccurate enough, and the model may have classification errors. Moreover, because there is no label control, the learning of data representations is not comprehensive enough, and the classification performance should be reduced. To solve this problem, we use a pseudo-data identification self-supervised learning task by reusing the unlabeled data with a self-supervised representation learning strategy to fully learn the data representations. Specifically, we use Resnet18 [22] as the encoder to extract the data representations and establish two network models with two fully connected network layers as our classification header and the authenticity prediction header, respectively.

3.1 Real and Fake Dataset Construction

Our method reuses data for self-supervised representation learning tasks to thoroughly learn all data representations. We judge the authenticity of the data through the encoder, $E(\cdot)$, and the authenticity prediction header, $G(\cdot)$. In the following, we describe the construction method of the dataset. The Fig. 2 shows our model in detail.

In our method, we extract the data representations through the encoder $E(\cdot)$ with shared weights. For two unlabeled data u_i and u_j in a batchsize dataset, U_B, we mix the two data with a hyperparameter, α, to generate the fake data u_i^{fake}:

$$u_i^{fake} = \alpha * u_i + (1 - \alpha) * u_j \tag{2}$$

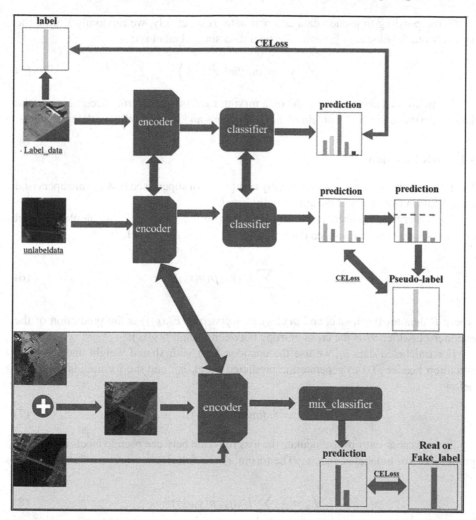

Fig. 2. Model framework: In the white background, we build a semi-supervised method using pseudo labels, and in the gray background, we create a self-supervised representation learning method for authenticity recognition.

Then we construct the real and fake datasets:

$$x^{fr} = \{u_i^{fake}, u_i\}_{i=1}^{B} \tag{3}$$

We set the label of fake data u_i^{fake} to 0 and the label of real data u_i to 1. The tag set is constructed as follows:

$$y^{fr} = \{0, \ldots, 0, 1, \ldots, 1\}^{2B} \tag{4}$$

Corresponding to pseudo data and real data, respectively, we randomly shuffle the data sets and label sets to generate the final data set and label set:

$$x^{fr}, y^{fr} = shuffle\left(x^{fr}, y^{fr}\right) \tag{5}$$

As mentioned above, we use the data mixing method to construct accurate and fake datasets to make the model obtain higher robustness and predictability with fewer labels.

3.2 Loss Function

The loss function of our method is mainly composed of supervised loss, L_x, unsupervised classification loss, L_u, and the authenticity loss, L_{fr}.

The supervised loss between the true and the predicted labels, L_x, is calculated based on cross-entropy on the labeled dataset. The formula is shown below:

$$L_x = \frac{1}{B} \sum_{b=1}^{B} H(y_b, p(y|x_b)) \tag{6}$$

where B denotes batch size, and $p(y|x_b) = softmax(f(E(x_b)))$ is the prediction of the encoder-classifier. H is the cross-entropy between y_b and $p(y|x_b)$.

For unlabeled data u_i, we use the encoder $E(\cdot)$ with shared weight and the classification header $f(\cdot)$ to generate the predicted label, q_u, and the formula is shown as below:

$$q_u = Softmax(h(f(u_i))) \tag{7}$$

L_u uses cross-entropy to calculate the loss function between pseudo labels and model predictions for unlabeled data, u_i. The formula is as follows

$$L_u = \frac{1}{B} \sum_{b=1}^{B} H(q_u, p(y|u_b)) \tag{8}$$

For the real and fake dataset, x^{fr}, we define its authenticity loss function as follows:

$$L_{fr} = \frac{1}{B} \sum_{b=1}^{B} H\left(y^{fr}, p\left(y|x^{fr}\right)\right) \tag{9}$$

where H is the cross-entropy loss between the authenticity label, y^{fr}, and the prediction, $p(y|x^{fr})$, generated by $E(\cdot)$ and $f^{fr}(\cdot)$.

To sum up, the final loss function of our model is shown below:

$$L = L_x + L_u + L_{fr} \tag{10}$$

The details of our model are shown in **Algorithm 1**.

Algorithm 1 Forest loss classification

Input: Labeled data, $x = \{(x_i, y_i)\}_{i=1}^{N}$; Unlabeled data, $U = \{u_b : b \in (1, ..., \mu B)\}$; Batch size, b; Epoch number, e; confidence threshold, τ

1. while $e<epoch$ do
2.   The supervised loss is calculated using Equation (6)
3.   for $i=1$ to b do
4.   The pseudo-label is computed using Equation (7)
5.   End for
6.   Equations (2), (3), (4), (5) are used to construct real and fake datasets
7.   The unsupervised classification loss is calculated using Equation (8)
8.   Equation (9) is used to calculate the authenticity loss
9. $L = L_x + L_u + \beta L_{fr}$ {total loss}
10. End while

---

4 Experiment

4.1 Dataset

We used the public dataset of the RSISC created by Northwestern Polytechnical University (NWPU) [11], which contains a total of 31,500 images covering 45 scene classes. In order to ensure the randomness of the experiment, we randomly selected 10 of these classes for training, and the classes are Airplane, Basketball Court, Bridge, River, mountain, Island, Forest, Thermal power station, Snow Berg, and Freeway. An example of each type is shown in Fig. 3.

We divided the complete dataset into a training set, validation set, and test set according to the ratio of 60%, 20%, and 20%. Since we use a semi-supervised method, we only use 10% and 20% labeled data for the supervised training, and the rest of the training data are processed as unlabeled data. The details of these datasets are shown in Tables 2 and 3.

4.2 Environment Setup

In this paper, we use PyTorch as our basic framework and apply NVIDIA GeForce RTX 3090 for training. In training stage, we set the initial learning rate to 0.001, use the stochastic gradient descent (SGD) method to optimize the supervised learning of the model, and use the Adam algorithm to optimize the semi-supervised learning and the self-supervised learning. We set the model to be trained for 150 epochs and set the the batch size to 16 in each epoch. For image data mixing, After our experiment, we believe that when $\alpha = 0.5$, the data can be well guaranteed not only to retain part of the original information but also not to be wrongly classified by the model.

Fig. 3. Samples of the dataset.

Table 2. Data partition details in the case of 10% labeled data

Type	Training		Validation	Test
	Label	Unlabel		
Sum Number	420	4200	1200	1200
Each class	42	420	120	120

4.3 Results

We test the performance of our model on a remote sensing image classification dataset created by Northwestern Polytechnical University [11] and compare it with the supervised and semi-supervised pseudo-label methods that only use label data and the same

Table 3. Data partition details in the case of 20% labeled data

Type	Training		Validation	Test
	Label	Unlabel		
Sum Number	840	4200	1200	1200
Each class	84	420	120	120

encoder and classifier framework. The experimental results are shown in Tables 4 and 5. It can be seen from Tables 4 and 5 that our model performs better than the comparative methods on each data scenarios. The experimental results directly reflect that our proposed model can accurately and efficiently classify remote sensing scene images. And from the perspective of the experiment process, adding fake data did not bring more burden to the experimental equipment.

Table 4. The results in the case of 10% labeled data method

Method	10%	
	Val	Test
Supervised	64.13	61.58
Pseudo-label [10]	66.69	63.78
Our	67.33	65.13

Table 5. The results in the case of 20% labeled data

Method	20%	
	Val	Test
Supervised	71.02	68.75
Pseudo-label [10]	72.44	72.16
Our	73.65	73.58

5 Conclusions

In this paper, we present a new semi-supervised classification model for 6G network remote sensing images. In view of the defects of previous models using pseudo-labels, our model applies unlabeled data for further representation learning by combining the pseudo-label methods with the real and fake data identification. The model can learn the data representations comprehensively. The experimental results show that our approach is superior to the baselines. Due to the continuous development of the 6G network, its interaction rate with the ground network will be faster and faster, and the frequency of obtaining image data will be higher and higher. Therefore, improving the interaction effects between the network model and the aerial remote sensing system and how to better connect them is the goal of our future efforts.

Acknowledgments. This work was supported by Heilongjiang Province Natural Science Foundation under Grant LH2022F034.

References

1. Cheng, G., Han, J., Guo, L., Liu, Z., Bu, S., Ren, J.: Effective and efficient midlevel visual elements-oriented land-use classification using VHR remote sensing images. IEEE Trans. Geosci. Remote Sens. **53**, 4238–4249 (2015)
2. Gómez-Chova, L., Tuia, D., Moser, G., Camps-Valls, G.: Multimodal classification of remote sensing images: a review and future directions. Proc. IEEE. **103**, 1560–1584 (2015)
3. Cheng, G., Han, J., Zhou, P., Guo, L.: Multi-class geospatial object detection and geographic image classification based on collection of part detectors. ISPRS J. Photogramm. Remote Sens. **98**, 119–132 (2014)
4. Lv, Y., Zhang, X., Xiong, W., et al.: An end-to-end local-global-fusion feature extraction network for remote sensing image scene classification. Remote Sens. **11**(24), 3006 (2019)
5. Lin, T.-Y., et al.: Microsoft COCO: common objects in context. In: Fleet, D., Pajdla, T., Schiele, B., Tuytelaars, T. (eds.) Computer Vision – ECCV 2014: 13th European Conference, Zurich, Switzerland, September 6-12, 2014, Proceedings, Part V, pp. 740–755. Springer, Cham (2014). https://doi.org/10.1007/978-3-319-10602-1_48
6. Zhou, S., Nie, D., Adeli, E., Yin, J., Shen, D.: High-resolution encoder-decoder networks for low-contrast medical image segmentation. IEEE Trans. Image Process. **99**, 461–475 (2019)
7. Xh, A., Yz, A., Xin, X., Sz, A., Li, L.: Robust semi-supervised classification based on data augmented online elms with deep features. Knowl.-Based Syst. **229**, 107307 (2021)
8. Sohn, K., Berthelot, D., Carlini, N., et al.: Fixmatch: simplifying semi-supervised learning with consistency and confidence. Adv. Neural. Inf. Process. Syst. **33**, 596–608 (2020)
9. Berthelot, D., Carlini, N., Goodfellow, I., et al.: Mixmatch: a holistic approach to semi-supervised learning. Adv. Neural Inf. Process. Syst. **32**, 1–11 (2019)
10. Lee, D.-H.: Pseudo-label: the simple and efficient semi-supervised learning method for deep neural networks. In: ICML Workshop on Challenges in Representation Learning (2013)
11. Cheng, G., Han, J., Xiaoqiang, L.: Remote sensing image scene classification: benchmark and state of the art. Proc. IEEE **105**(10), 1865–1883 (2017)
12. Chen, S., et al.: Vision, requirements, and technology trend of 6G—how to tackle the challenges of system coverage, capacity, user data-rate and movement speed. IEEE Wirel. Commun. **27**(2), 218–228 (2020)
13. Chen, S., Sun, S., Kang, S.: System integration of terrestrial mobile communication and satellite communication—the trends, challenges and key technologies in B5G and 6G. China Commun. **17**(12), 156–171 (2020)
14. Berthelot, D., Carlini, N., Cubuk, E.D., et al.: Remixmatch: semi-supervised learning with distribution alignment and augmentation anchoring. arXiv preprint arXiv:1911.09785 (2019)
15. Hu, Z., Yang, Z., Hu, H., Nevatia, R.: Simple: similar pseudo label exploitation for semisupervised classification. In: Proceedings of the IEEE/CVF Conference on Computer Vision and Pattern Recognition, pp. 15099–15108 (2021)

16. Arazo, E., Ortego, D., Albert,P., O'Connor, N.E., McGuinness, K.: Pseudo-labeling and confirmation bias in deep semi-supervised learning. In: 2020 International Joint Conference on Neural Networks (IJCNN), pp. 1–8. IEEE (2020)
17. Grandvalet, Y., Bengio, Y.: Entropy regularization. In: Semi-Supervised Learning, pp. 151–168. MIT Press, Cambridge (2006)
18. Bengio, Y., Simard, P., Frasconi, P.: Learning long-term dependencies with gradient descent is difficult. IEEE Trans. Neural Netw. 5(2), 157–166 (1994)
19. Glorot, X., Bengio, Y.: Understanding the difficulty of training deep feedforward neural networks. In: AISTATS (2010)
20. LeCun, Y., Bottou, L., Orr, G.B., Muller, K.R.: Efficient backprop. In: Orr, G.B., Müller, K.-R. (eds.) Neural Networks: Tricks of the Trade. LNCS, vol. 1524, pp. 9–50. Springer, Heidelberg (1998). https://doi.org/10.1007/3-540-49430-8_2
21. He, K., Zhang, X., Ren, S., Sun, J.: Delving deep into rectifiers: Surpassing human-level performance on imagenet classification. In: ICCV (2015)
22. He, K., Zhang, X., Ren, S., et al.: Deep residual learning for image recognition. In: Proceedings of the IEEE Conference on Computer Vision and Pattern Recognition, pp. 770–778 (2016)

Establishment of Soil Quantitative Detection Model Based on Sparrow Search Algorithm

Qiuduo Zhao[1,2(✉)], Ke Liu[1], Chen Xiong[1], and Fengyong Yang[1]

[1] College of Electronical and Information Engineering, Heilongjiang University of Science and Technology, Harbin 150022, Heilongjiang, China
22025744@qq.com
[2] Key Laboratory of Agricultural Renewable Resource Utilization Technology, Harbin 150030, China

Abstract. In recent years, with the rapid economic growth in my country, environmental problems have become more severe, among which the problem of heavy metal pollution in soil is particularly prominent. Soil is the material basis for human survival. In order to ensure human health and achieve sustainable development, the control and treatment of soil heavy metal pollution is imminent. Based on the sparrow search algorithm, this paper establishes a soil quantitative detection model, and uses the algorithm's population optimization performance to detect soil heavy metal content. And a detection model based on the improved algorithm was proposed, and the detection accuracy of the models under the two algorithms and the relative error of each heavy metal element were compared, and the effectiveness of the improved sparrow search algorithm in soil quantitative analysis was verified.

Keywords: Sparrow Search Algorithm · Soil Heavy Metals · Detection Model · Relative Error

1 Introduction

With the deepening of urbanization and the rapid development of modern agriculture, some soils have suffered from heavy metal pollution to varying degrees. Due to the absorption effect of plants, the heavy metals entering the soil may be absorbed by plants, thereby causing heavy metals in food. Pollution eventually endangers human health through the biological chain. Therefore, the detection of heavy metals in soil has important practical significance for evaluating soil quality, protecting human health and maintaining sustainable social and economic development.

At present, many scholars have achieved remarkable results in the research on the establishment of soil quantitative detection model based on the sparrow search algorithm. For example, a scholar used the LIBS method to study the copper pollution in the soil, and successfully obtained the content of copper in the soil. Relevant experiments show that this method fully meets the detection requirements of trace copper in the soil [1].

A. Li et al. (Eds.): 6GN 2022, LNICST 505, pp. 32–39, 2023.
https://doi.org/10.1007/978-3-031-36014-5_3

The related research combined LIBS with the sparrow search algorithm to quantitatively analyze the elements contained in the soil. By solving the matrix effect between soils, the quantitative detection of elements in different soils was successfully achieved, and the accuracy was higher than that of the internal standard method [2]. Some scholars first collect soil samples, and then use the fuzzy k-means algorithm to cluster the soil reflection spectrum, and then perform local modeling according to different categories, so that the detection accuracy is significantly improved [3]. Although the research results of the soil quantitative detection model based on the sparrow search algorithm are good, the validity of the model detection accuracy needs to be further improved.

This paper expounds the basic principle of the sparrow search algorithm, analyzes the shortcomings of the algorithm, and establishes a quantitative detection model based on the sparrow search algorithm and the improved sparrow search algorithm, and then uses these two algorithm models to detect heavy metal elements in soil. The detection accuracy verifies the detection advantage of the improved SSA model.

2   The Basic Principle of the Algorithm and the Mathematical Model

2.1   Quantitative Detection Model Based on Sparrow Search Algorithm

In nature, as a group of birds, sparrows have a clear internal division of labor in the process of foraging. The sparrows with stronger ability have a higher probability of finding food, and they are the main force to find food for the entire population, while the rest of the sparrows follow the first batch to find food [4]. The inspiration of the sparrow search algorithm is a meta-heuristic optimization algorithm proposed from the foraging behavior and vigilance behavior of sparrows, which is a kind of finder and joiner model. The selection of different foraging behaviors in sparrow populations is inextricably linked to energy reserves. All sparrows have a strong curiosity about everything in nature, but their vigilance is very high, and the sparrows will always observe the changes in the surrounding environment [5]. If we observe carefully in life, we will find that when there are sparrows in the group and there are predators around, one or more individuals in the group will make a chirping sound. Once such a sound is made, the whole group will immediately avoid danger, and then fly to other safe areas to forage.

The main behavioral rules of sparrow foraging can be described as: the ratio of finders to joiners is usually constant in the whole population. In other words, when joiners follow the finders to find food, the joiners find better Foraging area and direction, its identity shifts towards the finder. When individual sparrows are threatened externally, sparrows will act on alert. In order to obtain a better position, the sparrows farther away from the center of the group will quickly move to the individual sparrows that find the best food source, while the sparrows in the best food position perform random walk operations in order to get close to other sparrows [6, 7].

The SSA mathematical model is as follows:

Discoverer mathematical model:

$$X_{i,d}^{t+1} = \begin{cases} X_{i,d}^t \cdot exp(\frac{-i}{\alpha \cdot K}), & E < ST \\ X_{i,d}^t + Q \cdot L, & E \geq ST \end{cases} \tag{1}$$

where t is the current number of repetitions. i represents the sparrow, and X_1 represents the position information of the sparrow i in the d dimension. $\alpha \in (0, 1]$ is a random number. E is a random number in (0, 1), indicating the warning value, ST is the safety value, K is a constant, indicating the maximum number of repetitions of execution. Q is a random number, obeying the Normal distribution, L represents a $1 \times d$ matrix.

Joiner mathematical model:

$$X_{i,d}^{t+1} = \begin{cases} Q \cdot exp(\frac{X_1^t - X_{i,d}^t}{i^2}), & i > n/2 \\ X_P^{t+1} + \left| X_{i,d}^t + X_P^{t+1} \right| \cdot A^+ \cdot L, & otherwise \end{cases} \tag{2}$$

Among them, X_p is the finder, which indicates the position of the best food source it has found, and X_1 is the joiner, which is the worst in the sparrow population. Q is a random number following a standard Gaussian distribution. A represents a $1 \times d$ array where each element is randomly assigned a value of 1 or -1, and $A^+ = A(AA^T)^{-1}$.

As a new heuristic algorithm, SSA algorithm has the characteristics of fast convergence speed, easy implementation, few adjustable parameters, and good performance in local search, so it is easy to be used and studied by scholars [8]. However, the SSA algorithm still has shortcomings, as follows:

Precocious Convergence. It can be seen from the mathematical model of the SSA algorithm that when the discoverer in the SSA algorithm searches for the local optimal solution, the joiners will follow the discoverer to quickly gather near the local optimal solution, which is difficult to escape, and because the SSA algorithm itself does not have the ability to jump out of the local optimal solution. The mechanism of, which leads to the situation that the convergence accuracy is too low when facing high-dimensional problems [9]. On the other hand, in the general SSA algorithm, the ratio of discoverers to joiners is fixed. Once the parameters are fixed, the algorithm cannot make corresponding adjustments according to the real-time changing environment during iteration. When the algorithm is in the later stage of iteration, the population of the algorithm cannot be guaranteed Diversity further exacerbates the occurrence of algorithm stagnation in local optimal convergence [10].

Location Update. It can be seen from formula (2) that when the fitness of the joiner is poor, each position is updated to a regular normal distribution random number and multiplied by an exponential function based on natural logarithms. As the number of repetitions increases, its value will decrease to 0, and its position update is jumpy. When the extreme value of the test function is not at the origin, the convergence is poor; when the fitness of the joiner is good, the joiner The location update will be performed based on the individual with the best fitness, only considering the current location information of the individual and the optimal location information of the population, without considering the individual's own experience, indicating that it is relatively lacking in the individual's own location memory [11].

2.2 Quantitative Detection Model Based on Improved Sparrow Search Algorithm

Group Reverse Learning Mechanism. The advantages of the sparrow search algorithm are strong local search ability and fast convergence speed, but the disadvantages are also very obvious, mainly because the global search ability is not enough, the ability to deviate from the local optimum is weak, and it is easy to fall into the local optimum, showing that the sparrow individual seeks the best. The efficiency is not stable enough, and it is very effective to solve the problem of such optimization algorithms by introducing a reverse learning mechanism [12].

Elite Strategy. A set of optimal solutions including forward and reverse solutions can be obtained through the reverse learning mechanism, and the elite strategy is used to change the solution in the set, and the elite strategy is used to obtain the 20% solution with the best fitness value. A new solution is formed. At this time, the newly generated 20% solution is added to the total solution set, and the fitness values of all solutions in the solution set added to the new solution are sorted again, and the 20% ranking is removed first. The solution of the later fitness value, so we get a new optimization group [13, 14].

Membership Function. For the universe of discourse X, a fuzzy set $\overline{A}$ on it, for any $x \in X$, there is $u_{\overline{A}}(x) \in [0, 1]$ corresponding to x, where x is called the degree of membership to $\overline{A}$, and the mapping relationship is:

$$\overline{A} = \{(x, u_{\overline{A}}(x)) | x \in X\} \tag{3}$$

In particular, when $u_{\overline{A}}(x) = 0,\ x \neq \overline{A}$; when $u_{\overline{A}}(x) = 1,\ x \in \overline{A}$. The closer $u_{\overline{A}}(x)$ is to 1, the greater the degree that x belongs to $\overline{A}$. When $u_{\overline{A}}(x) = \{0, 1\}$, the fuzzy set $\overline{A}$ degenerates into an ordinary set.

In life, fuzzy mathematics uses precise mathematical methods to express fuzzy phenomena and deal with the actual objective fuzzy problems, and the primary problem is to solve the determination of membership functions. The establishment of the membership function is usually obtained by combining with the actual and fuzzy operations, such as union, intersection and remainder.

3 Experimental Research

3.1 Research Content

This paper is mainly divided into two experiments. One is to verify which detection model is better in the detection model established by using SSA and improved SSA algorithm, and the other is to verify the application of the detection model established based on the two algorithms in soil heavy metal detection. In both experiments, the relative error is used to judge the detection effectiveness of the model. The smaller the error, the higher the detection accuracy.

3.2 Obtaining Experimental Samples

In this paper, the soil near an abandoned factory on the outskirts of a city was collected, divided into 7 samples, and each sample was subjected to experimental pretreatment. The pretreatment is to use LIBS technology to extract the heavy metal content in the soil, and obtain eight elements that mainly cause heavy metal pollution in the soil, including Cu, Fe, Pb, Hg, Si, Cr, Ti, and Mn. Compare the detection relative errors of the two algorithm detection models on each element.

4 Detection Results of Quantitative Detection Model Based on Sparrow Search Algorithm

4.1 Model Validation

It can be seen from Table 1 that the detection models established based on the SSA algorithm and the improved SSA algorithm have relatively large relative errors in some samples, but the relative errors of the overall inspection samples are small, and the relative errors of most samples are within 5%. The relative error of one sample in the detection model established based on the SSA algorithm is slightly greater than 10%, and there is no sample relative error greater than 10% in the model established based on the improved SSA algorithm. The maximum relative error in each model is 13.41%, 9.73%, and the minimum relative error is 1.24%, 0.86%, respectively. Among them, the error of the SSA model is larger, indicating that the detection effect of the improved SSA model is better.

Table 1. Sample Test Results.

		1	2	3	4	5	6	7
SSA (%)	Detection value	11.24	15.36	7.15	10.84	9.21	16.47	12.65
	actual value	12.12	14.79	7.52	9.86	10.35	15.18	12.38
	Relative error	4.52	3.91	1.63	1.24	3.06	13.41	2.72
Improve SSA (%)	Detection value	10.38	14.67	7.04	10.23	8.57	14.82	11.59
	actual value	11.72	14.83	6.73	10.05	9.41	13.67	12.11
	Relative error	3.66	3.49	1.27	0.86	2.34	9.73	2.31

It can be seen from Fig. 1 that the comprehensive determination coefficient ($R2$), the average relative error (MRE), the posterior difference ratio (C) and the small probability error (P) are used to compare the model detection accuracy, and the improved sparrow search algorithm is used. The detection accuracy of the established detection model is the best, with a larger $R2$ value of 0.986, a smaller MRE value of 2.415, a C value of 0.277, and a P value of 1, indicating a higher detection accuracy level. The C of the model established based on the sparrow search algorithm is 0.213, which is less than 0.2774, and the P is 1, but the MRE value is larger, which is 7.284%, and the $R2$ value is 0.963, which is slightly worse than the corresponding accuracy index of the improved algorithm detection model. It can be seen that the improved sparrow search algorithm detection model can exert its unique advantages in the complex problem of soil quantitative detection.

4.2 Quantitative Detection Results of Heavy Metal Elements in Soil

The sparrow search algorithm was used to analyze the 8 elements in the soil, and compared with the detection results of the improved algorithm. Figure 2 shows the comparison results. It can be seen from Fig. 2 that the element with the largest relative error is

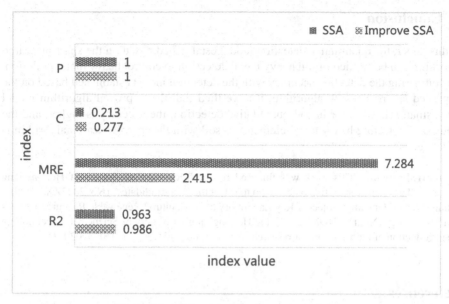

Fig. 1. Model detection accuracy comparison.

Cu, with a relative error of 19.34%, and the element with the smallest relative error is Si, with a relative error of 7.72%, and the soil metal content detected by the improved sparrow search algorithm is higher. Through the calculation of the contents of 8 elements in the soil samples, it is known that although the soil element detection and analysis results of the soil quantitative detection model based on the sparrow search algorithm have relatively large relative errors in some elements, it is effective and feasible to use the sparrow search algorithm to detect the element content in the soil.

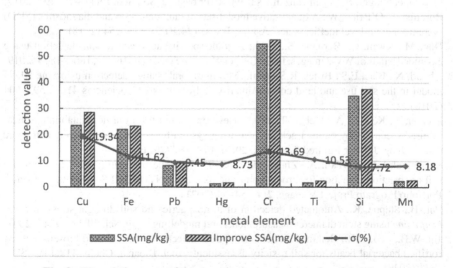

Fig. 2. The relative error of the quantitative analysis results of the algorithm.

5 Conclusion

In this paper, the quantitative detection model established based on the sparrow search algorithm can be applied to soil heavy metal detection to control heavy metal pollution. By comparing the detection accuracy with the detection model established based on the improved sparrow search algorithm, it is verified that the improved algorithm model has a small relative error in soil quantitative detection, the accuracy is higher, and the method of detecting heavy metal elements in soil with the sparrow search algorithm is effective.

Acknowledgements. This work was financed by the Technological Project of Heilongjiang Province "The open competition mechanism to select the best candidates" (No. 2022ZXJ05C01), Funding for the Opening Project of Key Laboratory of Agricultural Renewable Resource Utilization Technology (No. HLJHDNY2114) and Heilongjiang University of Science and Technology the introduction of high-level talent research start-up fund projects (No. 000009020315).

References

1. Minkina, T., Sushkova, S., Yadav, B.K., et al.: Accumulation and transformation of benzo[a]pyrene in Haplic Chernozem under artificial contamination. Environ. Geochem. Health 42(8), 2485–2494 (2020)
2. Park, K.H., Jung, Y.H.: Quantitative detection of contact force chains in a model particle assembly using digital RGB photoelastic measurements. KSCE J. Civ. Eng. 24(1), 63–72 (2020)
3. Maina, V.M., Boitt, M.K.: Hungarian association of agricultural informatics European Federation for information technology in agriculture. J. Agric. Inform. 11(2), 12–21 (2021)
4. Jantzi, S.C., Dutton, C.L., Saha, A., et al.: Novel 'filter pellet' sample preparation strategy for quantitative LA-ICP-MS analysis of filter-bound sediments: a 'green chemistry' alternative to sediment fingerprinting in Tanzania's Ruvu River basin. J. Soil Sed. 19(1), 478–490 (2019)
5. Berquist, J., O'Brien, W.: A quantitative model-based fault detection and diagnostics (FDD) system for zone-level inefficiencies. Ashrae Trans. 124(PT.2), 133–154 (2018)
6. Dao, M., Kwan, C., Bernabe, S., et al.: A joint sparsity approach to soil detection using expanded bands of WV-2 images. IEEE Geosci. Remote Sens. Lett. 16(12), 1869–1873 (2019)
7. Aboud, N., Bias, E.S., Brites, R.S., et al.: Multitemporal change detection using the NDVI model in the soil use and land cover. Anuario do Instituto de Geociencias 41(3), 592–604 (2018)
8. Richter, J., Kessler, A., Weber, T., et al.: Developing and testing a new quantitative near infrared spectroscopy online tracking measuring system for soil detection during automatic dishwashing. J. Near Infrared Spectrosc. 29(3), 179–187 (2021)
9. Kunderenko, D., Пугач, А., Zhukovskyy, V.: To the issue of creating models of precise soil compaction detection for production scale use. Bull. NTU KhPI Ser. Strateg. Manage. Portfolio Program Project Manage. 2(4), 54–59 (2021)
10. Put, H., Steppe, K.: Automated detection of atmospheric and soil drought stress in *Ficus benjamina* using stem diameter measurements and modelling. Irrig. Sci. 40(1), 29–43 (2021)
11. Jin, W.B., Seo, H.B., Belkin, S., et al.: An optical detection module-based biosensor using fortified bacterial beads for soil toxicity assessment. Anal. Bioanal. Chem. 412(14), 3373–3381 (2020)

12. Meena, R.: Modified Ulaby model on backscattering as a function of salinity, frequency and soil moisture. Indian J. Agric. Res. **53**, 646–654 (2019)
13. Harasaki, K., Asai, M., et al.: Validation of a fluid-solid multiphase flow simulation by a SPH-DEM coupled method and soil foundation scour simulation with a coarse graining particle model. Trans. Jpn. Soc. Comput. Eng. Sci. **2018**(2), 20182001–20182001 (2018)
14. Shabani, F., Aflaki, R., Minamide, T., et al.: Soil aquifer treatment to meet reclaimed water requirements. Water Environ. Res. **92**(2), 266–277 (2020)

Soil Temperature and Humidity Detection System Based on Machine Learning and Computer Vision

Qiuduo Zhao[1,2(✉)], Liu Zhao[1], Ke Liu[1], and Xudong Zhang[1]

[1] College of Electronical and Information Engineering, Heilongjiang University of Science and Technology, Harbin 150022, Heilongjiang, China
22025744@qq.com

[2] Key Laboratory of Agricultural Renewable Resource Utilization Technology, Harbin 150030, China

Abstract. In agricultural production, the growth of seeds is closely related to soil temperature and humidity. Different crops have different requirements on the temperature, humidity and humidity of the crop area, so soil temperature, humidity and humidity play an important role in the growth of seeds and increase productivity and income. This paper aims to study a soil temperature and humidity detection system based on computer learning and computer vision. The soil temperature and humidity detection system based on machine learning and computer vision has the characteristics of accurate data, real-time monitoring, and multiple storage. This article will divide the program into two parts: front-end and back-end. The front end is a part of the field of soil detection, which is mainly used to monitor, extract and transmit soil temperature and humidity data. In this case, sensors are used in conjunction with serial communication techniques to determine sensor data capture, and to receive and transmit data using short-circuit wireless transmission techniques and long-range wireless transmission techniques. End-to-end is used to process data from the front end, and the main purpose is to use data technology and related controls to store and retrieve data for users to use, using technologies such as OLEDB and VC to deploy data. Experiments have shown that the system constructed in this paper detects soil temperature and humidity about 20–100 times faster than traditional manual detection, and the system has high stability. In different weather environments, the detection time error does not exceed about 10%.

Keywords: Machine Learning · Computer Vision · Soil Temperature and Humidity · Wireless Transmission

1 Introduction

With the development of computer and wireless network technology, people are ushering in the era of artificial intelligence. Artificial intelligence is the intelligence created by human beings, and machine learning and computer vision are the supporting technologies

A. Li et al. (Eds.): 6GN 2022, LNICST 505, pp. 40–47, 2023.
https://doi.org/10.1007/978-3-031-36014-5_4

of artificial intelligence. Temperature and humidity are very important factors in agricultural production, which directly determine the productivity of agriculture. Custom-made room temperature and humidifiers could no longer meet the requirements, so a room temperature and humidity detection system with the help of computer technology was included in the search for this remote sensing system. The distance and acquisition of soil temperature and humidity data and maintenance data in this area make up for the lack of initial soil temperature and humidity detection [1, 2].

In the research of soil temperature and humidity detection system based on machine learning and computer vision, many scholars have studied it and achieved good results, for example, Servadei L records the moisture content and temperature and humidity in the air as a monitoring screen, designed A real-time monitoring system of rice field information based on hybrid antenna sensor network is proposed [3]. Elyan E stated that air temperature and humidity, total rainfall and maximum evaporation are typical input data for soil carbon dioxide models, i.e. the effects of thermal conductivity, humidity and humidity on soil performance. Carbon dioxide balance model and soil temperature, and humidity record time step and room temperature and humidity data to calculate soil properties [4].

Soil temperature and humidity detection system based on machine learning and computer vision has the characteristics of accurate data, real-time monitoring, and multiple storage. This article will divide the program into two parts: front-end and back-end, the front end is a part of the field of soil detection, which is mainly used to monitor, extract and transmit soil temperature and humidity data. In this case, sensors are used in conjunction with serial communication techniques to determine sensor data capture, and to receive and transmit data using short-circuit wireless transmission techniques and long-range wireless transmission techniques. End-to-end is used to process data from the front end, and the main purpose is to use data technology and related controls to store and retrieve data for users to use, using technologies such as OLEDB and VC to deploy data.

2 Research on Soil Temperature and Humidity Detection System Based on Machine Learning and Computer Vision

2.1 Application of Machine Learning and Computer Vision in the Field of Soil Temperature and Humidity Detection

The manual operation and calculation of temperature and humidity meter verification not only has a large workload, but also has low precision and many uncontrollable human errors. Therefore, it is very urgent to solve the requirements of automatic measurement and verification of temperature and humidity meters. With the development of computer digital vision technology, it has become possible to use mechanized automatic readings.

Based on this, this paper developed a set of glass temperature and humidity meter automatic verification system. The system is an integrated system of software and hardware including image acquisition and analysis, image identification and reading archive and process automatic control. The system software mainly includes a series of functions such as image processing and analysis, image enhancement and display, reading temperature and humidity indications from images, temperature and humidity table position control, temperature and humidity table database management, interactive man-machine interface, verification calculation and printing, etc. program. It is difficult to improve the image capture environment in the temperature and humidity tank, and during the capture process, the equipment cannot be stopped, the vibration is large, and the captured images are often seriously deteriorated. Therefore, it is difficult to process images efficiently and effectively [5, 6].

The extraction and identification of image features and parameters not only requires good accuracy, but also requires high speed. Otherwise, it is impossible to determine the position of key areas of the image during the movement of the temperature and humidity meter control. In addition to the grade of the machine, the system's requirements for speed are more important to develop faster and better algorithm programs. In order to study the image characteristics of the temperature and humidity table and improve the analysis accuracy and efficiency of the image, the system also includes the off-line image analysis program, data image storage and management program, manual comparison and other corresponding auxiliary programs, so as to extract the image for the system. Image processing models and test image algorithms provide convenience. After a certain amount of image accumulation, machine learning can be used to debug and improve the system without external acquisition equipment [7, 8].

2.2 Overall System Design

The soil temperature and humidity detection system is based on computer vision and machine learning to determine the wireless temperature and humidity detection function of the monitoring area. The system includes a data acquisition unit, a controller and a remote monitoring center. The data acquisition unit is composed of multiple sensor components distributed on the farmland, and regularly records the parameters of ambient temperature and humidity and soil temperature and humidity. All data sessions are eventually sent through the router to the registrar and then transferred to the screen. The computer in the monitoring center can display the room temperature and humidity data collected by the sensor, and the user can analyze the environment of the land based on the displayed data to determine whether irrigation is needed [9, 10].

2.3 Algorithm Selection

The similarity between data in cluster analysis is usually determined by calculating the distance between the corresponding two data. The Chebyshev distance used in this article is:

$$d(X, Y) = \max_{i=1}^{n}(|x_i - y_i|) \tag{1}$$

In the formula, X and Y both represent an n-dimensional data object. The most commonly used clustering criterion function (loss function) in clustering analysis is the error sum of squares function [11, 12].

$$E = \sum_{i=1}^{k} \sum_{x \in c_i} \|x - c_i\|^2 \tag{2}$$

3 Research Design Experiment of Soil Temperature and Humidity Detection System Based on Machine Learning and Computer Vision

3.1 Design of Soil Temperature and Humidity Sensor

Soil temperature and humidity sensor is the key to the entire soil temperature and humidity detection system. The accuracy of the measured soil temperature and humidity data depends entirely on the accuracy of the soil temperature and humidity sensor. Therefore, the selection of soil temperature and humidity sensors needs to be strictly screened.

Soil temperature and humidity sensors needs to meet the following criteria.

High stability, easy installation and operation. Because the transmission of room temperature and humidity data must be carried out at regular intervals, it is required that the room temperature and humidity sensors be accurate, and ensure that the data readings are accurate and resistant to environmental changes. At the same time, since the components of the indoor temperature and humidity sensor are very sensitive, if the installation is complicated, poor contact with the housing will result in incomplete data reading, so the simple installation of the sensor is also one of them.

The sensor is rugged and the box is solid. Since the sensor is in contact with cold ground for a long time, in order to avoid water damage, the sensor must have a strong resistance, which directly affects the life of the sensor.

High-precision measurements and accurate data. This is the most important condition for selecting a sensor, and the accuracy of the data is the most important indicator for the operation of the room temperature and humidity detection system. This requires the sensor to have very sensitive capacitive materials and a good transmission circuit to ensure the normal operation of the entire system.

The sensor needs to be less affected by the land quality, and the data transmission speed is fast. Since soil quality varies from place to place, sensors must have minimal requirements on soil texture, so it is best to ensure accurate data transmission. Likewise, data transfer speed is one of the prerequisites for programming. Extremely fast data transmission can ensure real-time monitoring of system data.

Select the sensor that meets the above conditions to meet the sensor requirements of the room temperature and humidity detection system. After comparing the ambient temperature and humidity sensors produced by various manufacturers, the TDR-3A ground humidity sensor and the (built-in) humidity sensor produced by a certain manufacturer were finally selected. For humidity and humidity.

3.2 Microprocessor

The role of the microprocessor in all wireless transmission nodes is very important. Your first task is to use the microcomputer's serial port to retrieve the information from the sensor, save it, and send it using the unit connected to the serial port. This requires the microprocessor to have powerful performance, data transmission capability and data storage capability. Also, since the microcontroller must run for a long time, it must have low power consumption to ensure long-term operation.

3.3 Experimental Design

This paper mainly compares the system constructed in this paper with the traditional manual detection, mainly for the detection speed and detection stability.

4 Experimental Analysis of Soil Temperature and Humidity Detection System Based on Machine Learning and Computer Vision

4.1 Detection Speed

This paper compares the detection speed between the algorithm system constructed in this paper and the traditional manual detection method. Under the same environment, two different algorithms are used to detect the temperature and humidity of 100, 500, 1000 m^2 of normal planting land. Comparing the detection time of the two algorithms, the experimental data are shown in Table 1.

Table 1. Comparison of two algorithms for soil temperature and humidity detection time of different sizes

	100	500	1000
Traditional algorithm	20	61	162
The algorithm in this paper	1.1	1.7	1.9

As can be seen from Fig. 1, the difference between the detection speeds of the two algorithms is very obvious, and as the detection land becomes larger and larger, the gap between the two is also increasing, from 20 times to more than 100 times. Therefore, the use of this algorithm can greatly reduce the detection time.

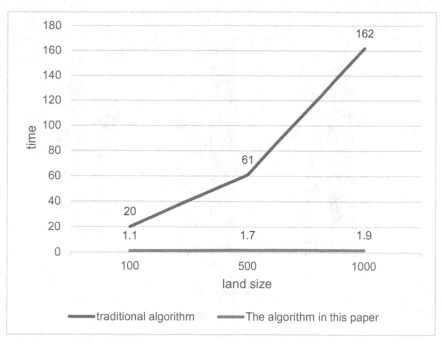

Fig. 1. Comparison of two algorithms for soil temperature and humidity detection time of different sizes.

4.2 Detection Stability

In order to test the stability of the system constructed in this paper, the speed of soil temperature and humidity testing by the system is tested in different weather environments, and the temperature and humidity testing is performed on two pieces of land of the same size in different environments, and the experimental results are shown in Table 2.

It can be seen from Fig. 2 that the detection speed of the system does not change much in different weather environments, so the system has high stability and can be adapted to detect work in different environments.

Table 2. Velocity changes detected by the system in different weathers

	rain	thunderstorm	hot sun
Test1	1.3	1.5	1.1
Test2	1.2	1.1	1.2

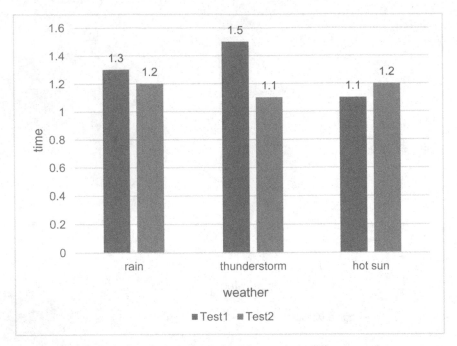

Fig. 2. Velocity changes detected by the system in different weathers.

5 Conclusions

With the advent of the era of artificial intelligence, applications based on machine learning and computer vision have received more and more development and attention. The soil temperature and humidity detection system based on machine learning and computer learning is a new application that marks the arrival of the era of artificial intelligence. This system uses the latest machine learning and computer vision technology to achieve the difficult goals of traditional soil temperature and humidity detection: remote monitoring, real-time control and data storage. This paper introduces the formation of this system and its ins and outs in detail. It truly combines machine learning and computer vision with traditional technologies, and innovatively designs and implements this system. Firstly, the definition, development and research status of soil temperature and humidity system are introduced, and the significance of soil temperature and humidity detection for agricultural production is emphasized, and the concepts and related technologies of machine learning and computer vision are expounded in detail. Secondly, the key technologies of the soil temperature and humidity detection system are described in detail, including machine learning and computer vision supporting technologies such as technology and technology. Finally, the design and implementation scheme of the system are described in detail, the new technology is combined with the traditional soil detection, and the whole system is finally completed. This soil temperature and humidity detection system based on machine learning and computer vision is the product of the combination of new technology and traditional technology. And technology is a new wireless technology, we creatively link these technologies with soil temperature and humidity detection, a traditional agricultural activity, and perfectly realize the improvement of traditional agricultural activities.

Acknowledgements. This work was financed by the Technological Project of Heilongjiang Province "The open competition mechanism to select the best candidates" (No. 2022ZXJ05C01), Funding for the Opening Project of Key Laboratory of Agricultural Renewable Resource Utilization Technology (No. HLJHDNY2114) and Heilongjiang University of Science and Technology the introduction of high-level talent research start-up fund projects (No. 000009020315).

References

1. Huang, C., Zhao, Y.: Research on temperature and humidity decoupling control of clean air conditioning system. IOP Conf. Ser. Earth Environ. Sci. **565**(1), 012034 (2020)
2. Ji, W., Liu, Y., Zhen, J.Q.: Prediction of soil humidity based on random weight Particle Swarm Optimized Extreme Learning Machine. J. Phys. Conf. Ser. **1486**(4), 042043 (2020)
3. Servadei, L., Mosca, E., Zennaro, E., et al.: Accurate cost estimation of memory systems utilizing machine learning and solutions from computer vision for design automation. IEEE Trans. Comput. **69**, 856–867 (2020)
4. Elyan, E., Vuttipittayamongkol, P., Johnston, P., et al.: Computer vision and machine learning for medical image analysis: recent advances, challenges, and way forward. Artif. Intell. Surg. **2**(1), 24–45 (2022)
5. Schultebraucks, K., Yadav, V., Galatzer-Levy, I.: Utilization of machine learning-based computer vision and voice analysis to derive digital biomarkers of cognitive functioning in trauma survivors. Digit. Biomark. **5**(1), 16–23 (2020)
6. Maitre, J., Bouchard, K., Bedard, L.P.: Mineral grains recognition using computer vision and machine learning. Comput. Geosci. **130**, 84–93 (2019)
7. As, A., Aja, B.: Determination of the oxidative stability of olive oil using an integrated system based on dielectric spectroscopy and computer vision. Inf. Process. Agric. **6**(1), 20–25 (2019)
8. Balakrishnan, S., Kumar, K.S., Ramanathan, L., et al.: IoT for health monitoring system based on machine learning algorithm. Wirel. Pers. Commun. **124**(1), 189–205 (2021)
9. Miloevi, N., Rackovi, M.: Synergy between traditional classification and classification based on negative features in deep convolutional neural networks. Neural Comput. Appl. **33**(8), 1–10 (2021)
10. Yu, Q., Jiang, P., Wang, Y., et al.: Research on first aid measures based on convolutional neural network recognition human actions. Zhonghua Wei Zhong Bing Ji Jiu Yi Xue **32**(11), 1385–1387 (2020)
11. Khan, W., Hussain, A.J., Kuru, K., et al.: Pupil localisation and eye centre estimation using machine learning and computer vision. Sensors **20**(13), 3785 (2020)
12. Rizkin, B.A., Popovich, K., Hartman, R.L.: Artificial Neural Network control of thermoelectrically-cooled microfluidics using computer vision based on IR thermography. Comput. Chem. Eng. **121**, 584–593 (2019)

Extraction of Soybean Pod Features Based on Computer Vision

Shan Ning, Qiuduo Zhao$^{(\boxtimes)}$, and Xudong Zhang

Heilongjiang University of Science and Technology, Harbin 150022, China
22025744@qq.com

Abstract. Getting agronomic traits of soybean is a labor-intensive and time-consuming operation. The technology of object detection based on image processing is the fundamental and significant link in the research of automatic accurate detection of crop phenotype. In this study, a solution based on computer vision was proposed, which could automatically and accurately detect the phenotype of crops. A fixed distance digital camera and two flash lighting were used for pod identification and automatic measurement of pod width and pod length. A novel proof of method for extraction of soybean pod characters was proposed for segmented soybean plant images. In the extraction of soybean pod characters, it was identified pod types and extracted length and width of pods. From the confusion matrix heat map, the mean of precision was 95.12%, the mean of recall was 97.06%, and the mean of F1-score value was 96.09%. Meanwhile, compared with the deep learning methods, the advantage of the method was that it did not need a large number of training samples and image annotation. The image preprocessing time of IM-Watered was 143.44 min, 21.36 min, and 17.01 min less than that of Vgg16, Alexnet, and GoogleNet. Mosreover, the agronomic characters of soybean could be obtained by one program.

Keywords: Computer Visio · Watershed Transform · Pod Identification · Soybean Breeding

1 Introduction

Soybean is one of the most important legume crops in the world. Crop phenotype investigation is a key task in the selection and breeding of crop varieties. In the investigation of soybean phenotypes, the correct identification of pod characteristics is the key and premise for the accurate extraction of phenotypes such as the number, length and width of pods. This study focused on the pictures of mature soybean pods by using phenotypes to identify one-pod, two-pod, three-pod, four-pod, and the length and width of pods. Agronomic traits of soybean plants are a major evaluation index for soybean yield [1, 2]. Getting agronomic traits of soybean is a labor-intensive and time-consuming operation. The technology of object detection based on image processing is the fundamental and significant link in the research of automatic accurate detection of crop phenotype [3,

A. Li et al. (Eds.): 6GN 2022, LNICST 505, pp. 48–58, 2023.
https://doi.org/10.1007/978-3-031-36014-5_5

4]. It is a typical object recognition task that detected the key organs (pods and stems) of soybean from images of the harvested plants [5, 6]. Therefore, it was particularly important to propose an effective method to detect the main organs of soybean plants. The automatic accurate detection could use the image understanding.

Image segmentation is based on the segmentation of regions with unique features such as color, gray scale and texture with other regions. The same features of the same region are extracted consistently and the differences of different regions are extracted. It is a process of dividing an image into disjoint regions. This process is also a process of marking, and pixels belonging to the same region are given the same number. Image segmentation is the image preprocessing of target recognition and classification. The purpose is to extract the features of the target area in the image and provide the basis for further processing and analysis. At present, image segmentation mainly includes: threshold based segmentation method [7], clustering based segmentation method [8–10], region based segmentation method [11–14], depth learning based segmentation method [15] and edge based segmentation method [16–18]. This paper uses watershed segmentation method to preprocess the image.

Following the image preprocessing, in this study, it was proposed a new extraction of phenotypes method, which used adaptive fitting curve of the pod and extraction of local extremum. After segmentation, the pixel size of the pod detected was transformed to the actual size of the pod in centimeters by using parameters calibration. And, it was used a new classification method to identify one-pod, two-pod, three-pod, and four-pod. The method did not require training processes. So the amount of data was reduced and the training time was saved. It could identify and measure the pod length and pod width automatically by computer vision.

2 Material and Methods

In this section, it was described how to get the data sources. Then, the main principles of the crop phenotypes were extracted from segmentation results.

2.1 Data Sources

For soybean plant image acquisition, Canon 5D Mark II camera and EF 24–105 mm/F4 is lens are used to vertically fix the position 2000 mm above the plant acquisition platform. The blue non-woven fabric is used as the background, and the purple dotted line is used as the reference line of cotyledon knot. The lighting system is a high angle lighting with an angle of 45 degrees with the horizontal direction. The high angle lighting has the characteristics of concentrated light beam, high brightness and good uniformity. The working room flash dpx-400 xenon lamp is used as the lighting source. The xenon lamp has the characteristics of wide spectrum range and high energy. The flash index is GN66, the color temperature is 5500k, the output is 3/8, and the lighting lampshade is 800 mm × 1200 mm rectangular soft light box with a resolution of 5616 × 3744 pixels, focal length of 55 mm, aperture value of F/11, exposure speed of 1/200 s, ISO of 100, exposure compensation of 0.

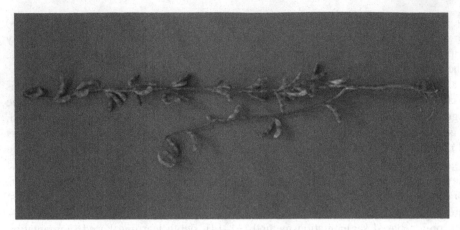

Fig. 1. A sample image of a soybean plant.

The images were saved in .jpg format. The sample image was shown in Fig. 1. Soybean plant samples for the test were from the Xiangyang experimental base of Northeast Agricultural University. The samples were collected at the end of September 2017 and at the beginning of October 2018. The total number of soybean plants was 695, including four varieties: Dongnong 52, Dongnong 251, Dongnong 252 and Dongnong 253.

2.2 MC-Watershed Algorithm

Watershed algorithm [13, 19–21] is an area segmentation method based on mathematical morphology. Its basic idea is to assume that the gradient image is a terrain surface, the gradient value of each image pixel indicates the altitude of the point, the area with a small gradient is a flat area, forming a basin, and the area with a large gradient at the edge is a ridge of the divided basin. The lower ridge is submerged by the rise of water level, and a dam is built on the higher ridge. To prevent regional merging, finally, image segmentation is realized according to the composition of isolated ponding basins, as shown in Fig. 2.

Watershed transform is an image segmentation based on regional gradient change. Even if the target region has low contrast and weak boundary, watershed transform can provide a closed contour. However, watershed algorithm will produce a large number of over segmentation and under segmentation for the segmentation of soybean plant images with more details. Watershed algorithm only considers the gray information and does not consider the spatial information, so it has weak ability to segment the image with complex texture or noise pollution. In order to solve these problems, a watershed image segmentation algorithm based on the fusion of multiple methods is designed.

The traditional watershed algorithm often produces a large number of over segmentation due to the complexity of the internal texture of the target. Compared with the traditional watershed algorithm, the marked watershed algorithm [20] can reduce the over segmentation by adding additional information to improve the gradient image, and conducting internal and external mark guided image segmentation on the image to prevent over segmentation. To segment the soybean plant image using the marker

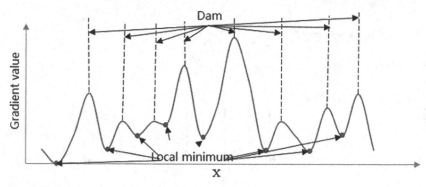

Fig. 2. Diagram of watershed segmentation. The blue line is the gradient image value.

watershed algorithm, it is necessary to find a group of markers to determine the positions of different pods and stems in the image. In order to obtain better markers, the erosion, expansion, open operation and close operation of mathematical morphology are used to process them. Corrosion operation is to eliminate small targets and narrow the range of large target area through the translation of structural elements on the target. Its essence is to shrink the target boundary. The expansion operation is to expand the range of the target area and expand the boundary to the outside through the translation of structural elements on the target, which can be used to fill some holes in the target area and eliminate small particle noise contained in the target area. The start operation is an operation of first eroding and then expanding the image. It is used to eliminate small noise targets, smooth the shape boundary, and do not change its area, which is helpful to break the adhesion between targets. The closed operation is an operation that expands the image first and then erodes it. It is used to fill small holes in the target, connect adjacent targets or contours, and smooth the target boundary without changing the area of the target. In order to better segment the target and the background, in the marking watershed algorithm, the gray-scale gradient image is used as the terrain surface, and each pixel lower than the given threshold is set as the foreground marker, and then the mathematical morphology operation is used to eliminate the small noise interference, providing better marks for the segmentation of the foreground and the background. Diagram of MC-Watershed segmentation was shown in Fig. 3. The selection of structural elements and mathematical morphology operation is the basis for obtaining better marks [22]. The gray-scale image is opened and closed based on reconstruction, and the local minimum value in the gradient image is set as the foreground marker.

In order to improve the segmentation accuracy of soybean pods and stems, an improved watershed algorithm is proposed, which divides the image segmentation process into three stages: image preprocessing, re-segmentation of under segmented regions and merging of over segmented regions [23]. The segmented image is shown in Fig. 4.

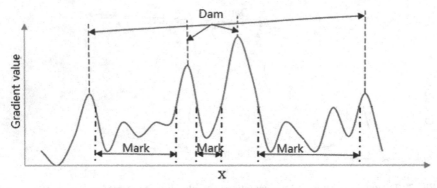

Fig. 3. Diagram of MC-Watershed segmentation. The blue line is the gradient image value.

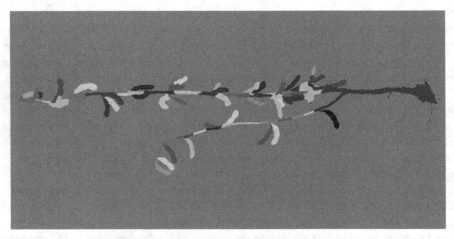

Fig. 4. The result of the IM-watered algorithm.

2.3 The Investigation of Soybean Phenotypes

In the study of soybean phenotype, it was the key and premise to correctly identify pod type and extract pod length and width. And, pod type was the number of seeds in pod. This section focused on the pictures of mature soybean pods by using adept curve regression analysis to identify one-pod, two-pod, three-pod, and four-pod.

Firstly, the segmented image of a pod was binarized, and the skeleton was extracted for it. Secondly, the skeleton was used LF for extracting line. The coordinate system was transformed according to the inclination angle of the extracting line for obtaining horizontal pods, as shown in Fig. 5. Thirdly, the binary image was calculated to obtain the pod characteristics ρ that was given by Eq. (1).

$$\rho = \rho_i \quad i = 1, 2 \ldots m$$
$$\rho_i = \sum_{j=1}^{m} x_{ij} \quad j = 1, 2 \ldots l \tag{1}$$

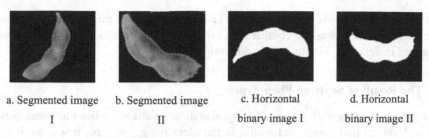

| a. Segmented image | b. Segmented image | c. Horizontal | d. Horizontal |
| I | II | binary image I | binary image II |

Fig. 5. Segmented pod image by binarization.

The size of binary image was $l \times m$. Where ρ_i was the ordinate of the characteristic value, x_{ij} was the value in the binary image.

The ρ was processed by adaptive linear regression. The mathematical model of linear regression was selected univariate τ times for improving accuracy, $\tau \in (1, 16)$. The linear regression function was given by Eq. (2) and Eq. (3).

$$y_e = c_0 + c_1 x_e + c_2 x_e^2 + \cdots + c_\tau x_e^\tau \tag{2}$$

$$\varepsilon_e = \frac{1}{m} \sum_{i=0}^{m} \frac{\sqrt{(y_{ei} - \rho_i)^2}}{y_{ei}} \quad i = 1, 2 \ldots m \tag{3}$$

where y_e was the ordinate of the curve regression, x_e was the abscissa of the curve regression, and $c_0, c_{1\ldots}c_\tau$ were the parameters of the linear regression function. The function was defined with the mean error rate ε_e less than $\theta\%$.

Found local maximums of linear regression, and deleted the maximum value smaller than δ. The pod category was estimated according to the number of the local maximums. The value at the absolute maximum was calculated and converted to pod width in mm. The pod width Pw could be obtained by Eq. (4). Estimation of pod length Pl according to the relation of x, y in linear regression could be obtained by Eq. (5).

$$Pw = Mw \times \varphi \tag{4}$$

$$Pl = Ml \times \varphi \tag{5}$$

$$y_e = \omega \tag{6}$$

where Mw was the value of the absolute maximum, Ml was the value of the distance from x_a to x_b. The x_a and x_b were the two points of intersection of the Eq. (1) and Eq. (6).

3   Results and Discussion

In this section, experimental results were presented using four varieties of soybean plant images. This section showed the feature extraction results of pods. It was used a new identification method to identify one-pod, two-pod, three-pod, and four-pod. Then, length and width of pods were extracted. The result of soybean phenotypes was shown in Sect. 3.1. Next, it was the comparative experiment, the results were described and compared in Sect. 3.2. Finally, it was discussion in Sect. 3.3.

3.1 The Result of Soybean Phenotypes

After the segmentation of a plant, the segmentation results were used to identify pod type and extract pod length and width. In the identifying pod type, it was set $\theta = 5$ for the upper line in the mean error ε_e. If the value of the local maximum of the curve regression y_e was smaller than $\delta = 5$, it was deleted. In calculating length and width of pods, it was set $\varphi = 0.05$ and $\omega = 3$. In Fig. 6, the number of black stars represented the type of pod that one black star was one-pod, two black stars were two-pod, three black stars were three-pod and four black stars were four-pod. Red points were the distribution of the pod characteristics. The blue line was linear regression for pod characteristics. The green dash-dotted line was the error of the linear regression function. In Fig. 6a, it showed the soybean phenotypes that was three-pod and width 10.7 mm, length 39.1 mm. In Fig. 6b, it showed the soybean phenotypes that was two-pod and width 10.1 mm, length 32.7 mm.

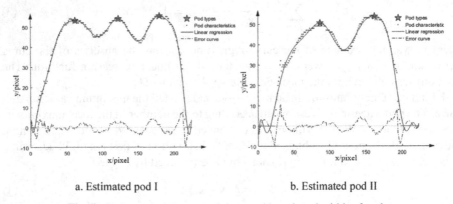

a. Estimated pod I   b. Estimated pod II

Fig. 6. Estimated pod type and extracted length and width of pods.

3.2 Comparative Experiment

Compared with neural network, this method did not require training data, and the parameters were fitted with the dataset to process.

The mean square value of the difference between the true value and the calculated value was computed, and the magnitude of the mean square error was used to evaluate the accuracy of the calculated error. The mean square error of the pod width MSEW and the pod length MSEL were calculated by Eq. (7) and Eq. (8).

$$\text{MSEW} = \frac{1}{M} \sum_{i=1}^{M} (pw(i) - rw(i))^2 \tag{7}$$

$$\text{MSEL} = \frac{1}{M} \sum_{i=1}^{M} (pl(i) - rl(i))^2 \tag{8}$$

where M was the number of pods, rw was the true value of the pod width , rl was the true value of the pod length, pw and pl were the measured value of the pod width and length. The average of MSEW was 0.89 mm^2, and MSEL was 1.94 mm^2.

The hit rate and the confusion matrix were commonly used metrics for assessing the quality of identification methods. In the case of identification, several metrics were used to obtain performance indicators. Some measures were based on the number of correct identification compared with the ground truth. These metrics were based on the spatial overlap and result from the four basic cardinalities of the confusion matrix: true positives (TP), false positives (FP), true negatives (TN), and false negatives (FN). Based on the cardinalities of the confusion matrix, it was obtained the following performance indicators: Precision (%), Recall (%), and F1-score (%) were calculated by Eq. (9), Eq. (10) and Eq. (11).

$$\text{Precision} = \frac{TP}{TP + FP} \tag{9}$$

$$\text{Recall} = \frac{TP}{TP + FN} \tag{10}$$

$$\text{F1-score} = 2 \times \frac{\text{Precision} \cdot \text{Recall}}{\text{Precision} + \text{Recall}} \tag{11}$$

Precision was the percentage of the correct classification of pods in all samples, reflecting the accuracy of the method. The recall was the percentage of the right sort of pods compare with the ground truth, reflecting the sensitivity of the method. F1-score values revealed an appropriate balance between precision and recall.

In Fig. 7, the columns of the confusion matrix heat map were predicted class, and its lines were true class; the two columns on the far right were the precision of the pod class, and the bottom two rows were the recall of the pod class. Overall, the mean of precision was 95.12%, the mean of recall was 97.06%, and the mean of F1-score value was 96.09%, in Table 1. It could be seen from the above mean value that identification of pod types is effective.

3.3 Discussion

To estimate the practicability of different algorithms, it was compared the training time, or preprocessing time, and precision of four algorithms. Among them, YAN Zhuang-Zhuang et al [24] provided the result of Vgg16, AlexNet, and GoogleNet for classification performance. All experiments were performed on a workstation with an Intel Core i7, NVIDIA Titan Xp 12 GHz CPU, and 16 G memory using MATLAB. From Table 2, the method was slightly lower than the precision of deep learning. However, the training cost of deep learning was high. IM-Watered method used preprocessing instead of network training, so its initial application time was the least among the four methods shown in

Confusion Matrix for the Classification of Pods

one-pod	416	32	2	0		92.44%	7.56%
two-pod	2	2065	30	5		98.24%	1.76%
three-pod	0	26	1767	15		97.73%	2.27%
four-pod	5	17	32	625		92.05%	7.95%
	98.35%	96.50%	96.50%	96.90%			
	1.65%	3.50%	3.50%	3.10%			
	one-pod	two-pod	three-pod	four-pod			

True class (left axis)

Predicted Class

Fig. 7. Confusion matrix heat map of the method.

Table 1. Classification performance of the method.

Pod class	Precision	Recall	F1-score
one-pod	92.44	98.35	95.39
two-pod	98.24	96.50	97.37
three-pod	97.73	96.50	97.12
four-pod	92.05	96.90	94.47
Mean	95.12	97.06	96.09

Table 2. The training cost of Vgg16, AlexNet, and GoogleNet were 144.56 min, 22.48 min, and 18.13 min. The preprocessing time of the IM-Watershed was only 1.12 min. The IM-Watershed did not need annotation, but deep learning needed time and effort for image annotation. The results showed that the identification method proposed in Sect. 2.3 was effective in soybean phenotypic research. The method could identification of pod types the number of seeds in the pod, measure pod width, and pod length, and its function was more perfect than the above deep learning network.

Table 2. Comparison of precision, training, or preprocessing time of four methods on identifying pods.

Model	Iteration/loop	Time/min	Precision/%
Vgg16	2000	144.56	98.41
AlexNet	2000	22.48	97.11
GoogleNet	2000	18.13	95.83
IM-Watershed	46	1.12	95.12

4 Conclusions

A method of soybean pod feature extraction based on computer vision is proposed. After the segmentation processing, it used parameters calibration and classification for extracting the agronomic traits of soybean. The segmentation results were used to identify pod type and extracting length and width of pod. Moreover, the pod identification method could provide similar precision compared with the above three deep learning methods in Sect. 3.3, and the initial cost of the identification method was very little. At the same time, the pod width and pod length could also be calculated by the method. At present, the research of deep learning in pod recognition did not include the research of pod size. The identification method didn't special requirements for the number of samples, and also could be used in small samples experiment. Nevertheless, the training of deep learning network needed a large number of training samples. If the number of training samples were insufficient, the network could be over fitted and could not be used. The result of the experiment showed that the proposed method could be applied to the actual identification of pods, and provide an important solution for further automatic extraction of pod phenotypes. However, some characteristics of pods have not been extracted. In addition, the method of phenotypic features is extended to feature extraction of other crops.

Acknowledgements. This work was financed by the Technological Project of Heilongjiang Province "The open competition mechanism to select the best candidates" (No. 2022ZXJ05C01), Funding for the Opening Project of Key Laboratory of Agricultural Renewable Resource Utilization Technology (No. HLJHDNY2114) and Heilongjiang University of Science and Technology the introduction of high-level talent research start-up fund projects (No. 000009020315).

References

1. Qiu, L., Chang, R., et al.: Description Specification and Data Standard of Soybean Germplasm Resources, vol. 3, pp. 18–74. China Agricultural Press, Beijing (2006)
2. Rahaman, M.M., Chen, D.J., Gillani, Z., et al.: Advanced phenotyping and phenotype data analysis for the study of plant growth and development. Front. Plant Sci. **6**(619), 1–15 (2015)
3. Cen, H., Zhu, Y., Sun, D., et al.: Current status and future perspective of the application of deep learning in plant phenotype research. Trans. Chin. Soc. Agricult. Eng. **36**(9), 1–16 (2020)
4. Zhu, F., Zheng, Z.: Image-based assessment of growth vigor for Phalaenopsis Aphrodite seedlings using convolutional neural network. Trans. Chin. Soc. Agricult. Eng. **36**(9) (2018)
5. Ma, X., Zhu, K., Guan, H., et al.: High-throughput phenotyping analysis of potted soybean plants using colorized depth images based on a proximal platform. Remote Sens. **11**(9), 1–24 (2019)
6. Wang, L., Dong, Q., Yang, L., et al.: Crop classification based on a novel feature filtering and enhancement method. Remote Sens. **11**(4), 1–18 (2019)
7. Otsu, N.: A threshold selection method from gray-level histograms. IEEE Trans. Syst. Man Cybern. **9**, 62–66 (1979)
8. Deng, B.: A survey on advanced K-means algorithm. Comput. Eng. Softw. **41**(02), 188–192 (2020)

9. Chatzis, S.P., Varvarigou, T.A.: A fuzzy clustering approach toward hidden Markov random field models for enhanced spatially constrained image segmentation. IEEE Trans. Fuzzy Syst. **16**(5), 1351–1361 (2008)

10. Zhu, L., Teng, Q., Gong, J.: Mineral particle segmentation algorithm based on improved fuzzy C-means and region merging. Sci. Technol. Eng. **20**(34), 14138–14145 (2020)

11. Bezdek, J.C., Ehrlich, R., Full, W.: FCM: The fuzzy c -means clustering algorithm. Comput. Geosci. **10**(2–3), 191–203 (1984)

12. Wang, H., Zong, Z., Zhang, W., et al.: An extraction xylem images of Caragana stenophylla Pojark based on K-means clustering and circle structure extraction algorithm. Trans. Chin. Soc. Agricult. Eng. **36**(1), 193–199 (2020)

13. Gamarra, M., Zurek, E., Escalante, H.J., et al.: Split and merge watershed: A two-step method for cell segmentation in fluorescence microscopy images. Biomed. Signal Process. Control **53**, 1–12 (2019)

14. Zhang, J., Han, S., Zhai, Z., et al.: Improved adaptive watershed method for segmentation of cotton leaf adhesion lesions. Trans. Chin. Soc. Agricult. Eng. **34**(24), 165–174 (2018)

15. Lu, X., Liu, Z.: A review of image semantic segmentation based on deep learning. Softw. Guide **20**(01), 242–244 (2021)

16. Canny J.: A computational approach to edge detection. IEEE Trans. Pattern Anal. Mach. Intell. **PAMI-8**(6):679–698 (1986

17. Zheng, H., Bai, Y., Zhang, Y.: An edge detection algorithm based on Sobel operator. Microcomput. Appl. **36**(10), 4–6 (2020)

18. Chen, S., Wang, X., Ge, Y., et al.: Application of image edge extraction algorithm in third national land survey. Computer Technology and Development **30**(10), 161–166 (2020)

19. Vincent, L., Soille, P.: Watersheds in digital spaces: an efficient algorithm based on immersion simulations. IEEE Trans. Pattern Anal. Mach. Intell. **13**(6), 583–598 (1991)

20. Zeng, Q., Miao, Y., Liu, C., et al.: Algorithm based on marker-controlled watershed transform for overlapping plant fruit segmentation. Opt. Eng. **48**(2), 1–10 (2009)

21. Hamarneh, G., Li, X.: Watershed segmentation using prior shape and appearance knowledge. Image Vis. Comput. **27**(1–2), 59–68 (2009)

22. Derivaux, S., Forestier, G., Wemmert, C., et al.: Supervised image segmentation using watershed transform, fuzzy classification and evolutionary computation. Pattern Recogn. Lett. **31**(15), 2364–2374 (2010)

23. Ning, S.: Research on Soybean Plant Phenotypic Feature Detection Method Based on Machine Vision, vol.6.. Northeast Agricultural University (2021)

24. Yan, Z.Z., Yan, X.H., Shi, J., et al.: Classification of soybean pods using deep learning. Acta Agron. Sin. **46**(11), 1771–1779 (2020)

Artificial Intelligence Cross-Domain Fusion Pattern Recognition Based on Intelligent Robot Algorithm

Yu Qiu and Zheqing Tang[✉]

Heilongjiang Vocational College, Harbin 150001, China
347493701@qq.com

Abstract. In recent years, the deep integration of new technology systems based on information and Internet technology and various industries has made product innovation increasingly diversified, compounded, intelligent and miniaturized. Technology integration is another aspect of industrial development. New and decisive factors have become the key way for enterprises to break through technological constraints, respond to market changes, and achieve innovative development. Based on the related application research of intelligent robot algorithm, this paper constructs the current artificial intelligence cross-domain fusion pattern recognition system to meet the needs of cross-domain fusion pattern recognition applications. This paper analyzes the formation and evolution of cross-domain technology fusion. In view of the complex correlation between cross-domains, we further consider multi-source data fusion scenarios, integrate user information in the field of e-commerce and social networks, and introduce an attention mechanism to Focus on the importance of different related information. The final result of the research shows that when the number of fusions of platform 5 is 96 times, its corresponding cross-domain fusion compatibility is 84.6%. The results show that when the number of fusions changes, the corresponding cross-domain fusion compatibility value does not change, and it always maintains a stable level of about 85%. The results show that the application of artificial intelligence cross-domain fusion pattern recognition based on intelligent robot algorithm is feasible.

Keywords: Intelligent Robot · Artificial Intelligence · Cross-Domain Fusion · Pattern Recognition

1 Introduction

Technology begins with the purposeful programming of realistic needs, and new technologies are generated thanks to the continuous integration and evolution of technologies in different fields, and the results of innovation. Technological integration is a phenomenon of technological integration and blurring of technological boundaries in different fields formed by technological innovation driven and demand structure upgrading [1]. The artificial intelligence system technology in a single field is very mature, but

A. Li et al. (Eds.): 6GN 2022, LNICST 505, pp. 59–66, 2023.
https://doi.org/10.1007/978-3-031-36014-5_6

in the era of big data, the artificial intelligence required by users is often not only reflected in a single field. There are also many limitations in solving the data sparsity and cold start problems of artificial intelligence in a certain field.

In recent years, many researchers have explored artificial intelligence cross-domain fusion pattern recognition, and achieved good results. For example, Lakshmi G V believes that cross-domain recommendation has great advantages in solving the problem of data sparseness and cold start, and combining data from two or more domains through different methods can often achieve different effects [2]. The most important core of Pal P's cross-domain recommendation is to find the relationship between two or more domains, and to generate more accurate personalized content for users by using the commonality between users' check-in behaviors in these domains [3]. At present, scholars at home and abroad have conducted a lot of research on the application of artificial intelligence cross-domain fusion pattern recognition. These previous theoretical and experimental results provide a theoretical basis for the research in this paper.

Based on the relevant theoretical research on intelligent robot algorithms, this paper designs a system for artificial intelligence cross-domain fusion pattern recognition, and has achieved relatively fruitful research results. The experimental results of cross-domain fusion compatibility analysis show that when the number of fusions changes, the corresponding cross-domain fusion compatibility value does not change, and it always maintains a stable level of about 85%. The results show that the application of artificial intelligence cross-domain fusion pattern recognition based on intelligent robot algorithm is feasible.

2 Related Theoretical Overview and Research

2.1 Cross-Domain Fusion Pattern Recognition

(1) **Cross-domain integration.** The development of cross-domain fusion theory focuses on using data from multiple domains to perform knowledge fusion to predict users' ratings on the target domain and provide users with recommendations. However, experience shows that ranking determines the lower bound of the model, and recall determines the upper bound of the model. Starting from the recall model to solve the cross-domain recommendation problem can achieve unexpected results [4]. At present, the theoretical development of intelligent robot algorithms mainly focuses on modeling the multi-behavior and multi-attribute of users, and there are relatively few researches on commodity fusion in different fields. This paper studies the combination of artificial intelligence cross-domain fusion pattern recognition and intelligent robot algorithm, and solves the neighbor sampling problem, node vector learning problem and feature mismatch problem generated in the combination process. While expanding the cross-domain recommendation research boundary, it enriches the intelligence The development of robotic algorithm theory.

(2) **Pattern recognition.** Pattern recognition means that the receiving end automatically recognizes the modulation mode of the received signal, and the demodulator uses the corresponding method to demodulate the information according to the recognition result [5]. In cross-domain integration, in order to realize the intercommunication of communication systems of different systems, pattern recognition is an indispensable

core technology and the basis for ensuring the smooth completion of communication. Before widespread application, the identification of modulation patterns of pattern recognition signals mainly relied on manual judgment through signal measurement equipment [6, 7]. Another way is to carry a variety of demodulators at the output, each demodulator demodulates a unique type of signal, and then analyzes the output of the demodulator to determine the presence or absence of each signal.

(3) **Construction of cross-domain fusion pattern recognition system.** In the era of rapid development of the Internet industry, a large number of platforms generate data every day, making the amount of data grow exponentially. The growth of data has also created many difficulties for people's daily processing. People can no longer use traditional statistical methods to complete data processing, so tools based on intelligent robot algorithms emerge as the times require [8]. With the development of intelligent robot algorithm technology and the improvement of people's needs, it has become a research hotspot. Therefore, cross-domain fusion pattern recognition technology has gradually attracted people's attention. In solving the problems of data sparseness and cold start, cross-domain fusion pattern recognition has great advantages, and the fusion of data from two or more domains through different methods can often achieve different effects.

In the construction process of the artificial intelligence cross-domain fusion pattern recognition system based on intelligent robot algorithm. The cross-domain knowledge representation learning based on collaborative filtering aims to integrate the information of the auxiliary domain and the target domain, and then adopts the centralized Methods such as collaborative filtering, joint matrix factorization, tensor factorization, etc. Perform knowledge representation learning while considering the differences between domains [9]. Using collaborative filtering to stitch the auxiliary field and the target field scoring matrix is equivalent to turning multiple fields into a single field, and a single field algorithm can be used. Although this method is simple to implement, it requires the scoring mechanism of the auxiliary field and the target field to be consistent, which is not suitable for scenarios with differences between domains [10]. The design loss function combines the loss functions of each matrix according to the weight coefficient, and the joint matrix decomposition obtains the feature matrix of the user and the item, and finally multiplies the original matrix.

2.2 Theoretical Introduction to Cross-Domain Integration

Cross-domain fusion technology fusion is the result of simultaneous efforts of innovation-driven and demand-driven. Technological innovation, industry-university-research cooperation and basic research are important prerequisites for the successful integration of cross-disciplinary technologies. The cross-integration of market demand and industry is also an important guarantee for technology integration. In addition, technological integration is also guided and constrained by technological system reforms, technological innovation activities and changes in user needs [11]. Therefore, we need to take a systematic view to gain a more accurate and comprehensive understanding of the technology integration process from basic disciplines, applied research, technology development to industrialization.

Most scholars believe that the process of cross-disciplinary integration technology integration runs through multiple links such as cross-disciplinary integration, cross-technology integration, market and industry penetration and integration [12]. When stakeholders from different fields aim to achieve the same goal or solve complex problems of common concern, the cross-border citation and flow of scientific knowledge and the cross-integration of research methods lead to the overlapping of knowledge paths in different disciplines. The close R&D cooperation makes the knowledge spillover effect gradually spread, promotes the mutual penetration of different technologies, produces technology integration, and further promotes the emergence of new products, which leads to market integration and inter-enterprise mergers, and finally promotes the successful realization of industrial integration.

3 Experiment and Research

3.1 Experimental Method

A low-dimensional network representation of all cross-domain neighbors of node v. Then use the low-dimensional representation h of the current node to perform preference fusion migration, which is completed through several fully connected layers, and finally obtain the low-dimensional representation of several cross-domain neighbor nodes j ∈ N(v) of node v. The calculation formula is:

$$h_v^c = leakyReLU\left([h_v \| n_c]\right) \tag{1}$$

$$h_v^c = leakyReLU\left(\beta W h_c^v + \theta h_v^n\right) \tag{2}$$

In the above formula, after obtaining the same domain node hn and the cross domain node hc, and finally using nonlinear mapping to fuse the two to obtain the new node representation hv of the final node v. where β is used to control how much cross-domain preference information is transferred into the existing framework, and θ is used to control how much current existing domain-effective information is retained.

3.2 Experimental Requirements

In the calculation process of the experiment, the degree of cross-domain transfer information can be flexibly controlled by β and θ. In particular, when β is set to 0 and θ is set to 1, the cross-domain information does not participate in the learning of the model, and does not use Any cross-domain item information is equivalent to the traditional graph neural network model; when β is set to 1 and θ is set to 0, the learning of the model is all derived from cross-domain model learning, and the model will not use the network in the same domain relationship to learn. The flexible use of β and θ enables the model to trade-off between accuracy and generalization, while also being suitable for various cross-domain tasks. And make the model achieve more obvious benefits in the final effect.

4 Analysis and Discussion

4.1 Cross-Domain Fusion Compatibility Analysis

By comparing and analyzing the relationship between the fusion times and fusion compatibility of the artificial intelligence cross-domain fusion pattern recognition platform based on intelligent robot algorithms, it is possible to judge whether the cross-domain fusion model is feasible. The experimental data are as follows:

Table 1. Cross-domain fusion compatibility analysis table.

Platform	Fusion times	Compatibility(%)
One	74	86.5
Two	85	83.7
Three	63	85.2
Four	41	85.9
Five	96	84.6

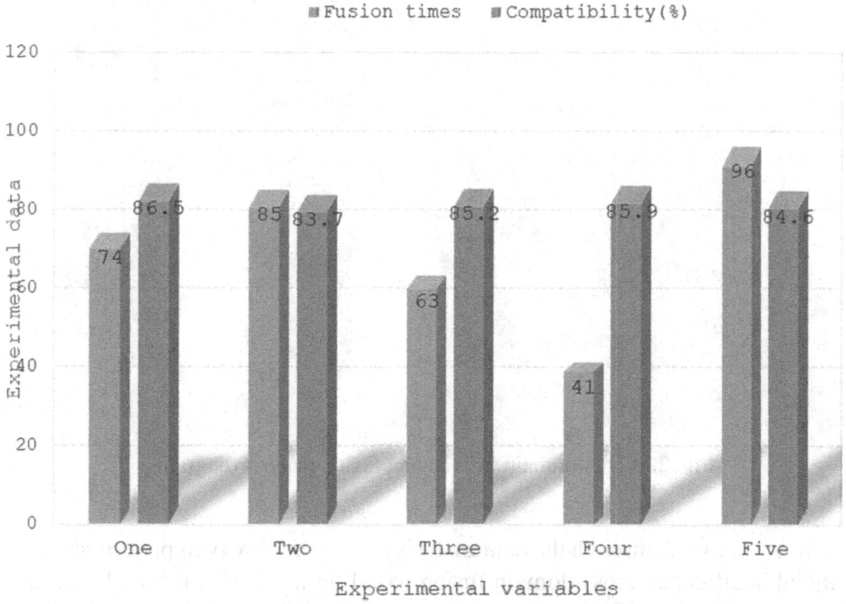

Fig. 1. Cross-domain fusion compatibility analysis diagram

From the data analysis in Table 1 and Fig. 1, it can be seen from the results that when the number of fusions of platform 1 is 74 times, the corresponding cross-domain fusion compatibility is 86.5%. When the number of fusions on platform 2 is 85, its corresponding cross-domain fusion compatibility is 83.7%. When the number of integrations of platform three is 63, its corresponding cross-domain integration compatibility is 85.2%. When the number of fusions of platform 4 is 41, its corresponding cross-domain fusion compatibility is 85.9%. When the number of fusions on platform 5 is 96, its corresponding cross-domain fusion compatibility is 84.6%. The experimental results show that when the number of fusions changes, the corresponding cross-domain fusion compatibility value does not change, and it always maintains a stable level of about 85%. The results show that the application of artificial intelligence cross-domain fusion pattern recognition based on intelligent robot algorithm is feasible.

4.2   Cross-Domain Fusion Complexity Analysis

Data analysis is carried out on the complexity of artificial intelligence cross-domain fusion pattern recognition based on intelligent robot algorithm. The experimental data is shown in Fig. 2.

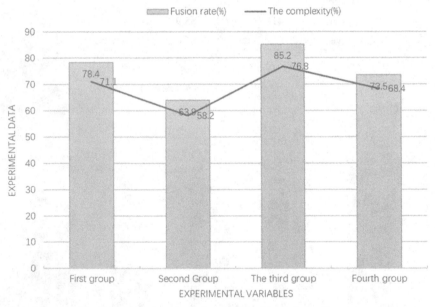

Fig. 2. Cross-domain fusion complexity analysis diagram

As shown in Fig. 2, through the data analysis of the complexity of pattern recognition of artificial intelligence cross-domain fusion based on intelligent robot algorithm, the results are as follows: the fusion rates of cross-domain fusion in the four sets of data are 78.4%, 63.9%, 85.2%, respectively. % and 73.5%, and the corresponding cross-domain fusion complexities are 71.1%, 58.2%, 76.8% and 68.4%, respectively. The results show that in the process of artificial intelligence cross-domain fusion pattern recognition based on intelligent robot algorithm, the fusion rate of cross-domain fusion and the complexity of cross-domain fusion change synchronously, and there is a positive correlation between them.

5 Conclusions

Based on the research background of intelligent robot algorithm, this paper firstly analyzes and designs artificial intelligence cross-domain fusion pattern recognition. During the identification process, the fusion rate of cross-domain fusion and the complexity of cross-domain fusion change synchronously, and there is a positive correlation between them. And in the experiment of cross-domain fusion compatibility analysis, the results show that when the number of fusions changes, the corresponding cross-domain fusion compatibility value does not change, and it always maintains a stable level of about 85%. The final experimental results show that the application of artificial intelligence cross-domain fusion pattern recognition based on intelligent robot algorithm has certain feasibility and has corresponding promotion and application value.

References

1. Fernandez, N., Lorenzo, A.J., Rickard, M., et al.: Digital pattern recognition for the identification and classification of hypospadias using artificial intelligence vs experienced pediatric urologist. Urology **9**(21), 40–74 (2020)
2. Lakshmi, G.V., Sharada, N.: Artificial intelligence based pattern recognition. Int. J. Eng. Manag. Res. **9**(2), 29–32 (2019)
3. Pal, P., Mukherjee, V., Bhakta, S.: Design of an intelligent heuristic algorithm-based optimised fuzzy controller for speed control of a separately excited DC motor. Aust. J. Electr. Electron. Eng. **4**, 1–10 (2020)
4. Bendimerad, L.S., Houacine, N.A., Drias, H.: Swarm Intelligent Approaches for Ambulance Dispatching and Emergency Calls Covering: Application to COVID-19 Spread in Saudi Arabia. In: Abraham, A., et al. (eds.) SoCPaR 2021. LNNS, vol. 417, pp. 617–626. Springer, Cham (2022). https://doi.org/10.1007/978-3-030-96302-6_58
5. Alimjan, G., Jiaermuhamaiti, Y., Jumahong, H., et al.: An image change detection algorithm based on multi-feature self-attention fusion mechanism UNet network. Int. J. Pattern Recogn. Artif. Intell. **35**(14), 971–985 (2021)
6. Bendimerad, L.S., Drias, H.: An efficient deep self-learning artificial orca algorithm for solving ambulance dispatching and calls covering problem. In: Abraham, A., et al. (eds.) SoCPaR 2021. LNNS, vol. 417, pp. 136–145. Springer, Cham (2022). https://doi.org/10.1007/978-3-030-96302-6_12
7. Tsai, C.M., Shih, F.Y.: An efficient detection and recognition system for multiple motorcycle license plates based on decision tree. Int. J. Pattern Recognit. Artif. Intell. **36**(5).135–148 (2022)
8. Kim, J., Kim, S., Lee, H.: Pattern recognition and classifier design of bio-signals based interface in human - artificial intelligence interaction (HAII) framework for real time evaluation of emotions. J. Korean Inst. Intell. Syst. **29**(3), 242–249 (2019)
9. Monika, B.A.: Automatic twitter crime prediction using hybrid wavelet convolutional neural network with world cup optimization. Int. J. Pattern Recogn. Artif. Intell. **36**(5).1–23 (2022)
10. Maitra, S., Akter, N., Zaha, N., Mithila, A., et al.: Apriori-Backed Fuzzy Unification and Statistical Inference in Feature Reduction: An Application in Prognosis of Autism in Toddlers. **115**(1), 120–150 (2021)

11. Zaldivar, M.S.: GPU Devices. International Workshop on Artificial Intelligence and Pattern Recognition, vol. 31, no. 5, pp. 1257–1273. Springer, Cham (2021)
12. Avila-Domenech, E., Taboada-Crispi, A.: Improving the robustness of DCT-based handwritten document image watermarking against JPEG-compression. In: Hernández Heredia, Y., Milián Núñez, V., Ruiz Shulcloper, J. (eds.) IWAIPR 2021. LNCS, vol. 13055, pp. 327–336. Springer, Cham (2021). https://doi.org/10.1007/978-3-030-89691-1_32

Cross-Border Technology Integration in the Field of Artificial Intelligence Based on Neural Network Algorithm

Yu Qiu, Zheqing Tang[✉], and Yang Luo

Heilongjiang Vocational College, Harbin 150001, China
347493701@qq.com

Abstract. In recent years, with the continuous development of my country's social science and technology level, people's research and exploration in the field of cross-border technology AI has become more and more in-depth, and the society's demand for cross-border technology integration and application in the field of artificial intelligence has also increased. Gradually increasing, only by investing more research and analysis, can there be greater breakthroughs and development in the application of cross-border technology AI. Based on the neural network algorithm, this paper takes the key point of the field of artificial intelligence as the starting point, and explores the application of cross-border technology AI from a new perspective. This paper briefly introduces the current cross-border technology AI and its development trend, studies the existing cross-border technology integration applications in the field of artificial intelligence, and conducts a series of experiments to prove the artificial intelligence based on neural network algorithm. Cross-border technology integration in the field of intelligence has specific advantages. The final results of the research show that the fusion coefficient of experiment 5 is 93, and the matching degree of cross-border technology fusion in the field of artificial intelligence is 98.7%. Through the comparison of experimental data, it is found that the matching degree of cross-border technology AI has always maintained a stable level, that is, it has remained around 99%. It shows that the matching degree of cross-border technology fusion in the field of artificial intelligence does not change with the change of the fusion coefficient.

Keywords: Neural Network · Artificial Intelligence · Cross-Domain · Technology Integration

1 Introduction

With the development of science and technology and productivity, the society's demand for cross-border technology AI is more and more urgent. The establishment of a more diverse and perfect application system for cross-border technology AI has become the focus of many researchers at home and abroad [1]. By building a demand-oriented cross-border technology integration model in the field of artificial intelligence, the application

A. Li et al. (Eds.): 6GN 2022, LNICST 505, pp. 67–74, 2023.
https://doi.org/10.1007/978-3-031-36014-5_7

process in the field of artificial intelligence can be optimized, the research capabilities in the field of artificial intelligence, the quality of decision-making support services and the driving force for sustainable development can be improved, and demand-oriented services in the field of artificial intelligence can also be guaranteed. Quality and level, expand the theory and application scope of services in the field of artificial intelligence, and promote the sustainable development of cross-border technology AI.

In recent years, many researchers have explored the research of cross-border technology fusion in the field of artificial intelligence based on neural network algorithms, and achieved good results. For example, Jenaibi B A takes the robot control system as the research object, and based on the traditional method, it proposes a neural network-based robot adaptive control strategy [2]. From the perspective of Hedayat B artificial intelligence, college teachers urgently need to have cross-border development thinking and teamwork spirit, comprehensively improve educational technology application and research capabilities, and continuously enhance data mining, processing and analysis capabilities [3]. At present, scholars at home and abroad have conducted a lot of research on the application of cross-border technology AI. These previous theoretical and experimental results provide a theoretical basis for the research in this paper.

Based on the theoretical basis of neural network algorithm, this paper reveals and defines the research process of cross-border technology fusion in the field of artificial intelligence. The measurement and analysis of cross-border technology AI has always been a difficult problem in academic research. In the past, most scholars research on cross-border technology AI mainly focused on qualitative descriptions, such as predicting industry technology development trends based on cross-border technology AI based on different tracks, and analyzing technology development through the combined structure of different technical elements. Characteristics, as well as the development and application of fusion technology in different fields.

2   Related Theoretical Overview and Research

2.1   The Development Process of Cross-Border Technology Integration

(1) **The status quo of cross-border technology integration.** Analyze the formation and evolution of cross-domain technology fusion. The essence of technology is the purposeful programming of phenomena and needs. The emergence of new technologies benefits from the continuous combination and evolution of technologies in different fields, and the results of innovation [4]. Starting from the essence of technology and the inherent characteristics of technological combination evolution; secondly, through the induction of technological innovation diffusion, the promotion of industry-university-research cooperation, the pull of demand structure upgrade, and the drive of business model innovation, it analyzes the formation motivation of modern cross-domain technology integration; From the perspective of cycle theory and knowledge reorganization and continuous acquisition of external knowledge, based on the dynamic analysis framework, it discusses the formation and evolution of cross-domain technology fusion, as well as the main characteristics of old technology fusion changes and new technology fusion.

(2) **The composition of the cross-border technology integration structure in the field of artificial intelligence.** Analyze the mediating effect of technology standardization ability on the relationship between cross-domain technology integration and enterprise new product development performance. Firstly, it analyzes the impact of complementary technology integration and alternative technology integration on enterprise technology standardization ability, and examines the impact of old technology integration changes and new technology integration on enterprise technology standardization ability, and puts forward corresponding hypotheses in turn [5, 6]. Secondly, it analyzes the relationship between enterprise technology standardization ability and new product development performance, and discusses the mediating effect of technology standardization ability on cross-domain technology integration and enterprise new product development performance based on static analysis framework and dynamic analysis framework, respectively and make corresponding assumptions.

(3) **System design of cross-border technology AI.** The cross-border technology AI is the result of the simultaneous efforts of innovation-driven and demand-driven. Cross-border technological innovation, industry-university-research cooperation and basic research in the field of artificial intelligence are important prerequisites for the successful integration of cross-field technologies, and the cross-integration of market demand and industry is also an important guarantee for technological integration [7, 8]. In addition, the cross-border technology AI is also guided and restricted by the reform of the scientific and technological system, technological innovation activities and changes in user needs. Therefore, we need to take a systematic view to gain a more accurate and comprehensive understanding of the process of cross-border technology AI from basic disciplines, applied research, technology development, and industrialization.

Guided by the demand for cross-border technology AI, there are many direct and indirect service elements for the formation, development and application of cross-border technology integration service models and capability evaluation systems [9]. Based on the needs of cross-border technology integration, the system service process of cross-border technology AI is analyzed, and the elements involved in the cross-border technology integration service process are determined as: the main body of the information agency, multi-source data, technical methods, From five aspects of smart platform and smart environment, and then extract and interpret the three key characteristics of data multi-source, technical intelligence and service scenario of cross-border technology integration services. Multi-source data acquisition is a key preliminary project in cross-border technology integration research activities.

2.2 Theoretical Introduction to Neural Network Algorithms

Neural network is a mathematical model based on the working principle of human brain. It has good system identification and nonlinear approximation capabilities. For this reason, neural network control algorithms are widely used to solve the problems of unknown parameters and system uncertainty in nonlinear systems [10]. The design idea of the neural network control algorithm is to first replace the uncertain part of the system model with a neural network, and then adjust the weight parameters of the neural network to keep the error between the output value of the neural network and the value of the function to be approximated within a certain range.

At present, for a neural network whose overall structure has been determined, how to select the optimal number of hidden layer nodes has always been the difficulty and key of structure design [11]. A neural network with only one hidden layer and a sufficient number of nodes can also approximate a nonlinear function with arbitrary precision. The parametric training algorithm is also an important bottleneck to be overcome. The selection of the number of hidden layer nodes will directly affect the optimization effect of the network. Introducing too many nodes will increase the difficulty of training and lead to the phenomenon of "overfitting"; while too few nodes may cause the network to not be able to fully learn the training. The sample features have poor fault tolerance [12]. For this kind of network that receives multi-dimensional input and obtains a single output through operation and activation function, it is called a perceptron. The perceptron has a simple structure and can only deal with linear problems, so to deal with nonlinear problems, a multi-layer neural network is generally used. In addition to the network structure, the activation function also has an important impact on the output of the neural network.

3   Experiment and Research

3.1   Experimental Method

The forward pass refers to calculating and storing the intermediate variables (including the output) of the model in sequence from the input layer to the output layer of the neural network, and finally calculating the fitting error through the loss function. In the forward pass, the most important process is the weight calculation of neuron nodes. The mathematical model that exists between the input and output of the lth layer is such as the formula:

$$x_j^l = \sum_k \omega_{jk}^l y_k^{l-1} + b_j^l \tag{1}$$

$$y_j^l = \sigma(x_j^l) \tag{2}$$

where x represents the input of the jth neuron in the lth layer, y represents the output of the jth neuron in the lth layer, and w represents the kth neuron in the l–1th layer pointing to the jth neuron in the lth layer The weight of each neuron, b represents the offset of the jth neuron in the lth layer, and the activation function is σ.

3.2   Experimental Requirements

In the control system, the mathematical models of many controlled objects are easy to change with the changes of the external environment, and the law of their parameter changes is usually difficult to grasp. Traditional control methods cannot eliminate or reduce the adverse effects caused by this change, so that the global stability of the system cannot be guaranteed. Therefore, in order to overcome this effect and keep the system in the optimal working state or close to the optimal working state, scholars have proposed an adaptive control algorithm. On the one hand, market integration guides the development of technology integration according to the actual market demand, and on the other hand, it is the basis for the successful realization of industrial integration. Therefore, market integration plays an important role as a bridge between technology integration and industrial integration. Its emergence not only means that the market size and scope have undergone significant changes, but also the nature of the market has undergone fundamental changes.

4 Analysis and Discussion

4.1 Matching Degree Analysis of Cross-Border Technology AI

This experiment is based on the neural network algorithm to study the matching degree of cross-border technology fusion in the field of artificial intelligence. By detecting the relationship between the fusion coefficient and matching degree of cross-border technology fusion in the field of artificial intelligence, the experimental data is as follows (Table 1):

Table 1. Matching degree analysis table of cross-border technology AI

Technical project	Fusion coefficien	Suitability(%)
Technical one	24	98.5
Technical two	46	99.1
Technical three	61	99.8
Technical four	79	99.6
Technical five	93	98.7

From the above data analysis, it can be seen from the results that when the fusion coefficient of experiment 1 is 24, the matching degree of cross-border technology fusion in the field of artificial intelligence is 98.5%. When the fusion coefficient of experiment 2 is 46, the matching degree of cross-border technology fusion in the field of artificial intelligence is 99.1%. When the fusion coefficient of experiment 3 is 61, the matching degree of cross-border technology fusion in the field of artificial intelligence is 99.8%. When the fusion coefficient of experiment 4 is 79, the matching degree of cross-border technology fusion in the field of artificial intelligence is 99.6%. The fusion coefficient of experiment 5 is 93, and the matching degree of cross-border technology fusion in the field of artificial intelligence is 98.7%. Through the comparison of experimental data, it is found that the matching degree of cross-border technology AI has always maintained a stable level, that is, it has remained around 99%. It shows that the matching degree of cross-border technology fusion in the field of artificial intelligence does not change with the change of the fusion coefficient (Fig. 1).

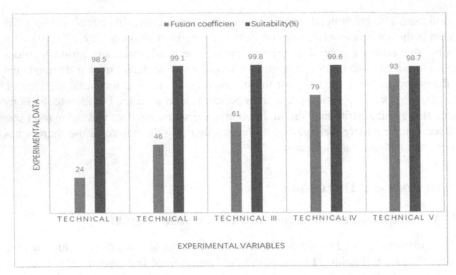

Fig. 1. Analysis of the matching degree of cross-border technology AI

4.2 Economic Applicability Analysis of Cross-Border Technology AI

By analyzing the economic applicability of cross-border technology AI, it is helpful to explore whether cross-border technology AI can meet the pursuit of economic applicability, so as to judge the feasibility of cross-border technology AI. The experimental data are shown in Fig. 2.

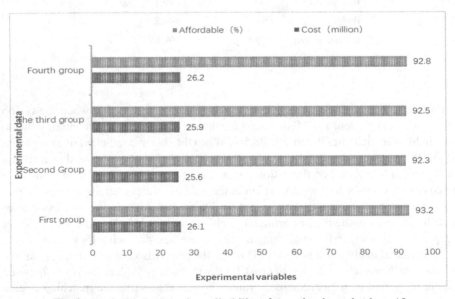

Fig. 2. Analysis of economic applicability of cross-border technology AI

As shown in the data in Fig. 2, through the comparative analysis of the economic applicability data of cross-border technology AI, when the costs of the four sets of data are 261,000 yuan, 256,000 yuan, 259,000 yuan, and 262,000 yuan, respectively, The corresponding economic applicability is 93.2%, 92.3%, 92.5% and 92.8%, respectively. The cost and economic applicability of the four sets of data are not much different, and the data is stable at the same level. The experimental data shows that the cross-border technology AI has good economic applicability and high feasibility.

5 Conclusions

This paper firstly studies and analyzes the current cross-border technology fusion application in the field of artificial intelligence based on neural network algorithm, and through a series of experiments to prove that the cross-border technology fusion application in the field of artificial intelligence based on neural network algorithm matches to a certain extent It has certain feasibility in terms of degree and economic applicability. From the experimental data of the matching degree of cross-border technology fusion applications in the field of artificial intelligence, it can be seen that the matching degree of cross-border technology fusion in the field of artificial intelligence has always been maintained at a stable level, that is Stay around the 99% level. It shows that the matching degree of cross-border technology fusion in the field of artificial intelligence does not change with the change of the fusion coefficient. Moreover, the data from the economic applicability analysis of cross-border technology AI indicates that the economic applicability of cross-border technology AI is relatively good and has high feasibility. The research results of the obtained three-dimensional model of film and television animation production meet the requirements of matching degree and economic applicability, and have the value of popularization and application.

References

1. Tarasov, I., Potekhin, D.: Calculation of activation functions in FPGA-based neuroprocessors using the cordic algorithm. In: Jordan, V., Tarasov, I., Faerman, V. (eds.) HPCST 2021. CCIS, vol. 1526, pp. 13–20. Springer, Cham (2022). https://doi.org/10.1007/978-3-030-94141-3_2
2. Jenaibi, B.A., Mansoori, A.A.: Information and communications technology is merging data science and advanced artificial intelligence towards the core of knowledge based society. **22**(5), 152–213 (2022)
3. Hedayat, B., Ahmadi, M.E., Nazerian, H., et al.: Feasibility of simultaneous application of fuzzy neural network and TOPSIS integrated method in potential mapping of lead and zinc mineralization in Isfahan-Khomein metallogeny zone. Open J. Geol. **12**(3), 19 (2022)
4. Nazir, A., Shabbir, G., Hussain, F., et al.: A note on classification of dust static plane symmetric space-times via proper curvature collineations inf (R)gravity. Int. J. Geomet. Methods Mod. Phys. **19**(6), 639–723 (2022)
5. Hartley, K., Andújar, A.: Smartphones and learning: An extension of M-learning or a distinct area of inquiry. Educ. Sci. **12**, 235–265 (2022)
6. Abdelbasset, W.K., Elsayed, S.H.: Study on cross-border fresh order and transport model based on profit maximization principle. **5**(15), 329–352 (2021)

7. Błasik, M.: Numerical method for the one phase 1D fractional stefan problem supported by an artificial neural network. In: Arai, K., Kapoor, S., Bhatia, R. (eds.) FTC 2020. AISC, vol. 1288, pp. 568–587. Springer, Cham (2021). https://doi.org/10.1007/978-3-030-63128-4_44

8. Saptalakar, B.K., Latte, M.V.: Effective reflection removal system for cognitive based convolutional neural networks. **55**(6), 522–533 (2022)

9. Satish, R., Kantarao, P., Vaisakh, K.: A new algorithm for harmonic impacts with renewable DG and non-linear loads in smart distribution networks. Technol. Econ. Smart Grids Sustain. Energy **7**(1), 1–19 (2022)

10. Herrmann, T., Pfeiffer, S.: Keeping the organization in the loop: a socio-technical extension of human-centered artificial intelligence. AI Society, 1–20 (2022)

11. Dehestani, H., Ordokhani, Y.: Numerical evaluation of variable-order fractional nonlinear Volterra functional-integro-differential equations with non-singular kernel derivative. Iranian J. Sci. Technol. Trans. A Sci. **46**(2), 405–419 (2022). https://doi.org/10.1007/s40995-022-01278-6

12. Hassan, A.S., Othman, E.S.A., Bendary, F.M., et al.: Improving the techno-economic pattern for distributed generation-based distribution networks via nature-inspired optimization algorithms. Technol. Econ. Smart Grids Sustain. Energy **7**(1), 1–25 (2022)

Research on Ad Hoc Network Routing Protocol for UAV Application

Zhenyu Xu$^{(\boxtimes)}$, Xinlu Li, and Xinyun Wang

Huizhou Engineering Vocational College, Huizhou, China
hitusa@126.com

Abstract. The realization of self-organized network communication based on OLSR protocol by multiple UAVs in the air is the core of this demonstration. Each UAV is equipped with a raspberry pie and a physical transmission device, and a ground station as the overall dispatching and command. After the UAV is powered on, it will automatically complete networking. Each UAV is a network node with equal status. The joining or leaving of any UAV will not affect the smoothness of the whole network. If a UAV quits the network midway due to power or network, other UAVs can still communicate normally, and when the UAV returns to normal status, it can rejoin the network after simple configuration. The UAV and the ground station can transmit videos, images and commands through ROS communication mechanism under the support of multi hop ad hoc network, and the UAV and the UAV can also exchange information as needed. The whole system can be used in agricultural detection, emergency rescue, regional coverage, small-scale operations and other application scenarios.

Keywords: UAV · ROS Communication · Routing Protocol · Unmanned Unit Network

1 Communication Principle of Unmanned Unit Network

1.1 Networking Principle

A stable and low collision probability wireless ad hoc network is the foundation of successful communication and various services of UAV network. In traditional wireless local area networks such as WiFi, there is a fixed AP in the network [1]. When a node in the network needs services, it sends a request to the AP, completes access and routing through the AP, and the AP records the IP of the requesting task node at the same time. After obtaining the requested service, it distributes the service to the requesting IP to complete the service. Each user only acts as the host, and a separate router completes the routing and addressing work [2]. The main difference between wireless ad hoc network and traditional wireless LAN is that each user in the ad hoc network is both a host and an AP, and each node not only requests services but also undertakes routing functions. Since each node is an AP, the deletion or addition of a node is only an update of the routing table in the node for other nodes [3]. After the route update process, the whole network can continue to run smoothly.

© ICST Institute for Computer Sciences, Social Informatics and Telecommunications Engineering 2023
Published by Springer Nature Switzerland AG 2023. All Rights Reserved
A. Li et al. (Eds.): 6GN 2022, LNICST 505, pp. 75–83, 2023.
https://doi.org/10.1007/978-3-031-36014-5_8

The networking process of the wireless ad hoc network is similar to that of the traditional wireless LAN. The traditional WiFi generates a WiFi name ESSID and password password by the AP. In ad-hoc networks, a network device generates an ESSID and a LAN cell value in ad-hoc mode. Other devices connected to the same ESSID will also generate the same cell value. This means that connected to the same LAN, all nodes in the network can ping each other, which is similar to that each node in the network is connected to a virtual AP. At this time, each node in the network runs a unified routing protocol [4, 5]. After the route discovery process, if the active routing protocol such as OLSR is running, each node has maintained a routing table, and the source node and the destination node can carry out multi hop forwarding according to the routing table. However, multi hop will lead to competition in the link layer and greatly increase the transmission delay. Therefore, how to select the channel is worth studying [6].

The routing protocol adopted in this paper is the OLSR protocol, which reduces the forwarding information in the network through the selection of the set of MPR nodes, and limits the maximum number of hops that each node can communicate to 2 hops, which improves the reliability of the network and is suitable for applications in large-scale networks with dense node distribution [7]. The OLSR maintains the Hello packet and the TC packet. The Hello packet is used for broadcasting and the TC packet is used for maintaining the node MPR set. The OLSR protocol has a complete demo of the embedded implementation in Ubuntu 16.04. According to the actual test, it takes about 20s from the route establishment to the basic stability of the network state under the condition of using the wireless network card, which is related to the electromagnetic interference and occlusion of the environment [8]. The precondition for running the OLSR protocol is that each node running the protocol must be in the same local area network, that is, the cell value of each node in the network must be the same. Otherwise, the IP of the node cannot be detected after running the protocol. When all nodes in the network successfully run the OLSR protocol, a wireless ad hoc network based on the OLSR routing protocol is successfully established. The schematic diagram of UAV network networking is shown in Fig. 1.

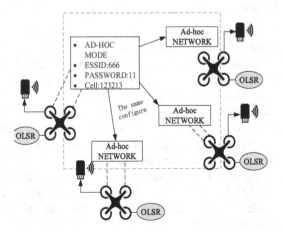

Fig. 1. Principle of unmanned unit network.

1.2 Transmission Principle

After each UAV node and the ground station are networked, this ad hoc network will carry tasks such as flight control command transmission and video service transmission. The transmission of flight control commands is realized through the ROS system. Firstly, the communication and transmission principle of the ROS system is introduced. The system is composed of multiple ROS, and each ROS node is the smallest unit of an executable program [9]. The ROS node exchanges data with other nodes through messages, which are divided into the following three types: topics of one-way message sending and receiving mode, which are mainly used for communication in our flight control program; A service of two-way message request and response mode; Two way messages are actions in the form of goal, result and feedback (Fig. 2).

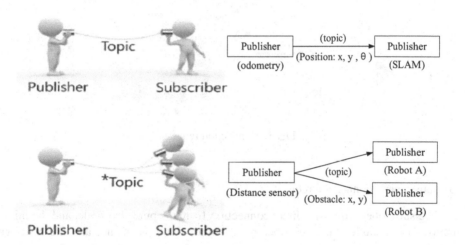

Fig. 2. Transmission mode

Taking topic as an example, the establishment process of message communication is as follows:

(1) rescore establishes the master node

It is used to register the name, topic (service, action) name, message type, URI address and port of the node; Notify other nodes of this information when requested.

(2) establish publisher node publisher

It is used to register the publisher node name, topic name, message type, URI address and port with the master node.

(3) establish a subscriber node

Register its subscriber node name, topic name, message type, URI address and port with the master node.

(4) notify the publisher

The master node sends information such as the name of the publisher, the topic name, the message type, the URI address and the port that the subscriber wants to access to the subscriber node (Fig. 3).

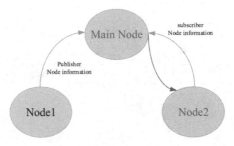

Fig. 3. Connection request

(5) subscriber's connection request

The subscriber requests a direct connection from the publisher node, and the information sent includes the subscriber node name, the topic name, and the message type.

(6) the connection of the publisher is corresponding

The publisher node sends the URI address and port of the TCP server to the subscriber node as a connection response (Fig. 4).

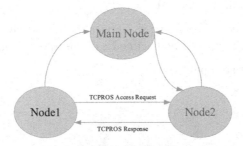

Fig. 4. Connection establishment

Note: a ROS node can be either a subscriber or a publisher; You can subscribe to or publish multiple messages at the same time.

In our ad hoc network demonstration scheme, each UAV node can be regarded as a ROS node (in fact, it is two ROS nodes under the same group), and the ground side is a ROS node and a ROS master node integrating multiple publish and subscribe functions. Each ROS node communicates messages in the ROS system through the ad hoc network, thereby realizing the transmission of flight control instructions.

2 Analysis of Overall Communication Behavior of the System

Now, the overall communication behavior of the system is analyzed in detail by combining the networking principle and ROS communication transmission principle. The overall communication flow chart is shown in Fig. 5.

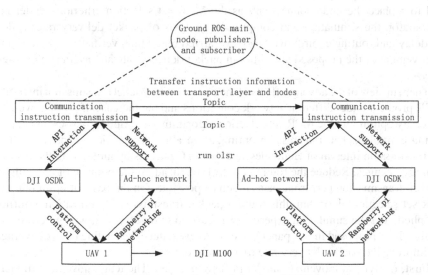

Fig. 5. Overall communication behavior of UAV network

The UAV interacts with the raspberry pie through the serial port. The raspberry pie is first networked through the wireless network card/physical transmission device to provide support for ROS communication transmission. Direct control of UAV is realized by downloading DJI osdk in raspberry pie. Osdk includes APIs that encapsulate flight control and ROS applicable to UAV platforms. After installing the ROS environment in the raspberry, declare the ground station as the master node. The slave node, i.e. UAV, declares itself as an ROS slave node through the ROS API in osdk, defines the topic to be published and the topic group, and registers with the master node. After the registration is completed, the communication between the slave node and the slave node can be independent of the master node. The slave node is connected with the master node through an IP address through an ad hoc network based on the OLSR protocol. ROS nodes transmit data through topic, which is an asynchronous communication mode. The whole system uses raspberry pie to carry OLSR protocol to form an ad hoc network. On the basis of the network, ROS communication mechanism is used to transmit data, and osdk is used to control the UAV.

3   Design of Routing Protocol for UAV Ad Hoc Network

In view of the characteristics of UAV ad hoc network such as network topology and movement speed, it is necessary to improve the traditional ground ad-hoc routing protocol and design a low overhead and high reliability UAV ad hoc network routing protocol with task adaptive ability. Starting from the OLSR protocol, add speed and location information to the Hello packet to calculate a new link evaluation standard to guide route selection. The multi point relay (MPR) mechanism of OLSR protocol is optimized, and an optimized MPR set selection algorithm based on node link transmission quality and mobility similarity is proposed. The weighted comprehensive link evaluation index is used to replace the node connectivity as the MPR set selection criterion. Under NS-2 simulator, the simulation and comparison analysis of packet delivery rate, end-to-end delay and routing control overhead are carried out, which verifies the performance improvement of the proposed algorithm in packet delivery rate and average end-to-end delay.

Then, in view of the adverse effects of the fixed routing packet transmission interval of OLSR protocol under different network conditions and the increase of routing overhead caused by optimizing the MPR set selection algorithm, this paper proposes an adaptive routing control packet transmission optimization algorithm, which adaptively adjusts the transmission interval of Hello messages and TC packets by monitoring the network topology changes, Reduce the routing control overhead on the premise of ensuring the network transmission performance as much as possible. On the basis of optimizing the MPR set selection algorithm, this routing packet transmission optimization algorithm is applied, and the simulation experiment is carried out with NS-2, which verifies that the algorithm proposed in this paper can effectively reduce the routing control overhead and improve the packet delivery rate to a certain extent.

First, the typical movement model in fanet is given. The team movement model is designed based on the open-source software and hardware system paparazzi UAS system of Ecole Nationale de l'aviation Civil (ENaC). Similar to the RWP model, pprzm model is also a path based random movement model. However, pprzm model has more node movement behaviors closer to fanets, and the distribution uniformity of UAV nodes Regional communication frequency, link connection number and other parameters are more in line with the actual situation. In the pprzm model, as shown in Fig. 6, there are five possible movements of nodes:

circling, i.e. nodes make circular motion around a fixed position;

Figure 8, i.e. flying around two fixed areas, with node trajectory of Fig. 8;

ellipse, i.e. elliptical flight around two fixed positions;

scanning, that is, the UAV performs scanning of the area defined by two points along the two-way trajectory;

way point flight, i.e. straight-line flight of UAV from the starting point to the target position.

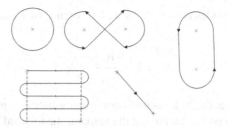

Fig. 6. Five node motions of pprzm mobile model

All these motions have their own occurrence probabilities. This model considers that "circling", "ellipse" and "scanning" are the actions that generate the most in the mission flight. Therefore, the occurrence probabilities of each flight behavior set in the model are fixed as follows: for each node, the probability of "circling", "ellipse" and "scanning" is equal to 30%, and the probability of "Fig. 8" and "waypoint" is equal to 5%, but this probability is not unalterable, The user can change the transmission probability of each type of motion as needed. In addition, there are some connection oriented mobility models, such as group force mobility model (GFMM), coverage oriented multi pheromone UAV mobility model (MPU), and so on.

In fanets, the relative movement between nodes can usually represent the link lifetime and stability between nodes, and it is easy to obtain and calculate. Therefore, this paper introduces the node mobility similarity and the link transmission quality as the criteria to measure the link performance between nodes and select the MPR set. By comprehensively considering the relative mobility between each pair of nodes and the actual transmission quality of the link, the algorithm for selecting the MPR set is optimized. In this way, the nodes with high connectivity and poor link quality are bypassed, and the nodes with high mobility similarity or high link transmission quality are selected as MPR nodes to improve the robustness of the entire network, improve the effective utilization of bandwidth, avoid the reduction of transmission quality, and thus improve the network communication performance to a certain extent.

In this paper, it is assumed that each UAV is equipped with a GPS (Global Positioning System) system, so that each node can know its real-time position and speed information, so as to calculate the mobile similarity between nodes. The mobility similarity of a node refers to the mobility speed similarity between a UAV node and another neighboring UAV node. Generally speaking, the greater the mobility behavior similarity between nodes, the longer the link between the two nodes will exist, and then the two nodes are considered to be able to maintain a good connection state. Otherwise, the link between the two nodes is considered to be prone to fracture. Because this paper is more concerned about the topological change of fanets network on the two-dimensional plane, and the height of UAV will not change frequently in practical application, the vertical velocity component of UAV is ignored for the sake of appropriately simplifying the model and facilitating the simulation work. Assuming that there are two UAV nodes I and j, and their movement speeds are respectively and, the calculation formula of the mobility similarity of these two nodes is as follows with reference to the mobility measurement of Euclidean distance:

$$\theta_{ij} = 1 - \frac{|v_i - v_j|}{|v_i| + |v_j|} \tag{3.1}$$

As mentioned above, the link transmission quality between nodes is calculated by ETX, and ETX is obtained by calculating the value of the forward link quality (LQ) and the reverse link quality (neighbor link quality, NLQ) according to the proportion of Hello messages sent by the neighbor nodes received by the two nodes within a certain period. The smaller the value of ETX, the higher the link quality of network communication. The link quality of node i and the calculation formula of ETX are as follows:

$$
\begin{aligned}
LQ &= \frac{HELLO_{jreceive}}{HELLO_{isend}} \\
NLQ &= \frac{HELLO_{ireceive}}{HELLO_{jsend}}
\end{aligned} \tag{3.2}
$$

$$ETX = \frac{1}{LQ \times NLQ} \tag{3.3}$$

Through analysis, it is found that for node i, the number of Hello messages I can obtain is only "the number of Hello messages I sent to j" and "the number of Hello messages I received from J". LQ and NLQ cannot be calculated based on this data alone, and ETX cannot be calculated further. Therefore, this paper defines mutual link quality (MLQ) as an intermediate quantity to calculate the ETX of two nodes. Then for the local node i, the link quality ETX calculation formula is shown in formula and formula:

$$
\begin{aligned}
MLQ\_L &= \frac{HELLO_{jreceive}}{HELLO_{isend}} \\
MLQ &= \frac{HELLO_{ireceive}}{HELLO_{jsend}}
\end{aligned} \tag{3.4}
$$

$$ETX = \frac{1}{MLQ\_L \times MLQ} \tag{3.5}$$

4 Conclusion

Through further analysis, it is found that the value range of node mobility similarity is [0, 1], and the larger the value, the better the link stability, while the value range of ETX is [1, +∞], but the smaller the value, the higher the link transmission quality, which makes it inconvenient to normalize the two indicators and the weighted average of the two, thus affecting the calculation of the optimal link performance indicators. Therefore, this paper defines a new link transmission.

References

1. Yong, Z., Rui, Z., Teng, J.L.: Wireless communications with unmanned aerial vehicles: Opportunities and challenges. IEEE Commun. Mag. **54**(5), 36–42 (2016)
2. Lei, L., Shen, X., Dohler, M., Lin, C., Zhong, Z.: Queuing models with applications to mode selection in device-to-device communications underlaying cellular networks. IEEE Trans. Wirel. Commun. **13**(12), 6697–6715 (2014)
3. Moretti, M.: Distributed power allocation for D2D communications underlaying/overlaying OFDMA cellular networks. IEEE Trans. Wirel. Commun. **16**(3), 1466–1479 (2017)
4. Wang, H., Chen, J., Ding, G., Wang, S.: D2D communications underlaying UAV-assisted access networks. IEEE Access **6**, 46244–46255 (2018)
5. Gomez, K., Hourani, A., Goratti, L., Riggio, R., Kandeepan, S., Bucaille, I.: Capacity evaluation of aerial LTE base-stations for public safety communications. In: 2015 European Conference on Networks and Communications (EuCNC), pp. 133–138. IEEE (2015)
6. Xie, L., Xu, J., Zhang, R.: Throughput maximization for UAV-enabled wireless powered communication networks. IEEE Internet Things J. **6**(2), 1690–1703 (2018)
7. Hu, Q., Cai, Y., Yu, G., Qin, Z., Zhao, M., Li, G.Y.: Joint offloading and trajectory design for UAV-enabled mobile edge computing systems. IEEE Internet Things J. **6**(2), 1879–1892 (2018)
8. Feng, D., et al.: Device-to-device communications underlaying cellular networks. IEEE Trans. Commun. **61**(8), 3541–3551 (2013)
9. Kha, H.H., Tuan, H.D., Nguyen, H.H.: Fast global optimal power allocation in wireless networks by local dc programming. IEEE Trans. Wirel. Commun. **11**(2), 510–515 (2011)

Research on Emergency Communication Technology of UAV Based on D2D

Zhenyu Xu[⊠], Jinfang Li, and Xun Xu

Huizhou Engineering Vocational College, Huizhou, China
hitusa@126.com

Abstract. In recent years, wireless communication technology plays an important role in the development of national economy. However, while enjoying the benefits of the growing development of communication technology, people are also facing various potential risks and challenges, such as various natural disasters, public security emergencies, etc. Traditional ground communication is generally deployed based on long-term data traffic and user distribution. The infrastructure is usually fixed and cannot be moved immediately. Emergency communication is an important part of public network communication. It is the combination and unification of emergency methods and means. The tasks to be undertaken are emergency services and emergency support. This paper focuses on the construction of a fast and stable emergency communication network from the air and ground dimensions when local networks are paralyzed due to terrorist attacks or earthquakes in emergency services, Expand network coverage and improve network reliability.

Keywords: UAV · D2D · Emergency Communication

1 Introduction

On the way of communication construction in China, the development of emergency communication system is a very important part, which is closely related to the production and life of the people. However, there are still some very important problems. The details are as follows: First, the coverage of emergency communication construction is not enough. China has a vast territory and a large population, so it is very difficult to carry out the overall emergency communication coverage. Economically speaking, it is also difficult to achieve full coverage. Therefore, once problems occur in grass-roots areas, it is difficult to timely resume communication and assist in rescue; Secondly, China's emergency communication means rely on communication infrastructure, and the network has low survivability and disaster tolerance. However, the emergency communication application scenarios are diverse, and the forms of communication needs are diverse, and any single communication technology cannot meet the requirements; Finally, in the current public security network standards, such as Terrestrial Trunked Radio (TETRA), Project25, etc., the main technology is still based on the old 2G technology, seriously lagging behind today's mobile communication technology, and has long been unable to

A. Li et al. (Eds.): 6GN 2022, LNICST 505, pp. 84–99, 2023.
https://doi.org/10.1007/978-3-031-36014-5_9

meet the nature and requirements of emergency communication in today's information society. Therefore, it is necessary to fully integrate various communication technologies to meet the demand for fast and reliable communication in emergency situations.

With the rapid popularization of intelligent terminal equipment and the continuous innovation of Internet of Things (IoTs) technology, business requirements and application scenarios emerge in endlessly, and data traffic shows an explosive growth trend. The contradiction between people's urgent demand for high-speed data transmission and the scarcity of spectrum resources is increasingly prominent. In this case, 3GPP (Third Generation Partnership Project) has proposed a device to device (D2D) communication technology, that is, terminal direct connection communication technology, which allows two adjacent terminal nodes to exchange data through the direct connection link without passing the forwarding of the base station (BS) or access point (AP) and sharing spectrum resources with cellular users, It can effectively improve the efficiency of resource utilization. As a short-range direct connection technology, D2D communication has the advantages of high frequency spectral efficiency, low communication delay and low power consumption, providing technical support for building a future network architecture with higher data transmission rate, wider coverage and better quality of service [1, 2]. Since it was first proposed at the International Computer Communication Conference in 2000, it has received extensive attention from scholars [3]. In 3GPP Release - 12, D2D communication technology has been officially established as the standard technology in the field of emergency communication.

The unprecedented development of aviation and electronic technology has led to the gradual transition of unmanned aerial vehicles (UAVs) from military to civilian, such as UAVs, aircraft, balloons and airships [4–6]. At present, UAV has become an important part of wireless network by virtue of its high mobility and flexible deployment, and it is also a key driver of 5G and future wireless Internet of Things. If properly planned and deployed, UAVs can provide reliable and cost-effective wireless communication solutions for various scenarios. On the one hand, UAVs can be used as aerial base stations to provide reliable wireless communication to scenes without wireless access infrastructure, such as areas where cellular infrastructure is damaged due to natural disasters. On the other hand, it can also be used as a mobile relay to provide network coverage in hard to reach rural, mountainous and other areas, so as to quickly provide wireless connectivity for ground wireless equipment and supplement the existing cellular system. The application of UAV in the public security scenario is shown in Fig. 1. UAV can unload excessive traffic in the traditional cellular network and reduce the load on the base station; In emergency scenarios (such as high-rise fire, flood, earthquake and other areas), communication facilities can also be carried for temporary networking to quickly establish emergency rescue communication network [7]. At the World Mobile Conference in February 2018, China Mobile exhibited the UAV high-altitude base station independently developed for emergency communication, which greatly promoted the development of UAV emergency communication.

To sum up, UAV and D2D communication help to build a fast and stable emergency communication network from the air and ground dimensions, expand network coverage and improve network reliability. On the one hand, UAVs make full use of air resources and break through the limitations of geographic and topographic conditions, costs and

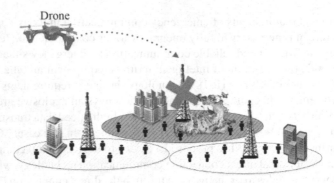

Fig. 1. Schematic Diagram of UAV Application in Public Safety Scenarios.

time delay on communication technology; On the other hand, D2D communication makes full use of the distance advantage of ground users and gets rid of the dependence of traditional cellular users on base stations. It can be seen that the combination of UAV and D2D technology is a promising emergency means, and it is necessary to further study and tap the potential.

2 Research Significance

When natural disasters occur, communication is interrupted, and the disaster area and the outside world cannot be interconnected. The emergency communication guarantee system can provide a strong security guarantee for people's lives and property. At present, the relatively mature emergency communication system in China mainly focuses on mobile command vehicles, such as mobile emergency command system based on vehicle. The mobile command vehicle and mobile access point are deployed to the emergency area to build a temporary wireless communication network. At the same time, the domestic research on emergency response mechanism under the public emergency scenario mainly stays in the traditional methods, such as emergency material scheduling, emergency facility selection and path optimization. In addition, satellite network is also an important means of emergency communication. It covers a wide range of communication, is not limited by ground conditions, and has independent communication capability and strong survivability.

At present, the existing traditional emergency communication means are often affected by some restrictive factors when dealing with emergencies, such as "disconnection, power failure, network disconnection" and other unexpected situations, which cause people, materials, emergency communication vehicles unable to reach the site, facilities and equipment unable to supply power, etc. The low popularity of satellite terminals, poor signal quality and large time delay make it difficult to meet the needs of large-scale communication. On the other hand, the traditional emergency system can no longer meet the current real-time communication requirements of large bandwidth and low delay [8, 9]. Therefore, the current research results cannot be applied to the requirements of user emergency communication in the situation without basic communication equipment. A more effective emergency communication guarantee system is urgently needed to establish an emergency communication guarantee system with large communication area, wide coverage and strong recovery capability.

As one of the key technologies of 5G communication, applying D2D communication technology to emergency communication network to improve the reliability and throughput of emergency communication network is attracting more and more researchers' attention. For example, the European METIS (Mobile and Wireless Communications Enablers for the Twenty Twenty Information Society) project team has studied and developed the D2D technology applicable to emergency situations [10]. In the event of major natural disasters or man-made emergencies, the infrastructure in the region is usually damaged or paralyzed due to sudden growth in communication demand. If a reliable communication network can be quickly established after the incident, the rescue efficiency will be greatly improved. Moreover, before the external rescue, the communication between survivors is smooth, and timely understanding of the external situation is particularly important for mutual self-help. The existing emergency communication technology requires professional personnel to cooperate with professional equipment to complete communication, but ordinary people do not have the conditions to use this technology. At this time, if the D2D technology can be used to establish an emergency D2D communication network among users through the intelligent devices in the hands of survivors, communication can be quickly restored.

In addition to the introduction of D2D communication technology, it is another promising auxiliary means to use UAVs as relay nodes or temporary base stations to assist in the construction of emergency communication networks to maintain the communication capability in the damaged areas of base stations. Compared with traditional emergency communication technology, UAV emergency communication technology has the following advantages. First of all, the UAV emergency communication deployment is simple, and it does not require real-time maintenance. It only needs to set the daily maintenance cycle at ordinary times. In addition, compared with the deployment of a huge emergency communication network, it has low economic cost and strong communication capability, and can be combined with LTE to achieve modern and information-based emergency communication and real-time video transmission. At present, there are landing applications of UAV emergency communication. For example, after the earthquake in Jiuzhaigou, Sichuan Province in 2017, China Mobile urgently dispatched a set of UAV high-altitude base stations, which were delivered to the disaster area overnight to restore mobile phone signals in the surrounding disaster area of more than 30 square kilometers. This is also the first application of UAV high-altitude base stations in earthquake relief in China. In July 2021, there will be a sudden rainstorm in Henan Province. China Mobile and AVIC will use the "pterosaur" fixed wing UAV to provide 5-h communication support for the disaster area. At 1089.89M, a maximum of 648 users can be accessed at a single time, and more than 2500 users can be connected in total, generating a flow of 1089.89M, effectively supporting emergency rescue operations in the disaster area.

Moreover, UAV and D2D communication can also complement each other, breaking the limitations of traditional emergency communication schemes in many ways. On the one hand, the UAV with communication transfer function can change its position according to the flight path and communication requirements of other UAVs to maintain connectivity between ground congestion and assist D2D users to communicate with cellular users; On the other hand, as a temporary base station, the UAV can flexibly adjust its position and height according to the changes of user information (number of end users, flux, location information, etc.). The direct connection communication between D2D users can effectively reduce the load of the UAV base station and reduce the capacity requirements for backhaul. At the same time, D2D communication technology can also help UAV base stations expand their coverage and accommodate more users.

Although the communication between UAV and D2D brings new opportunities for emergency communication, new challenges also follow. First of all, the horizontal position and height of the UAV are adjustable, which means that the channel characteristics will be different from the traditional cellular base station. Secondly, the increase in the distance between the UAV and its ground users will lead to greater path loss. Therefore, reasonable resource allocation and UAV trajectory planning are essential for achieving the goal of greater coverage and high throughput performance. In addition, another major challenge is the interference problem caused by the coexistence of ground users and UAVs in flight. On the one hand, when D2D users and users associated with UAVs share the same spectrum, the mobility of UAVs will change the topology of the network, so the interference analysis will become more complex; On the other hand, D2D users may not only interfere with users associated with UAVs, but also interfere with each other in the same channel. Therefore, on the basis of considering the requirements of different types of users for communication quality of service and the matching channel conditions and mode selection, the research focus of the subject is to explore new and efficient resource allocation technology and UAV deployment scheme, suppress interference between different types of users, and improve the performance of the system.

3   Research Status at Home and Abroad

(1) Interference management of D2D communication in traditional cellular networks.

Analysis of the current situation of D2D communication assisted emergency scenario research.

According to the TR36 and 843 technical reports, the application of D2D in specific scenarios can be divided into public security and non-public security scenarios according to the differences in business and system levels [11]. Non public security refers to general scenarios, such as commercial activities. The public security scenario refers to the use of D2D technology to enable disaster affected users to gain communication capability without network coverage under special circumstances, such as floods, earthquakes and hurricanes, when the internal infrastructure of the disaster area is damaged, and when network service facilities such as insufficient power supply are damaged. The research on D2D technology in emergency situations is of great value and has received extensive attention.

In addition, some researchers proposed that some regions could not communicate due to the impact of disasters, so the communication regions were divided into different parts for better analysis. In [12], the author divided the communication area into healthy area and unhealthy area, and set up relay nodes in the unhealthy area to recover the communication between D2D users. In the literature [13], the author studied the disaster management and recovery using D2D communication. The whole scene is divided into energy collection area and damaged area. The transmitting node collects energy from the energy collection area and sends signals to the relay node in the damaged area. After several times of communication, it arrives at the receiving end to recover communication.

(2) Analysis of the status quo of traditional D2D interference management research

The D2D communication mechanism is introduced into the traditional cellular network to form a cellular and hybrid network (referred to as hybrid network). In the hybrid network, the D2D communication mode with the highest spectrum utilization is the in band sharing mode, that is, D2D communication and cellular communication share the cellular spectrum. This mode is the most concerned D2D communication mode at present. However, after introducing the D2D communication into the cellular network, three new interference types will appear in the hybrid network: the interference of the D2D link to the cellular link, the interference of the cellular link to the D2D link, and the mutual interference between the D2D links. These interferences seriously affect the performance of the network. Therefore, interference management technology has become an important technical topic in the cellular and D2D hybrid network.

Resource allocation and power control are important means to solve the problem of co frequency interference. Resource allocation is one of the methods to effectively coordinate interference problems. Through reasonable and effective allocation of resources, resource allocation can reduce the transmission power of user equipment, ensure user demand, and improve system performance. Many technologies such as spatial reuse gain, game theory, matching theory and graph theory are used to improve energy efficiency and reduce outage probability. One literature proposed an effective interference cognitive spectrum resource sharing method to select users of reusable resources based on distance, so as to solve the problem of co frequency interference. One literature proposed a reasonable and effective channel resource allocation method, using interference sensing strategy and network aided management to reduce the co frequency interference between D2D users, thus improving energy efficiency. One literature proposed a distributed resource allocation algorithm based on matching theory to minimize these interferences and optimize network performance. The results show that the algorithm can achieve more than 90% of the best network performance with lower overhead and complexity. For many to many multiplexing scenarios, the resource allocation strategy based on matching theory in [14] also solves the problem of co frequency interference between authorized and unauthorized channels, and improves the system throughput. One literature proposed a new channel allocation algorithm based on greed to allocate the best channel for each communication link to mitigate system interference. Different from the previous literature, one literature proposed a new resource allocation consisting of two stages to maximize the total capacity of D2D communication.

Power control is another effective interference management method. By controlling the transmission power of users, it can effectively reduce the power consumption of devices, reduce the interference between users, and ultimately effectively improve the system performance such as throughput, energy efficiency and coverage probability. For the system throughput of a single cell, one literature studied how to maximize the system throughput of a single cell by limiting the real-time link state information and the average link state information in a many to one multiplexing scenario. Reference proposed a power control method based on a single cell, and obtained the optimal power allocation result by referring to the performance measurement of the system model. One literature proposed a distributed D2D power allocation framework, in which D2D attempts to maximize its own time average throughput utility independently, and simultaneously jointly guarantees the time average coverage probability of cellular users in multiple cells. However, one literature gives a D2D management scheme based on interference limited area (ILA), derives the closed form expression of the average coverage probability of cellular and D2D links under the proposed ILA scheme, and then proposes a resource allocation algorithm constrained by power control mechanism. Convex optimization is a common approach when the optimization objective is system energy efficiency. One literature proposed an energy-saving power control method, which considered the problem of energy efficiency maximization as a non convex function optimization problem on the premise of ensuring the maximum allowable transmission power and minimum data rate requirements, and finally realized the improvement of system energy efficiency. Reference uses convex optimization to control the transmission power of D2D users, uses Lagrangian optimization to control the power loss of users, improves the original auction algorithm to optimize the working time, and improves the system energy efficiency. One literature improves the quality of service (QoS) through power control and applies it to nonlinear planning for interference management. In addition, the coexistence of D2D and large scale Multiple Input Multiple Output (MIMO) is also one of the key scenarios of 5G. One literature proposed a spatial dynamic power control solution to reduce the interference between cells to D2D and D2D to cells, which can flexibly and effectively reduce the interference between cells and D2D layers.

Moreover, the joint optimization of resource allocation and power control is also a common interference management method. Some articles proposed resource allocation and power control algorithms based on auction theory to optimize system energy efficiency and throughput respectively. Reference proposed a joint power control and resource matching algorithm extended to multi-user scenarios, which optimizes user power and effectively improves the overall system rate under the condition of guaranteeing the minimum threshold of user signal to noise ratio (SINR). [15] defines the optimization problem of maximizing the links supported by the network, and proposes a D2D resource allocation and power control framework to improve network performance and ensure fairness between links. In addition, D2D mode selection is another powerful entry point for interference management. [16] Consider a mode selection scheme based on the maximum received signal strength of each user equipment to control D2D to cell interference. To solve the problem that the bottom layer D2D communication may introduce additional interference to undermine the execution conditions of continuous interference cancellation decoding in non orthogonal multiple access (NOMA) cellular networks, one literature proposed a joint D2D mode selection and resource allocation scheme, which significantly improved the overall system rate and D2D access rate. In addition, space division, interference map and link scheduling are also common interference coordination methods.

(3) Wireless communication network assisted by UAV

As an air wireless relay platform, UAV can improve the connectivity of ground users and help expand the coverage of ground cellular BS. In particular, in the earthquake stricken area where communication facilities are damaged or in the communication blind area caused by channel blockage, deploying the UAV air relay platform can establish a reliable temporary communication link between the ground users in the remote disaster area or the blind area users with channel blockage and the ground cellular BS. In addition, for temporary dense user scenarios, the UAV air relay platform can also be temporarily deployed to provide relay coverage services for ground users in the coverage area to enhance user connectivity. Compared with the land relay system, the rapid deployment capability, environmental adaptability and air ground channel characteristics of high line of sight (LoS) probability of the UAV are widely used in the communication relay of post disaster emergency response and the coverage enhancement of overload BS in hot areas. How to use the UAV air relay platform to establish temporary connections to help complete the data transmission of two or more remote users without reliable direct connection.

On the other hand, for rotor static relay, the adjustable height and hovering characteristics of rotor UAV provide additional design freedom for effective deployment of UAV static relay. The rotor static relay system is studied in [17]. Specifically, [17] analyzed the optimal flight altitude for single UAV downlink coverage, proposed a single antenna air ground channel model with pitch angle correlation, and obtained the optimal hover altitude through numerical calculation. Reference maximizes the reliability of relay communication by optimizing the position of UAV. Reliability is measured by power loss, outage probability, bit error rate and other performance indicators. One literature maximizes the throughput of rotor UAV single line static relay through joint optimization of transmission power, bandwidth, transmission rate and UAV hovering position. One literature studied the multi-user relay system, maximizing the sum rate of all ground users under the condition of considering the QoS requirements of each ground user, LoS probability and information causality constraints, and proposed an effective algorithm to obtain the optimal deployment position of UAV based on the continuous convex optimization approximation and optimization problem architecture.

However, similar to fixed wing UAV half duplex mobile relay, literature [17] only studies single antenna relay, and the impact of deploying multiple antennas at UAV on the optimal deployment position of rotor half duplex static relay needs further study. In addition, literature [17] assumes that UAVs can perfectly obtain global CSI or use free space propagation channels, but in practice, channel estimation will have errors, and the impact of channel estimation errors on the optimal deployment position of rotor UAV static relay remains to be further studied.

As a mobile relay, UAV has good mobility and is flexible and easy to deploy with good air to air and air to ground LOS links. Compared with traditional fixed relay, UAV as a mobile relay adds flexible 3D position, flight path and other optimization dimensions, so it can better assist in wireless communication performance optimization. At present, the research on UAV as mobile relay mainly includes the following aspects, such as mobile relay assisting in enhancing the link reliability of the network, reducing the data transmission delay, optimizing the throughput, and related research on data transmission between the original node and the destination node connected by mobile relay.

Next, it mainly analyzes and expounds the relevant research of single UAV as mobile relay and multiple UAVs as mobile relay. The research results of single UAV as mobile relay are relatively rich, one literature studied the throughput optimization of single

UAV as mobile relay. One document proposed the problem of optimizing the position between two ground nodes in a multi rate network as a mobile relay to obtain better signal throughput, in which the height of the UAV as a mobile relay and the distance from the source node are optimized. However, one literature rarely involves the trajectory optimization of a single UAV as a mobile relay, mainly optimizing the position of the UAV as a mobile relay.

The research on a single UAV as a mobile relay in one literature mainly considers the situation that the UAV provides services for direct flight, while one literature considers the situation that a single UAV provides services by flying in a circular trajectory when it acts as a mobile relay. In document, UAV uses circular trajectory for flight. Considering the propulsion energy consumption of UAV flying in circular trajectory, the flight trajectory, flight speed and time allocation of UAV are jointly optimized to maximize energy efficiency and spectral efficiency. One document also studied that a single UAV can provide communication services by flying in a circular path as a mobile relay. The main difference is that the mobile relay optimization communication performance under variable rate is considered.

The above literature mainly studies the situation of a single UAV as mobile relay, while one literature studies the situation of multiple UAVs as mobile relay. One document studied the same problem of communication cooperation among multiple UAVs. Each UAV flies in a circular trajectory, and jointly optimized the flight trajectory radius and center of UAV as mobile relay to reduce communication delay and enhance the reliability of communication link. Reference optimizes the location of multiple UAVs as mobile relays to enhance the connectivity of existing networks. One literature studied that UAV serves as a mobile relay auxiliary ground base station for massive machine type communications (MTC). Considering the factors of frequency reuse, interference, backhaul link resource allocation and coverage of UAV, an algorithm for optimizing mobile relay deployment is proposed.

(4) Research status of UAV base station

When natural disasters such as earthquakes, volcanoes and floods occur, ground base stations are often destroyed, and communication infrastructure in disaster areas is damaged to provide communication services, which greatly hinders rescue operations. The traditional emergency communication vehicle will be affected by the terrain. If the road is damaged, it will not be able to reach the disaster area in time to provide communication services, which will delay the precious time of rescue. Although the aerial base station balloon on the high platform is not affected by the terrain and terrain, it can provide communication services for the disaster area, but it takes a long time to deploy, which is not suitable for such a short burst of urgent communication services. UAV has good mobility, is easy to deploy, and is very suitable for such emergency communication services. Therefore, it is very valuable for UAVs to provide communication services for natural disaster areas or hot spots as aerial base stations. The research on UAV as air base station mainly includes the following aspects, such as coverage of UAV as air base station, energy efficiency maximization, air to ground channel modeling, data unloading and throughput optimization. When the UAV is used as the air base station, the rotary wing UAV can hover in the air to provide communication services for ground users, while the fixed wing UAV can only provide communication services for ground users through continuous flight. Next, the research and analysis of static or dynamic communication services provided by UAV as an aerial base station will be described respectively.

One Literature analyzes and optimizes the 3D position of UAV to maximize the minimum number of users served. Among them, one literature proposed a maximum weighted area algorithm to constrain and optimize the 3D position of the UAV in order to optimize the 3D position of the UAV as the aerial base station to maximize the minimum number of users in consideration of different quality of service (QoS) of users. Similarly, one literature also uses the idea of dimension reduction to optimize the 3D position of the UAV, that is, first optimize the flight height of the UAV to maximize the users covered, then optimize the water half position of the UAV to maximize the minimum number of users served. At this time, the optimization problem is a mixed integer nonlinear problem. Finally, under the condition of ensuring a certain QoS, iteratively optimize the horizontal position to minimize the transmission power. One literature analyzed that when the backhaul link data rate is limited, optimizing the 3D position of the UAV can maximize the number of service users under its proposed network centric scheme, and the user centric scheme can maximize the throughput. In addition, one literature considers the relationship between flight altitude and coverage radius of air base stations in different environments under different road losses.

The problem studied in the above literature is mainly to maximize the minimum number of users to serve, while the problem studied in literature is to optimize the 3D position of UAVs to minimize the number of UAVs used, in which UAVs provide communication coverage as aerial base stations. One document considered the constraint of minimum distance between UAV and user, transformed the geometric circular coverage problem into a p-center problem, and proposed a spiral algorithm, which has lower complexity compared with traditional strip algorithm, random algorithm and K-means clustering algorithm. However, one literature mainly considers the optimal deployment of UAV horizontal position under the condition of given UAV flight altitude. In reference, a particle swarm optimization algorithm is proposed to optimize the 3D position of UAVs in order to minimize the number of UAVs in use when a region to be served is given.

It is worth noting that when using a rotary wing UAV as an aerial base station, the energy loss will be greater than that of a fixed wing UAV, because more energy needs to be consumed to maintain a certain flight height when hovering. If it is a fixed wing UAV, it will maintain a certain flight height through direct flight. At this time, the inertia in flight can be used to offset some of the gravity, so the energy consumed will be less. Therefore, in addition to maximizing the minimum number of users served and minimizing the number of UAVs used, minimizing the transmission power of UAVs is also a meaningful research on the research of UAVs as aerial base stations. One literature analyzed and optimized the 3D position of the UAV as the aerial base station to minimize the transmission power and extend the service time of the UAV.

In fact, compared with the traditional ground base station, the flight path of UAV is one of the unique optimization dimensions. When UAV is used as an aerial base station to dynamically provide communication services for users, it has high flexibility and good LOS link, so it can obtain better communication performance.

One literature proposed the flight path optimization design of UAV as an aerial base station to maximize and minimize throughput. Among them, literature studies that a single UAV assists existing ground base stations to provide communication services for cell edge users in hot areas. One document considers that a single UAV uses a circular trajectory to provide communication services for users, and maximizes the minimum throughput by optimizing the flight trajectory radius of the UAV, bandwidth allocation between the UAV and the ground base station, and user allocation. Reference considers optimizing the flight path, transmission power and user allocation of multiple UAVs to maximize the minimum throughput.

The above literature mainly focuses on optimizing the flight path of UAV as air base station to maximize the minimum throughput. When the UAV flies, the energy loss is greater than when it is stationary, and because the airborne energy of the UAV is limited, the time to execute the task is also limited. At present, there are some international literatures on optimizing the flight path of UAV to shorten the task completion time. Although optimizing the flight path of UAV can improve throughput and shorten task completion time, the communication link between UAV and users is not stable due to UAV flying in high altitude and high mobility during flight, so the reliability of communication link when UAV serves as an air base station for users needs to be further studied. One literature analyzed and studied the reliability of air to ground links between UAVs and users when unmanned aerial base stations provide communication services for users, optimized the flight altitude and position of UAVs, and maximized the coverage of communication services while ensuring a certain reliability.

In 2016, one literature first proposed a heterogeneous network model in which UAV base stations serve D2D users and cellular users. The author first studied the coverage capability of deploying static UAV base stations, and then proposed a deployment strategy for the minimum number of hovering points required for mobile single UAV base stations to cover the ground network. Reference proposed a UAV auxiliary access system, which enables UAV as a static air base station to serve multiple ground terminals, and optimizes the power control of the underlying D2D communication to maximize throughput. Considering the mobility of UAV, literature jointly optimizes the transmission power of UAV and D2D users, the flight altitude and position of UAV, and the bandwidth allocated by ground terminals to maximize the reachable rate of D2D terminal.

In emergency communication, D2D's multi hop communication advantage is the main means to improve coverage. In one literature, the author proposed a new type of D2D multi hop multicast network based on UAV. The UAV initially broadcasts emergency information to all ground D2D users, and then D2D users who successfully receive the emergency information will send information to the outside. On the basis of the model proposed in one literature and one literature obtained the outage probability expression of D2D users in the uplink and downlink multi hop, and then proposed an optimal transceiver design scheme to maximize the total downlink transmission rate between the UAV and the source node of the multi hop D2D link. In one literature, the author applied UAV to assist information transmission in emergency situations. When the user received the alarm information from UAV, the user sent the received data packet to adjacent users in D2D mode, and applied game theory and dynamic hypergraph coloring methods to solve the problems of dynamic cluster formation and spectrum sharing in random environments respectively.

Another major advantage of D2D communication is to reuse the spectrum resources of cellular users. Therefore, [18] considers the cognitive communication network consisting of a UAV flight base station serving multiple downlink ground terminals (GTs) and multiple bottom layer D2D users, proposes a joint design of D2D allocation, bandwidth and power allocation, and reformulates the mixed binary optimization problem as a continuous optimization problem to support the throughput of GTs, At the same time, the service quality of D2D users is guaranteed. In addition, system energy efficiency (EE) is also an important indicator to evaluate the emergency network with bottom D2D communication that enables UAV base stations. One literature deduced the successful transmission probability, average total rate and easy to handle expression of EE in the coexistence network of UAV and D2D communication based on the principle of random geometry. It also solved the impact of D2D users and user density connected with UAV on EE, and optimized the sum rate as a performance index in the uplink scheme. Reference studied the problem of maximizing the energy efficiency of the D2D UAV assisted 5G system at the bottom layer of interference perception. Considering all interference scenarios, the constraint function was reconstructed by using the cubic inequality method, and the non convex problem was transformed into a convex problem for solution. In addition, security is also an important measure of system construction. For example, literature [19] studied the security of wireless power supply D2D communication network in the emergency communication system with multiple eavesdroppers. UAV acts as a cooperative jammer to interfere with eavesdroppers, and the proposed scheme can effectively improve the security capability of D2D communication.

However, the wireless coverage of a single static UAV is limited. Taking full advantage of the mobility of the UAV, it is also a common method to use dynamic base stations to assist D2D communication. Reference analyzed the task execution scenarios of UAV applicable to S-shaped trajectory, circular trajectory, Z-shaped trajectory and square trajectory respectively, and analyzed the minimum task completion time and energy loss. In addition to utilizing the mobility of UAVs, increasing the number of UAVs to serve more ground users at the same time is also one of the topics faced by UAV emergency communication. One literature considered the communication scenario of dual UAVs connected by D2D in disaster scenarios. In order to obtain better performance, the author proposed a learning based clustering algorithm and optimization algorithm to optimize user association to maximize the weighted sum rate of UAV service users and the total number of D2D connected users.

On the other hand, UAV as a relay assisted ground network with low-level D2D communication is also a research hotspot at present. In most cases, UAV communication links reuse the existing spectrum of ground communication services. In the low-level mode, the coexistence of UAV and D2D communication will cause serious interference, which will inevitably reduce the system performance. Similar to one document, it considers the problem of power allocation and trajectory optimization in the network where UAVs share the spectrum with ground D2D communication as flight relays. Due to the limited energy capacity and flight time of UAVs, an important issue in deploying UAVs is to manage the energy consumption in real time, which is proportional to the launching power of UAVs. To solve this important problem, one literature proposed a real-time resource allocation algorithm to maximize energy efficiency by jointly optimizing energy collection time and power control. One literature designed an effective resource allocation algorithm to maximize the average throughput in a time range on the premise of meeting the energy causality constraints. One literature maximizes the capacity of relay network by jointly optimizing relay deployment, channel allocation and relay allocation. Considering the coupling relationship between the three optimization variables, an alternative optimization method is proposed to solve this problem. For the application scenario of multi UAV relay, in [20], the author considered the impact of users' dynamic selection and transmission mode on network performance, including multi UAV selection, time allocation of data loading and unloading, and channel access competition. A hierarchical game model is designed to analyze the complex relationship between devices, which improves the global network performance.

In addition to the aerial base station and relay, UAVs are also often used as flight communication nodes to interact with auxiliary ground D2D users. For example, deploying UAVs can expand the communication range of the D2D network. One literature studied the application scenario where three nodes (one UAV and two D2D users) are equipped with multiple antennas and communicate with each other in a multi-channel manner, and compared the performance of various transmission schemes in terms of total rate. Due to the scarcity of spectrum resources, when UAV and D2D are both communication nodes, the allocation of radio channels is a challenging research topic. The dynamic topology and high mobility of nodes in the combined network based on UAV and D2D make the traditional channel allocation algorithm no longer applicable. One literature uses partially overlapping channels and game theory to alleviate the above problems. One literature studied the problem of three-dimensional spectrum sharing between D2D users and UAV communication, aiming to maximize the regional spectrum efficiency of UAV network and ensure the minimum regional spectrum efficiency required by D2D network. One document introduced NOMA technology into UAV network and proposed a D2D enhanced UAV-NOMA network architecture to further improve spectral efficiency.

4 Conclusion

At present, the traditional emergency D2D communication is mainly embodied in information collection, information sharing and expanding cellular coverage. By taking advantage of D2D technology and its application mode, users in disaster affected areas can transfer information to each other through D2D to achieve the purpose of information sharing. Furthermore, D2D can transmit the information of the affected area to the area covered by the basic network in the form of multi hop, so as to quickly send out the distress signal at the early stage of the disaster, bringing great convenience to the rescue work. Due to the particularity of D2D direct connection communication, D2D related technologies under cellular network coverage mainly include mode selection, transmission scheduling, power control, energy consumption analysis, etc. However, with the increase of the number and distribution density of D2D, the advantages and contradictions of D2D are gradually highlighted. More and more D2D users will reuse cellular frequency resources in the way of bottom communication, and the diversity and complexity of information will also aggravate the interference between users. Finally, with the high standards and strict requirements of emergency communication on time delay and energy consumption, how to reasonably plan D2D communication and give full play to the advantages of D2D communication in emergency communication is an important topic at present.

(1) Compared with the traditional ground wireless relay communication system, the relay system based on UAV platform brings new possibilities and challenges for resource optimization design. On the one hand, because UAV flies at a certain altitude, it is easy to avoid obstacles on the transmission path, which will bring a better LoS transmission channel; On the other hand, UAV can flexibly change its position in the air, which brings a new way of thinking for optimizing system performance. Since the position, altitude, speed and heading direction of the UAV can be dynamically changed, the flight state of the UAV can be designed according to the corresponding communication requirements to obtain better communication performance. In addition, resources such as power and time also determine the performance of communication system based on UAV platform. Reliability, throughput and fairness are still important evaluation criteria for communication system based on UAV. Therefore, the joint optimization of UAV relay flight path and time, power and other resources is a key problem.

(2) The deployment strategy of UAV base station is the primary task of using UAV for data communication service, and its deployment performance is directly related to the system service quality and effective utilization of resources. The deployment strategy of UAV mainly includes network planning, static space deployment and dynamic space deployment. For the deployment of UAV base station, domestic and foreign scholars have made theoretical analysis from multiple perspectives, but compared with the actual application situation, the current analysis still has some limitations. On the one hand, how to plan the number and task division of UAVs when the distribution and demand of ground users are known; On the other hand, according to the communication environment and user distribution, how to reasonably plan the static base station deployment location or dynamic flight path of (multiple) UAVs to obtain the optimal communication performance on the premise of meeting the user communication needs. Therefore, the flexibility of UAV brings more possibilities and innovations to the communication network as well as more challenges.

(3) UAV and D2D communication respectively assist emergency communication from two dimensions of air and ground, breaking through the constraints of ground infrastructure damage and geographical and topographic environment on emergency communication. As mentioned earlier, the UAV can not only serve as a relay to assist the original cellular users in an emergency scenario, but also serve as a base station to provide continuous and wide coverage communications. However, D2D may interfere with other users sharing spectrum resources while assisting ground communication and expanding coverage. The current literature on the interference and cooperation between UAV and D2D communication is not sufficient, and the advantages of the combination of the two have not been brought into play to provide more reliable and stable services for emergency scenarios. Moreover, for the scenario of

widely distributed D2D users, there is no literature to explore the communication network assisted by multiple UAVs.

References

1. Lin, Y.D., Hsu, Y.C.: Multihop cellular: a new architecture for wireless communications. In: Proceedings IEEE INFOCOM 2000. Conference on Computer Communications. Nineteenth Annual Joint Conference of the IEEE Computer and Communications Societies, Tel Aviv, Israel, March, 2000, pp. 1273–1282 (2000)
2. Bucaille, I., H´lethuin, S., Munari, et al.: Rapidly deployable network for tactical applications: aerial base station with opportunistic links for unattended and temporary events, absolute example. In: Military Communications Conference (2014)
3. Ding, G., Wu, Q., Zhang, L., et al.: An amateur drone surveillance system based on the cognitive internet of things. IEEE Commun. Mag. **56**(1), 29–35 (2018)
4. Hossein Motlagh, N., Taleb, T., Arouk, O.: Low-altitude unmanned aerial vehicles-based internet of things services: comprehensive survey and future perspectives. IEEE Internet Things J. 1–1 (2016)
5. Bucaille, I., et al.: Rapidly deployable network for tactical applications: Aerial base station with opportunistic links for unattended and temporary events absolute example. In: MILCOM 2013–2013 IEEE military communications conference. IEEE (2013)
6. Ada, S., Sharman, R., Han, W., et al.: Factors impacting the intention to use emergency notification services in campus emergencies: an empirical investigation. IEEE Trans. Prof. Commun. **59**(2), 89–109 (2016)
7. Lei, C., Lin, W., Miao, L.: A stochastic emergency vehicle redeployment model for an effective response to traffic incidents. IEEE Trans. Intell. Transport. Syst. **16**(2), 898–909 (2015)
8. Lakshman, T.R., Sui, Y., Svensson, T.: EU FP7 INFSO-ICT-317669 METIS, D 4.1 Summary on preliminary trade-off investigations and first set of potential network-level solutions (2013)
9. 3GPP TR 36.843 V12. 0.0. Study on LTE Device to Device Proximity Services: Radio Aspects (2014)
10. Asadi, A., Wang, Q., Mancuso, V.: A survey on device-to-device communication in cellular networks. IEEE Commun. Surv. Tutor. **16**(4), 1801–1819 (2014)
11. Hunukumbure, M., Moulsley, T., Oyawoye, A., et al.: D2D for energy efficient communications in disaster and emergency situations. In: 2013 21st International Conference on Software, Telecommunications and Computer Networks-(SoftCOM 2013). IEEE, pp. 1–5 (2013)
12. Li, Y., Kaleem, Z., Chang, K.: Interference-Aware Resource-Sharing Scheme for Multiple D2D Group Communications Underlaying Cellular Networks. Kluwer Academic Publishers (2016)
13. Swain, S.N., Mishra, S., Murthy, C.S.R.: A novel spectrum reuse scheme for interference mitigation in a dense overlay D2D network. In: IEEE, International Symposium on Personal, Indoor, and Mobile Radio Communications. IEEE, pp. 1201–1205 (2015)
14. Mach, P., Becvar, Z., Najla, M.: Resource allocation for D2D communication with multiple D2D pairs reusing multiple channels. IEEE Wireless Commun. Lett. **8**(4), 1008–1011 (2019)
15. Dai, Y., Sheng, M., Liu, J., et al.: Joint mode selection and resource allocation for D2D-enabled NOMA cellular networks. IEEE Trans. Veh. Technol. **68**(7), 6721–6733 (2019)
16. Min, H., Lee, J., Park, S., et al.: Capacity enhancement using an interference limited area for device-to-device uplink underlaying cellular networks. IEEE Trans. Wireless Commun. **10**(12), 3995–4000 (2011)
17. Fan, R., Cui, J., Jin, S., et al.: Optimal node placement and resource allocation for UAV relaying network. IEEE Commun. Lett. **22**(4), 808–811 (2018)

18. Huq, K.M.S, Mumtaz, S., Zhou, Z., et al.: Energy-Efficiency Maximization for D2D-Enabled UAV-Aided 5G Networks. In: ICC 2020–2020 IEEE International Conference on Communications (ICC). IEEE, pp. 1–6 (2020)
19. Zeng, Y., Zhang, R., Lim, T.J.: Wireless communications with unmanned aerial vehicles: Opportunities and challenges. IEEE Commun. Mag. 54(5), 36–42 (2016)
20. Tang, F., Fadlullah, Z.M., Kato, N., et al.: AC-POCA: Anticoordination game based partially overlapping channels assignment in combined UAV and D2D-based networks. IEEE Trans. Veh. Technol. 67(2), 1672–1683 (2017)

China Mobile Network Architecture for 6G

Baorong Zhan[1] ⓘ, Xichang Yu[2](✉) ⓘ, Zhaojiang Zeng[1] ⓘ, Shuai Shao[1] ⓘ,
Xiao Han[2], and Qingxin Lu[3]

[1] Guangdong Innovative Technical College, Dongguan 523960, China
[2] China Mobile Group Guangdong CO LTD., Dongguan Branch, Dongguan 523129, China
yuxichang@gd.chinamobile.com
[3] Deptartment of Electronic Engineering, Jinan University, Guangzhou 510632, China

Abstract. With the large-scale commercial deployment of the 5G network in the world, more and more researchers and organizations have already begun to study the sixth generation of mobile communication systems. Network architecture is not only the skeleton and backbone of mobile communication system, but also the core of the 6G system. The concept, key technologies, design ideology and key factors of 6G are explored in this article. The network architecture for 6G called "three-entity, four-layer, and five-plane" is presented, which is proposed by China Mobile. As the first systematic 6G network architecture proposed in the industry, it shows a full view of cross-domain, cross-layer, and multidimensional 6G network architecture from three perspectives: spatial view, logical view, and functional view. The "three-entity" includes network entity, management orchestration entity, and digital twin entity; the "four-layer" includes resource & computing layer, routing & connection layer, servitization function layer, and open & enablement layer; The "five-plane" includes control plane, user plane, data plane, intelligence plane, and security plane.

Keywords: 6G · network architecture · three-entity · four-layer · five-plane · China Mobile

1 Introduction

The pace of scientific and technological innovation in the field of mobile communication has never stopped. From the first generation of analog communication system (1G) to the fifth generation of the Internet of everything (5G), mobile communication has not only profoundly changed people's way of life, but also become a new engine for the acceleration of social and economic digitalization and informatization [1]. 5G has entered the fast track of commercial deployment. It will open a new era of the Internet of Everything, enabling industrial, transportation, agriculture, and other industries [2].

In order to promote the full integration of 5G with the economy and society, China Mobile has begun to fully implement the "5G+ " plan, including coordinated development of 5G + 4G, 5G + AICDE and ecology of 5G+ to maximize the influence of 5G in all aspects [3]. Based on 5G, "5G+ " will generate a series of innovative solutions

Published by Springer Nature Switzerland AG 2023. All Rights Reserved
A. Li et al. (Eds.): 6GN 2022, LNICST 505, pp. 100–117, 2023.
https://doi.org/10.1007/978-3-031-36014-5_10

covering many aspects of people's life, production and social governance, and create new experiences, new driving forces, and new models to boost overall national strength, high-quality economic development, and social transformation and upgrading [4].

According to the pace of development of the mobile communication industry, it is expected that 6G will be commercially available around 2030. The Finnish government is the first in the world to launch a large-scale 6G research program. The US Federal Communications Commission has opened up the terahertz spectrum for 6G research, and China started 6G research in 2018 [5]. As the leader of operators, China Mobile proposed a 6G network architecture called "three-entity, four-layer, and five-plane" [6]. With the new architecture, 6G will further create a new technological ecology, promote the society to a "digital twin" world, to achieve the grand goal of "6G innovation world".

In this paper, the concept of 6G is briefly introduced and the design concept and key factors of the 6G network architecture are discussed. Combined with the new services and applications in the future, the overall design and function of each module of the China Mobile 6G network architecture are described in detail.

2   6G Concepts

2.1   6G Vision

The goal of 6G is to meet the demands of the information society in 10 years, which would go significantly beyond what 5G can offer. The vision of 6G can be summarized into four key aspects, 'intelligent connectivity', 'deep connectivity', 'holographic connectivity', and 'ubiquitous connectivity', which constitute the overall vision of 6G, which is 'Wherever you think, everything follows your heart'.

'Intelligent connectivity' refers to the inherent intelligence of communication systems: the intelligence of network elements and network architecture, the intelligence of connected objects (terminal devices), and the support of intelligent services information. 6G networks will face many challenges, such as super-complex and immense networks, myriad types of terminals and network devices, and extremely complex and diverse business types. 'Intelligent connectivity' will meet two requirements simultaneously [7]: (1) each of the connected devices related to the network itself is intelligent and the related services are intelligent; (2) the complex network itself needs intelligent management. 'Intelligent connectivity' will be the fundamental characteristic for supporting the other three main characteristics of the 6G network: 'deep connectivity', 'holographic connectivity' , and 'ubiquitous connectivity'.

2.2   Requirements and KPIs

To realize the vision of the 6G network and to meet the demand for future communications, the following key requirements and challenges must be considered, particularly compared to some KPIs of 5G [8].

Peak rate: terabit era, ~ 10 terabits per second, which is ~ 10 times higher than 1 terabits per second for 5G networks with a system bandwidth of ~ hundred MHz.

Universal connection with low delay, reliability, and high rate.

Higher energy efficiency, compared to no definite requirements in 5G either at the network side, or the terminal side if for eMBB and URLLC.

Connection everywhere and anytime, as opposed to a million devices per square kilometer for 5G which may not be very challenging, depending on the assumptions of traffic models, system bandwidths, etc.

Ubiquitous intelligence, vs. no such requirement in 5G.

Native security, more trustable than 5G.

Versatility: to accommodate various networks in a dynamic and organic manner.

Convergence of communication, computing, sensing, and control.

Non-technical challenges: industry barriers, policy and regulation, and consumer habits.

2.3 Enabling Technologies

Currently, the concept of 6G is still in the early stage of discussion, and the views expressed by different countries are quite diverse. To achieve the 6G vision mentioned above and considering the development status and trends of related technologies, we believe that the potential key technical features of 6G would include the aspects shown in Fig. 1. Among them, for example, terahertz communications, visible light communications, very large-scale antenna, advanced channel coding would be crucial to achieve the peak rate of ~ 10 terabits per second and the extreme low latency [9, 10]. Advanced channel coding & modulation and space-air-ground-sea integrated communications can help to truly fulfill the massive connection (everywhere and anytime). The holographic radio and the large intelligent surface are promising in significantly improving energy efficiency and reducing the hardware cost of 6G networks [11].

In previous generations of mobile communications, it would sometimes be difficult to clearly categorize whether a technology should belong to the a-th or b-th generation. Similarly, some technologies may be envisioned as the evolution of 5G, since the level of maturity is higher and the related study has been conducted for many years; for example, the problems, challenges, and general approaches are well known. Depending on the demand for future releases, there is a chance that some of these technologies may end up being part of 6G [12].

However, several technologies are still in the exploratory stage; strictly speaking, some of them are still science, not technology. Some may be highly dependent on the advancement of other fields, such as material science, physics, chemistry, and semiconductor manufacturing. However, they may not reach maturity before 2030 [13].

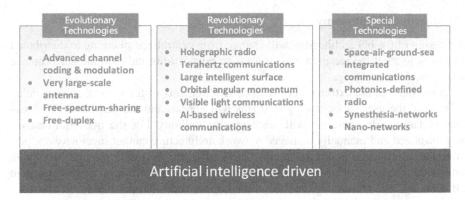

Fig. 1. Key technologies of 6G.

3 Design Ideology of 6G Network Architecture

3.1 Compatibility

The mobile communication network is evolving along the direction of IP, cloud, and service. The 6G architecture design will continue these soft development directions and achieve forward and backward compatibility.

In terms of connectivity flexibility, the 6G architecture will further realize deterministic IP on the basis of end-to-end IP; In terms of resource flexibility, the 6G architecture will further realize the integration of computing network on the basis of cloud; In terms of functional flexibility, the 6G architecture will further realize the whole-domain servitization and its technological evolution on the basis of servitization of the core network. The continuous development of these three flexibility directions will fully continue the architectural advantages of 5G and will support the smooth development and evolution of the 5G network into the 6G network [14].

3.2 Cross-Domain

The 6G architecture design will support the management of fixed, mobile, satellite and other access, support the management of public/industry, physical/digital networks, and support the collaboration of different domains within the network.

The 6G architecture is required to integrate multiple access systems, such as fixed access, mobile access, and satellite access, and to realize multi-access control integration, service integration, and management integration at the architecture level [15]. For the diverse application scenarios facing the public and industries, the 6G architecture must carry out the cross-layer and integrated design of the core network, the transmission network, and the access network for different modes of networking and functional requirements, in order to realize the integration of the network organization at the architecture level.

3.3 Distributed Autonomy

The design of the 6G architecture will change from centralized planning to distributed autonomy to meet the requirements of massive connections and extreme performance in large-scale networking.

In the 6G era, the extreme performance requirements of the control surface delay < 1ms and the user surface delay < 0.1ms will appear, and the number of base stations of large-scale operators will reach tens of millions. For the 6G requirements, the centralized and manually managed network architecture cannot meet network performance. Centralized and distributed collaborative networking is required to realize distributed management of resources, routes, functions, and services, and then realize self-growing, self-optimizing, and self-evolving network autonomy [16]. In this way, network resources and capabilities can be optimally scheduled in a large-scale, complex network environment.

3.4 Endogenous

The 6G architecture design will transform from external to endogenous, including endogenous security and AI, which are built into the core capabilities of the architecture.

For multiple domain convergence, ubiquitous connections, and heterogeneous resources in 6G, the incremental or patched ability is difficult to meet the requirement of diversification and diversified service under the large-scale network. It needs the security and AI to be built into the core capabilities of 6G architecture, and penetrated into various areas, various networks and the whole life cycle of each unit. Through endogenous design, security, AI, and other core technical capabilities can be fully integrated with the communication network [17].

3.5 Simplicity

The 6G architecture design will be transformed from complex incremental to simple and integrated, presenting as an integrated system externally and micro-servitization internally.

In the 6G architecture, the complex internal logic, the operation commands and the service parameters will be encapsulated and exposed, the integrated architecture will be easy to implement and deploy, the interface will be clear and the cost will be controllable, so it will be convenient for operation and maintenance, external system interconnection and user calls. To achieve the aim, on the one hand, it is necessary to restructure and simplify the set of functions, integrate scattered service functions, and reduce the complexity of the network. On the other hand, there is also need to refine the services and functions, reduce the coupling of services, support intelligent organizational ability, and reduce the difficulty of system maintenance.

3.6 Digital Twin

The 6G architecture design will evolve from a simple physical network entity to the direction of physical + digital twin, realizing virtual-real mapping and virtual-real interaction.

The 6G network needs to build parallel physical and digital networks to provide a virtual-real integrated management method. This means that it not only supports real-time modeling of different network and service patterns, but also supports flexible, real-time control policy and physical systems prediction based on digital systems [18].

4 Key Factors in the Architecture of the 6G Network

4.1 Holistic Service-Based Component

In order to support the SAGIN network, the SBA will evolve to a holistic service-based architecture to provide more flexible and efficient architecture and protocols. It supports the modular and servitization design of network functions to meet the requirements of flexible construction and networking. The modules should be able to meet an easy to call loosely coupled requirement for orchestration, supporting a balance of capabilities, efficiency, and cost [19].

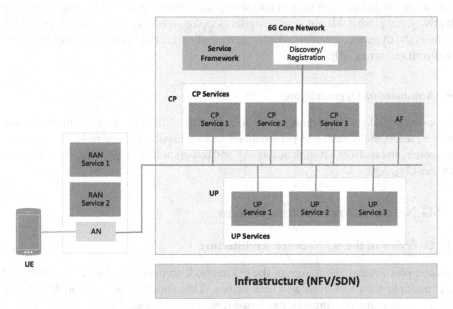

Fig. 2. Holistic service-based architecture.

4.2 Opened Protocol

Provides protocols that are easy to construct, easy to maintain and efficient to meet the requirements of intergenerational system access and upgrade evolution capabilities, as well as the flexible docking requirements for future applications, different levels communication systems or communication and external systems.

4.3 Distributed Networking

It enables to support building of global + local, centralized + distributed networks. It supports general management and customization of network functions, realizes self-inclusion, and self-organization networking.

4.4 Flexible Connection

It enables fast, robust, and ubiquitous connections between networks, between terminals, and between different functions, realizes routing of data and computing capability, so that it can meet the requirement of multisystem, multifunction, and multidomain resources sharing.

4.5 Mechanism of Twinization

For multidimensional resources such as data, storage, forwarding and computing, the twinization mechanism can realize reusability, easy management, light customization, adaptivity, and predictable physical + digital mapping, feedback, and closed-loop, which can meet the dynamic, automatic deployment, and optimization of the overall and local multiform resources [20].

4.6 Autonomous Organization

It supports digital and intelligent means to reduce the difficulty of operation and maintenance, meets the overall and personalized service capability of visible, manageable, and secure, and realizes network autonomy and integration of cloud, edge, terminal and services [21].

5 6G Network Architecture Design

5.1 Overview of the 6G Network Architecture

As a complex system, the design of the 6G network architecture should be considered from multiple points of view and dimensions. This paper introduces the 6G overall logical architecture of "three-entity, four-layer, and five-plane" from spatial, logical, and functional views, which was issued by China Mobile in June 2022.

In the China Mobile 6G overall logical architecture:

(1) "Three-entity" is the spatial view of architecture, describing the objective existence form of 6G network entities, which is divided into network entity, management & orchestration entity and digital twin entity.
(2) "Four-layer" is the logical view of the architecture, showing the structure and organization of the 6G network design, which consists of the resource & computing power layer, the routing & connection layer, the servitization function layer, and the open & enablement layer.

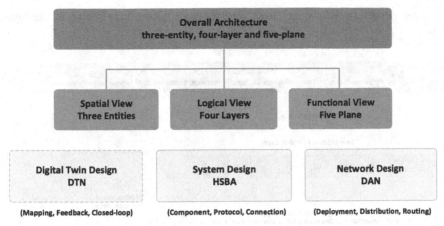

Fig. 3. Overview of the 6G network architecture.

(3) "Five-plane" is the functional view of the architecture, showing the division and composition of 6G network functions, including the control plane, user plane, data plane, intelligence plane, and security plane.

Based on the overall architecture of "three-entity, four-layer, and five-plane", the Digital Twin Network (DTN) is constructed from the design perspective of the combination of physical space and digital virtual space. The twin architecture of 6G network includes spatial design of mapping, feedback, and closed-loop. This part of the architecture has been initially defined, which can be seen in the white paper "Digital Twin Network (DTN)" issued by China Mobile in 2021.

Based on the overall architecture of "three-entity, four-layer, and five-plane", the Holistic service-based architecture (HSBA) was constructed by defining an end-to-end system through services. HSBA designs the interactive mode of the whole end-to-end system, including components, protocols, and connections, and carries out information transmission and business processing based on servitization interfaces, which reflects the system design method of the entire 6G network architecture.

Based on the overall architecture of "three-entity, four-layer, and five-plane", the network achieves flexible and intelligent design, and constitutes the distributed autonomous network architecture (DAN). The networking design shows the connection relationship and the form of the network along 6G networks. It is composed of Small Cloud units (SCU) with self-contained, homogenous, and self-closed functions, which are deployed in a centralized and distributed way. The distributed SCU is designed in a minimalist way and acts as the front desk close to users. The centralized SCU is fully functional and acts as the middle and back end.

5.2 The "Three-Entity, Four-Layer, and Five-Plane" Architecture

China Mobile proposed the 6G overall architecture of "three-entity, four-layer and five-plane", which presents a cross-domain, cross-layer and multidimensional 6G network from three perspectives of space, logic and function. Details are shown in the figure below:

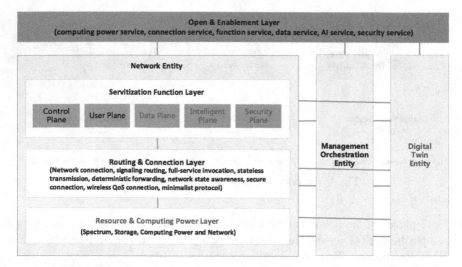

Fig. 4. The "three-entity, four-layer, and five-plane" architecture of 6G.

The "Entity" is the spatial view of the architecture that describes the composition of the network in three dimensions. "Layer" is a logical view of the architecture which logically describes the layered architecture of the network and can be integrated in the implementation process. "Plane" is the functional view of the architecture, mainly refers to the functional category, and follows the concept of "plane" in the traditional 3GPP network,e.g. control plane and user plane.

In the spatial view, the 6G network includes three entities: the network entity, the management orchestration entity, and the digital twin entity. The management orchestration entity and the digital twin entity are two new entities defined in 6G. The network entity is the most important entity that realizes the function of the network and the operation of the network. The management orchestration entity instantiates and modifies the network to realize the whole life cycle management; The digital twin entity builds the digital space of the network and realizes the mapping between virtual and real. As operating networks become more complex, network testings and malfunctions become more costly. To ensure the operation and maintenance of the network, a new development system named digital twin entity is built, which is a mapping to the traditional physical network. Through a digital twin entity, the operator can modify the rules of network planning, building and maintenance, optimize the network in real time, and then realize network autonomy in the future.

In the logical view, the 6G network includes four layers, which are the resource & computing power layer, the routing & connection layer, the servitization function layer, and the open & enablement layer from bottom to top. The design of "four layers" shows the different kinds of capabilities in 6G architecture, and it reflects the concept of cross-domain connectivity, multi-domain collaboration, and integrated development.

The design concept of resource & computing power layer highlights the resource element of "computing power", which will provide basic resources for further integration of spectrum, storage, computing power, and network for 6G. The routing & connectivity layer continues the design concept of open protocols, continuously absorbing new mechanisms and protocols (such as deterministic IP and SRv6), and evolving to programmable and deterministic. The servitization function layer continues the design concept of servitization, and SBA expands from the core network to the end-to-end field, supporting the construction of different functions. The open & enablement layer further enriches the information and communication capabilities, and provides services for its own business and third-party applications through extraction, encapsulation, orchestration, and combination.

In the functional view, the 6G network enhances the functions of traditional control plane and user plane, and introduces new data plane, intelligence plane, and security plane, which constitute the "five planes". The control plane is further enhanced, evolving to the direction of full service and implementing the integration control of multiple access modes. The user plane is enhanced, evolving into the direction of programmability, serviced, cross-domain deterministic, and realizing flexible, high-performance forwarding. The new data plane solves the problem of user data migration, and systematically provides trusted data service. The new intelligence plane provides global AI capability through the collaboration of distributed intelligent nodes to realize endogenous intelligence. The new security plane builds a security system with security awareness and active protection, which are driven by "security data + AI", realizing endogenous security.

5.3 The "Three-Entity": Network Entity, Management Orchestration Entity, and Digital Twin Entity

With the development of digital twin technology and the increasing complexity of network operation and maintenance, it is necessary to carry out external abstract mapping to traditional physical network entity, which means establishing a new development system by constructing a new digital twin entity and realizing closed-loop control of physical network through management orchestration entity.

5.3.1 Network Entity

The network entity includes physical devices such as base station, core network, bearer network in the conventional sense. The network entity is a real and operational network that provides information services for users and is the carrier of architecture implementation.

(1) In terms of basic resources, "computing power" is introduced as a new resource element in 6G. The network expands from scheduling connections to scheduling computing resources, which providing the foundation for new 6G network capabilities, such as sensing capabilities and intelligent endogenous capabilities.

(2) In terms of the provision method, it will continue to evolve from cloud-enabled and software-oriented to pooling. The network entity gradually develops into a

schedulable, fluid, and flexible entity, which provides capabilities of connectivity, computing, and storage in an integrating, pooling method.

(3) In terms of service capability, it will further develop into a service-oriented and platform-based network. Network entity constructs functions and service capabilities oriented to specific scenarios by basic modular services such as user management, connection management, service management, and mobility management. So 6G will deepen the network platform capabilities of 5G.

5.3.2 Management Orchestration Entity

The management orchestration entity is a functional entity that performs intelligent orchestration and management for network resources and network capabilities, and realizes network lifecycle management.

(1) The management orchestration entity not only operates the network entity, but also arranges and optimizes the digital twin entity. The management orchestration entity arranges resources and functions based on their service and network operation requirements and provides required capabilities to ensure users' service experience. The management orchestration entity arranges resources and functions required by users and the network based on their service and network operation requirements, and provides required capabilities to ensure users' service experience. By interacting with the digital twin entity, the management orchestration entity accepts the network configuration parameters from the digital twin, then orchestrates and manages the physical network entity, so as to realize automatic network operation and improve the adaptability of the network to new services, new scenarios, and new differentiated requirements.

(2) The management orchestration entity integrates resources of multiparties by end-to-end configuration, so as to realize the renewal of the management system. For network resource, the management orchestration entity needs to be able to coordinate and manage resources such as spectrum, storage, and computing power. For network capability, the management orchestration entity needs to link all layers and planes of the end-to-end network, and arrange connectivity capabilities, computing capabilities, intelligence capabilities, and security capabilities into services that can be exposed and called externally through the open & enablement layer. In other words, the management orchestration entity realizes the closed-loop management of network autonomy by means of network intelligence and automation.

5.3.3 Digital Twin Entity

The digital twin entity is the mapping of the physical network entity in the virtual space, which realizes the low-cost trial and error, intelligent decision making and high-efficiency innovation in the network. Building a network digital twin requires four key elements: data, model, mapping, and interaction.

(1) The digital twin entity can partially or completely mirror the network entity. All network functions in the 6G network architecture can be constructed as required, corresponding network function twins, which can exchange data with the physical network in real time. By modeling and mapping the running status and environment

of the physical network in digital twin entity, operator can pre-verify the network before deployment, so as to provide the optimal solution of network policies and improve the reliability of network decision-making and deployment.

(2) The digital twin entity assists the 6G network to realize the intelligence plane and achieve the goals of flexible network and intelligent endogenous through the inner and outer closed loop. The requirements of network operation & optimization, network intelligent application, network intelligent autonomy, network new technology & service innovation can all be input to the digital twin entity through the northbound interface, and their relative services can be deployed and verified through the model instance of the entity. After verification, the digital twin entity sends the update control to the physical network entity through the southbound interface.

5.4 The "Four-Layer": Resource & Computing Power Layer, Routing & Connection Layer, Servitization Function Layer, and Open & Enablement Layer

5.4.1 Resource and Computing Power Layer

Resources & computing power layer is the physical resources of the 6G network, including spectrum, storage, computing power, the network, and other basic resources. Software and hardware are decoupled in the 4G core network, and cloud technology is introduced into 5G core network. On this basis, the 6G network evolves into an integrated network with a computing power network as its typical feature. The cross-domain design and distributed design of the 6G network require the integration of wireless & network architecture and the sharing of resources. Therefore, with computing power as its core, the 6G network aggregates physical resources of end, edge, network, and cloud, and provides them for upper-layer services. It not only realizes the deep integration of network, computing power, and storage, but also realizes the intelligent scheduling and optimal utilization of information and communication resources.

5.4.2 Routing and Connection Layer

The routing & connection layer connects the physical nodes in the 6G network to a network to realize state awareness, deterministic forwarding, and flexible service call.

(1) Realize physical connection for the lower layer. The routing & connection layer connects various physical nodes in the resource & computing power layer by means of static or dynamic connections according to the factors of time and space to form an organic network. It can dynamically detect node state and link state, adjust network connection in real time, and realize the optimal network path and real-time reachability.

(2) Build logical connections for the upper layer. The routing & connection layer provides secure and QoS-guaranteed logical connections for the servitization function layer and builds an efficient, intelligent, secure, and reliable connection base. It detects the working state and load of the servitization functional layer in real time, receives and analyzes the microservice messages and data packets from the upper layer, and realizes efficient routing, stateless transmission, and deterministic forwarding. According to the principle of minimalist design, general and unified

interface protocols can be used in the specific design of the routing & connection layer.

5.4.3 Servitization Function Layer

In order to inherit the architectural advantages of SBA, this layer continues the flexible design concept of 5G services, which means that it has basic functions such as access control, mobility management, session management, network security, data packet processing and forwarding, and can support enhanced capabilities such as cross-domain integration, roaming & interworking, and artificial intelligence. The different planes in this layer should support flexible combination to form micro-cloud units on demand and support distributed deployment and independent work. The logical function definition of the servitization function layer will be explained in the "five-plane" section.

5.4.4 Open and Enablement Layer

As is well known, open communication capability has become the core content of future network development. The open & enablement layer provides capabilities and services for its own business and third-party applications by extracting, encapsulating, arranging, and combining the information and communication capabilities of the lower layers. Through the open & enablement layer, the computing services, connectivity services, functional services, data services, AI services, and security services of the operator network are opened, which brings more value-added services to the operator and a better service experience to users. Capabilities and services can be exposed through capability components, service plug-ins, customized services, APIs, and Software Development Kit (SDK).

5.5 The "Fine-PLane": Control Plane, User Plane, Data Plane, Intelligence Plane, and Security Plane

In the servitization function layer of the 6G system architecture, there are many core links and capabilities of the network that need to be added and considered. Therefore, on the basis of strengthening the traditional control plane and user plane, independent data plane, intelligence plane, and security plane are added to achieve endogenous intelligence and endogenous security.

5.5.1 Control Plane

The 6G network should realize the integration control of multiple access modes and evolve to full-service direction. To realize the unified, efficient, and precise control of wireless and core network resources, as well as fixed, mobile, and satellite resources, China Mobile's 6G network architecture will be further enhanced in the following aspects on the basis of the traditional control plane:

(1) Cross-domain integration, flexible control. Access network functions are reconstructed into services to improve the integration and collaboration capabilities of the access network and the core network, as well as the customization and response capability of the service. To improve the utilization of network resources and guarantee

service continuity and quality of service, it is necessary to implement the integration control of multiple access modes. Through the atomization and segmentation of network functions, the dynamic arrangement and combination of network elements, and the dynamic cooperation of heterogeneous network elements, 6G realizes the dynamic segmentation, deployment, cooperation, and integration control of network functions in integrated fixed, mobile, and satellite networks.

(2) Multidimensional sensing and precise control. On the premise that the communication function is not affected as much as possible, the ability of the communication technology itself can be used for sensing detection, so as to realize intelligent adaptive sensing of the target, environment, or content. This can improve the performance of network communication or enable new capabilities for communication systems. Through the sensed information, combined with new technologies such as artificial intelligence, 6G achieves more precise network control.

5.5.2 User Plane

Based on the traditional network user plane, 6G evolves into a programmable, servitization, deterministic cross-domain direction, realizing flexible and high-performance forwarding and comprehensively improving the capability of the user plane.

(1) Programmable: By using protocol-independent programming language, we can flexibly define the group processing logic of the user plane, realize the flexible definition of network functions and optimize the arrangement on each programmable network element in the user plane. Network programmability provides innovative communication services with increased agility and flexibility, and supports a faster deployment of services.

(2) Servitization: The evolution of servitization makes the data plane agile, simplified, and open. However, the 6G service development will be implemented in different scenarios, because the user plane must meet the fast forwarding requirement. In the centralized scenario that requires heavy traffic forwarding, software and hardware can still be more coupled. In the distributed edge scenario, servitization is preferred for flexible deployment.

(3) Cross-domain deterministic: In user plane, resource reservation, traffic shaping, queue scheduling, and other technologies are used to achieve predictable and planable traffic scheduling, which means the delay, jitter, and packet loss rate are controlled within a certain range. In this way, it not only meets the diversified requirements of new services, such as high bandwidth, low latency, and high reliability, but also ensures the quality of traffic forwarding for common service.

5.5.3 Data Plane

The data plane is a new plane in the 6G network architecture, which aims to achieve efficient and secure iteration of massive user data, reliable migration of the network state, and introduction of data services in a trusted way. The plane provides efficient and unified data management functions, supports refined data collection, efficient data transmission, flexible data storage, and distributed data collaboration, ensures data reliability, data privacy, and security, and realizes closed-loop management of the entire data life cycle. At the same time, it takes data as a service product, constructs the business logic based on data provider and consumer, and provides diversified data value-added services. Specifically, the data plane needs to have the following three capabilities:

(1) Data integration capability: User data network elements are defined as different types of network elements in 2G, 3G, 4G, 5G and IMS, and store different user data and related interfaces. For example, the identity information, the authentication information, and the service information of mobile users are different. Communication networks of different generations also use different user data management protocols. To implement the capabilities of authentication data reuse, authentication synchronization, and called party domain selection, user data must be integrated between different systems. In the traditional user data integration mode, user data network elements need to be created or upgraded, and then the existing data of all network users are transferred to the new data network elements, which causes problems such as waste of network resources, huge amounts of data transfer, and long upgrade time. Therefore, the 6G data plane must have efficient data integration capabilities, adopt centralized and distributed storage mode, support unification, authentication, and authentication between different networks, and provide a unified user view to the service platform.

(2) Data continuity capability: In addition to static contract data and configuration data, users also generate context data, such as semistatic data like location and ID assigned by the network, as well as dynamic data such as signaling messages and transient context generated during communication. If the related network element is malfunctioning, the above data need to be quickly migrated from the old network entity to the new network entity to ensure rapid communication recovery. Therefore, the 6G data plane has reliability and flexible migration capability. Combined with blockchain, IPFS, and other decentralized storage methods, it can realize the reliability of distributed data storage and transfer.

(3) Data service capability: 6G networks are rich in "gold mines" of data, but these data are scattered across different operators' systems like gold sand. Therefore, by introducing data service capabilities and building a trusted data service framework, the 6G data plane can collect, process, analyze and share network operation data, business data, user contract data, perception data, AI model data, etc., to find new values.

5.5.4 Intelligence Plane

As a physical carrier to realize intelligent services, the intelligence plane can not only provide local AI capabilities for service objects, but also provide global AI capabilities through the collaboration of distributed intelligent nodes. It achieves the following three capabilities:

(1) Automatic integration of AI elements and their workflows: By means of AI engineering, computing network integration, and other technologies, AI element resources (computing power, algorithms, data) can be utilized in the whole network. 6G supports the interaction and integration of AI elements, provides a local automated integrated AI running environment, realizes the efficient running of the AI workflow, and meets the real-time feedback requirement of AI service calling. To solve

the problem of low efficiency of current AI technology in network applications, the deployment design of a nearby data source and nearby service object can meet the real-time demand of the AI service.

(2) Efficient collaboration of intelligent services: 6G supports atomized abstraction of AI services and distributed deployment and collaboration. Through distributed training & inference and multi-agent collaboration technology, intelligent service collaboration among multinodes is realized, such as intelligent service cooperation among terminals, wireless access, core network and application services, federated learning and cooperate reasoning of multiregional nodes, etc. 6G realizes the evolution from single-node intelligence to distributed multi-node intelligence, and solves the upgrade from single-domain problems to complex system problems. It reduces the large amount of data transmission overhead caused by traditional centralized AI computing mode, and alleviates the data privacy problem in data transmission.

(3) Collaboration along intelligence plane, other planes, and other entities: The management orchestration entity arranges AI services for the intelligence plane. The control plane provides the control and QoS guarantee of AI services for the intelligence plane; the user plane provides the transmission connection between the elements required by AI services for the intelligence plane; the data plane provides a data base for data acquisition and processing for the intelligence plane; as a digital mirror of the network, the digital twin entity provides intelligent services for the intelligence plane to build the required network multidimensional data model, such as traffic data model, network feature business model, etc. At the same time, the digital twin entity provides the pre-verification environment of intelligent services for the intelligence plane, and provides quality assurance for the intelligent services before the network entity runs.

5.5.5 Security Plane

The security plane in a 6G network is an active, intelligent, flexible, and efficient security system based on various security capabilities built inside the network. It provides a high security protection capability in different network integration scenarios and enables applications. On the basis of traditional security protection, the main new functions are as follows.

(1) Endogenous high-security capability: The security capability is fully integrated with network elements/network features to achieve the "high security immunity" capability of the network, and further form a 6G endogenous security system. At the same time, based on the characteristics of mobile communication network, it realizes the network native security capabilities based on identity, such as identity management, authentication, and high security password services.

(2) Perception of safety and active protection: On the basis of the existing passive security protection, the active security capability is added. The key points include: sensing threats and discovering unknown attacks by means of "security data + AI"; analyzing and deducing security policies by means of "safety data + DTN + AI". With the above means, the 6G network not only realizes active security capability and global optimal configuration, but also realizes the transformation from passive defense to active defense.

(3) Flexible and collaborative security capabilities and services: First, based on trust and by means of security measurement, security measures are deployed after a comprehensive analysis of "security + trust", so as to break the concept of "either zero or one" in security and promote a dynamic and appropriate security concept. Second, on the basis of collaboration and by means of orchestration, all kinds of distributed security capabilities and security-related mechanisms are fully coordinated to maximize security capabilities. Third, flexible and schedulable security services are provided based on business requirements.

6 Conclusions

There is a strong upcoming need for communication on the 2030 horizon, with the transformation begun by 5G spurring increasing expectations in society, accelerated by advances in enabling technology, and leading to new services and use cases that will improve our lives.

Development is ramping up in formulating capability targets for the 6G era and investigating a range of promising technology components that may become part of 2030 networks. The key elements for this transformation will be the extreme performance of the adaptability of the radio access network with global and widespread reach. Going beyond connectivity, 6G should become a trusted platform for data and compute, encouraging innovation and serving as the information backbone of society.

This is the right time to start advanced research on 6G technology to expand the capabilities for the needs of 2030. To achieve ubiquitous intelligent communication, China Mobile has designed an advanced 6G network architecture. In this paper, the concept of 6G is briefly introduced, the design concept and key factors of 6G network architecture are described, and the "three-entity, four-layer, and five-plane" architecture of China Mobile is discussed in detail, which provides useful reference for the research and implementation of 6G network in the future.

Acknowledgments. The authors acknowledge the financial support of the University Recognized Scientific Research Foundation in Guangdong Province (Grant: 2022KTSCX384), the University-Level Scientific Research Project Foundation in the Guangdong Innovative Technical College (Grant: 2022ZDYY01).

References

1. Shafi, M., Molisch, A.F., Smith, P.J., et al.: 5G: a tutorial overview of standards, trials, challenges, deployment, and practice. IEEE J. Sel. Areas Commun. **35**(6), 1201–1221 (2017)
2. IMT-2020: (5G) Promotion Group: White Paper on 5G Network Technology Architecture (2018). http://www.imt2020.org.cn/zh/documents/download/18
3. Raghavan, V., Li, J.: Evolution of physical-layer communications research in the post-5G era. IEEE Access, pp. 1–11 (2019). https://doi.org/10.1109/access.2019.2891218
4. IEEE Future Networks.: IEEE 5G and beyond technology roadmap - WHITE PAPER (2017). https://5g.ieee.org/

5. Zhao, Y.J., Yu, G.H., Xu, H.Q., et al.: 6G mobile communication networks: vision, challenges, and key technologies. Sci. Sin. Inform. **49**(8), 963–987 (2019). https://doi.org/ https://doi.org/ 10.1360/N112019-00033

6. China Mobile Communications Group Inc.: White paper on 6G network architecture, section. 3. 6G network architecture "three-entity, four-layer and five-plane", Beijing (2022)

7. Zhang, P., Niu, K., Tian, H., et al.: Technology prospect of 6G mobile communications. J. Commun. **41**(1), 141–148 (2019)

8. You, X.H., Yin, H., Wu, H.Q.: On 6G and wide-area IoT. Chinese J. Internet Things **4**(1), 3–11 (2020)

9. Xie, S., Li, H.R., Li, L.X., et al.: Survey of terahertz communication technology. J. Commun. **41**(5), 168–186 (2020)

10. Lemic, F., Abadal, S., Tavernier, W., et al.: Survey on terahertz nanocommunication and networking: a top-down perspective. IEEE J. Sel. Areas Commun. **39**(6), 1506–1543 (2021)

11. Sheikh, F., Gao, Y., Kaiser, T.: A study of diffuse scattering in massive MIMO channels at terahertz frequencies. IEEE Trans. Antennas Propag. **68**(2), 997–1008 (2020)

12. Gustavsson, U., Frenger, P., Fager, C., et al.: Implementation challenges and opportunities in beyond-5G and 6G communication. IEEE J. Microwaves **1**(1), 86–100 (2021). https://doi. org/10.1109/jmw.2020.3034648

13. Zhang, H.J., Chen, A.Q., Li, Y.B., et al.: Key technologies of 6G mobile networks. J. Commun. (2022). https://kns.cnki.net/kcms/detail/11.2102.TN.20220706.1402.002.html

14. Tataria, H., Shafi, M., Dohler, M., et al.: Six Critical Challenges for 6G Wireless Systems. arXiv e-prints (2021). https://doi.org/10.1109/JMW.2020.3034648

15. Garzon, S., Yildiz, H., Küpper, A.: Decentralized Identifiers and Self-sovereign Identity in 6G. arXiv e-prints (2021). https://doi.org/10.48550/arXiv.2112.09450

16. Peltonen, E., Leppänen, T., Lovén, L.: Edge-native Distributed Platform for Artificial Intelligence. In: 6G Wireless Summit (2019)

17. Chen, Y., Liu, W., Niu, Z., et al.: Pervasive intelligent endogenous 6g wireless systems: prospects, theories and key technologies. Digital Commun. Netw. **6**(3), 312–320 (2020). https://doi.org/10.1016/j.dcan.2020.07.002

18. Khan, L., Saad, W., Niyato, D., et al.: Digital-Twin-Enabled 6G: Vision, Architectural Trends, and Future Directions. arXiv e-prints, (2021). https://doi.org/10.48550/arXiv.2102.12169

19. Wang, X.Y., Sun, T., Duan, X.D., et al.: Holistic service-based architecture for space-air-ground integrated network for 5g-advanced and beyond. China Commun. **19**(01), 14–28 (2022)

20. Lu, Y.L., Huang, X.H., Zhang, K., et al.: Low-latency federated learning and blockchain for edge association in digital twin empowered 6G networks. IEEE Trans. Industr. Inf. (2020). https://doi.org/10.1109/TII.2020.3017668

21. Li, C., Guo, W., Sun, C., et al.: Trustworthy deep learning in 6G enabled mass autonomy: from concept to quality-of-trust key performance indicators. IEEE Veh. Technol. Mag. (2020). https://doi.org/10.1109/MVT.2020.3017181

Mobile Edge Computing for 6G Networks

3D Battlefield Radiation Source Location Tracking Algorithm

Ziqi Sun[1], Weichao Yang[2], Yifan Ping[2], Ruofei Ma[1], and Gongliang Liu[1(✉)]

[1] Harbin Institute of Technology, Weihai 264200, Shandong, China
liugl@hit.edu.cn
[2] China Academy of Space Technology (Xi'an), Xi'an 710100, Shanxi, China

Abstract. Under the framework of multi-domain grid in battlefield environment, in order to make better use of battlefield electromagnetic domain information to perceive and manage electromagnetic radiation sources in the area, this paper proposes a three-dimensional battlefield radiation source location tracking algorithm (BRSLTA). Different from the existing methods, the proposed BRSLTA considers the influence of the battlefield terrain, utilizes the Euclidean distance of the signal space to maximize the location of the signal monitoring station, and builds a fingerprint database in a large area by drawing on the idea of indoor fingerprint positioning. Deep learning is used to search and match electromagnetic energy, and realize the tracking of radiation sources through real-time positioning. The simulation results show that the proposed algorithm can roughly simulate the trajectory of the radiation source in the battlefield area with high accuracy and precision.

Keywords: Radiation Source · Location Tracking · Deep Learning

1 Introduction

Electromagnetic information is mainly used to describe the movement trajectory and path changes of the electromagnetic radiation source, and is a representation of the relationship between the electromagnetic radiation source and other things or the environment. At present, our army's traditional methods of data analysis cannot meet the needs of current military operations. The collected electromagnetic data needs to be stored more effectively. It is necessary to make full use of this information to carry out a series of applications and conduct accurate analysis in the electromagnetic environment, so as to make decisions during the war. Correct and timely decisions. Therefore, this paper studies the application of battlefield electromagnetic information management and radiation source positioning and tracking.

The principle of the fingerprint positioning method is to establish a map storing the signal strength fingerprint data in a designated area. In the gridded area, the signal strengths in each grid are calculated and stored uniformly in a fingerprint database. During online positioning, the monitoring station measures the intensity of the electromagnetic radiation source signal, and compares it with the fingerprint database to

A. Li et al. (Eds.): 6GN 2022, LNICST 505, pp. 121–141, 2023.
https://doi.org/10.1007/978-3-031-36014-5_11

find the closest grid node coordinates as the final positioning result of the radiation source. Received Signal Strength (RSS)-based localization methods have been used in many researches because the method is easy to configure the system [1]. Reference [2] proposed a two-step indoor location estimation method based on the received signal strength in wireless sensor networks, measuring the received signal strength of radio signals transmitted by multiple training points in the wireless sensor network, and applying the least squares method to determine the signal propagation model. Parameter. Reference [3] proposed a set of methods to improve the accuracy of RSS-based location estimation. Considering that the transmitter power is unknown, PDOA (Power Difference of Arrival) technique is used together with ML (Maximum Likelihood) algorithm to predict the transmitter location. By weighting the probabilistic calculations of ML, the contradiction between the received and expected signal levels of each receiver is exploited, and low-precision estimates are eliminated. Based on RSS positioning algorithm and Zigbee wireless communication module, literature [4] proposes an indoor positioning system based on multi-level Transmission-Signal-Strength (TSS) technology, which can effectively improve positioning accuracy. References [5, 6] use a physical model-based localization method. Different from fingerprint localization, it uses a path loss model to represent RF signal attenuation. However, due to factors such as multipath, metal reflection and interference noise, the propagation distance and The relationship between radio signal strengths becomes so complex that the accuracy of the predictions cannot be judged. The above positioning algorithms are only suitable for positioning in a small range, especially indoor positioning, and do not consider the positioning of electromagnetic radiation sources in a large range outdoors.

Deep learning has the characteristics of strong learning ability and good nonlinear fitting ability. There are also many studies that introduce learning ideas in fingerprint positioning. Reference [7] proposed a hybrid neural network, which uses multiple access points to receive channel state information from the network, reduces the non-line-of-sight propagation effect, and significantly improves the robustness of indoor positioning systems, but this study fixed The power of the signal transmitting source has poor positioning effect for unknown signal sources. Literature [8] proposed a solution for deep neural network (DNN), which can adjust the weight of neurons through the learning process to represent any mathematical function, and can automatically capture the characteristics of the data during the learning process, solving the data required for feature extraction. However, only one access point is used in this study, the network is relatively simple, and the accuracy is low for the case of multiple reference points. Reference [9] proposed an indoor positioning machine learning location tracking system based on Bluetooth Low Energy (BLE), and the average estimation error of this method is 50 cm. Other references proposed a nonlinear relationship between the signal strength measured by deep neural network learning and the location of the signal source for the indoor positioning of cellular signals, but in these studies, the input of training data in the neural network is the reception measured by different base stations. Signal strength, for a signal source with unknown signal strength, there may be a large error when searching for a match.

It can be seen from the above analysis that for the positioning and tracking of electromagnetic radiation sources, there are many studies on indoor positioning, and outdoor positioning mostly relies on satellite positioning systems such as GPS, which cannot be related to the electromagnetic environment of the battlefield at present. In terms of positioning, the model researched by deep learning is relatively simple, which is not suitable for large-scale positioning scenarios, and there are few studies on electromagnetic radiation sources of unknown intensity.

In order to make better use of battlefield electromagnetic domain information to perceive and manage electromagnetic radiation sources in the area, this paper proposes a three-dimensional battlefield radiation source location and tracking algorithm. This algorithm is divided into two stages, namely offline training data stage and online radiation source location stage. The specific process is to create a regular grid in the selected battlefield area in the offline phase, reasonably deploy multiple monitoring stations in the grid area, collect the electromagnetic energy information of each grid node corresponding to each monitoring station, and store it in the corresponding network. In the grid, the fingerprint database is established. In the online stage, the frequency and energy of the unknown electromagnetic signal are detected by the radar of the monitoring station, and the corresponding fingerprint database is searched and matched to obtain the approximate position of the electromagnetic radiation source, and the movement path of the electromagnetic radiation source can be predicted by updating the position in real time. The simulation results show that the proposed algorithm can roughly simulate the trajectory of the radiation source in the battlefield area with high accuracy and precision.

2 System Model

2.1 Fingerprint Localization Model

Fingerprint positioning method has been studied by more and more scholars due to its advantages of high positioning accuracy and low hardware complexity. The fingerprint positioning method was first proposed when studying indoor positioning. According to the characteristics of the WiFi signal, the strength of the WiFi signal was monitored in multiple different locations and stored as a fingerprint database. When an unknown electromagnetic device was detected in the positioning area, each monitoring Detect the electromagnetic signal strength emitted by the radiation source, search and match the measured signal strength of the unknown radiation source with the fingerprint data of each position in the database, and select the most matching position coordinates as the positioning result. The fingerprint positioning method mainly includes two processes, namely the offline data acquisition process and the online signal source positioning process. The offline data collection process is mainly responsible for collecting the position coordinates of each reference point set in advance and the received signal strength vector RSSI (Received Signal Strength Indicator) measured at the position, and storing the data information of these reference points to establish a fingerprint database. The online signal source location process is mainly responsible for using the monitoring station to measure the RSSI of the target signal source and searching and matching it with the signal strength vector in the database. The matching algorithm can be used to select a relatively close reference point position as the positioning result. The structural principal block diagram of the fingerprint positioning method is shown in Fig. 1.

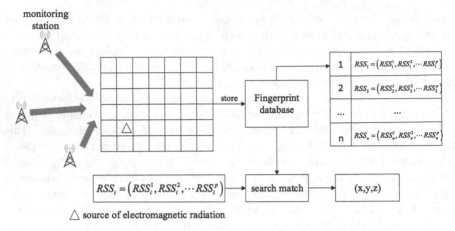

Fig. 1. Schematic diagram of fingerprint positioning model

Offline Stage

The task of the offline phase is to obtain the position coordinates of each reference point and the signal strength vector corresponding to each monitoring point AP, and save it as a fingerprint database. The first step is to select the positions of all reference points and APs in the specified model area, and use multiple APs to monitor the signal strength corresponding to each reference point and form a vector RSSI. The collected location information and RSSI corresponding to each reference point are stored to establish a signal strength fingerprint database. The signal strength vector of each fingerprint is in one-to-one correspondence with its position coordinates, and the position coordinates of the point can be found by retrieving one of the signal strength data. Therefore, as long as the close signal strength vector data is provided, the position coordinates of the closest reference point can be obtained.

Online Stage

In the process of online radiation source positioning, under the premise that the fingerprint database of the designated area has been established in the offline phase, when the electromagnetic radiation source appears in the area and the location coordinates are unknown, each pre-deployed monitoring point AP in the area is The measurement calculates the signal strength vector RSSI for this source of electromagnetic radiation. The RSSI is provided as an input to the positioning system for search and matching, and a certain algorithm can be used to find one or more fingerprint vectors that are closest to the unknown position RSSI in the established fingerprint database, and the reference point positions corresponding to these vectors are reflected the location area where the source is located. In the process of searching for matches in the database, the Euclidean distance between vectors is often compared to represent the proximity between vectors or the similarity between fingerprint data. Among them, the main search and matching methods when comparing Euclidean distance are the nearest neighbor method (NN), K-neighbor method, neural network method and so on.

2.2 Deep Learning Search Matching Model

In this paper, the idea of deep learning is introduced, and the signal strength attenuation vector of each reference point in the fingerprint database corresponding to the monitoring station is used as the training data input, and the three-dimensional position coordinates of each reference point are output. The schematic diagram is shown in Fig. 2. In the offline stage, a suitable neural network is first trained using the database information. In the online stage, the signal intensity of the radiation source measured by each monitoring station is input into the network, and the approximate three-dimensional position coordinates of the radiation source can be predicted.

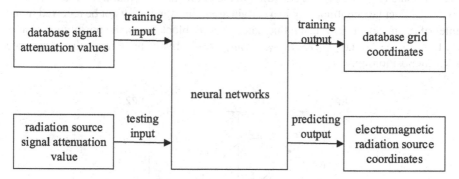

Fig. 2. Deep learning search matching diagram

Using the regression network structure can predict the approximate position of the electromagnetic radiation source instead of the coordinates of the nearby reference point, and can obtain higher accuracy by adjusting the network structure and parameters.

2.3 Optimal Deployment of Monitoring Stations

In order to solve the problem of optimal deployment of monitoring stations, this paper first proposes a deployment scheme based on Euclidean distance in signal space. The electromagnetic signal distribution in the grid area is judged by observing the signal Euclidean distance between the grid nodes. Equation (1) gives the definition of the Euclidean distance in the signal space. It is assumed that the grid node numbers are the signal strength vectors of i and j are $RSS_i = \left(RSS_i^1, RSS_i^2, \cdots RSS_i^p\right)$ and $RSS_j = \left(RSS_j^1, RSS_j^2, \cdots RSS_j^p\right)$, respectively, the Euclidean distance between the two grid nodes $d_{i,j}$ is expressed as:

$$d_{i,j} = \sqrt{\sum_{k=1}^{p} \left(RSS_i^k - RSS_j^k\right)^2} \tag{1}$$

Among them, RSS_i^k represents the signal strength value from the i-th grid node received by the k-th monitoring station, and p represents the number of monitoring stations, that is, the dimension of the signal space. Search and match the calculated p-dimensional signal strength vector with the signal strength vector of each grid node in the fingerprint database.

Next, we focus on analyzing the principle of Euclidean distance to measure the optimal deployment. Here, it is assumed that the point to be measured receives a random signal, which will fluctuate after being interfered by noise. Let the mean center of the electromagnetic signal be located at point S, σ indicating the fluctuation range of the signal, then the circular area is the possible signal for the signal. Distribution space. It can be seen from Fig. 3 that the grid node closest to the mean center is RP1, so the electromagnetic signal will be located at the RP1 point with a high probability, and the coordinate is (x_{RP1}, y_{RP1}). According to the characteristics that the electromagnetic signal will fluctuate continuously in a certain area, the signal may not be received in the center of the mean value. When it fluctuates to other block areas, the positioning results may be (x_{RP2}, y_{RP2}), (x_{RP3}, y_{RP3}), (x_{RP4}, y_{RP4}), respectively, resulting in the occurrence of wrong positioning.

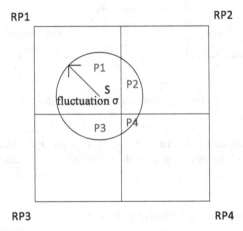

Fig. 3. Schematic diagram of grid error location

It is assumed that the radiation source to be located will be located in two grid nodes RP1 or RP2, and the electromagnetic signal obeys the Rayleigh distribution. Assuming that the mean centers of the amplitude probability density curves of the electromagnetic signals received at the two grid nodes are σ_1, σ_2, respectively, then the distance between the centers of the two curves is $\Delta r = \sigma_2 - \sigma_1$. As shown in Fig. 4, set the decision threshold to be r_0, and analyze the probability of wrong decision when the received signal r changes around the decision threshold. If the intensity of the electromagnetic signal received by the radiation source that should be positioned at RP1 satisfies the condition $r_0 > r$, the positioning result will be misjudged as RP2.

It can be seen from Fig. 4 that the area of the shaded part under the probability density distribution curve represents the probability of being wrongly judged as RP2

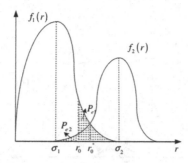

Fig. 4. Schematic diagram of the probability of wrong localization

point, denoted as P_{e1}, then P_{e1} can be expressed as:

$$P_{e1} = P(RP2|RP1) = \int_{r_0}^{\infty} f_1(r)dr = \int_{r_0}^{\infty} \frac{r}{\sigma_1^2} \exp\left(\frac{-r^2}{2\sigma_1^2}\right)dr \tag{2}$$

The same can be seen:

$$P_{e2} = P(RP1|RP2) = \int_{0}^{r_0} f_2(r)dr = \int_{0}^{r_0} \frac{r}{\sigma_2^2} \exp\left(\frac{-r^2}{2\sigma_2^2}\right)dr \tag{3}$$

If the probabilities of receiving electromagnetic signals from RP1 and RP2 points are $P(RP1)$ and $P(RP2)$, and $P(RP1) = P(RP2) = 1/2$, respectively, then the total probability of possible misjudgment is:

$$P_e = P(RP1)P_{e1} + P(RP2)P_{e2} = \frac{1}{2}(P_{e1} + P_{e2}) \tag{4}$$

According to the characteristics of the probability density distribution curve, it can be found from Fig. 4 that the probability of wrong positioning P_e is composed of two shaded parts, and the size of the total probability is the sum of the area of P_{e1} and P_{e2}. The sum is the smallest, which means that the probability of wrong positioning is the smallest when $r_0 = r^*$, so it is the best threshold. According to the characteristics of the Rayleigh distribution probability density curve, if the mean centers of the two probability density curves are respectively σ_1 and σ_2, then when the distance between the two mean centers $\sigma_2 - \sigma_1$ increases, the distance between the mean centers of the two curves also increases, such as shown in Fig. 5.

It can be seen from Fig. 5 that when $f_2(r)$ moving to $f_2'(r)$, the intersection of the two curves moves to the right as the distance from the center of the mean increases, and the total area of the shadow part also gradually decreases, which can effectively reduce the probability of wrong positioning. It can be seen that when the Euclidean distance between the mean values of grid node signals increases, the mean center distance between the two probability density function curves increases, which reduces the probability of wrong positioning and can effectively reduce the positioning error. On this theoretical basis,

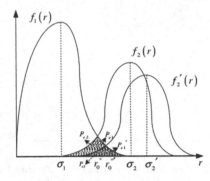

Fig. 5. Changes in the probability of mislocalization after the center of the mean is shifted

the optimal deployment of monitoring stations can be achieved by using the maximum constraint of the Euclidean distance between the reference points in the signal space.

The increase of the Euclidean distance of the signal space between grid nodes will reduce the incidence of wrong positioning. According to the definition of the Euclidean distance, it can be seen that when the dimension of the signal strength vector increases, the signal Euclidean distance will also increase. Therefore, in theory, the larger the number of monitoring stations, the larger the Euclidean distance of the electromagnetic signal space, and the smaller the probability of wrong positioning. However, considering the actual situation, when the number of monitoring stations increases, the dimension of the signal vector will increase, and at the same time, it will also generate greater interference, which will affect the positioning accuracy. Therefore, it should not be too large when setting the number of monitoring stations. The solution in this paper is to find the optimal number and position of monitoring stations, so that the maximum value of the Euclidean distance of all grid nodes in the specified area exceeds the threshold S set in advance, and the Euclidean distance The minimum number of monitoring stations whose maximum distance exceeds the threshold is determined as the optimal number. The threshold S needs to be determined comprehensively by observing the effects of multiple simulations and analyzing the degree of interference between signals. The specific objective function in this paper is expressed as formula (5):

$$
\begin{cases}
\min_{p}\left\{\max_{\alpha} f_1(p)\right\} \geq S \\
f_1(p) = \dfrac{1}{n}\sum_{i=1}^{n}\overline{d}_i \\
\overline{d}_i = \sum_{j\in N(i)} \left\|RSS_i - RSS_j\right\|_2 / length(N) \\
\alpha = \left\{(X_1, Y_1), (X_2, Y_2), \cdots, (X_p, Y_p)\right\}
\end{cases}
\tag{5}
$$

Among them, n is the total number of nodes; p is the number of monitoring stations, that is, the signal dimension; $N(i)$ represents the set of all grid nodes whose distance from the i-th grid node is less than a certain value; $length(N)$ represents the number of elements in the set N; $\overline{d}_i$ represents the p-dimensional average electromagnetic signal Euclidean distance of the i-th grid node, α is a possible deployment scheme of p monitoring stations, $(X_1, Y_1), (X_2, Y_2), \cdots, (X_p, Y_p)$ is the deployment position of p monitoring stations under the scheme, f_1 is The p-dimensional mean signal strength Euclidean distance of all grid nodes. After the threshold value S is determined, there are two variables in the objective function: the signal dimension p and the placement method α of the monitoring station. The number of monitoring stations is gradually increased, and the average value of the signal space Euclidean distance of each reference point in the placement mode of all monitoring stations under the signal dimension is calculated, and the placement mode when the Euclidean distance is the largest is selected and compared with the threshold S, until a value greater than The minimum number of monitoring stations for the threshold and the placement method when the average signal Euclidean distance is the largest under the signal dimension, the final output result is the optimal monitoring station deployment plan.

2.4 Radiation Source Location Tracking Based on Deep Learning

When an electromagnetic radiation source emits an electromagnetic signal, the monitoring station will receive the signal through frequency detection technology and obtain the signal strength. Since the signal transmission power is unknown, it is difficult to know the signal attenuation value. Therefore, it is necessary to preprocess the data before learning, and use the difference of signal attenuation corresponding to the difference of signal reception strength as the input of training data, and finally obtain its grid position through the neural network. This subject will use the signal strength difference measured by each monitoring station as the input and the difference value of the signal vector dimension of each reference point in the database to search and match.

In terms of data set collection, a $10 \times 10 \times 10$ three-dimensional grid model from coordinates $(0, 0, 0)$ to $(10, 10, 10)$ is established in the region, and the measured signal attenuation difference vector and its corresponding grid nodes are substituted into the model as training data. It will take a lot of time to recalculate the signal attenuation difference vector for the data points other than the grid nodes. Here, the interpolation method will be used to interpolate the four-dimensional data. Creates an interpolation for a set of scattered sample points, then computes the interpolation at a set of 3D query points. Interpolate the center positions of each grid, and finally obtain the position coordinates of all grid nodes and center points and the signal attenuation difference vector, complete the collection of all data sets, and send them to the neural network for training.

In the BP neural network, the original data enters the neural network from the input layer, completes the linear or nonlinear mapping combination layer by layer through each hidden layer, and finally propagates to the output layer. In the neural network of this paper, the original data is the signal intensity attenuation difference vector of each reference point corresponding to multiple monitoring stations after preprocessing, and the three-dimensional vector corresponds to the three nodes of the input layer. The final output of the output layer is three-dimensional coordinates, which are also three nodes. In the hidden layer, parameters such as the number of hidden layers, the number of neurons, and the learning rate are adjusted according to the actual simulation effect to achieve a better fitting effect. The general structure of the BP neural network is shown in Fig. 6. The input x is the n-dimensional signal strength attenuation difference vector, and the output z is the corresponding three-dimensional position coordinate. In the research model of this paper, n is 3. After adjusting the network parameters, the simulation results are analyzed and compared, and the network structure and parameters with the best performance are selected as the final application scheme.

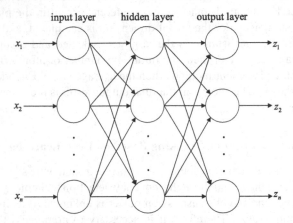

Fig. 6. BP neural network structure

3   Model Establishment

The model used in the simulation is a $10 \times 10 \times 10$ grid established in a certain area in Shandong, where the grid scale is 1 km long, and the two-dimensional top view is shown in Fig. 7. The selection of grid scale will affect the size of subsequent calculations and the accuracy of positioning. According to the empirical data of multiple measurements and calculations, and after comprehensively considering the interference from multi-dimensional signals, the threshold S is set to 17 dB, and the deployment range of monitoring stations is reduced to 6 km $\times$ 6 km in the middle of the ground grid to accelerate convergence.

To solve the problem of optimal deployment of monitoring stations, this paper uses the heuristic search algorithm genetic algorithm. Genetic algorithm is a natural process of simulating the survival of the fittest in the biological world. An initial population undergoes generations of genetic variation and other processes to become a more survivable group through continuous evolution, just like the survival law of survival of the fittest in nature. Have a greater chance of surviving to reproduce. Populations retain some of the most resilient individuals after hundreds of generations of reproduction. After adjusting the algorithm parameters, the simulation results are analyzed and compared, and the algorithm and parameters with the fastest convergence speed are selected as the final application scheme.

The flowchart of the genetic algorithm to solve the optimal deployment of monitoring stations is shown in Fig. 8, which mainly includes processes such as initialization,

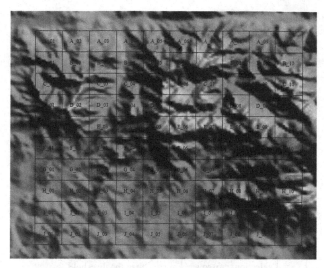

Fig. 7. 2D top view of mesh model

encoding and decoding, selection, crossover, mutation, and calculation of fitness. First initialize the system parameters and set the number of monitoring stations to increase from 0, randomly generate an initial population, perform selection, crossover, mutation and other operations on the population, record the optimal individual and its objective function value in the current population, and keep looping When the program runs beyond the set maximum number of iterations or the objective function does not change significantly within a certain genetic algebra, it is judged whether the objective function is greater than the threshold S set in advance, and if it is greater than the threshold S, the final number of monitoring stations and the maximum number of monitoring stations are output. The optimal individual is the set of optimal monitoring station deployment locations, otherwise the number of monitoring stations is increased and the iteration continues. Finally, the location information of the optimal monitoring station is output to complete the deployment of the monitoring station.

After completing the optimal deployment of multiple monitoring stations, calculate and store the attenuation values of electromagnetic radiation signals from each reference point to each monitoring station, build a fingerprint database, and update the database information regularly to grasp the electromagnetic distribution in each time period.

When testing the genetic algorithm, the population size and crossover rate are used as variable parameters, the average signal Euclidean distance of the reference point is used as the fitness function, and the operation time and genetic algebra are used as the observation data. Initialize the genetic parameters as the population size is 50, the total genetic generation is 100, the crossover probability is 0.8, the mutation probability is 0.05, the tolerance constraint is 0.001, and the maximum tolerance algebra is 50.

In the grid model designed in this paper, the three-dimensional coordinates of the area are divided into new rectangular coordinates, the xyz axes are 0–10, and the unit is km. The signal attenuation difference vector of all reference points is set as the input of the training data, and the position coordinates are set as the output of the training

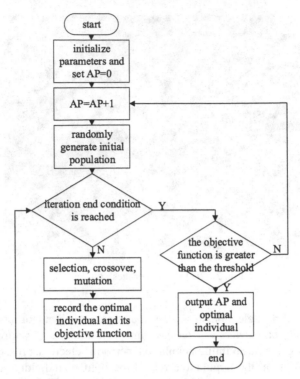

Fig. 8. Genetic algorithm for optimal deployment

data. Some fixed simulation parameters are initialized before simulation, including the maximum number of training iterations is 200, the maximum continuous performance unimproved algebra to prevent overfitting is 10, and the performance target value is 0.00001.

4   Simulation Results and Analysis

The simulation results of the optimal deployment algorithm of the monitoring station are shown in Figs. 9 and 10. When the number of APs gradually increases from 0 to 3, the Euclidean distance of the average signal of the reference point is 45.8111 (16.6 dB), and when the number of APs is 4, the Euclidean distance of the average signal of the reference point is 53.3883 (17.2 dB), which is the minimum value exceeding the threshold S. The number of APs, so the positions of 4 monitoring stations in the optimal deployment scheme are determined. Figure 11 is the rendering of the optimal deployment scheme, in which the white part is the ground location of the model, and the four points correspond to the locations of the four monitoring stations. Using these four monitoring stations to calculate the signal attenuation vectors of all grid nodes and save them to establish a signal attenuation fingerprint database.

Finally, the attenuation values of electromagnetic signals from all grid nodes to each deployed monitoring station are calculated in batches in the model area, and different

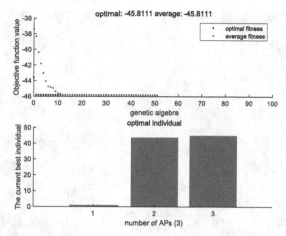

Fig. 9. Simulation results when the AP number is 3

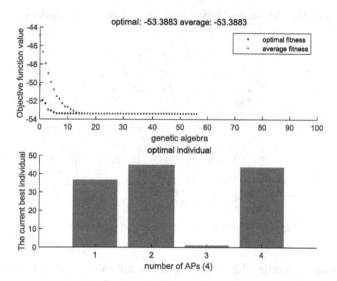

Fig. 10. Simulation results when the AP number is 4

attenuation values are calculated according to the signals of different frequency bands, and stored in the database together with the position coordinates of the grid nodes. The basic information in the fingerprint database is shown in Fig. 12, in which the first row of date and time represents the database update time, the signal frequency f is in MHz, and the databases of different frequency bands are updated at the same time. The first column is the grid number, with a total of $11 \times 11 \times 11$ grid nodes, and the real geographic coordinates corresponding to each grid node can be derived according to the corresponding node information in the model. The last four columns are the electromagnetic signal attenuation values predicted by each grid node corresponding to the four deployed monitoring stations, and the unit is dB.

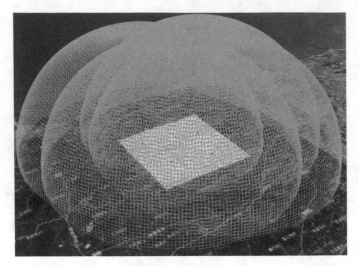

Fig. 11. Optimal deployment renderings of monitoring stations

2022.5.1 15: 18	f=460		
1	165.9547	144.105	139.5472	144.1737
2	182.6061	166.0641	169.2825	164.5952
3	146.9411	139.9544	136.2221	135.3023
4	196.9419	170.2851	171.8172	172.6864
5	154.295	122.5986	123.0992	123.1026
6	163.0968	128.0629	119.7551	129.636
7	169.7434	156.0892	154.8075	148.3867
8	154.1301	113.9898	110.1535	111.3688
9	151.0931	114.33	113.7011	105.8317
10	153.6439	124.9971	113.4526	113.8563

Fig. 12. Basic information of fingerprint database

By continuously adjusting the network structure and corresponding parameters, comparative simulation experiments were carried out on the fitting effects of different numbers of hidden layers, neurons and learning rates. The experimental results are shown in Figs. 13, 14, and 15.

Figure 13 compares the network performance when simulating different numbers of neurons, in which the number of hidden layers is controlled to 1 layer, the learning rate is controlled to 0.01, and each network structure is trained five times for comparison. From the simulation results in the figure, it can be seen that with the increase of the number of neurons in the hidden layer, the generalization error of the neural network is also gradually decreasing. The training results are better but it also means that the training time increases. The added simulation results show that the experimental results show that the network performance optimization is not obvious, the optimal generalization error is about 0.04 km, and it will take more time for data training, so the subsequent simulations will set the number of neurons to 20.

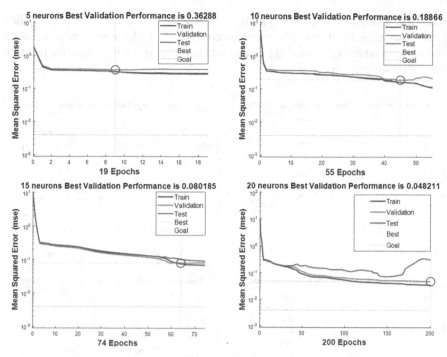

Fig. 13. Comparative simulation of different numbers of neurons

Figure 14 compares and simulates the network performance with different numbers of hidden layers, in which the number of neurons in each layer is controlled to 20, the learning rate is controlled to 0.01, and each network structure is trained five times to compare the best. From the simulation results in the figure, it can be seen that the fitting effect of three hidden layers is better, and the mean square error is about 0.02 km. When the number of hidden layers continues to increase, the training effect is unstable and the performance improvement is not obvious, and the training time will also increase, so the subsequent simulation sets the number of hidden layers to 3.

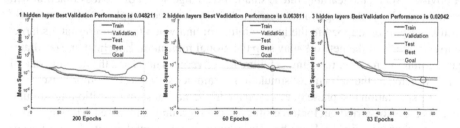

Fig. 14. Comparative simulation of different number of hidden layers

Figure 15 compares the network performance when simulating different learning rates, in which the number of neurons in each layer is controlled to 20, the number of hidden layers is controlled to 3, and each network structure is trained five times to compare the best. As an important parameter in supervised learning, the learning rate determines whether the objective function can converge to the local minimum and when it converges. In addition, a suitable learning rate can also make the objective function converge in a suitable time.

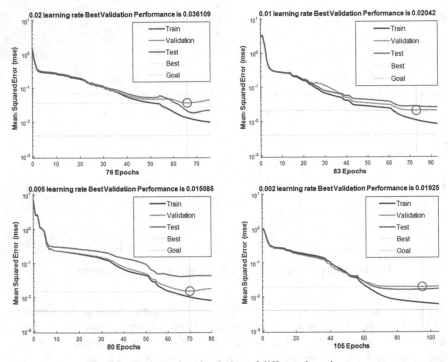

Fig. 15. Comparative simulation of different learning rates

It can be seen from the simulation results that when the learning rate is properly adjusted, the performance of the network will also change slightly, but the change is not obvious. When the learning rate is small, the change speed of the loss function will become very slow, resulting in an increase in the convergence complexity of the network, and it is easy to be trapped in the local minimum; and when the learning rate is large, the loss function of the network may skip the global minimum. Excellent and oscillates near the minimum value, resulting in failure to converge. Therefore, the learning rate of 0.01 is selected as the subsequent simulation parameter setting after compromise.

In the simulation test phase of electromagnetic radiation source positioning, simulation tests are also carried out for three situations: air, ground, and mixed. The simulation results are shown in Fig. 16. It can be seen from the experimental results that for the situation in the air, the positioning accuracy and precision are high, and the generalization error can reach the order of magnitude; while the situation involving ground positioning may result in incorrect positioning leading to low accuracy. For ground training data only The positioning accuracy of the network is lower, and the optimal generalization error can only reach about 0.05 km. The possible reason is that for the attenuation of electromagnetic signals in the air, only the loss of free space is generally considered, while the ground situation needs to consider the influence of terrain. Small changes in position may cause changes in obstacles on the path, thereby affecting the measured signal attenuation. There are large changes that lead to the appearance of wrong positioning. In addition, a large amount of data may also cause some data to overlap, resulting in insufficient data characteristics of each reference point. These are also the reasons why it is divided into ground, air, and ground-air mixed situations in advance in the testing phase.

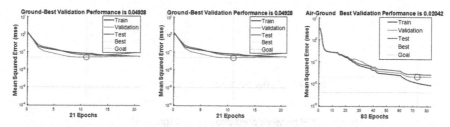

Fig. 16. Comparison of training network performance under three terrains

A large number of test points are selected for the above three situations, and the corresponding electromagnetic signal attenuation difference vector is calculated to test the accuracy and positioning accuracy of the training network. The test results for aerial positioning are shown in Fig. 17. The figure shows the actual and predicted positions of the test points in the 3D grid model. It can be seen from the figure that the data fitting effect of aerial training is better and can be accurately Locate unknown sources of electromagnetic radiation in the air. 1% of the grid model scale is used as the correct positioning standard. If the error is less than 100 m, it is regarded as correct positioning, otherwise, it is regarded as wrong positioning. Through a large number of tests, it can be concluded that the neural network trained in the air can make its positioning accuracy reach more than 95%, and the positioning accuracy is within 20 m on average.

The test results for ground positioning are shown in Fig. 18. The figure shows the actual and predicted positions of the test points in the grid model. It can be seen from the figure that the data fitting effect of ground training is worse than that of the air, and it can be compared Roughly locate unknown sources of electromagnetic radiation on the ground. Through a large number of tests, it can be concluded that the neural network trained on the ground can make its positioning accuracy reach more than 75%, and the positioning accuracy is within 80 m on average.

The test results of the ground-air hybrid positioning are shown in Fig. 19. The figure shows the actual and predicted positions of the test points in the grid model. Half of the ground and air test points are selected for simulation. The fitting effect of the training data is obviously better than that of the ground data, and the predicted position basically coincides with the actual position. Through a large number of tests, it can be seen that the neural network trained by ground-air hybrid training can achieve a positioning accuracy of more than 90%, and the average positioning accuracy is within 40 m.

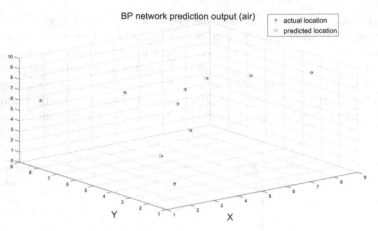

Fig. 17. Aerial positioning test results

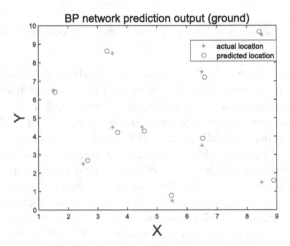

Fig. 18. Ground positioning test results

For the test of electromagnetic radiation source tracking, the above three cases are still used for simulation analysis. The specific simulation process is to first set a trajectory of the electromagnetic radiation source, sample the route at equal time intervals, measure the signal attenuation difference vector of each sampling point corresponding to each monitoring station, and input these vectors into the neural network to predict its approximate position. The multiple prediction points are smoothly connected to represent the predicted trajectory of the electromagnetic radiation source. Compared with the original set trajectory route, the observed value is the average value of the error between the actual and predicted positions of each sampling point. Figure 20 shows the results of the tracking test of the electromagnetic radiation source in the air. Set a trajectory of the electromagnetic radiation source in the air, and take ten sampling points to locate the target. The line connecting the predicted positions of the sampling points can roughly

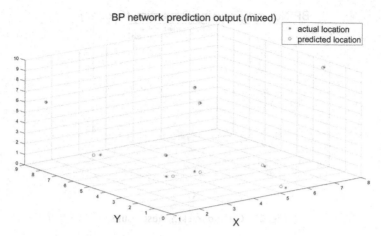

Fig. 19. Ground-air hybrid positioning test results

simulate the action route of the radiation source. The positioning accuracy of the points is within 20 m, and the average positioning error is 17.926 m.

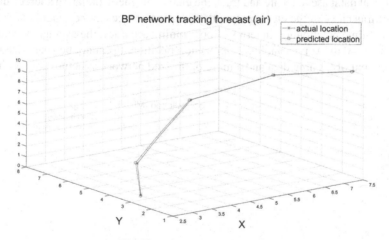

Fig. 20. Air tracking test results

Figure 21 shows the results of the ground electromagnetic radiation source tracking test. Set a movement trajectory of the electromagnetic radiation source on the ground, and take ten sampling points to locate the target. The line connecting the predicted positions of the sampling points can roughly simulate the action route of the radiation source. The positioning accuracy of the points is within 80 m, and the average positioning error is 74.513 m.

Figure 22 shows the tracking test results of the ground-air hybrid electromagnetic radiation source. Set a trajectory of the electromagnetic radiation source from the ground to the air, and take ten sampling points to locate the target. The connection between the

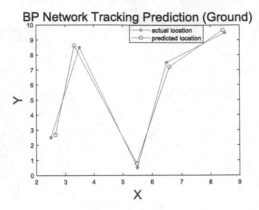

Fig. 21. Ground tracking test results

predicted positions of the sampling points can roughly simulate the radiation source. The positioning accuracy of the positioning point is within 40 m, and the average positioning error is 31.925 m. Through the simulation analysis of the above positioning and tracking, it can be seen that it is theoretically feasible to use the BP neural network trained by the fingerprint database to locate and track the electromagnetic radiation source, and the movement trajectory of the electromagnetic radiation source can be roughly simulated through real-time positioning. In terms of positioning accuracy, the average positioning error is within 40 m. At present, higher-precision positioning cannot be guaranteed, and a larger amount of training data and a more optimized network structure are required.

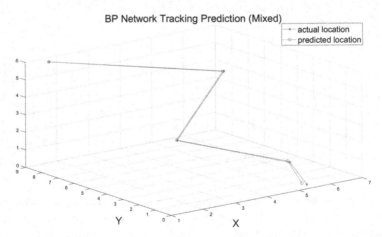

Fig. 22. Ground-air hybrid tracking results

5   Conclusion

In this paper, the objective function is designed by using the Euclidean distance in the signal space through theoretical analysis, and the optimal number and position of monitoring stations in the model area are obtained through the heuristic search algorithm, and the fingerprint database is established. In terms of positioning and tracking of radiation sources in three-dimensional battlefields, this paper draws on the method of indoor fingerprint positioning, and introduces the idea of deep learning in the search and matching stage, and finally realizes the positioning and tracking of electromagnetic radiation sources. In the simulation test stage, the feasibility and accuracy of the algorithm in this paper are verified by multiple positioning and tracking tests of electromagnetic radiation sources.

References

1. Madigan, D., Einahrawy, E., Martin, R., et al.: Bayesian indoor positioning systems. In: Proceedings IEEE 24th Annual Joint Conference of the IEEE Computer and Communications Societies. IEEE vol. 2, pp. 1217–1227 (2005)
2. Cheng, Y., Lin, Y.: A new received signal strength based location estimation scheme for wireless sensor network. IEEE Trans. Consum. Electron. **55**(3), 1295–1299 (2009)
3. Doğru, E.: Methods for minimizing error in location estimation using received signal strength. In: 2018 26th Signal Processing and Communications Applications Conference (SIU). IEEE, pp. 2–4 (2018)
4. Lee, M., Gim, J., Lee, S.: Probabilistic location determination methods using multi-level transmission signal strength technique. In: 2014 International Conference on Information and Communication Technology Convergence (ICTC). IEEE, pp. 630–631 (2014)
5. Singh, R., Macchi, L., Regazzoni, C., et al.: A statistical modelling based location determination method using fusion technique in WLAN. In: Proceedings of IEEE IWWAN, pp. 256–260 (2005)
6. Halder, S., Choi, T., Park, J., et al.: Enhanced ranging using adaptive filter of zigbee RSSI and LQI measurement. In: Proceedings of the 10th International Conference on Information Integration and Web-based Applications & Services, pp. 367–373 (2008)
7. Zhang, Z., Lee, M., Choi, S.: Deep learning-based indoor positioning system using multiple fingerprints. In: 2020 International Conference on Information and Communication Technology Convergence (ICTC). IEEE, pp. 491–493 (2020)
8. Zhou, R., Hao, M, Lu, X., et al.: Device-free localization based on CSI fingerprints and deep neural networks. In: 2018 15th Annual IEEE International Conference on Sensing, Communication, and Networking (SECON). IEEE, pp. 4–9 (2018)
9. Sthapit, P., Gang, H., Pyun, J.: Bluetooth based indoor positioning using machine learning algorithms. In: 2018 IEEE International Conference on Consumer Electronics-Asia (ICCE-Asia). IEEE, pp. 206–212 (2018)

Server Selection and Resource Allocation for Energy Minimization in Satellite Edge Computing

Weichen Zhu[1], Weichao Yang[2], and Gongliang Liu[1(✉)]

[1] Harbin Institute of Technology, Weihai 264209, Shandong, China
liugl@hit.edu.cn
[2] China Academy of Space Technology, Xi'an 710100, Shanxi, China

Abstract. In this paper we construct a double layer satellite network and let MEO satellites carry computing servers to execute computation tasks generated by LEO satellites. The main purpose is to find a task offloading scheme and resource allocation strategy to minimize the energy consumption of the dynamic network which is formulated as a mixed-integer programming problem. To solve it efficiency, we research a suboptimal resource allocation and computation offloading scheme. Specifically, the original problem is divided into three subproblems. The first subproblem is a convex problem which is easy to solve it. Then for the next subproblem, we propose a terminal satellites and edge satellites matching strategy (TEMS). For the last one, random adjustment execution algorithm is applied. Finally, the simulation results have be given to verify the effectiveness of proposed algorithm.

Keywords: Resource allocation · edge computing · dynamic satellite networks · computation offloading

1 Introduction

Satellite communication has been paid much attention due to wide coverage, wide frequency band, freedom from geographical conditions and strong survivability [1–3]. It is an important part of the future 6G communication. Nowadays, in order to achieve global seamless coverage, high-capacity, low delay communication and network services, many researches are devoted to building satellite edge networks by taking advantage of the advantages of edge computing itself in improving the integrity of the network by arranging servers with computing and storage functions near network terminals. The purpose of reducing communication delay is to provide computing services for other satellites by networking

This work was supported partially by National Natural Science Foundation of China (Grant Nos. 61971156, 61801144), Shandong Provincial Natural Science Foundation, China (Grant Nos. ZR2019QF003, ZR2019MF035, ZR2020MF141), the Fundamental Research Funds for the Central Universities, China (Grant No. HIT.NSRIF.2019081).

© ICST Institute for Computer Sciences, Social Informatics and Telecommunications Engineering 2023
Published by Springer Nature Switzerland AG 2023. All Rights Reserved
A. Li et al. (Eds.): 6GN 2022, LNICST 505, pp. 142–154, 2023.
https://doi.org/10.1007/978-3-031-36014-5_12

some satellites containing computing and storage resources. However, this has led to an increase in the energy consumption of the entire satellite network and an increase in the difficulty of satellite network re-source allocation.

Recently, there has been several works considering resource optimization problem in the satellite network. In [4], the authors propose a satellite edge computing network combined with the NFV technology and implement a decentralized resource allocation algorithm based on a potential game (PGRA) to maximize the overall network payoff. In [5], the authors utilize the deep reinforcement learning based method to learn the optimal offloading decision for satellite assisted vehicle-to-vehicle (V2V) communication networks. Similarly, in [6], the authors demonstrate a method based on deep Q-learning to allocate resource for satellite-terrestrial networks. In addition, the authors in [7] consider a double auction mechanism for resource allocation in satellite mobile edge computing (MEC).

However, above solutions are based on the relative stationarity of satellite, without considering the dynamics of satellite network. At present, a few work has been devoted to the research of collaborative computation offloading based on scenarios of dynamic satellite edge computing networks. In [8] the authors consider a space-aerial-assisted mixed cloud-edge computing framework, and demonstrate an alternating optimization algorithm with guaranteed convergence, to solve the formulated problem. The authors in [9] proposed a game-theoretic approach to the optimization of computation offloading strategy in satellite edge computing.

Motivated by the existing work above, this article investigates the computing resource allocation and computation offloading in satellite edge computing to reduce network energy consumption. The contributions of this article are summarized as follows:

- The computing resource allocation and computation offloading problems considering the dynamics of satellite network were formulated as a mixed-integer programming problem.
- To decrease the computation complexity, the original problem is divided into three subproblems, and an effective algorithm was proposed to solve it.
- The simulation results have been provided for showing the validity of the proposed algorithm.

The remainder of this article is organized as follows. Section 2 introduces the system model and problem formulation. Section 3 provided the main solution method of energy minimization problem which can be decoupled into three subproblems In Sect. 4, we analyze the simulation results with different parameters. Finally, a conclusion was given in Sect. 5.

2   System Model and Problem Formulation

2.1   System Model

As depicted in Fig. 1, this paper takes into account a computation offloading scenario for low earth orbit (LEO) satellite networks with N terminal satellites and

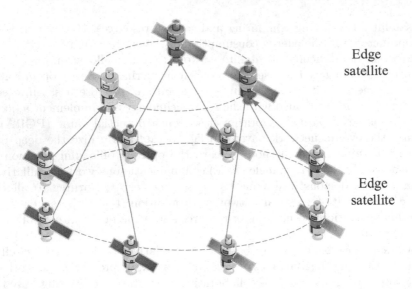

Fig. 1. The satellite network model.

M edge satellites. Suppose that the edge satellites and LEO satellites both carry computing servers, but the edge satellites possess far more computing capacities than LEO satellites. At first, the terminal satellites such as military satellites, military meteorological satellites and so on, generate some computing tasks with specific delay requirements. However, in order to avoid task incompletion due to limitations on terminal satellite computing resources, the terminal satellites have to divide the task into two parts, one executed locally, the other offloaded to the edge satellites within its visible range. Compared to traditional ground edge computing network, the method that usually selects the nearest edge node as the offloading node, may not be applicable to satellite networks owing to the time varying net-work topology and large number of unexpected tasks in a short period of time. Consequently, this paper proposes a bidirectional selection algorithm based on time-slot variation to solve the offloading problem. Topological relationships between satellites are time-varying. To solve it, this paper divides the duration of the satellite networks into multiple time slots represented by $\mathcal{T} = \{1, 2, \ldots, T\}$ during which the satellite networks can be seemed as static, and the length of each slot is τ. We supposed that the task can be successfully offloaded and processed in one time slot in which it is scheduled to be executed.

2.2 Problem Formulation

For the terminal satellite n, it has local computing capability of $z_{n,j}$ and transmission power $p_{n,trans}$. This paper give a feature $\langle X_n, T_n^{max} \rangle$ to represent the task generated by the terminal satellite n in which X_n represents the amount of the task and T_n^{max} represent maximum delay to complete the task. As mentioned before, we divide the task into two parts and apply $x_{n,l}$ and $x_{n,e}$ representing the part executed locally and the other part offloaded to the edge satellite respectively. Thus, the relationship between total computing task and two parts can be expressed as follows.

$$x_{n,l} + x_{n,e} = X_n \tag{1}$$

Inter-satellite communication is generally carried out through inter-satellite links (ISL). Thus, the terminal satellites can apply ISL to offload part of its task to edge satellites. The transmission rate in slot t can be calculated as

$$C_{n,m}^t = B \log(1 + \frac{p_{n,trans} G_{r,m} G_{tr,n} L_{n,m}^t}{\kappa T B}) \tag{2}$$

where B is the channel bandwidth, $G_{r,m}$ and $G_{tr,n}$ are respectively the acceptance gain of antenna of edge satellite m and transmission antenna gain of terminal satellite n, κ represents the Boltzmann constant. T refers to the noise temperature. $L_{n,m}^t$ is the pathloss of the ISL between edge satellite m and terminal satellite n in time slot t and expressed as

$$L_{i,j}^t = \left(\frac{c}{4\pi f d_{n,m}^t}\right)^2 \tag{3}$$

where constant c refers to the light speed, f is the carrier frequency, $d_{n,m}^t$ is the distance between edge satellite m and terminal satellite n in time slot t.

In addition, due to different types of tasks with different delay requirements, if all the tasks are arranged to be executed in one time slot, it may lead to the overload of edge servers. For convenience we use $\mathcal{A} = \{a_n^t \mid n \in N, t \in \mathcal{T}\}$ to donate the decision variables on task execution, where $a_n^t = 1$ if terminal satellite n executes its task in time slot t, and $a_n^t = 0$ otherwise.

We can calculate the transmission delay denoted by $T_{n,m,tr}^t$ for the computation task that terminal satellite n offloads to edge satellite m in time slot t based on the communication model analyzed above. The transmission delay can be calculated as follows.

$$T_{n,m,tr}^t = \frac{x_{n,e}^t}{C_{n,m}^t} \tag{4}$$

where $x_{n,e}^t = a_n^t x_{n,e}$. Similarly $x_{n,l}^t = a_n^t x_{n,l}$. Then the energy consumed by transmission is proposed by:

$$E_{n,m,tr}^t = P_{n,l} T_{n,m,tr}^t = P_{n,l} \frac{x_{n,e}^t}{C_{n,m}^t} \tag{5}$$

It is obvious that the communication delay and energy consumption depend on the offloaded task size which is related to the local executed task size.

The computing delay and energy consumption of local task can be given respectively as follow.

$$T_{n,l}^t = \frac{x_{n,l}^t}{Z_l} \tag{6}$$

$$E_{n,l}^t = x_{n,l}^t \xi \kappa Z_l^2 \tag{7}$$

where ξ is the number of cycles required per bit, κ is the constant coefficient depending on chip architecture.

On the other hand, the edge satellites will execute the received tasks and then re-turn the results to the terminal satellites. Since the size of the results is much smaller than the original task, we generally ignore it. Then the computing resources allocated to the task from terminal satellite n by the edge satellite m in time slot t is donated by $z_{n,m}^t$. Furthermore, the computing delay and energy consumption can be given respectively as follow.

$$T_{n,m,com}^t = \frac{x_{n,e}^t}{z_{n,m}^t} \tag{8}$$

$$E_{n,m,com} = x_{n,e}^t \xi \kappa (z_{n,m}^t)^2 \tag{9}$$

Moreover, the total delay of the terminal satellite n's task offloaded to the edge satellite m in time slot t is donated by $T_{n,m}^t$, and can be obtained as

$$T_{n,m}^t = T_{n,m,tr}^t + T_{n,m,com}^t \tag{10}$$

Besides, the computing capacity of edge satellites is far more than the terminal satellites', but it is also considered to be limited. Hence, the sum of computation allocated to complete the offloaded tasks in time slot t cannot exceed the computing capacity.

$$\sum_{n=1} z_{n,m}^t \leq Z_m \tag{11}$$

$B = \{b_{n,m}^t | n \in N, m \in M, t \in T\}$ denotes the decision variables on task offloading, where $b_{n,m,t} = 1$ if terminal satellite n offloads its task to edge satellite m in time slot t, and $b_{n,m,t} = 0$ otherwise. Each terminal satellite can only choose one edge satellite to offload if it decides to execute in time slot t, which can be expressed as follow:

$$\sum_{m=1}^M b_{n,m,t} = a_n^t \tag{12}$$

Based on the above, we can calculate the delay of subtask offloaded to the edge server. On the other hand, the terminal satellites execute local task and transmit the other part at the same time. Therefore, the execution delay of computation task X_n equals to the maximal delays of the two parts. As mentioned earlier, we need to en-sure that the task can be successfully offloaded and processed in one time slot which can be expressed as

$$\max_{m,l}(T_{n,l}^t, b_{n,m,t}(T_{n,m,tr}^t + T_{n,m,com}^t)) \leq \tau \tag{13}$$

It is noticed that the total delay of the computation task X_n is also related to the execution time slot, namely the decision variables a_n^t. Meanwhile the total de-lay needs to meet the delay requirement T_n^{max}:

$$\max_{m,l}(T_{n,l}^t, b_{n,m,t}(T_{n,m,tr}^t + T_{n,m,com}^t)) + a_n^t(t-1)\tau \leq T_n^{max} \tag{14}$$

Now, it's time to analyze the total energy consumption of each computation task X_n. For simplicity, we donate $x_n^t = a_n^t x_n$ as the date size of computation task x_n in time slot t, we can find $x_n^t = x_{n,e}^t + x_{n,l}^t$. The energy consumption of x_n^t can be given by

$$E_n^t = E_{n,l}^t + \sum_m b_{n,m,t}(E_{n,m,tr}^t + E_{n,m,com}^t) \tag{15}$$

And the total energy consumption of each computation task X_n can be calculated as $\sum_t E_n^t$. In this paper, we aim to minimize the energy consumption of all computation tasks while satisfying the maximum available computation resource and tolerable delay constrains. Then the final optimization problem can be written as

$$\mathcal{P} : min \ \sum_t \sum_n E_n^t$$

$$s.t. \ x_{n,l}^t + x_{n,e}^t = a_n^t x_n$$

$$\sum_n z_{n,m}^t = Z_m$$

$$\max_{m,l}(T_{n,l}^t, b_{n,m,t}(T_{n,m,tr}^t + T_{n,m,com}^t)) \leq \tau$$

$$\max_{m,l}(T_{n,l}^t, b_{n,m,t}(T_{n,m,tr}^t + T_{n,m,com}^t)) + a_n^t(t-1)\tau \leq T_n^{max} \tag{16}$$

$$\sum_{t=1}^T a_n^t = 1$$

$$\sum_{m=1}^M b_{n,m,t} = a_n^t$$

$$a_n^t \in \{0,1\}, b_{n,m,t} \in \{0,1\}, z_{n,m}^t \geq 0, x_{n,l}^t \geq 0, x_{n,e}^t \geq 0$$

The a_n^t and $b_{n,m,t}$ are 0–1 variables and $x_{n,l}^t, x_{n,e}^t$ are continuous variables. All of them are coupled. Thus the optimization problem $\mathcal{P}$ is a mixed-integer programming problem which is difficult to solve directly. In order to reduce the complexity of the problem, we provide an effective algorithm by decompose problem $\mathcal{P}$ into three subproblems in the next section.

3 Optimal Computation Offloading and Resource Allocation

In this section, we mainly elaborate the algorithms to solve subproblems decomposed from $\mathcal{P}$ respectively.

3.1 Optimal Task Offloading and Computing Resource Allocation Scheme

For terminal satellite n, when the slot of the task execution and the unloading edge satellite m are determined, i.e., $a_n^t = 1, b_{n,m,t} = 1$, problem $\mathcal{P}$ turns into a task offloading and computing resource allocation problem. We can adjust the computing resources allocated to satellite n $\mathbf{x_{n,l}^t}, \mathbf{x_{n,e}^t}$ and the amount of tasks unloaded to satellite m $\mathbf{z_{n,m}^t}$ to minimize the energy consumption while meeting the delay requirements, which can be written as:

$$\mathcal{P}1 : \min_{\mathbf{z,x}} \; x_{n,l}^t \xi \kappa Z_l^2 + P_{n,m}^t \frac{x_{n,e}^t}{C_{n,m,tr}^t} + x_{n,e}^t \xi \kappa (z_{n,m}^t)^2$$

$$s.t. \; x_{n,l}^t + x_{n,e}^t = x_n^t \tag{17}$$

$$\max_{m,l}(\frac{x_{n,l}^t}{Z_l}, b_{n,m,t} x_{n,e}^t (\frac{1}{C_{n,m,tr}^t} + \frac{1}{z_{n,m}^t})) \leq \min(\tau, T_{n,max}^t)$$

where $T_{n,max}^t = T_{n,max} - a_n^t(t-1)\tau$ donates the maximum tolerable delay in time slot t. Obviously, the problem $\mathcal{P}1$ is a convex optimization problem. It's easy to get the optimal solution $x_{n,l}^{t*}, x_{n,e}^{t*}, z_{n,m}^{t*}$

3.2 Terminal Satellites and Edge Satellites Matching Strategy

For problem $\mathcal{P}$ with fixed $\{x_{n,l}^{t*}, x_{n,e}^{t*}, z_{n,m}^{t*}, a_n^t\}$ the terminal satellites and edge satellites matching problem can be written as:

$$\mathcal{P}2 : \min_{b_{m,n,t}} \; \sum_t \sum_n a_n^t (x_{n,l}^t \xi \kappa Z_l^2 + \sum_m b_{m,n,t}(P_{n,m}^t \frac{x_{n,e}^t}{C_{n,m,tr}^t} + x_{n,e}^t \xi \kappa (z_{n,m}^t)^2))$$

$$s.t. \; \sum_n z_{n,m}^t \leq Z_m \tag{18}$$

$$\sum_{m=1}^M b_{n,m,t} \leq a_n^t$$

As problem $\mathcal{P}1$ described, terminal satellites can generate corresponding unloading strategies and computing resource requirements according to the task size, unloading edge satellite and offloading time slot. Thus, when a task exists and offloading time slot is determined, the terminal satellite can send the unloading strategies $x_{n,l}^{t*}, x_{n,e}^{t*}$ and computing resource requirements $z_{n,m}^{t*}$ to all the edge satellites within the visible range. The edge satellites and terminal satellites can generate matching lists donated by $\mathcal{ML}_{terminal,n}^t(m)$ and $\mathcal{ML}_{edge,m}^t(n)$ respectively, which is designed by the unloading strategies and computing re-source requirements.

Previously mentioned, the energy consumption can be calculated by $x_{n,l}^{t*} \xi \kappa Z_l^2 + P_{n,m}^t \frac{x_{n,e}^{t*}}{C_{n,m,tr}^t} + x_{n,e}^{t*} \xi \kappa (z_{n,m}^{t*})^2$. The energy consumption can be divided into two parts, one expended by terminal satellites and the other expended by edge satellites which calculated by $E_{n,m,l}^{t*} = x_{n,l}^{t*}\xi\kappa Z_l^2 + P_{n,m}^t \frac{x_{n,e}^{t*}}{C_{n,m,tr}^t}$, $E_{n,m,e}^{t*} = x_{n,e}^{t*}\xi\kappa(z_{n,m}^{t*})^2$ respectively. Each terminal satellite ranks all edge satellites within its visible range by $E_{n,m,l}^{t*}$, which is the smaller, the higher ranking. Similarly, each edge satellite ranks all terminal satellites by $E_{n,m,e}^{t*}$. No matter terminal satellites and edge satellites will preference the top ranked in the list.

The terminal satellites and edge satellites matching strategy is described in Algorithm 1. At first, initial the $\mathcal{ML}_{terminal,n}^t(m)$, $\mathcal{ML}_{edge,m}^t(n)$ and $\mathcal{N}_{unmatched}^t$ which donates the unmatched terminal satellites within the tasks that must be executed in time slot t by the given $\{x_{n,l}^{t*}, x_{n,e}^{t*}, z_{n,m}^{t*}, a_n^t\}$. Then terminal satellite n with task chooses the first edge satellite in the list $\mathcal{ML}_{terminal,n}^t(m)$ and remove the selected edge satellite from the list. Next in importance, we set $b_{m,n,t} = 1$. After all the terminal satellites select the edge satellites, the edge satellites will decide whether accept the task offloading. If the sum of all tasks offloaded to edge satellite m does not exceed the computing resource, the edge satellite m will process all the tasks offloaded to it and we will remove the terminal satellites whose tasks have be offloaded from the $\mathcal{ML}_{terminal,n}^t(m)$. If the sum of all tasks offloaded to edge satellite m exceeds the computing re-source, edge satellite m will reject the terminal satellites at the lower ranking in the list $\mathcal{ML}_{edge,m}^t(n)$ until up to its computing capacity and set $b_{m,n,t} = 0$ where n is the rejected terminal satellite. Repeat the above steps until $\mathcal{N}_{unmatched}^t = \emptyset$.

Algorithm 1. Terminal satellites and edge satellites matching strategy

---

1: Initialize the edge satellites and terminal satellites matching lists $\mathcal{ML}_{terminal,n}^t(m)$
   and $\mathcal{ML}_{edge,m}^t(n)$ and let $\mathcal{ML}_{terminal,n}^t(m) =\mid a_n^t = 1 \mid$.
2: Set the edge satellite as the destination.
3: **while** $\mathcal{N}_{unmatched}^t = \emptyset$ **do**
4:    **for** $n \in \mathcal{N}_{unmatched}^t$ **do**
5:       Chooses the first edge satellite in the list $\mathcal{ML}_{terminal,n}^t(m)$.
6:       Remove the selected edge satellite from the list.
7:       Set $b_{m,n,t} = 1$.
8:    **end for**
9:    **for** $m \in M$ **do**
10:      **if** $\sum_n b_{m,n,t} z_{n,m}^t \leq Z_m$ **then**
11:         Edge satellite m selects all terminal satellites
12:         Moves all received terminal satellites out of $\mathcal{N}_{unmatched}^t$
13:      **else**
14:         Move the terminal satellites that meet the calculation resource allocation
            in the table out of $\mathcal{N}_{unmatched}^t$;
15:         Reject the remaining terminal satellites and set $b_{m,n,t} = 0$
16:      **end if**
17:   **end for**
18: **end while**

3.3   Task Execution Slot Decision

Bringing the terminal satellites and edge satellites matching strategy into the problem $\mathcal{P}$, the optimization problem can be rewritten as

$$\mathcal{P}3 : \min \sum_t \sum_n a_n^t (x_{n,l}^t \xi \kappa Z_l^2 + P_{n,m}^t \frac{x_{n,e}^t}{C_{n,m,tr}^t} + x_{n,e}^t \xi \kappa (z_{n,m}^t)^2)$$

$$s.t. \ a_n^t \in \{0,1\} \tag{19}$$

$$\sum_{t=1}^T a_n^t = 1$$

Observing that adjusting the task executing time slot of a terminal satellite may lead to the whole terminal satellites and edge satellites matching strategy(TEMS) change. Thus, the problem is a NP-hard problem which is difficult to find optimal solution. Hence, we propose Random adjustment execution Algorithm to obtain suboptimal execution slot decision. We donate $\mathcal{N}_t$ as the set of terminal satellites executing tasks in time slot t.

$Definition1$: $E(a)$ is the energy consumption under the execution decision **a**, whose TEMS is given by the above strategy.

Random adjustment execution Algorithm(RAEA) is shown as Algorithm 2.: Firstly, find an initial feasible solution $a_{initial}$. We randomly rank $\mathcal{N}_t$ in each time slot and obtain new ordered permutation set $\mathcal{N}_t^*$ through $a_{initial}$. According to the order of $\mathcal{N}_t^*$, adjust the executing time slot of the terminal satellite through calculating the energy consumption while execution time of the terminal satellite changed and get a new execution slot decision a^*. If $E(a^* \leq E(a))$, we update the $\mathcal{N}_t^*$ and a. Carry out the adjustment in each time slot set. Repeat above steps until the $E(a)$ unchanged.

Algorithm 2. Task Execution Slot Decision

1: Initialize an initial feasible solution $a_{initial}$ and the set of terminal satellites executing tasks in time slot t: $\mathcal{N}_t$.
2: randomly rank $\mathcal{N}_t$ in each time slot and obtain new ordered permutation set $\mathcal{N}_t^*$ according to $a_{initial}$
3: **while** $\mid E(a) - E(a^*) \mid \leq \varepsilon$ **do**
4:    **for** $t \in \mathcal{T}$ **do**
5:        **for** $n \in \mathcal{N}_{unmatched}^t$ **do**
6:            Adjust the executing time slot of the terminal satellite n a_n^t according to the T_n^{max} and get a new execution slot decision a^*.
7:            **if** $E(a^* \leq E(a))$ **then**
8:                $a = a^*$.
9:            **end if**
10:        **end for**
11:    **end for**
12: **end while**

3.4 Solution Reconstruction Method

Although the relaxed solution is close to the optimal solution of problem (15), the relaxed solution may be not feasible. To find an optimized feasible solution, an efficient reconstruction method needs to be investigated. It can be seen that the optimal solution a of problem $\mathcal{P}2$ is always feasible. Hence, we only need to make sure the optimal solution x feasible by keeping the optimal solution a fixed. Specifically, for the given optimal solution a, update the link capacity as $\tau a_{t,i,j} C_{t,i,j}$. Then, solve the min-cost max-flow problem again and obtain the new optimal solution x^*. The whole detailed solution process can be referred to Algorithm 1.

4 Simulation Results

This section provides the simulation results to evaluate the effectiveness of the proposed algorithms. For obtaining the inter satellite link status, we use Satellite Tool Kit(STK) to create a Walker constellation with the type "Delta" of 30 satellites which includes 5 satellite planes and 6 satellites per plane as the terminal satellites network. We set the Orbit altitude to 1000 km, the inclination to 45°, the right ascension of ascending node to 0 and the true anomaly to 120°. The edge satellite network is also a Walker constellation with the type "Delta". Different from terminal satellite network, the Orbit altitude is 3500km and true anomaly is 0°. The other simulation parameters are set as follows: the carrier frequency $f = 12\,\text{Ghz}$, the transmission antenna gain $G_{tr} = 27\,\text{dBi}$, the receiving antenna gain $G_{re} = 24\,\text{dBi}$, the noise temperature $T = 350\,\text{K}$, the bandwidth $B = 30\,\text{MHz}$, the computational intensity $\xi = 1000 cycle/bit$ and the computational coefficient $\kappa = 3 * 10^{-24} J/(cycle \cdot bit^2)$. To verify the effectiveness of the computing offloading based on Terminal satellites and edge satellites matching strategy with optimized resource allocation (COTEMS-ORA), we also propose the following benchmark method.

Closest edge satellites and equal computational resource allocation method (CES-ECRA): The terminal satellites select the closest edge satellite to offload their tasks. After receiving all the tasks, the edge satellites will determine the amount of computation resource used to be allocated equally according to the delay requirement and task size.

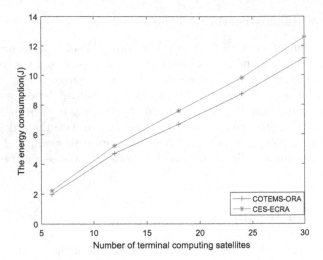

Fig. 2. The energy consumption versus the number of terminal computing satellites.

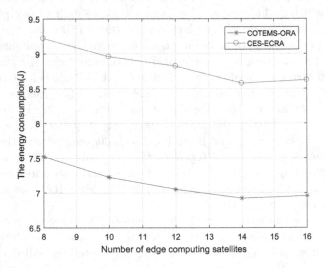

Fig. 3. The energy consumption versus the number of edge computing satellites.

In Fig. 2, we plot the relationship between the total energy consumption and the number of the edge satellites. It can be seen that the proposed algorithm can achieve low-er total cost than the CES-ECRA and the total energy consumption reduces as the number of the edge satellites increasing. As we can see, the trend of both curves tends to be flat when the edge satellite number is larger than 15 which means that the computation resource is sufficient. The result is consistent with our expectation. Hence the optimal computation offloading and resource allocation is necessary for improving energy efficiency.

The total energy consumption versus total number of the terminal satellites with tasks to be executed is presented in Fig. 3. It is observed that the total energy consumption of the network increases with the data size for both algorithms since more data needs to be computed and more computational power and transmission power is used to satisfy the latency constraints. Moreover, it is found that the proposed algorithm always outperforms the CES-ECRA, especially for large terminal satellites number.

In Fig. 4 we illustrate the total energy consumption versus the transmission power of the terminal satellites. From this figure, we find that the total energy consumption of both algorithms first decreases and then increase because the transmission power is low at first, which causes the excessive transmission delay and a large amount of computing resources to be required to meet the time delay requirements. With the increase of transmission power, the demand for computing resources will reduce which lead to the total energy consumption decrease. But when the transmission power increases to a certain extent, transmission energy consumption will become the main influencing factor and the total energy consumption will increase. Moreover, when transmission power is less than 12 W, there is even no feasible allocation strategy of the CES-ECRA to ensure that the tasks is successfully implemented at the required time. It is also shown that, compared with the CES-ECRA, the proposed algorithm can significantly reduce the total energy consumption. Hence, the optimal computation offloading and resource allocation is crucial to make full use of the resource.

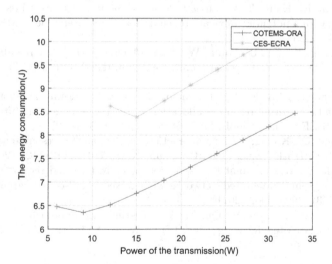

Fig. 4. The energy consumption versus the transmission power.

5   Conclusions

In this paper, we have presented the total energy consumption minimization problem for a MEC satellite network. The proposed problem is modeled as a mixed-integer programming problem about task allocation, computing resource allocation and execution time decision. We provide an effective algorithm to solve three subproblems decomposed from original question. For task offloading and computing re-source allocation problem, it is a convex problem. For selection problem of unloading edge satellites, we utilize matching algorithm to get best uninstall policy. For task execution timeslot problem, random adjustment execution Algorithm was applied to obtain suboptimal execution slot decision. Simulation results indicate the energy consumption was obviously reduced by using the proposed method.

References

1. Zhou, D., Sheng, M., Liu, R., Wang, Y., Li, J.: Channel-aware mission scheduling in broadband data relay satellite networks. IEEE J. Sel. Areas Commun. **36**(5), 1052–1064 (2018)
2. Leyva-Mayorga, I., Soret, B., Popovski, P.: Inter-plane inter-satellite connectivity in dense LEO constellations. IEEE Trans. Wirel. Commun. **20**(6), 3430–3443 (2021)
3. Zhang, S., Cui, G., Wang, W.: Joint data downloading and resource management for small satellite cluster networks. IEEE Trans. Veh. Technol. **71**(1), 887–901 (2022)
4. Gao, X., Liu, R., Kaushik, A.: Virtual network function placement in satellite edge computing with a potential game approach. IEEE Trans. Netw. Serv. Manag. **19**(2), 1243–1259 (2022)
5. Cui, G., Long, Y., Xu, L., Wang, W.: Joint offloading and resource allocation for satellite assisted vehicle-to-vehicle communication. IEEE Syst. J. **15**(3), 3958–3969 (2021)
6. Qiu, C., Yao, H., Yu, F., Xu, F., Zhao, C.: Deep Q-learning aided networking, caching, and computing resources allocation in software-defined satellite-terrestrial networks. IEEE Trans. Veh. Technol. **68**(8), 5871–5883 (2019)
7. Li, Z., Jiang, C., Kuang, L.: Double auction mechanism for resource allocation in satellite MEC. IEEE Trans. Cogn. Commun. Netw. **7**(4), 1112–1125 (2021)
8. Mao, S., He, S., Wu, J.: Joint UAV position optimization and resource scheduling in space-air-ground integrated networks with mixed cloud-edge computing. IEEE Syst. J. **15**(3), 3992–4002 (2021)
9. Wang, Y., Yang, J., Guo, X., Qu, Z.: A game-theoretic approach to computation offloading in satellite edge computing. IEEE Access. **8**, 12510–12520 (2020)

Comprehensive Interference Analysis for ZC-NOMA

Mingyi Wang[1] , Yifan Ping[2], and Gongliang Liu[1(✉)]

[1] Harbin Institute of Technology, Weihai, Shandong 264209, China
liugl@hit.edu.cn
[2] China Academy of Space Technology (Xi'an), Xi'an, Shanxi 710100, China

Abstract. In order to realize the integration of communication and navigation on LEO, a new waveform named ZC-NOMA was proposed in the previous study, which was proved to achieve reliable navigation function without significantly affecting the communication performance. In this paper, factors affecting the performance of ZC-NOMA signals, including inter-satellite asynchronous access interference and interference between communication and navigation components, are comprehensively discussed. In addition, the whole process of communication signal processing is also clearly demonstrated in the form of simulation. The analysis results show that through reasonable parameter configuration, the interference level can be effectively controlled and the integration of communication and navigation functions can be realized.

Keywords: ZC-NOMA · satellite communication · LEO navigation · ICAN

1 Introduction

With the rise of an emerging mass user base represented by autonomous driving, positioning, navigation and timing (PNT) requirements now exceed what GNSS can provide today. Specifically, they seek to improve resiliency, accuracy, and security. Perhaps the most demanding are the requirements for self-driving systems (such as SAE Level 4 self-driving cars), with some proposals calling for 30cm horizontal position protection, 99.99999% reliability, or one failure in a billion miles of driving. Reliable decimeter positioning unlocks a new generation of applications that enable humans and machines to interoperate in a shared physical space [3].

This kind of high-precision location and time-based services have higher expectations for real-time high precision, high integrity, high availability, and high security performance of PNT services, which makes it difficult to meet

This work was supported partially by National Natural Science Foundation of China (Grant Nos. 61971156, 61801144), Shandong Provincial Natural Science Foundation, China (Grant Nos. ZR2019QF003, ZR2019MF035, ZR2020MF141), the Fundamental Research Funds for the Central Universities, China (Grant No. HIT.NSRIF.2019081).

A. Li et al. (Eds.): 6GN 2022, LNICST 505, pp. 155–165, 2023.
https://doi.org/10.1007/978-3-031-36014-5_13

the limitations of the traditional "ground-based monitoring with information enhancement" enhancement system [2]. Therefore, whether from the perspective of commercial development or the standardization process, high-precision positioning will have a position that cannot be ignored.

From the communication perspective, providing ubiquitous connectivity and high data rate communication services is one of the main goals of communication networks. To accomplish this goal, satellite communication have gained widespread attention in the B5G era. AlHouraniAkram.2021.

In addition, satellite networks will also provide support for M2M/IoT in 5G networks as well as on high-speed mobile carriers. Passengers provide services to ensure omnipresent network services, and also provide multicast or broadcast information transmission for network edge network elements and user terminals. LEO satellite systems are distributed at altitudes ranging from a few hundred kilometers (from the Earth's surface) to several thousand kilometers. Due to the closeness of the LEO orbit to the Earth, the LEO constellation is characterized by lower propagation delays and generally higher landing power relative to the MEO and GEO constellations, LEO-based satellite networks stand out as a promising solution. As a result, many companies have announced ambitious plans [4, 7], by deploying LEO satellite mega-constellations to provide broadband Internet access on a global scale, these built constellations are mainly used for communication functions, considering their widespread deployment, while providing traditional communication services, the popularity of high-precision location and time-based services opens up new opportunities for low-orbit satellite networks, making the sheer number of LEO satellites offer predictable new possibilities for low-orbit satellite navigation. Higher signal strength and lower propagation delay have led to expectations for seamless high-precision positioning using LEO satellite communication networks. This makes the precise point positioning technology (Precise Point Positioning, PPP) based on ultra-dense LEO have a faster convergence speed. If the LEO constellation capable of sending navigation signals is applied to the current GNSS, it will be a major improvement for the current PPP technology. However, most communication and positioning systems are currently designed separately. Using LEO satellites to carry dedicated navigation payloads and broadcast dedicated navigation signals will inevitably lead to insufficient utilization of radio resources and reduced network performance. To circumvent this problem, Integrated Communication and Navigation (ICAN) was proposed, which specifically refers to the use of the co-design and optimization of communication and navigation components in terms of signal form, transmitter and receiver, etc., to share network infrastructure and radio in an optimal way resources to fully utilize the advantages of next-generation wireless networks.

The ICAN model based on the LEO satellite network shows some innate advantages that traditional GNSS cannot match, which can be summarized as:

- ICAN signal has high landing power and strong anti-interference ability.
- Larger number of satellites observed at the same time, with better geometric accuracy: considering GDOP, the geometry of LEO constellation is at least three times better than current GPS [6].

- Low-orbit satellites have high dynamics and speed up the convergence of precision positioning.

Especially in the context of ultra-dense LEO satellite networks, the ICAN paradigm shows some of the following clear benefits. From the perspective of navigation, adding communication signals can not only enhance the communication capability of the navigation system, but also improve the positioning speed by allowing the communication signals to carry navigation information at a higher transmission rate. From the communication point of view, the navigation signal can assist the synchronization of the communication signal, and can simplify the detection and demodulation of the communication signal. Therefore, such a signal structure design can be regarded as a real fusion of navigation and communication signals, which can achieve the effect of mutual reinforcement. From this point of view, ICAN based on the low-orbit satellite network seems to be the development trend of PNT services in the future.

In this paper, based on the ZC-NOMA signal proposed in our previous work, we propose a multi-access communication-navigation integration architecture. Furthermore, we analyze the correlated interference between the navigation and communication components. Finally, we demonstrated and verified through a series of simulations.

2   Mutual Promotion of Communication and Navigation Components

Next-generation networks beyond 5G are expected to provide terabit-per-second data rate communication services and centimeter-level accuracy positioning services in an efficient, seamless and cost-effective manner. However, most communication and positioning systems are currently designed separately, resulting in underutilized radio resources and degraded network performance. Low Earth Orbit (LEO) navigation augmentation satellites can achieve the key goals of navigation services such as global coverage, strong landing capability, and rapid convergence of high-precision positioning. In recent years, with the rise of low-orbit communication constellations, the low-orbit satellite navigation enhancement technology developed in combination with low-orbit communication satellites has become popular in the field of satellite navigation enhancement.

Global macro trends will drive the use of GNSS by industries and individuals requiring greater PNT accuracy and security. However, the low power consumption and limited bandwidth of signals are inherent characteristics of current GNSS, which limit the achievable accuracy and threaten robustness against both intentional (jamming) and unintentional interference. MEO and GSO do suffer from large free-space losses for broadcast GNSS signals due to their great distances from Earth, and they both transmit in the overcrowded L-band, where bandwidth availability is scarce [5]. With the booming low-orbit communication satellite constellation, the integration of communication and navigation can fully utilize the advantages of low-orbit satellite navigation through the co-design and optimization of communication and navigation components. In addition to the sharing of network infrastructure and radio resources, more importantly, the integration of communication and navigation can also achieve mutual promotion between navigation and communication functions [1].

The effect of navigation on communication is

- random access
- frequency synchronization
- time synchronization
- Beam alignment and star chasing

The effect of communication on navigation is

- Ephemeris transmission
- Clock Skew Elimination

3   The Proposed Waveform

The time-frequency structure of ZC-NOMA is shown in Fig. 1. The main idea of ZC-NOMA is to use the ZC sequence as a navigation signal to superimpose it into the F-OFDM signal that can realize asynchronous access. Considering the clock deviation, the navigation user requires at least the reception of signals from four navigation satellites located at different positions. The four colors in the figure correspond to the integrated communication and navigation signals broadcast by the four satellites.

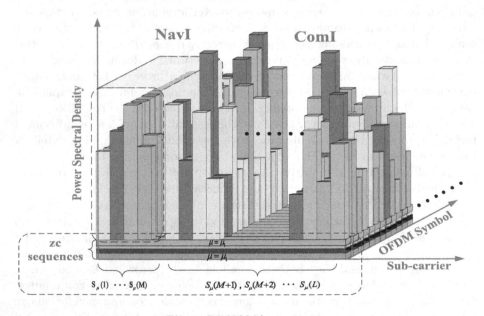

Fig. 1. ZC-NOMA structure

The Zadoff-Chu (ZC) sequence is accepted as the primary synchronization signal (PSS) for downlink time synchronization due to its zero autocorrelation and low peak-to-average power ratio (PAPR) properties [9], which can be expressed as

$$X_\mu[m] = e^{j\phi_\mu[m]} \tag{1}$$

where $\phi_\mu[m]$ is

$$\phi_\mu[m] = \begin{cases} \frac{\mu\pi}{N}m(m+1), & \text{if } N \text{ is odd} \\ \frac{\mu\pi m^2}{N}, & \text{if } N \text{ is even} \end{cases} \tag{2}$$

where μ is the root of the sequence, and N is the length of the sequence, and μ and N are relatively prime.

The satellite navigation message is a message broadcasted by the navigation satellite to describe the operating status parameters of the navigation satellite, including the system time, ephemeris, almanac, correction parameters of the satellite clock, the health status of the navigation satellite and the parameters of the ionospheric delay model. The parameters of the navigation message provide the user with time information, and the position coordinates and speed of user can be calculated by using the parameters of the navigation message. ZC-NOMA provides dedicated sub-carriers for broadcasting navigation messages, namely NavI, signal form of which is

$$s_{k,\ell}^{nav}(n) \triangleq \sum_{m=m'_{k,nav}}^{m'_{k,nav}+M_{k,nav}-1} d_{\ell,k,m}^{nav} e^{j2\pi mn/N}, \quad -N_{\text{cp}} \leq n < N \tag{3}$$

Among them, $m'_{k,nav}$ represents the starting subcarrier sequence number of the navigation message from the k satellite, and $M_{k,nav}$ represents the k satellite The number of sub-carriers occupied by the navigation message. General data will be transmitted using ComI subcarriers

$$s_{k,\ell}^{com}(n) \triangleq \sum_{m=m'_{k,com}}^{m'_{k,com}+M_{k,com}-1} d_{\ell,k,m}^{com} e^{j2\pi mn/N}, \quad -N_{\text{cp}} \leq n < N \tag{4}$$

Among them, $m'_{k,com}$ represents the starting subcarrier sequence number of the general data from the k satellite, and $M_{k,nav}$ represents the k satellite The number of subcarriers occupied by the general data.

In order to deal with the inter-carrier interference when multiple satellites are connected asynchronously, we apply a soft truncation filter to the subcarrier group corresponding to the navigation message and general data. The soft truncation filter of the navigation message is

$$f_k^{nav}(n) \triangleq p_k^{nav}(n) \cdot w(n) \tag{5}$$

The soft truncation filter corresponding to the general data subcarrier group is

$$f_k^{com}(n) \triangleq p_k^{com}(n) \cdot w(n) \tag{6}$$

where $p_k^{nav}(n)$ and $p_k^{com}(n)$ correspond to the rectangular frequency response, $w(t)$ is the time-windowing mask, expressed as

$$w(t) = \begin{cases} 0.5\left[1 + \cos\left(2\pi|t|/T_w\right)\right], & |t| \leq \frac{T_w}{2} \\ 0, & |t| > \frac{T_w}{2} \end{cases} \tag{7}$$

The navigation signal of one symbol length is expressed as

$$x_{k,\ell}(n) \triangleq \sum_{m=1}^{N} X_{\mu_k}[m]e^{j2\pi mn/N}, \quad -N_{\mathrm{cp}} \leq n < N \tag{8}$$

A set of conjugated sequence pairs is represented as

$$\tilde{x}_{k,\ell}(n) = \mathrm{real}\left(x_{k,\ell}(n)\right) + j(-1)^{\ell}\,\mathrm{imag}\left(x_{k,\ell}(n)\right) \tag{9}$$

The filtered NavI block is

$$\tilde{s}_{k,\ell}^{nav}(n) = s_{k,\ell}^{nav}(n) * f_k^{nav}(n) \tag{10}$$

The filtered ComI is

$$\tilde{s}_{k,\ell}^{com}(n) = s_{k,\ell}^{com}(n) * f_k^{com}(n) \tag{11}$$

Therefore, the l ZC-NOMA symbol is expressed as

$$s_{k,\ell}(n) = \tilde{s}_{k,\ell}^{nav}(n) + \tilde{s}_{k,\ell}^{com}(n) + \tilde{x}_{k,\ell}(n) \tag{12}$$

For continuous ZC-NOMA, it can be expressed as

$$s_k(n) = \sum_{\ell=0}^{L-1} s_{k,\ell}\left(n - \ell\left(N + N_{\mathrm{cp}}\right)\right) \tag{13}$$

After channel transmission, the receiver will simultaneously receive the ZC-NOMA signals from K satellites, which are expressed as

$$y(n) = \sum_{i=1}^{k} h_k s_k(n - n_i)e^{\frac{j2(n-n_i)\pi\Delta f_k}{F_S}} + \omega(n) \tag{14}$$

3.1   Interference Analysis

We analyzed the interference present in ZC-NOMA through the signal processing procedure.

The communication signal sent by satellite k is shown in the Fig. 2. Satellite k occupies a part of all sub-carriers, but since the OFDM signal is a truncation of an infinite-length signal, the signal spectrum of satellite k will leak to other sub-carriers, causing inter-carrier interference to other satellite signals.

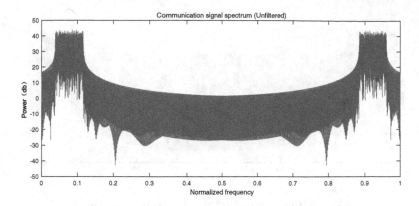

Fig. 2. Communication signal spectrum (Unfiltered)

In order to overcome inter-carrier interference and realize multi-satellite asynchronous access, ZC-NOMA applies band-pass filter to band-pass the in-band signal to suppress out-of-band leakage of spectrum. The spectrum of the signal after passing through the band-pass filter is shown in Fig. 3.

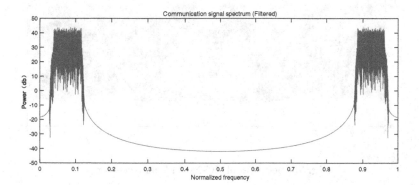

Fig. 3. Communication signal spectrum (Filted)

The low-power navigation signal is superimposed on the communication channel through the band-pass filter to form the ZC-NOMA signal broadcast by satellite k, and its frequency spectrum is shown in Fig. 4.

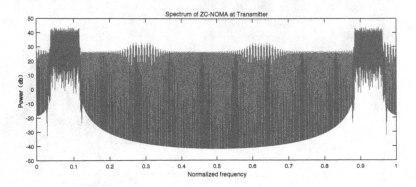

Fig. 4. Spectrum of ZC-NOMA at Transmitter

According to the same process, the receiver will simultaneously receive the ZC-NOMA signals from K satellites. After channel transmission, the spectrum structure of the receiver at this time is shown in Fig. 5.

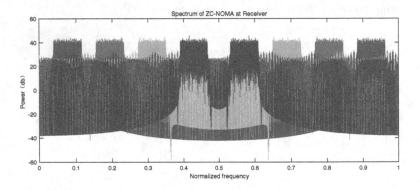

Fig. 5. Spectrum of ZC-NOMA at Receiver

It should be noted that even after bandpass filtering, satellite k will still be affected by frequency leakage from other satellites, so an appropriate guard interval is necessary. As can be seen from Fig. 5, in addition to the impact of spectrum leakage, the communication channel of satellite 1 will also be interfered by the navigation signals from K satellites. These two forms of interference are called inter-carrier interference and navigation communication mutual interference respectively in ZC-NOMA.

Inter-Satellite Asynchronous Interference. Considering the clock deviation between the navigation satellite and the system reference, it is necessary to receive the navigation signals of at least four satellites to determine the three-dimensional coordinates of the navigation user. For signals broadcast by satellites, the transmission times of these signals are not synchronized, and the propagation paths they travel through are not nearly the same, so it is impossible to achieve time synchronization between multiple signals. For ZC-OFDM, the orthogonality of subcarriers is only satisfied within the set of subcarriers broadcast by a satellite, OFDM-like sinc transfer function decays at frequencies f down to $1/f$, this will result in frequency leakage between different satellite sub-carrier groups, sub-carriers from one satellite can interfere with sub-carriers in the sub-carrier groups of other satellites [8].

In order to overcome the mutual interference between different satellite sub-carrier groups, the additional signal processing of ZC-NOMA on the traditional CP-OFDM waveform can suppress the interference leakage to achieve good spectral efficiency in the case of asynchronous access.

$$SI_{k,m} = \sum_{k=1}^{K} \sum_{m=1}^{M_k} \frac{p_{k,m,v}^2}{M_k^2} \left| \frac{\sin\left[\pi((m-1)-(n-1))\right]}{\sin\left[\frac{\pi}{2N_1}\left((m-1)-(n-1)+M_k\right)\right]} \right|^2 \tag{15}$$

where $SI_{k,m}$ represents the interference of other satellite subcarriers received by the m-th subcarrier in the k satellite subcarrier group, and $SI_{k,m}$ measures the inter-satellite interference in a quantitative manner. A clear representation is provided, which shows that reasonable subcarrier power allocation can effectively suppress the asynchronous interference between satellites.

Navigation-Communication Mutual Interference. In addition to the inter-carrier interference caused by the asynchronous access of different satellites, there is also mutual interference between navigation and communication in the ZC-NOMA signal. For the receiving end, the communication signals that need to be demodulated will suffer from navigation interference. Without considering the mutual interference between satellites, the SNR of the received communication channel of user g can be expressed as

$$\gamma_{g,m} = \frac{\sum_{k=1}^{K} P_{m,k} \left|h_m^{k\to g}\right|^2}{\sum_{k=1}^{K} P_{zc}^i \left|h_m^{k\to g}\right|^2 + \sigma_g^2} \tag{16}$$

where $P_{m,k}$ represents the power of the m subcarrier of the k satellite. It should be noted that for the same satellite, the navigation signals carried on different subcarriers have the same power value, P_{zc}^k does not need to be distinguished according to subcarriers, $h_m^{k\to g}$ represents the channel coefficient from satellite k to user g on the m subcarrier.

In order to extract the communication signal of satellite k, user g filters the sub-carrier group corresponding to satellite k, and the filtered spectrum is shown in Fig. 7. It can be seen from the figure that the communication signals of other satellites are effective suppression, but the navigation signal located at the corresponding sub-carrier position cannot be eliminated.

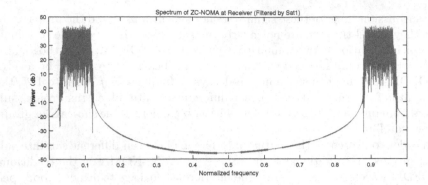

Fig. 6. Spectrum of ZC-NOMA at Receiver (Filtered by Sat1)

After DFT with filtered signals, a constellation diagram as shown in the Fig. 7 can be obtained, and it can be judged. After demodulation, the communication information carried by the satellite k can be obtained.

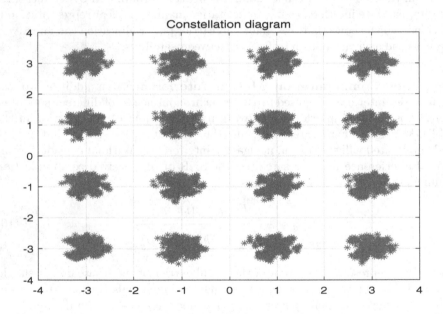

Fig. 7. Constellation diagram of Sat1

4   Conclusion

Through the signal level simulation, the interference of ZC-NOMA can be observed intuitively, that is, the inter-carrier interference and the mutual interference between the navigation and communication components caused by the non-orthogonality of the satellite due to asynchronous access. Through mathematical analysis, we quantitatively represent these two interferences, and we believe that based on this result, efficient allocation of resources can be achieved, and communication and navigation functions can be coordinated.

References

1. Aravanis, A.I., Shankar, M.R.B., Arapoglou, P.D., Danoy, G., Cottis, P.G., Ottersten, B.: Power allocation in multibeam satellite systems: A two-stage multi-objective optimization. IEEE Trans. Wireless Commun. **14**(6), 3171–3182 (2015). https://doi.org/10.1109/TWC.2015.2402682
2. Centenaro, M., Costa, C.E., Granelli, F., Sacchi, C., Vangelista, L.: A survey on technologies, standards and open challenges in satellite iot. IEEE Commun. Surv. Tutorials **23**(3), 1693–1720 (2021). https://doi.org/10.1109/COMST.2021.3078433
3. Darwish, T., Kurt, G.K., Yanikomeroglu, H., Bellemare, M., Lamontagne, G.: Leo satellites in 5g and beyond networks: A review from a standardization perspective (2021). https://doi.org/10.48550/ARXIV.2110.08654
4. Hanson, W.A.: In their own words: Oneweb's internet constellation as described in their fcc form 312 application. New Space **4**(3), 153–167 (2016)
5. Park, U., Kim, H.W., Oh, D.S., Ku, B.J.: A dynamic bandwidth allocation scheme for a multi-spot-beam satellite system. ETRI J. **34**(4), 613–616 (2012)
6. Reid, T.G.R., Neish, A.M., Walter, T., Enge, P.K.: Broadband leo constellations for navigation. Navigation, J. Inst. Navigation **65**(2), 205–220 (2018)
7. de Selding, P.B.: Spacex to build 4000 broadband satellites in seattle. Space News **19** (2015)
8. Zhang, X., Zhang, L., Xiao, P., Ma, D., Wei, J., Xin, Y.: Mixed numerologies interference analysis and inter-numerology interference cancellation for windowed ofdm systems. IEEE Trans. Veh. Technol. **67**(8), 7047–7061 (2018). https://doi.org/10.1109/TVT.2018.2826047
9. Zhao, Y., Cao, J., Li, Y.: An improved timing synchronization method for eliminating large doppler shift in leo satellite system. In: 2018 IEEE 18th International Conference on Communication Technology (ICCT), pp. 762–766 (2018). https://doi.org/10.1109/ICCT.2018.8600170

Soybean Pods and Stems Segmentation Based on an Improved Watershed

Shan Ning$^{(\boxtimes)}$, Qiuduo Zhao, and Ke Liu

Heilongjiang University of Science and Technology, Harbin 150022, China
4127756@qq.com

Abstract. The technology of object detection based on image processing is the fundamental and significant link in the research of automatic accurate detection of crop phenotype. The shape of pods is different at different angles, which brings difficulties to the segmentation of pods. In this study, a solution based on computer vision was proposed, which could automatically and accurately detect the phenotype of crops. A fixed distance digital camera and two flash lighting were used for pod identification and automatic measurement of pod width and pod length. A novel proof of method for key organ segmentation was proposed for harvested soybean plant images. With the improved watershed algorithm (IM-watershed), the famous Marker-Controlled watershed algorithm (MC-watershed) was combined with two stages that were split and merge processes. Under-segmented regions were split using adapted size of structural elements (ASSE) and fast and robust fuzzy c-means clustering (FRFCM).

Keywords: Image Processing · Image Segmentation · Watershed Transform · Soybean Phenotype

1 Introduction

Soybean contains high-quality plant protein, which is an important source of protein in people's daily diet. The research of soybean germplasm resources is the basic guarantee for the sustainable development of soybean industry. Crop phenotype research provides high-quality, high-precision and repeatable plant shape data for germplasm resources research. In soybean phenotype research, it is one of the important methods to master the relationship between different factors by investigating the characteristics of soybean plants and seeds at maturity and understanding the effects of different varieties or different treatment factors on the characteristics of plants and seeds. Experts and scholars are focusing on studying the detection of plant phenotypic characteristics due to the advancement of artificial intelligence and machine vision. The technology of object detection based on image processing is the fundamental and significant link in the research of automatic accurate detection of crop phenotype [1, 2]. An important application of image understanding is the identification of meaningful objects within an image based on segmentation.

© ICST Institute for Computer Sciences, Social Informatics and Telecommunications Engineering 2023
Published by Springer Nature Switzerland AG 2023. All Rights Reserved
A. Li et al. (Eds.): 6GN 2022, LNICST 505, pp. 166–181, 2023.
https://doi.org/10.1007/978-3-031-36014-5_14

At this phase, pixels were grouped into regions, whereas in classification, they were categorized into different classes. Each region consists of a set of pixels that could be segmented to extract rich features. It was expected that these features, which could not be extracted at the pixel level, would enhance accuracy of separation. Currently, the type of approach was commonly adopted for comprehending pictures [3–6]. Numerous approaches to image segmentation were proposed. Although relatively robust and efficient, these methods failed to segment similar objects adequately. Image segmentation technologies include clustering [7–9], watershed transform [10–12], region growth [13, 14], dynamic contour model [15], mean shift [16, 17], consensus segmentations [18], spectral cluster [19], neural network [20], Markov random field [21], etc. On the one side, clustering was a method of effectiveness and rapidity for using image segmentation. A clustering of pixels aimed to partition a set of pixels into groups in such a way that members of the same group were similar, and those in different groups were dissimilar. Image segmentation should, however, be affected by target regions with low contrast and weak boundaries. On the other side, watershed transform was another popular image segmentation technology. Because of its simple, fast and complete image segmentation, it was more and more considered as an effective segmentation method. Watershed transform could provide a closed contour even if the target region had low contrast and weak boundary. But, over-segmentation and under-segmentation plagued watershed transform with concerning to images of soybean plants. By reason of it only considered gray-level codes without paying attention to space structure, it was susceptible to image segmentation with complex textures. It was decided to design an algorithm that clusters connected pixels on the basis of their inherent characteristics rather than on the basis of a homogeneity criterion in order to deal with these problems.

As mentioned above, in this study, it was proposed a new segmentation method, which combined the MC watered algorithm to separate the pod from the plant and the background. For better segmentation results, the split and merge processes were used to deal with the part of excessive segmentation and insufficient segmentation, respectively. Through the two steps of IM-watershed (split and merge), appropriate tradeoffs were dealt with between excessive and insufficient segmentation. To adapt the shape of the pod, Skeleton Extraction (SE) was used for Linear Fitting (LF).

2 Material and Methods

In this section, it was described how to get the data sources. After that, MC-watershed transforms and FRFCM algorithms for image segmentation should be reviewed. It also presented the related work that attempted to introduce ASSE for splitting under-segmentation, SE and LF for merging over-segmentation. Besides, crop phenotypes were extracted from segmentation results.

2.1 Data Sources

A total of 524 RGB images of four varieties of soybean plants which was Dongnong 25, Dongnong 251, Dongnong 252, Dongnong 253 separately were collected from the Xiangyang Farm of Northeast Agricultural University in October 2018. The plant ranged in length from 900 mm to 1,200 mm and a width of 300 mm to 500 mm. In addition to a high-quality image, proper lighting was key to achieving optimal pictures shot with Canon EOS 5D Mark II with CANON ZOOM LENS EF 24-105 mm 1:4 L IS USM. The most common machine vision arrangements utilize structured lighting, front lighting or back lighting. Front lighting was used to detect surface features or textures. However, the structure of a soybean plant was complex and easy to produce shadows

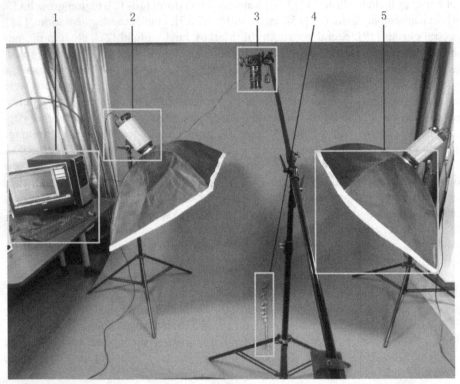

Note:1. Computer   2. Flash lighting   3. Camera and LENS 4. Soybean plant 5. Soft box

a. Experimental setup

b. Control panel of flash   c. A sample image of soybean plant
   lighting

Fig. 1. Experimental setup and images obtained of a soybean plant under front lighting. In this study, there were two 60° studio flashes on both sides for reducing shadows. The photo was taken in the laboratory environment, two meters away from the plant, as shown in Fig. 1. All images were 5,616 × 3,744 pixels. The focus was 55 mm. The aperture value was f/11. Exposure time was 0.005s. ISO was 100. Exposure compensation was 0. Flash lighting HM-400 was guide number GN66, and color temperature was 5,500k, accounting for 0.4% of the output power. Soft box was 800 mm × 1,200 mm. Images were preprocessed with the size of 5,400 × 2,700 pixels by cutting the edge. To prevent the poor performance of the model caused by interference with a complex background, soybean plants were photographed under blue nonwoven background. To improve the detection accuracy, the background value of the image was preprocessed to (0,0,0). The images were saved in .jpg format.

2.2 MC-Watershed Algorithm

It is normally applying segmented process of an image to use the MC-watershed algorithm as a base segmentation algorithm. The standard watershed segmentation algorithm used a topographic surface built from image gradients in this approach. Due to the fact that target edges (i.e., watershed lines) were probably located at picture element of high gradient value. Submerging it from the minimum value of the surface generates different catchment basins. Dams were built to prevent the confluence of water from two varying gathering areas. For each pixel in picture, the elevation was determined by the intensity of gradients, which is defined by the location of the dams when the whole image is flooded. In addition, amplitude gradient image, transform distance map and intensity grayscale map can be used with the standard watershed. Nevertheless, over-segmentation frequently occurred when applying the classical watershed algorithm.

MC-watershed extracted signs for the locations of the targets in the image to lower over-segmentation. To obtain good markers, morphological operations were required. Erosion, expansion, opening, and closing were basic morphological operations used in MC-watershed method. The method of morphological opening that was dilation following erosion. And, the method of morphological closing that was erosion following dilation. There was an interlinkage between figure and structural element that determined the precision of picture restoration in both conditions. MC-watershed used these operations to acquire well foreground signs and split them from the background. A gray-scale gradient image was used as a topographic surface. Each pixel was lower than a given threshold, then set it to zero. In this stage, little heterogeneity was deleted [20]. In the gray-scale image, foreground markers were created by selecting the regional maximum to open and close images based on reconstruction. Foreground markers were produced by reconstructed opening and closing images on the gray-scale image. The values of foreground markers were set to local minimums in the gradient image. MC-watershed method pierces holes in each minimum, and then slowly immerses the surface into a lake. Starting from the minimum of the lowest altitude, different catchment basins gradually filled up with water. There was now a dam to prevent merging of water from different minima, as the water gradually filled up the different catchment basins. The minimums were surrounded by dams, which delineated the catchment basins. These dams corresponded to the required watersheds. However, due to the irregularity of light, shadow and shape, it is a challenge to accurately extract markers.

To improve the segmentation accuracy, it was proposed an improved watershed (IM-watershed) algorithm, which divided the segmentation into three stages. Segmentation of pods, stems, and the background was the first step in obtaining an initial segmentation. Segmenting as many pods as possible was the goal of this block. As shown in Fig. 2a, this process follows a flowchart. MC-watershed comprises five steps: background preprocessing, grayscale conversion, reconstruction, marking foreground objects, and computation of the watershed transform.

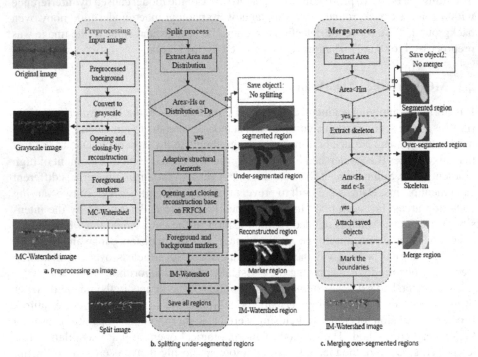

Fig. 2. Flowchart of the IM-watershed algorithm. Hs was the minimum pixel number of under-segmented region; Ds was the minimum number of picture elements distribution of under-segmented region; FRFCM was the fast and robust fuzzy c-means clustering method; Hm was the maximum number of picture elements in over-segmented area; Ha was the maximum number of picture elements in the merging area; Is was skeleton of the line fitting maximum error. (Color figure online)

To adjust input image and get foreground signs, the preprocessing stage was necessary. RGB color model was used for background processing, which determined whether each pixel was a background based on its red, green, and blue brightness. If the brightness of blue was greater than the other two components, it was regarded as a background pixel and the pixel was deleted. In this step, an input image was processed into a grayscale image. The Sobel operator computed the gradient magnitude to generate gradient image. Objects with higher gradients were bordering the objects, and objects with lower gradients were inside. To eliminate small pixels, each pixel in the gradient image was set to zero under a given threshold. However, the incomplete boundary of a pod could lead to subsequent incorrect information, such as pod texture. In addition, the algorithm of morphological operations improved the contrast between pods, stems, and backgrounds. In order to improve the picture and get the signs, morphological operations such as opening and closing reconstructions were performed. Foreground markers were the output of the fourth step. Foreground marker pixels were adjusted so that the gradient magnitude image's regional minima appeared there. Based on this modified gradient, which was identified as an image of segmentation with pods and stems in backdrop. The watershed transform was computed. As result of the preprocessing block, the MC-watershed image was generated, but there were a lot of pods not separated and a lot of noise (Fig. 3a).

a. The segmentation result of the   b. The segmentation result of the splitting
preprocessing stage   stage

Fig. 3. The results of processing and splitting stages in the IM-watershed

2.3   Base on ASSE and FRFCM Split Process

The split process was integrated into four stages: extracting the *Area* and *Distribution*, the close and open reconstruction based on FRFCM, signing targets and background, in addition, calculating watershed transform.

In the preprocessing stage, the values of *Area* and *Distribution* were obtained. Underseparated pods were identified utilizing *Area* and *Distribution* values. The Distribution number of each close region was calculated by Eq. (1).

$$Distribution = \frac{MER}{Area} \tag{1}$$

where *Area* was the pixel number of the closed region and *MER* was the area of the minimum enclosing rectangle that contained the closed region. If *Area* > *Hs* or *Distribution* > *Ds*, a new image was generated for the split process. *Hs* was the minimum pixel number of under-segmented regions. *Ds* was the minimum number of the picture element distribution in under-segmented regions.

As a result of its validity and rapidity, clustering has been one of the most popular methods for segmenting images. Using clustering, it attempted to partition a set into some groups that were similar, and different clusters that were dissimilar. Bezdek proposed fuzzy C-Means clustering by minimizing the sum-of-squares criterion based on fuzzy set theory [13]. K-means was a clustering method that minimizes the sum-of-squares criterion. The FCM method retained more data from the original picture than hard clustering because it was more tolerant of ambiguity in the image. However, it failed to segment pictures with complex geometric structures or noise. The FRFCM algorithm employs morphological reconstruction (MR) to replace mean or median filters due to its robustness to noise in order to improve the FCM algorithm's drawback of being sensitive to noise[11]. A gray-level histogram was used to cluster group, and the objective function in Eq. (2) and Eq. (3) were expressed as the number of noise spectra suppressed.

$$J_m = \sum_{l=1}^{q} \sum_{k=1}^{c} r_l u_{kl}^m \|\theta_l - v_k\|^2 \tag{2}$$

$$\sum_{l=1}^{q} r_l = N \tag{3}$$

where u_{kl} was the fuzzy membership of gray number l with treat as group k. v_k was prototype number of the kth group. N was a picture reconstructed by MR, and θ_l was gray level, l was greater than 1 but less than q, q meant the quantity of the gray levels included in picture, it was θ normally much lower than N. θ was expressed as Eq. (4).

$$\theta = R^c(f) \tag{4}$$

where R^c denoted morphologically closing reconstruction and f was an original image.

MR was an image transformation that required two input pictures, a marker picture and a mask picture [22]. The marker picture was the starting point for the transformation. And, the mask picture constrained the transformation. Used FRFCM to create the mask image for reducing interference with noise, complex texture, and background. In this stage, we used FRFCM opening and closing reconstruction for under-segmentation pods to separate them. Figure 2b shows a flowchart of this process, by reason of just one working was essential achieve an appropriate separation. For the split process, the input image was the result image of the preprocessing stage. This stage consisted of two core processes: ASSE and FRFCM reconstruction.

In this study, it was proposed ASSE for mathematical morphology operation that could improve image segmentation. Firstly, ASSE employed multiscale square structuring elements to basic morphological operations: erosion, dilatation, opening, and closing. IM-watershed used these operations to generate good target signs and split target and background. Secondly, small structural elements were used to deal with great gradient magnitudes in a gradient image, while low gradient deformation was generally used in large structural element, ASSE could get superior sign pictures to improve pod segmentation [23].

The size of the structure element was generally determined by combing a specific target with experiment effect [24, 25]. As for the size of the window, the small one brought the over-segmentation, while the larger one took the loss in precision to the under-segmentation in basic operations of morphological transform. Due to the various size of the object in the image, the structure element size should be chosen reasonably. Using ASSE could help to get an effective segmentation image.

The structure element set was a. The size of a structural element was defined as τ. Supposed segmentation image set was A, open operation was expressed as Eq. (5).

$$A \cdot a = (A \ominus a) \oplus a \tag{5}$$

where a was the size of a with reference to *Area* and *Distribution*, $\ominus$ was erosion operation, and $\oplus$ was expansion operation. τ could be calculated by Eq. (6).

$$\tau = \begin{cases} \frac{\gamma}{x_1} & \beta > y_2 \\ \frac{\gamma}{x_2} & y_2 > \beta > y_1 \\ \frac{\gamma}{x_3} & \beta < y_1 \end{cases} \tag{6}$$

where $\beta = $ *Distribution*, $\gamma = $ *Area*, y_1, y_2 were the predetermined threshold value. x_1, x_2 and x_3 were predetermined parameters. It was focused on a set of parameters for processes given in Sect. 3.2.

Close operation was expressed as Eq. (7).

$$A \cdot a = (A \oplus a) \ominus a \tag{7}$$

Performed opening and closing reconstruction to identify high-intensity objects. In reconstruction, there was a structuring ingredients (defining the connectivity), a marker picture (starting point), and a mask picture (constraining the transformation). Combined ASSE method with reconstruction, ASSE-based opening and closing process eliminated small imperfections much better than general opening and closing process without influencing the form of the targets. In the reconstruction operation, the FRFCM image mask was used to reconstruct the morphological features of the image marker and the foreground markers were returned to the image. The FRFCM image restored the forms of the objects, and the number of values in the FRFCM image was less than the original image. Therefore, the elements of marker were better than the ones under the regular image mask. It was necessary to remove some small parts generated by the split process owing to excessive segmentation originated from watershed. Split image was then used as the input for merging image

2.4 Base on SE and LF for Merge Process

By utilizing the FRFCM, it could be coped with the under-segmentation problem of the MC-watershed. Merging objects in over-segmentation pods was another way of improving segmentation quality.

Over-segmentation and sensitivity to noise continued to plague the MC-watershed with respect to soybean plant image. Generally, the gradient amplitude of the original image was calculated before applying the MC-watershed. Fluctuations in gradient amplitude images and negative impulse noise could lead to undesired additional watershed segments.

The third stage involved finding over-segmentation regions that would allow for a successful merging process. The merging process was performed once, since only a single application was required. Figure 2c shows a flowchart of this process. Split image was then used as the input for merging image. This stage consisted of two core processes: merge process by SE and LF [26, 27].

It used the values of *Area*, *Am*, and ε judge whether it was over-segmentation. If *Area* < *Hm*, the closed region was marked for waiting to be processed. *Hm* was the maximum number of pixels in the over-segmented region. Supposed that 2 to 5 adjacent regions satisfying the condition could be merged into one object, and calculated the *Am* value. *Am* was the total quantity of pixels in the merged region. If *Am* < H_a, a new image should be produced for the merge process. H_a was the maximum number of pixels in the merged region.

The skeleton was essential to the representation and recognition of an object. Image segmentation could be aided by the skeleton [28, 29]. SE model was based on thinning algorithm for extraction skeleton. The skeleton model was constant connectivity by gradually and uniformly denuding the boundary voxels. Object skeletons were derived by removing boundary points or iteratively moving towards their inner parts. This algorithm could preserve the topologies of objects. A binary picture was given. If it was one class picture element encoded one, else background element encoded zero. A sequential iterative algorithm was used for thinning the image: the iterations were repeated until the image was unchanged throughout the process. Iterations were performed to remove pixels from the boundaries of objects while preventing them from breaking apart. The remaining pixels form the skeleton of the image. After the iterations were finished, a supplemental procedure was removed spur pixels of iteration. The spur pixel operation removed endpoints of lines without removing small objects. This was reason the iterative section of the calculation was pointed at producing a well skeleton and hence the method could output one-pixel width skeleton without spurs (Fig. 4c).

The skeleton of these classes could be replaced by a linear fitting approach. It was used a method of the principle of the least square method to calculate the total error ε of the linear regression equation. The ε was calculated by Eq. (8). If the total error of LF was less than I_s, , adjacent classes could be clustering together (Fig. 4d), experimental parameters were presented in Sect. 3.3.

$$\begin{cases} \varepsilon = \sum_{i=1}^{n} |y_i - bx_i - a| \\ y = bx + a \\ b = \frac{\sum_{i=1}^{n}(x_i - \bar{x})(y_i - \bar{y})}{\sum_{i=1}^{n}(x_i - \bar{x})^2} \\ a = \bar{y} - b\bar{x} \end{cases} \tag{8}$$

where y was the ordinate of the skeleton, x was the abscissa of the skeleton, n was the number of pixels in the skeleton. b was the correlation parameter, and a was the intercept in the function. $\bar{x}$ was the average of x, $\bar{y}$ was the average of y.

3 Results and Discussion

3.1 MC-Watershed Results

This example shows two core results from IM-watershed preprocessing: foreground marker and segmentation. It shows the foreground maxima on the original image. Foreground markers were obtained by morphological operations and opening-closing reconstructions before the gray-scale conversion was performed. A constant intensity value was assigned to the pixels at the regional maxima and a lower value was assigned to the pixels at the external boundary. In order to get the foreground marker, it was necessary to delete the divided pixels after performing the performance. Using regional maxima, only pixels with density surround of a high level by low density pixels were deleted. The results of the preprocessing stage were shown in Fig. 3a. The ellipses indicate those pods that did not separate during the process.

In this experiment, a fixed square structure element with the size of 20×20 pixels was used for reconstruction. And, a fixed structuring element of square was size 5×5 pixels that was used to the morphological operations for the foreground markers. The gray-level scale was zero that the dark pixels belonged to the background.

3.2 Split Process Results

For the results of the MC-watershed process, many pods had not been separated. The second stage was the split process, to achieve the separation of the under-segmentation. As shown in Fig. 3a, a split image was generated using the MC-watershed step. A slight under-segmentation was obvious. Each of these areas was confirmed using data of *Area* and *Distribution* provided by the MC-watershed. *Hs* was calculated by Eq. (9), and *Ds* was calculated by Eq. (10). If the *Hs* was too large, it could lead to the missing selection of the under-segmented region. Otherwise, if the *Hs* was too small, it could lead to the selection of the not under-segmented region. Similarly, too large *Ds* led to the loss of under-segmented regions, while too small *Ds* led to the selection of not under-segmented regions. The complementary value of *Hs* and *Ds* could select the under-segmented region more accurately. If the parameters met the criteria, then the under-segmented pods were split.

$$Hs = \frac{\sum_{i=1}^{n} \gamma_i}{n \times 1.5} \tag{9}$$

$$Ds = \frac{\sum_{i=1}^{n} \beta_i}{n \times 1.2} \tag{10}$$

where n was the number of the classes in the separated image, γ_i was the *Area* of the ith class, and β_i was the *Distribution* of the ith class.

In the split process, it was set $y_1=0.3 \times Ds$, $y_2=0.5 \times Ds$, $x_1=10^3$, $x_2=1.4 \times 10^3$, $x_3=1.7\times10^3$ for ASSE.

In the FRFCM, the mask picture of rebuild was the initial picture, and a square structuring element of size 3×3 pixels was used to get marker picture. Also the size of the filtering window used by mean and median filter that was also 3×3 pixels.

Some objects with foreground markers were influenced by multiple highlights. Figure 3b was the result of the split process. Some over-separated pods were highlighted by white ellipses.

3.3 Merge Process Results

This process read the split image and identifies the regions to merge using the information from *Area* for merge step. H_m was calculated according to Eq. (11), and H_a was calculated by Eq. (12). Too small H_m led to less selection of over-segmented regions, while too large H_m led to wrong selection. Similarly, if H_a was too small, it could lead to the missing regions to merge. Conversely, if H_a was too large, it could lead to be merged regions that should not be merged. And, set $I_s=15$.

$$H_m = \frac{\sum_{i=1}^{n^s} \gamma_i^s}{n^s \times 4} \tag{11}$$

$$H_a = \frac{\sum_{i=1}^{n^s} \gamma_i^s}{n^s \times 1.5} \tag{12}$$

$$\varepsilon_s = \varepsilon \div n_{sp} \tag{13}$$

where n^s was the number of the classes in the image. ε_s was described by Eq. (13) that was the average error of linear regression for the skeleton. Figure 4a was the original image. Figure 4b was the result of the split process. Figure 4c was the skeleton extraction of the classes. Figure 4d was the result of the merge process. The final output of the IM-watershed was the image was shown in Fig. 5.

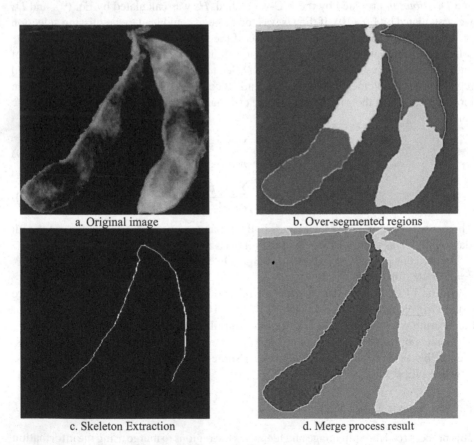

a. Original image   b. Over-segmented regions

c. Skeleton Extraction   d. Merge process result

Fig. 4. The result of merge process

Fig. 5. The result of the IM-watered algorithm

3.4 Comparative Experiment

In this part, test results were gotten by the IM-Watered in comparison with the MC-watershed for detecting the pods of soybean plants. The section was consisted into the MC-watershed, the IM-watershed, and manual segmentation results. The indicators were obtained by comparing these methods with ground truth.

Precision of visual estimation was undertaken occupying the definition of visual accuracy (VAC) [30] as outlined in Eq. (14).

$$
\begin{cases}
VAC = \dfrac{N_{segment}}{N_{segment}+N_{split}+N_{merge}+N_{add}+N_{missing}} \\
N_{segment} = \sum_{i=1}^{n^m} N_{segment}^i \\
N_{split} = \sum_{i=1}^{n^m} N_{split}^i \\
N_{merge} = \sum_{i=1}^{n^m} N_{merge}^i \\
N_{add} = \sum_{i=1}^{n^m} N_{add}^i \\
N_{missing} = \sum_{i=1}^{n^m} N_{missing}^i
\end{cases}
\tag{14}
$$

where N_{split}^i was the number of errors that a single pod was split into several pods, N_{merge}^i was the number of errors overlapping pods were merge into a single pod, N_{add}^i was the number of errors adding pods in background, $N_{missing}^i$ was the amount of errors assigning pods into the background, and $N_{segment}^i$ was the amount of errors in precisely splitting pod.

With the new method, the primary goal was to make sure pods were not over- or under-segmented and that they maintained their original shape. Pods with irregular shapes and low overlap were effectively shaped according to the visible part of the cluster due to the inclusion of geometrical recuperation in the method. Segmentation results of soybean plants by different methods was represented in Fig. 6.

The qualitative assessment of soybean segmentation was presented in Table 1, which compares the results to ground truth. The values of Table 1 were obtained from the

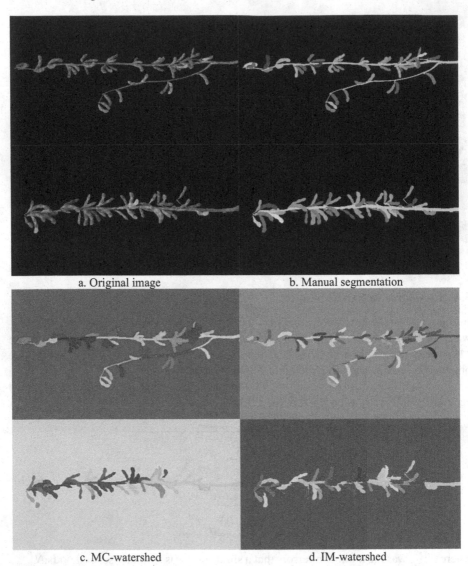

a. Original image   b. Manual segmentation

c. MC-watershed   d. IM-watershed

Fig. 6. Segmentation outcome of soybean plants by different methods.

number of corrected pods by three methods. The manual segmentation was the highest accuracy of the VAC, nevertheless, the number of overlapping pods (N_{merge}) was similar to the IM-watershed method. In terms of percentage accuracy, the IM-watershed method outperformed the MC-watershed method; the overlapping pods (N_{merge}) were much lower in the IM-watershed method. However, this step could result in excessive segmentation of partially good segmentation pods obtaining in the MC-watershed phase since it only took clumped objects out of range according to the value of *Area* or *Distribution*. This resulted in an indicator for over-segmentation (N_{split}) that was not lower

Table 1. Performance indicators for soybean plants

Indicator	Manual segmentation/%	MC-watershed/%	IM-watershed/%
VAC	93.68	55.72	80.81
$N_{segment}$	54.29	32.29	46.83
N_{split}	0.47	2.12	4.73
N_{merge}	2.45	21.5	4.35
N_{add}	0.21	0.98	0.98
$N_{missing}$	0.53	1.06	1.06

than in the MC-watershed method. However, in general, it was still a low level. The amount of missing ($N_{missing}$) and adding (N_{add}) pods was similar in both methods.

4 Conclusions

The IM-watershed method for separating soybean plants images was developed. It was obtained satisfactory results: VAC of the IM-watered algorithm was 25.09% higher than that of the MC-watershed method within segmentation of pods. It was suitable for pods separation, which allowed getting agronomic traits of soybean plants for complex studies. After the segmentation processing, it used parameters calibration and classification for extracting the agronomic traits of soybean. There was still a need for more research on the overlapping pod phenotypes, as well as the addition of noise to the indicator. In addition, soybean phenotypes need to be extracted correctly for further investigation of other crops.

Acknowledgements. This work was financed by the Technological Project of Heilongjiang Province "The open competition mechanism to select the best candidates" (No. 2022ZXJ05C01), Funding for the Opening Project of Key Laboratory of Agricultural Renewable Resource Utilization Technology (No. HLJHDNY2114) and Heilongjiang University of Science and Technology the introduction of high-level talent research start-up fund projects (No. 000009020315).

References

1. Cen, H., Zhu, Y., Sun, D., et al.: Current status and future perspective of the application of deep learning in plant phenotype research. Trans, Chin. Soc. Agricultural Eng. **36**(9), 1–16 (2020)
2. Zhu, F., Zheng, Z.: Image-based assessment of growth vigor for Phalaenopsis Aphrodite seedlings using convolutional neural network. Trans. Chin. Soc. Agricul. Eng. **36**(9) (2018)
3. Pont-, J., Arbelaez, P., Barron, J.T., et al.: Multiscale combinatorial grouping for image segmentation and object proposal generation. IEEE Trans. Pattern Anal. Mach. Intell. **39**(1), 128–140 (2017)

4. Hasnat, M.A., Alata, O., Tremeau, A.: Joint color-spatial-directional clustering and region merging (JCSD-RM) for unsupervised RGB-D image segmentation. IEEE Trans. Pattern Anal. Mach. Intell. **38**(11), 2255–2268 (2016)
5. Bampis, C.G., Maragos, P., Bovik, A.C.: Graph-driven diffusion and random walk schemes for image segmentation. IEEE Trans. Image Process. **26**(1), 35–50 (2017)
6. Saha, P.K., Basu, S., Hoffman, E.A.: Multiscale opening of conjoined fuzzy objects: theory and applications. IEEE Trans. Fuzzy Syst. **24**(5), 1121–1133 (2016)
7. Masulli, F., Rovetta, S.: Soft transition from probabilistic to possibilistic fuzzy clustering. IEEE Trans. Fuzzy Syst. **14**(4), 516–527 (2006)
8. Lei, T., Jia, X., Zhang, Y., et al.: Significantly fast and robust fuzzy C-Means clustering algorithm based on morphological reconstruction and membership filtering. IEEE Trans. Fuzzy Syst. **26**(5), 3027–3041 (2018)
9. Chatzis, S.P., Varvarigou, T.A.: A fuzzy clustering approach toward hidden markov random Field Models for Enhanced Spatially Constrained Image Segmentation. IEEE Trans. Fuzzy Syst. **16**(5), 1351–1361 (2008)
10. Vincent, L., Soille, P.: Watersheds in digital spaces: an efficient algorithm based on immersion simulations. IEEE Trans. Pattern Anal. Mach. Intell. **13**(6), 583–598 (1991)
11. Zeng, Q., Miao, Y., Liu, C., et al.: Algorithm based on marker-controlled watershed transform for overlapping plant fruit segmentation. Opt. Eng. **48**(2), 1–10 (2009)
12. Hamarneh, G., Li, X.: Watershed segmentation using prior shape and appearance knowledge. Image Vis. Comput. **27**(1–2), 59–68 (2009)
13. Lee, S.H.: Object-based classification using region growing segmentation. In: Geoscience & Remote Sensing Symposium, vol. 7, pp. 621–624. IEEE (2011)
14. Pan, C., Xiao, D., Lin. T., et al.: Classification and recognition for major vegetable pests in Southern China using SVM and region growing algorithm. Trans. Chin. Soc. Agricult. Eng. **34**(8), 192–199 (2018)
15. Gong, M., Li, H., Zhang, X., Zhao, Q., et al.: Nonparametric statistical active contour based on inclusion degree of fuzzy sets. IEEE Trans. Fuzzy Syst. **24**(5), 1176–1192 (2016)
16. Mahajan, P.K., Dewasthale, M.M:. An Improved Mean-Shift Algorithm with Self-Scaling Tracking Window. In: 2017 International Conference on Computing, Communication, Control and Automation (ICCUBEA), vol. 7, pp. 17–18 (2017)
17. Hongling, W., Bo, Y., Guodong, T., et al.: Object tracking by applying mean-shift algorithm into particle filtering. In: IEEE International Conference on Broadband Network & Multimedia Technology, vol. 10, pp. 550–554 (2009)
18. Mahapatra, D.: Semi-supervised learning and graph cuts for consensus based medical image segmentation. Pattern Recogn. **63**, 700–709 (2017)
19. Pang, Y., Xie, J., Nie, F., et al.: Spectral clustering by joint spectral embedding and spectral rotation. IEEE Trans. Cybern. **50**(1), 247–258 (2020)
20. Derivaux, S., Forestier, G., Wemmert, C., et al.: Supervised image segmentation using watershed transform, fuzzy classification and evolutionary computation. Pattern Recogn. Lett. **31**(15), 2364–2374 (2010)
21. Zhou, G., Shi, P.: Markov random field magnetic resonance image segmentation. J. Shanghai Jiaotong Univ. (Chin. Ed.) **11**, 1655–1657 (2001)
22. Tao, L., Xiaohong, J., Tongliang, L.: Adaptive morphological reconstruction for seeded image segmentation. IEEE Trans. Image Process. **28**(11), 5510–5523 (2019)
23. Li, Y., Xu, M., Liang, X., et al.: Application of Bandwidth EMD and Adaptive Multiscale Morphology Analysis for Incipient Fault Diagnosis of Rolling Bearings. IEEE Trans. Industr. Electron. **64**(8), 6506–6517 (2017)
24. Wang, K., Gao, L., Guo, L., et al.: Mathematical morphology based image detection for multi-scale structural elements. Journal of Northeastern University **04**, 473–476 (2008)

25. Filyak, M.M., Chetverikova, A.G., Kanygina, O.N., et al.: Wavelet analysis of ceramic surface images as a method for measuring the size of structural elements. Meas. Tech. **63**(2), 130–134 (2020)
26. Zhou, Y., Zhao, T., Wang, Y., et al.: A Linear Fitting Density Peaks Clustering Algorithm for Image Segmentation. Tehnicki Vjesnik **25**(3), 808–812 (2018)
27. Xu, L., Dong, M., Wang, J., et al.: An accuracy evaluating method for image point location based on linear fitting. In: Sixth International Symposium on Precision Mechanical Measurements, vol. 8916, pp. 182–185. International Society for Optics and Photonics (2013)
28. Youqing, X., Cai, Z., Yuan, X.: An improved skeleton extraction method via multi-task and variable Coefficient loss function in natural images. IEEE Access **99**, 1 (2019)
29. Saeed, K., Tabedzki, R., Rybnik, R., et al.: K3M: A universal algorithm for image skeletonization and a review of thinning techniques. Int. J. Appl. Math. Comput. Sci. **20**(2), 317–335 (2010)
30. Liao, M., Zhao, Y.Q., Li, X.H., et al.: Automatic segmentation for cell images based on bottleneck detection and ellipse fitting. Neurocomputing **173**(3), 615–622 (2016)

Design and Implementation of Garbage Classification System Based on Convolutional Neural Network

Qiuduo Zhao[✉], Chen Xiong, and Ke Liu

College of Electronical and Information Engineering, Heilongjiang University of Science and Technology, Harbin 150022, China
duoduo666z@163.com

Abstract. With the development of society, intelligent garbage classification was totally indispensable in life, and it was the key to intelligent garbage classification for the more superior image recognition technology. In order to solve the key problem of garbage identification technology, this paper designed a garbage image classification system based on transfer learning network model to recognize and classify a variety of common garbage images. By comparing the performance of the pretrained models of Alexnet, VGG, Res-Net and Mobile-Net, the optimal recognition accuracy reached more than 93%, and the most suitable network model for deployment and Mobile Terminal was selected, which provided technical support for intelligent garbage identification.

Keywords: Convolutional neural network · Garbage classification · Lightweight network · Transfer learning

1 Introduction

At present, artificial intelligence is a hot topic, and deep learning technology under artificial intelligence is booming. A growing number of industries are researching deep learning and its related technologies. Moreover, the convolutional neural network technology in deep learning has outstanding effects on image processing and recognition.

With the improvement of living standards and the development of urbanization, the amount of domestic garbage has increased sharply, and many cities around the world are facing the crisis of "garbage siege". And garbage classification is considered to be the main measure to solve the garbage dilemma and improve the utilization rate of resources in the existing environment. However, the implementation of garbage classification is not optimistic, mainly because the relevant laws and regulations are not perfect, the residents' awareness of garbage classification is not strong, and there are too many types of garbage that are difficult to accurately classify. Therefore, it is necessary to study the application of related technologies to improve the efficiency and accuracy of garbage classification, as well as to further develop related smart devices and garbage classification applications. This can not only improve the efficiency of garbage classification,

A. Li et al. (Eds.): 6GN 2022, LNICST 505, pp. 182–193, 2023.
https://doi.org/10.1007/978-3-031-36014-5_15

but also solve the disadvantages of high labor intensity and poor working environment in related work. Applying deep learning technology to garbage classification can also protect the ecological environment and promote economic development. The core technology of garbage classification is the identification and classification of garbage images. At present, deep learning has made remarkable progress in the field of computer vision, surpassing the human eye in image classification accuracy. Therefore, it is necessary to study the use of deep learning technology to classify garbage. For example, the research on garbage classification based on machine vision proposed by Jian Wu et al. [1], HSV algorithm and K-means clustering algorithm proposed by Huiling Huang et al. [2] can identify and classify construction waste images in real time. Bicheng Wu et al. [3] proposed to use InceptionV3 as the feature extraction of junk images, which are not suitable for mobile phones and embedded devices. Ling Wu et al. [4] proposed the Inception-ResnetV2 garbage classification and designed it for Web application invocation model. Zhuang Kang et al. [5] proposed a garbage type identification method based on the combination of Inception v3 network feature extraction model and transfer learning.

This paper selects a network model that can be deployed on mobile devices and embedded devices, which should have a small amount of computation, few implementation parameters, and a good performance in recognition accuracy.

2 Relevant Technical Basis

2.1 Model Selection

According to the current convolutional neural network technology, we choose to build AlexNet, which brings the neural network into the popular research field again, and VGG, which has a deep network layer depth. As well as Resnet, which surpasses the level of human recognition in one fell swoop, and MobileNet, which has a smaller model and fewer parameters, these four network models carry out related experiments and practices.

2.2 Image Classification Pre-model

Convolutional neural networks which is the most commonly used models for detection and classification currently have important features that weight sharing and local connection in deep learning. And there are less parameters and higher accuracy than other network models. Lecun et al. [6] proposed a convolutional neural network, which is a deep neural network model that operates on convolutional layers. At present, convolutional neural networks have achieved unprecedented success in the field of computer vision. Since Krizhevsky et al. [7] proposed the AlexNet network, various classification networks have been proposed continuously, among which the typical representatives are VGG [8], GoogleNet [9], ResNet [10] and so on. However, as the number of network layers continues to deepen, the phenomenon of gradient explosion appears. At the same time, the amount of parameters and the amount of computation continue to increase, and the running time of the network also continues to increase. MobileNetv2 [11] is a lightweight neural network proposed by the Google team in 2018. Compared with the MobileNetv1 version, the model parameters are reduced by 20%, but its accuracy exceeds that of MobileNetv1. The main features of Mobile Netv2 include: 1) Use depthwise separable convolutions to replace ordinary convolutions to reduce the amount of computation and parameters of the model; 2) Propose a reverse residual structure to deepen the number of network layers and enhance the expressiveness of features; 3) Adopt The linear bottleneck structure replaces the nonlinear bottleneck and reduces the loss of low-dimensional feature information. MobileNetv3 [12] is a lightweight network model proposed by the Google team in 2019. It has two versions, small and large, and has an SE module. It uses neural structure search to search for network configurations and parameters. Both accuracy and speed are better than the v2 version.

3 Structural Modules

3.1 Residual Structure

With the deepening of the network layers, the objective function is more and more likely to fall into the local optimal solution. At the same time, as the number of layers increases, the problem of gradient disappearance becomes more serious, especially when the activation function is sigmoid/softmax/tanh, etc., so that the network parameters of the principle output layer cannot be effectively learned. Therefore, many methods were born to improve this problem, such as regularization, dropout, designing special networks, modifying training algorithms, etc. Residual Network is a very effective network to alleviate the gradient disappearance problem, which greatly improves the depth of the network that can be effectively trained. Residual units can be implemented in the form of skip-layer connections, where the input of the unit is directly added to the output of the unit, and then activated. Figure 1 shows the standard network structure and residual network structure. Therefore, the residual network can be easily implemented with the mainstream automatic differential deep learning framework, and the gradient of the output of a certain low-level output by directly using the BP algorithm to update the parameter loss is decomposed into two items.

3.2 Separate Convolution

Depthwise separable convolution consists of depthwise convolution and pointwise convolution. Depthwise convolution is different from ordinary convolution. In the convolution process, one channel of the feature map is convolved by only one convolution kernel. The number is equal to the number of channels. The expression of depthwise convolution is as follows:

$$G_{i,j,m} = \sum_{W,h}^{W,H} K_{w,h,m} * X_{i+w+h,m} \tag{1}$$

The above formula G is the output feature map, and K is the convolution kernel with width W and height H. X is the input feature map, and m represents the mth channel of the feature map. i, j represent the i, j coordinates of the output feature map on the mth

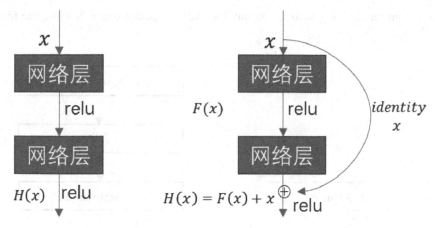

Fig. 1. Standard network structure and residual network structure

channel. w and h are the weight element coordinates of the convolution kernel of the mth channel. Point-by-point convolution is basically the same as normal convolution, except that the size of the convolution kernel is set to 1×1. Among them, the first depth convolution function is to use a single convolution kernel for each input channel, and the calculation process is only a convolution operation corresponding to the number of channels. The 1×1 convolution kernel combines the feature maps after depthwise convolution to change the number of channels. The comparison calculation process of the two convolutions is shown in the following figure.

In the standard convolution calculation process, a large convolution kernel can increase the receptive field of the convolution kernel on the input feature map, so that the feature extraction accuracy is higher. However, at the same time, the large convolution kernel is also relatively large in terms of parameters, which is not conducive to the operation of mobile phones, embedded devices and other devices.

3.3 SE Channel Attention Mechanism

By modeling the dependence of each channel to improve the representation ability of the network, and the features can be adjusted channel by channel. The SE network can learn to selectively enhance the features containing useful information and suppress useless features through global information. The basic structure of SE block [13] is shown in Fig. 3. The first step of squeezing is to use the global spatial features of each channel as the representation of the channel to form a channel descriptor. The second step of the excitation operation is to learn the degree of dependence on each channel, and adjust the feature map according to the degree of dependence. The adjusted feature map is the output of the SE block.

The core idea of SE is to automatically learn the feature weights according to the loss loss through the fully connected network, instead of directly judging according to the numerical distribution of the feature channels, so that the weights of the effective feature channels are large. Of course, the SE attention mechanism inevitably increases some parameters and calculation amount, but the cost performance is still quite high (Fig. 2).

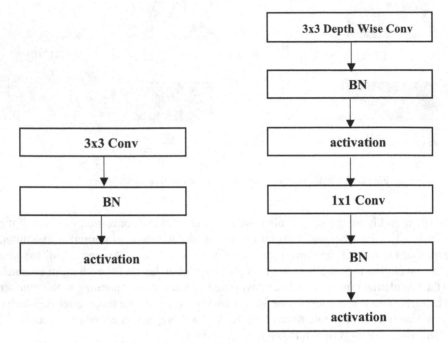

Fig. 2. Normal convolution and separable convolution

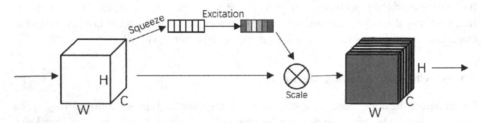

Fig. 3. Squeeze-and-Excitation block.

4   Experimental Analysis

4.1   Dataset Establishment

The data set is based on the data set published by Huawei. Choosing nine according to the daily life of the family. Also adding toothpaste hose as a data set which from Baidu photo library. A mobile phone camera was used to collect 100 pictures as a test set. The collected data needs to be cleaned and the image size adjusted to fit the training model.

Use 3271 images as training set, 358 images as validation set, and 100 photos as test set (10 for each item). The specific quantity of each garbage item is shown in Table 1 below. There are a total of 10 types, and they are also marked with secondary classification, according to dry garbage, recyclable garbage, harmful garbage and wet garbage.

Table 1. The sample distribution of the dataset

List	number/piece
Cans-recycle	309
carton-recycle	318
dry cell-harmful	320
fruit peel-wet	381
garbage bag-recycle	363
kitchen garbage-wet	576
medicine box-recycle	364
plastic bottle-recycle	318
shoe-recycle	376
tootpaste-dry	227

4.2 Development Environment Construction

The experimental training environment is an online server. Under the Linux system, the CPU is 6-core Intel(R) Xeon(R) Silver 4310@2.10 GHZ, the graphics card is RTX A4000, and the video memory is 16 G to complete the training and testing. The model optimizer chooses Adam, and the loss function is the cross-entropy loss function. The network training parameters are all set to bitch size set to 32, Epoch set to 30, and Learning-rate set to 0.0002.

4.3 Ablation Experiment

In order to select a network model more suitable for deployment in mobile terminals, it is necessary to verify the performance of each network model. In the ablation experiment, the accuracy of the model in the test set top1 is mainly used as an indicator. it includes the effect verification of each network model, transfer learning and the effect improvement under data enhancement.

For training four network models, choose AlexNet, VGG model choose VGG-16, ResNet choose Resnet-34, MobileNet choose v2 and v3-small version. Compare the training accuracy and runtime of five different network models. For ResNet, MobileNet performs transfer learning to train the network model and compares it with the model without transfer learning. Among the two models, ResNet selects ResNet34, ResNet101, and MobileNet selects MobilNetv2, MobilNetv3-small and MobilNetv3-large to compare the training set and test set accuracy and running time of the transfer learning network model. In order to verify the effect of the dataset size on the network model, we used data augmentation to expand the dataset, and selected 10 of them to perform dataset filling contrast experiments, using brightness enhancement, contrast enhancement, rotation angle, and flipping images. A total of 16355 images are used as training set and 358 images are used as validation set. Finally, 100 self-built datasets are used to test the model effect to select the most suitable model for mobile terminals and embedded devices (Fig. 4).

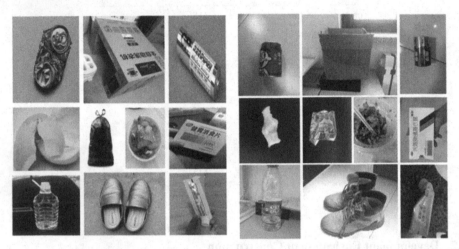

Fig. 4. The training set (left) and testing set (right) are displayed

4.4 Comparative Analysis of Model Methods

In Table 2, it can be seen that the maximum error of VGG-16 in the training error term is 1.222, and the best performance is Resnet-34 which adds residual module, and the training error is 0.776. The reason is that the VGG model is large, and there are many parameters to be trained, so the number of iterations needs to be increased. It can be predicted that with the increase of the number of iterations or the increase of the data set, the training error of the VGG model will also decrease, and the model performance will also become better, and it will be better than AlexNet. Under the same data set and 30 iterations, the Resnet network model has the best effect, with an accuracy rate of 0.709 on the validation set, followed by the related model of MobileNet, which uses an inverted residual structure, so it also has a good performance. Under the same training task, it can be seen that the entire training process of VGG-16 takes the longest, reaching 1088.4 s. Under the same dataset and 30 iterations, the ResNet network model performs the best, with an accuracy of 0.709 on the validation set. The second is the related model of MobileNet, which uses an inverted residual structure. So there is also a good performance. Under the same training task, it can be seen that the entire training process of VGG-16 takes the longest, reaching 1088.4 s. AlexNet's network layer model is small and takes the shortest time to complete training. In contrast, the MobileNet network uses convolutions with separable depths for computation, so it has fewer parameters. The MobileNetv3-small network model in the table has more advantages, its training time is short, and the accuracy of the validation set is relatively high.

In Table 3, it can be seen that in the training error term, the MobileNetv3-large error is the smallest at 0.094, while the worst performance is the best performing Resnet-34 without transfer learning, with a training error of 0.22. The ResNet-101 model is large and deep, and requires a lot of parameters to be trained, which takes a long time. When the data set is large and the number of iterations is sufficient, the effect of the model trained by it is theoretically the best. MobileNetv3-small is more suitable for the dataset used in this experiment in terms of network model size. In terms of validation set accuracy, the MobileNetv3-small network model performs the best, with a validation set accuracy rate of 0.961, followed by the large model. Under the same training task, it can be seen that the training time of the ResNet model is higher than that of the related models of MobileNet. The entire training process of ResNet-101 takes the longest, reaching 1175.2 s. The network layer model of MobileNetv3-small is smaller, the shortest time to complete the training. In Table 4, when the data set is enlarged, the test set error of each model is also better, and the best is 0.063 of MobileNetv3-large. By comparison, it can be obtained that the accuracy rate of the validation set is 0.941, which is the MobileNetv3-large network. In the case of sufficient data sets, the model effect will have better performance. After using data augmentation, the generalization ability is enhanced.

Table 2. The result of network model

Net	train_loss	val_accuracy	Full time(s)
AlexNet	0.922	0.693	228.5
VGG-16	1.222	0.617	1088.4
ResNet-34	0.776	0.709	441.1
MobileNetv2	1.022	0.687	359.2
MobileNetv3-small	1.000	0.707	275.6

Tested with 100 photos from the self-built test dataset. Figure 5 shows the test results. As shown in Table 5, MobileNetv3-small has the best effect, with an accuracy rate of 79% and a model size of 5.96 MB. The model takes into account the small amount of parameters and high accuracy, thanks to the addition of the SE attention mechanism. Its parameters are indeed less than the v2 model, and it is better than other compared models, which is consistent with the conclusions of v3 and the original paper.

For the convolutional neural network, the network model using the residual structure or the inverted residual structure is indeed better than the unused model (such as the model selection in Table 2). When the network model has advantages, even if the modulus parameters are small, the effect can also be better than the network effect of the large

Table 3. The result of transfer learning

Net	train_loss	val_accuracy	Full time(s)
ResNet-34	0.222	0.913	451.3
ResNet-101	0.183	0.919	1175.2
MobileNetv2	0.143	0.933	355.2
MobileNetv3-small	0.110	0.961	269.3
MobileNetv3-large	0.094	0.953	330.5

Table 4. The result of data augmentation

Net	train_loss	T-enhance	val_accuracy
Resnet-34	0.222	0.131	0.913
ResNet-101	0.183	0.114	0.919
MobileNetv2	0.143	0.113	0.933
MobileNetv3-small	0.110	0.086	0.961
MobileNetv3-large	0.094	0.063	0.953

model. This is consistent with the conclusion of the original paper of ResNet [7] proposed by Kaiming He. In the case of insufficient data sets, it will affect the performance of the model. For fewer datasets, small models tend to perform better than large models. We need to choose the network model according to the actual situation of the project. The effect of using transfer learning is better than that without transfer learning. And it is friendly to small data sets, and it can get good recognition results without multiple exercises, which saves time and is economical. Transfer learning has become one of the most important and commonly used augmentation techniques. In data preprocessing, data augmentation is used to expand the data set, which can improve the effect of the network model and enhance the generalization ability of the network. In choosing the network model, it is obvious that the MobileNet-related network model is more suitable for the purpose of this paper. The above conclusions are more suitable for the garbage classification task to choose MobileNetv3-small.

Fig. 5. The result of testing set displayed

Table 5. The result of test set

Net	Weight size(MB)	Test
AlexNet	55.71	43%
VGG-16	512.33	/
ResNet-34	81.35	74%
ResNet-101	162.81	/
MobileNetv2	8.77	74%
MobileNetv3-small	5.96	79%
MobileNetv3-large	16.31	78%

5 Conclusion

This paper compares the four network models of AlexNet, VGG, ResNet, and MobileNet. After continuous comparative experiments, the MobileNetv3-small model was finally selected to develop a garbage classification model. It has fewer parameters, less memory consumption, and shorter computing time, making it more suitable for deployment in mobile terminals. In addition to the effect of transfer learning, it has a very good effect, and the accuracy rate on the data set has reached 96.1%. After expanding the scale of the data set by means of image enhancement, the accuracy of model recognition can reach 91.9%, and the accuracy on the test data set can reach 79%. In the future, if the data set is increased, it is believed that the improvement of accuracy will be even higher. The network is deployed on mobile phones and embedded devices for garbage identification and classification.

Acknowledgements. This work was financed by the Technological Project of Heilongjiang Province "The open competition mechanism to select the best candidates" (No. 2022ZXJ05C01), Funding for the Opening Project of Key Laboratory of Agricultural Renewable Resource Utilization Technology (No. HLJHDNY2114), Key project of the 14th Five-Year Plan of Education Science of Heilongjiang Province in 2021(No.GJB1421563), and Heilongjiang University of Science and Technology the introduction of high-level talent research start-up fund projects (No. 000009020315).

References

1. Jian, W., Hao, C., Wu, F.: Research on analysis and identification of waste based on computer vision. Inf. Technol. Inf. **10**, 81–83 (2016)
2. Huang, H., Han, J., Feibin, W., et al.: Research on color feature extraction and classification of construction waste. Optics Optoelect. Technol. **16**(1), 53–57 (2018)
3. Wu, B., Deng, X., et al.: Intelligent garbage classification system based on convolutional neural network. Phys. Experim. **39**(11) (2019)
4. Ling, W., Wang, H., Zhang, X., et al.: Design and implementation of garbage classification system based on deep transfer learning. J. Shenyang Univ. Nat. Sci. Edn, **32**(6), 496–502 (2020)
5. Kang, Z., Yang, J., et al.: Design of automatic garbage classification system based on machine vision. J. Zhejiang Univ. (Eng. Sci. Edn.) **54**(07) (2020)
6. LeCun, Y., Boser, B., Denker, J.S., et al.: Backpropagation applied to handwritten zip code recognition. Neural Comput. **1**(4), 541–551 (1989)
7. Krizhevsky, A., Sutskever, I., Hinton, G.E.: Imagenet classification with deep convolutional neural networks. Commun. ACM **60**(6), 84–90 (2017)
8. Simonyan, K., Zisserman, A.: Very deep convolutional networks for large-scale image recognition. arXiv preprint arXiv:1409.1556. (2014)
9. Szegedy. C., Liu, W., Jia, Y., et al.: Going deeper with convolutions. In: Proceedings of the IEEE Conference on Computer Vision and Pattern Recognition, pp. 1–9 (2015)
10. He, K., Zhang, X., Ren, S., et al.: Deep residual learning for image recognition. In: Proceedings of the IEEE Conference on Computer Vision and Pattern Recognition, pp. 770–778 (2016)
11. Sandler, M., Howard, A., Zhu, M., et al.: Mobilenetv2: Inverted residuals and linear bottlenecks. In: Proceedings of the IEEE Conference on Computer Vision and Pattern Recognition, pp. 4510–4520 (2018)

12. Howard, A., Sandler, M., Chu, G., et al.: Searching for mobilenetv3. In: Proceedings of the IEEE/CVF International Conference on Computer Vision, pp. 1314–1324 (2019)
13. Hu. J., Shen, L., Sun, G.: Squeeze-and-excitation networks. In: Proceedings of the IEEE Conference on Computer Vision and Pattern Recognition, pp. 7132–7141 (2018)

Study on the Effect of Total Se Content of Chinese Cabbage Fermentation Broth on Its Quality Evaluation Based on Wireless Environmental Monitoring

Liming Wang[1] and Qiuduo Zhao[2](✉)

[1] Heilongjiang University of Finance and Economics, Harbin 150030, China
[2] College of Electronical and Information Engineering, Heilongjiang University of Science and Technology, Harbin 150022, China
duoduo666z@163.com

Abstract. Selenium is an indispensable trace element in bodies. Se has both promoting and inhibiting effects on fermentation broth. Therefore, the wireless sensor was used to collect and effectively adjust the environmental change parameters in the fermentation process of Se-rich raw materials. The potential of Se-rich Chinese cabbage in Hailun City, China as raw materials for fermentation broth preparation can be found. The different total Se, the influence of it on other indexes was analyzed, and the correlation analysis was used to study the influence of different total Se on the quality factors of the fermentation broth, which was used to determine the quality evaluation index of Chinese cabbage. Firstly, the differences of total Se content in Chinese cabbage samples from 25 different towns in Hailun City, China were collected under the monitoring and regulation of wireless environmental monitoring system. In order to better evaluate the fermentation broth of Chinese cabbage, the correlation between the total Se and the pH, soluble sugar, protein and antioxidant activity was studied. Considering the influence factors of the regional soil Se-enriched degree on the total Se of Chinese cabbage fermentation broth, the PCA was used to reduce the dimension of it evaluation index. Variables to achieve the optimization of the evaluation system, It can provide new ideas for the quality evaluation of Se-enriched Chinese cabbage fermentation broth in this region and similar regions.

Keywords: PCA · Chinese cabbage enzyme · Total selenium content · Evaluation index

1 Introduction

Selenium(Se) is an indispensable trace element in the body [1–4]. Although there is still no conclusion on whether Se is an essential element for plants, it was found that Se had an effect on seed germination, root vitality, plant growth, fruit yield and quality, etc. Se can promote plant growth and improve plant stress resistance. Li et al. [5] Soybean seeds had

A. Li et al. (Eds.): 6GN 2022, LNICST 505, pp. 194–205, 2023.
https://doi.org/10.1007/978-3-031-36014-5_16

been treated with 0.05 mol·L^{-1} Se, which significantly improved the germination rate, germination potential, germination index and vigor index of soybean. Li [6] Also under low-concentration Se treatment, it was found that the application of Se could promote the growth of pakchoi, and some studies found that Se m promoted the formation and accumulation of active ingredients such as protein and nicotine in tobacco. However, due to the very narrow threshold of Se, the danger of toxicity has occurred at high concentrations [7, 8], causing Se poisoning in plants, resulting in poor plant growth and plant diseases [9]. At the same time, Se has a dual character, which not only promotes the growth of microorganisms, but also inhibits the growth of microorganisms. Kenward et al. [10] and Lee et al. [11] they all found that the level of Se concentration has a great effect on the activity of microorganisms. Low concentrations of Se has a promoting effect on microorganisms, while high concentrations of Se is more toxic and will rapidly weaken the activity and diversity of microorganisms.

2 Materials and Methods

2.1 Materials to Be Tested Structural Modules

The experiment was carried out in a demonstration base in Harbin City, Heilongjiang Province. Chinese cabbage was selected from Hailun City, Heilongjiang Province. The wireless sensor environment monitoring system was designed and provided by the laboratory of Heilongjiang University of Finance and Economics.

The test materials were all selected from Hailun City, Heilongjiang Province, China, and were purchased from vegetable markets in 25 regions. The sampling information of Chinese cabbage is shown in Table 1.

Water, brown sugar and fermentation containers were purchased from Liming Market, Xiangfang District, Harbin City.

2.2 Experimental Design

Chinese cabbage from 25 towns in Hailun City was selected as the fermentation raw material for the Se-enriched agricultural fermentation broth. According to the ratio of brown sugar: fresh fruit and vegetable: water = 1:3:10, the fresh Chinese cabbage was removed from the mud and rot, and then cut into pieces and brown sugar, water into the fermentation bucket, stir gently until the brown sugar is completely dissolved in the water. Each experiment repeated 3 times, and the fermentation process managed uniformly: the fermentation device, fermentation environment, treatment method, and fermentation time were all the same.

2.3 Test Methods

Determination of environmental parameters: In this experiment, the wireless sensor environmental monitoring system was selected for acquisition and measurement. The system mainly included: the wireless communication module was composed of CC2530 and Zigbee, and the environmental data acquisition module includes temperature sensor, Hall sensor and photosensitive sensor. The MCU of the monitoring system was 89C51.

Table 1. Information of Chinese Cabbage samples

Materials	Sampling location	Time
Chinese cabbage1	No. 1 town	2018.10
Chinese cabbage2	No. 2 town	2018.10
Chinese cabbage3	No. 3 town	2018.10
Chinese cabbage4	No. 4 town	2018.10
Chinese cabbage5	No. 5 town	2018.10
Chinese cabbage6	No. 6 town	2018.10
Chinese cabbage7	No. 7 town	2018.10
Chinese cabbage8	No. 8 town	2018.10
Chinese cabbage9	No. 9 town	2018.10
Chinese cabbage10	No. 10 town	2018.10
Chinese cabbage11	No. 11 town	2018.10
Chinese cabbage12	No. 12 town	2018.10
Chinese cabbage13	No. 13 town	2018.10
Chinese cabbage14	No. 14 town	2018.10
Chinese cabbage15	No. 15 town	2018.10
Chinese cabbage16	No. 16 town	2018.10
Chinese cabbage17	No. 17 town	2018.10
Chinese cabbage18	No. 18 town	2018.10
Chinese cabbage19	No. 19 town	2018.10
Chinese cabbage20	No. 20 town	2018.10
Chinese cabbage21	No. 21 town	2018.10
Chinese cabbage22	No. 22 town	2018.10
Chinese cabbage23	No. 23 town	2018.10
Chinese cabbage24	No. 24 town	2018.10
Chinese cabbage25	No. 25 town	2018.10

Determination of physicochemical properties of enzymes: The physicochemical properties of samples were determined using the measurement method of Zhao [13, 14].

2.4 Data Analysis

Choose Excel2013, SPSS, IBM SPSS Statistics 26, Origin2016 and other analysis software. The main analysis methods include: variance analysis, correlation analysis, principal component analysis and so on.

3   Results and Discussion

3.1   Influence of Towns in Hailun City on Total Se Content in Chinese Cabbage Fermentation Broth

The distribution of soil Se content in different towns of Hailun City was different. The principle of raw material sample selection was to select 25 representative samples according to the administrative division. Figure 1 showed that the total selenium content in the fermentation broth of each treatment ranged from 0.097 mg·kg^{-1}–0.178 mg·kg^{-1}. The total Se content of Chinese cabbage fermentation broth was the highest in No. 14 town of Hailun City. The second was the fermentation broth of Chinese cabbage in No. 7, 6 and 9 towns of Hailun City. The total Se content of the Chinese cabbage fermentation broth in No. 4 town of Hailun City is the lowest, and the selenium content in other areas is similar. This result was due to the difference in soil Se content in different regions, among which the average Se-enriched level of soil in towns (No. 5, 6, 7, 9, 14, 17, and 19) was higher than that in other regions. But there were exceptions. Such as the Se-enriched level of soil in towns (No. 21 and No. 22) were lower than that in the above-mentioned areas. This was because Chinese cabbage had liquidity when it was sold, resulting in errors. The total Se level of the fermentation broth prepared from the Chinese cabbage in the farmer's vegetable garden tended to be stable, and it tended to be consistent with the Se level of soil, such as the Chinese cabbage fermentation broth in No. 1 Town, Hailun City. Based on the total Se level of Chinese cabbage fermentation broth in all towns in Hailun City, the average Se-enriched level of Chinese cabbage fermentation broth in all towns in Hailun City was 0.134 ± 0.012 mg·kg^{-1}, This shown that the Se level of Chinese cabbage fermentation broth in Hailun meets the Se content level of Se products in my country.

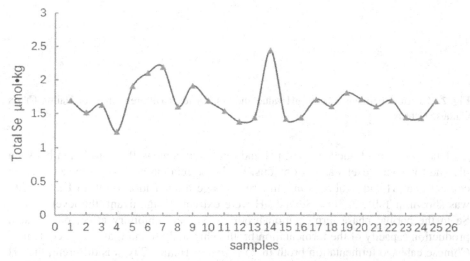

Fig. 1. Fermented broth Total Se of Different areas of Hailun City's Chinese Cabbage

3.2 The Effect of Total Se Content on pH and Total Acid Content in Chinese Cabbage Fermentation Broth in Hailun City

pH and total acid content was important evaluation indicators of fermentation broth products. As Fig. 2, it shown that the pH level range of 25 areas in Hailun City is between 3.09–3.28, and the overall fluctuation was small. The lowest was the fermentation broth of Chinese cabbage in Town No. 4, the highest was the fermentation broth of Chinese cabbage in Town No. 14, and the pH levels of the fermentation broth of Chinese cabbage in other towns were between them. The average pH level of Chinese cabbage fermentation broth in the towns of Hailun City was: 3.19 ± 0.14, which indicated that the origin of Chinese cabbage had little effect on the pH value of Chinese cabbage fermentation broth, The total acid level of the fermentation broth in these towns, it ranged from 0.13 g·100 mL^{-1}–0.25 g·100 mL^{-1} (calculated as acetic acid). The highest total acid content of Chinese cabbage fermentation broth were No. 4 and No. 8 towns, and the lowest were No. 14 and No. 18 towns. The average total acid content was: 0.17 ± 0.147 g·100 mL^{-1}, which indicated that the total acid level of Chinese cabbage fermentation broth in Hailun City was close.

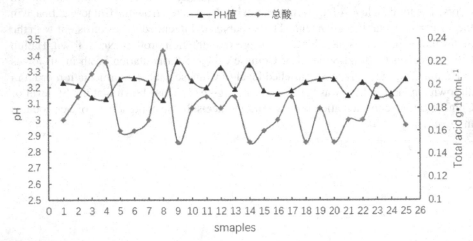

Fig. 2. Different Fermented broth pH value and Total acid of Different areas of Hailun City's Chinese Cabbage.

Due to the small fluctuation of pH and total acid content, the correlation between pH and total acid level was not obvious. So the correlation analysis between total Se content and pH and total acid in Chinese cabbage fermentation broth in Hailun City was shown in Table 2. Total Se and pH were extremely significant, the level of total Se in the normal phase fermentation broth showed an inhibitory effect on the acid production capacity of the fermentation broth. This study found that the Se content of Chinese cabbage fermentation broth in 25 towns of Hailun City was different, the pH value increased with the increase of Se content, the total acid content decreased with the increase of Se content. Through correlation analysis, the decrease of total acid content could be used as an evaluation index of Se content in Chinese cabbage fermentation broth (Correlation coefficient: -0.866^{**}). By monitoring the pH and total acid level of the Chinese cabbage fermentation broth, the total Se level in the Chinese cabbage fermentation broth was judged initially.

Table 2. Correlation coefficient between Total Se and pH value and Total acid of Chinese Cabbrage Fermented liquid

Factors	Total Se	Total acid	pH
Total Se	1	-0.866^{**}	0.766^{**}
Total acid		1	-0.819^{*}
pH			1

* $P < 0.05$, ** $P < 0.01$, the correlation is significant.

3.3 Effect of Total Se Content of Chinese Cabbage Fermentation Broth on Soluble Sugar Content in Hailun City

According to Chinese industry standards, soluble sugar is an important evaluation index for fruit and vegetable fermentation broth. Its level not only determined the quality of fermentation broth, but also provided quality assurance for fruit and vegetable breeding. As shown Fig. 3: except that the soluble sugar content of Chinese cabbage fermentation broth in No. 3 and No. 6 towns in Hailun City was significantly higher than others, the distribution of soluble sugar content in other towns was not significantly different. The average level of soluble sugar content in Chinese cabbage fermentation broth was 4.11 $\pm$ 0.109 $\mu g \cdot mL^{-1}$.

In order to further understood the effect of total Se content in Chinese cabbage fermentation broth on soluble sugar in Hailun City, The analysis of variance was performed on the soluble sugar. As Table 3, there was a significant difference between the total Se level in the Chinese cabbage fermentation broth and the soluble sugar content ($P < 0.05$), and the correlation was poor, which indicated that the judgment of soluble sugar could not be used as a Evaluation index of Se-enriched Chinese cabbage fermentation broth. Because Se content maybe have a great influence on microorganisms, but the critical threshold was very narrow, which was reflected in the changes in the number of microorganisms such as lactic acid bacteria and yeast, which had a large fluctuation effect on the metabolic capacity of soluble sugar.

3.4 Effect of Total Se Content in Chinese Cabbage Fermentation Broth on Protein Concentration in Hailun City

As Fig. 4, the protein concentration range of Chinese cabbage fermentation broth in 25 towns of Hailun City is: 4063.12–5065.84 $\mu g \cdot mL^{-1}$, The highest protein concentration of Chinese cabbage fermentation broth was in the towns No. 14 and 19, and the lowest was in the towns No. 14 and 19. The protein concentration of the fermentation broth in

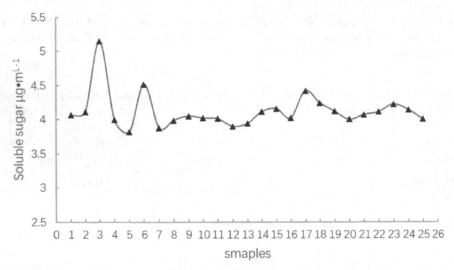

Fig. 3. Different Fermented liquid Soluble sugar of Different areas of Hailun City's Chinese.

Table 3. Analysis of variance for influence between Total Se and Soluble sugar of Chinese Cabbrage Fermented liquid

Source	SS	Df	Ms	F	salience
Deal with	1.652a	20	.083	8.743	0.024
error	0.038	4	0.009		
total variation	1.689	24		1	

other towns was between them, and the protein concentration in each region fluctuated greatly. The overall analysis showed that the average protein concentration level of Chinese cabbage fermentation broth in various regions of Hailun City was 4672.56 ± 253.66 $\mu g \cdot mL^{-1}$, The total Se level in the fermentation broth ($P < 0.01$) of Chinese cabbage in various regions of Hailun City was positively correlated with the protein content, and the correlation coefficient was 0.695(Table 4). This showed that there was a correlation between the total Se level and the protein content in the fermentation broth of Chinese cabbage, and the total Se played a role in promoting the protein content. Studies had also shown that the macromolecular Se present in plants mainly exists in the form of selenoprotein, Se polysaccharide, and Se nucleic acid. It showed that applying Se fertilizer to soybean leaves can significantly increased the content of selenoprotein in soybean [15], Se had a promoting effect on protein concentration. It showd that a part of Se in the fermentation broth of Chinese cabbage exists in the form of selenoprotein, which had great reference significance for the use of Se-enriched fermentation broth to supplement Se for plants.

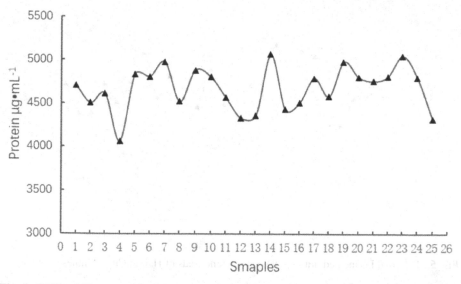

Fig. 4. Different Fermented liquid Protein of Different areas of Hailun City's Chinese Cabbage.

Table 4. Correlation coefficient between Total Se and Protein of Chinese Cabbrage Fermented liquid.

	Total Se	Protein
Total Se	1	0.695^{**}
Protein		1

**. $P < 0.01$, the correlation is significant.

3.5 Effect of Total Se Content in Chinese Cabbage Fermentation Broth on Antioxidant Activity in Hailun City

3.5.1 Effect of Total Se Content in Chinese Cabbage Fermentation Broth on SOD in Hailun City

Superoxide dismutase (SOD) is an important antioxidant enzyme in life, which can scavenge free radicals in living organisms. SOD was a protective enzyme that reduces superoxide anion, and its level directly affects the antioxidant capacity of Chinese cabbage fermentation broth (Fig. 5). The influence range of SOD of Chinese cabbage fermentation broth in 25 towns of Hailun City was: 230.22–259.68 $U \cdot g^{-1}$. The SOD activity of Chinese cabbage fermentation broth was the highest in No. 9 towns, and the lowest in No. 4 and No. 3 towns. This showed that the SOD activity level of the Chinese cabbage fermentation broth in Hailun City was higher, indicating that the anti-aging and antioxidant capacity of the Chinese cabbage fermentation broth in Hailun City was better, and had a protective effect on plants.

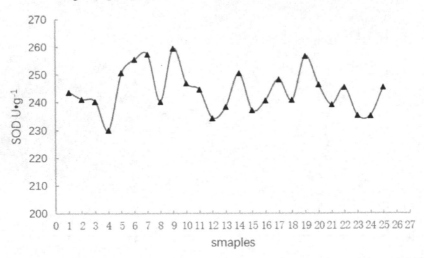

Fig. 5. Different Fermented liquid SOD of Different areas of Hailun City's Chinese Cabbage.

3.5.2 Effect of Total Se Content in Chinese Cabbage Fermentation Broth on Total Antioxidant Capacity in Hailun City

The total antioxidant capacity of Chinese cabbage fermentation broth in different towns of Hailun City was not consistent (Fig. 6), and the variation range was: 0.256–0.326U·mL^{-1}. The reason why the total antioxidant capacity of Chinese cabbage fermentation broth was the lowest in No. 4 town,it was that there was a risk of non-local Chinese cabbage in the vegetable market. The average total antioxidant capacity of Chinese cabbage fermentation broth was 0.301U·mL^{-1}, and a total of 16 towns (No. 1, 2, 3, etc.), It showed that the antioxidant capacity of Chinese cabbage fermentation broth was similar in different regions of Hailun City.

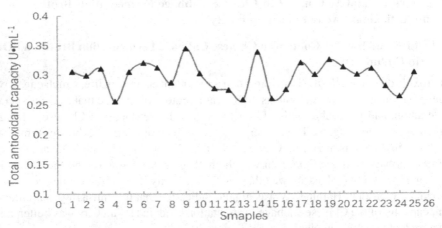

Fig. 6. Different Fermented liquid Total antioxidant capacity of Different areas of Hailun City's Chinese Cabbage

3.5.3   Correlation Analysis Between Total Se Content and Antioxidant Activity in Chinese Cabbage Fermentation Broth in Hailun City

The correlation analysis between total Se level and antioxidant activity in Chinese cabbage fermentation broth was shown in Table 5. The total Se level was significantly positively correlated with SOD, and was extremely significantly negatively correlated with the total antioxidant capacity, which indicated that the total Se level in the Chinese cabbage fermentation broth increased the antioxidant components in the fermentation broth, reduced the Se toxicity, and increased the Se toxicity. Promoting effect of Se on the antioxidant activity of fermentation broth. In this study, the Se content of the fermentation broth of Chinese cabbage in 25 towns of Hailun City was different. SOD increased with the increase of Se content, and the total antioxidant capacity decreased with the increase of Se content. When the Se concentration reached the threshold, its antioxidant capacity increased. Oxidation was significantly reduced. When the total Se content was between $0.097\text{–}0.134$ $\mu mol \cdot kg^{-1}$, Se could improve the body's antioxidant capacity. Studies showed that supplementing an appropriate amount of plant active Se to athletes reduced lipid peroxidation in athletes, improved athletes' endurance and the body's antioxidant capacity. The correlation analysis showed that the change of antioxidant activity was used as the evaluation index of Se content in Chinese cabbage fermentation broth (very significant positive correlation coefficients: 0.893^{**} and 0.873^{**}) to determine the level of Se in Chinese cabbage fermentation broth.

Table 5. Correlation coefficient between Total Se and Antioxidant of Chinese Cabbrage Fermented liquid

	Total Se	SOD	Total antioxidant capacity
Total Se	1	$0.8.93^{**}$	0.873^{**}
SOD		1	0.856^{**}
Total antioxidant capacity			1

* $P < 0.05$, ** $P < 0.01$, the correlation is significant.

3.6   Comprehensive Evaluation Index of Helen Chinese Cabbage Fermentation Broth Based on PCA

Through principal component analysis of total Se, pH, total acid, protein, soluble sugar, SOD and total antioxidant capacity of Chinese cabbage fermentation broth in Hailun City. From Table 6, It showed that in the first principal component, total Se, SOD enzyme activity, total antioxidant capacity, protein concentration, and pH. They were positive correlation coefficients, total acid had a negative correlation coefficient. While soluble sugar has a small negative correlation coefficient (-0.012), and the contribution rate of the first principal component was 58.664%, indicating that in the first principal component, soluble sugar was not the main reference component, indicating that the first principal component can be used as HaiLun city was the fermentation of Chinese cabbage. A measure of broth Se levels. In the second principal component, the positive correlation coefficient of soluble sugar (0.878), the positive correlation coefficient of total acid (0.427), the positive correlation coefficient of protein concentration (0.313), the negative correlation coefficient of pH (−0.438), the The public contribution rate was 19.09, and the cumulative contribution rate was 77.744%. The second component was used as a measure of nutrients in enzymes. The total contribution rate of the third index was 8.953%, which was used as a measure to measure other factors of the fermentation broth.

Table 6. Principal Component Analysis

Component	Total	Variance %	Cumulative contribution rate %
1	4.106	58.664	58.664
2	1.336	19.080	77.744
3	0.629	8.983	86.727

4 Conclusion

Taking the fermentation broth of Chinese cabbage from 25 towns in Hailun City, Heilongjiang Province, China as the research object, it was prepared based on wireless environmental monitoring. The influence of different total Se content on the quality factors of fermentation broth was studied, and the quality evaluation index of Chinese cabbage fermentation broth was determined in Hailun City, China. By PCA analysis to reduce the dimensionality of the evaluation index of fermentation broth. It was proposed that the amount of principal components screened by PCA, it was used as an excellent input variable for the model to optimize the evaluation system of fermentation broth.This provided a new idea for the quality evaluation of Se-enriched Chinese cabbage fermentation broth in Helen city and similar areas.

Acknowledgements. This work was financed by Key project of the 14th Five-Year Plan of Education Science of Heilongjiang Province in 2021 (No. GJB1421563), the Technological Project of Heilongjiang Province "The open competition mechanism to select the best candidates" (No. 2022ZXJ05C01), Funding for the Opening Project of Key Laboratory of Agricultural Renewable Resource Utilization Technology (No. HLJHDNY2114), Heilongjiang University of Science and Technology the introduction of high-level talent research start-up fund projects (No. 000009020315), and Logistics teaching reform and research project of national colleges and vocational colleges(No. JZW2022021) .

References

1. Li, Z., Liang, D.L., Peng, Q., et al.: Interaction between selenium and soil organic matter and its impact on soil selenium bioavailability: a review. Geoderma **295**, 69–79 (2017)
2. Natasha, S.M., Niazi, N.K., et al.: A critical review of selenium biogeochemical behavior in soil-plant system with an inference to human health. Environ. Pollut. **234**, 915–934 (2018)

3. Zhang, C.M., Zhou, X.B.: Effects of different selenium application methods on selenium utilization efficiency of rice. J. soil **56**, 186–194 (2019)
4. Du, Z.Y., Shi, Y.X., Wang, Q.H.: Absorption of selenium in vegetables and the appropriate amount of selenium supplement. Ecol. Environ. **13**(2), 230–231 (2004)
5. Li, H.F., Bai, Y.S., Fan, W.H., et al.: Effects of different concentrations of selenium on seed germination rate and seedling growth of soybean. J. Shanxi Agric. Univ. **26**(3), 256–258 (2006)
6. Li, D.C., Zhu, Z.J., Xu, Z.H., et al.: Effects of selenium on growth and nutrient uptake of Chinese cabbage. J. Plant Nutr. Fertil. **9**(3), 353–358 (2003)
7. Tegeder, M.: Transporters for amino acids in plant cells: some functions and many unknowns. Curr. Opin. Plant Biol. **15**, 315–321 (2012)
8. Wang, Q., Yu, Y., Li, J.X., et al.: Effects of different forms of selenium fertilizers on se accumulation, distribution and residual effect in winter wheat-summer maize rotation system. J. Agric. Food Chem. **65**, 1116–1123 (2017)
9. Terry, N., Zayed, A.M., de Souza, M.P., et al.: Selenium in higher plants. Ann. Rev. Plant Physiol. Plant Mol. Biol. **51**, 401–432 (2000)
10. Kenward, P.A., Fowle, D.A., Yee, N.: Microbial selenate sorption and reduction in nutrient limited systems. Environ. Sci. Technol. **40**, 3782–3786 (2006)
11. Lee, J.H., Han, J., Choi, H., et al.: Effects of temperature and dissolved oxygen on Se(IV) removal and Se(0) precipitation by Shewanella sp. HN-41. Chemosphere **68**, 1898–1905 (2007)
12. Fan, W.H., Li, L.: Effects of combined application of selenium and cobalt on tomato seedling growth and soil microorganisms. In: Proceedings of the 11th National Congress of Chinese Soil Society and the 7th Cross-Strait Symposium on Soil and Fertilizer Academic Exchange (Part 2), pp. 376–380. China Agricultural University Press (2008)
13. BQ/T5323–2018 Light industry Standard enzyme product classification guide "Plant enzyme". Ministry of Industry and Information Technology of the People's Republic of China (2018)
14. Zhao, Q.D.: Study on the Preparation of Se-enriched Agricultural Fermentation Broth (SAFB) and the Mechanism of Barrier Soil Remediation, vol. 6. Northeast Agricultural University (2021)
15. Zhou, X.B., Wu, H.Y., Zhang, H.J., et al.: Effects of spraying selenium fertilizer on growth and physiological and ecological parameters of soybean. North China J. Agric. Sci. **19**(4), 77–80 (2004)

Development Road Map and Planning Mode of Artificial Intelligence Technology Under the Background of Internet Information

Zheqing Tang$^{(\boxtimes)}$, Xiqiang Sun, and Yang Luo

School of Information Engineering, Heilongjiang Vocational College, Harbin 150022, China
347493701@qq.com

Abstract. With the progress of various software and hardware technologies, the data processing and computing power of the computer are further enhanced. Artificial intelligence technology has entered a period of rapid development. The current "Internet + " boom and the continued prosperity of the big data industry have further accelerated the integration of artificial intelligence technology with other related industries. This paper summarizes the Internet information, static information collection technology and artificial intelligence technology, analyzes the neural network, puts forward RRT path planning, and studies the pheromone increment dynamic update strategy. The results show that when LK is less than lbest, the increase of the difference will sharply increase the pheromone increment on the path, which makes the algorithm easy to fall into local optimization.

Keywords: Internet Information · Artificial Intelligence Technology · Development Road-map Planning Model · Neural Network

1 Introduction

With the development of China's economy and society and the increase of people's travel activities, the development of road map planning has been unable to meet people's travel needs, gradually forming a bottleneck restricting the development of the national economy.

With the continuous progress of science and technology, many experts have studied the development roadmap planning model of artificial intelligence technology. For example, Palade V, Wolff J, G described the development roadmap of SP machine based on SP intelligence theory and its implementation in SP computer model. SP machine was originally developed as a software virtual machine with advanced parallel processing and hosted on a high-performance computer. It is suggested that SP machine system help users visualize knowledge structure and processing [1]. Elkawkagy m, Heba e proposed a new method combining hierarchical artificial intelligence planning with map reduce paradigm. In the mapping part, the proposed clustering technology will be applied to divide the hierarchical planning problem into smaller problems, that is, the so-called sub

A. Li et al. (Eds.): 6GN 2022, LNICST 505, pp. 206–213, 2023.
https://doi.org/10.1007/978-3-031-36014-5_17

problems. Preprocess each sub problem to simplify the declarative hierarchical planning domain model, and then find a separate solution for each so-called sub problem sub plan [2]. Long KF discussed the construction of interstellar strategy and technology roadmap. In particular, assuming that the launch date is 2111, the specific path of human interstellar mission will be studied [3]. Although this paper has a lot of research results on the development roadmap planning model of artificial intelligence technology, there are still deficiencies in the research on the development roadmap planning model of artificial intelligence technology under the background of Internet information.

In order to study the development roadmap planning mode of artificial intelligence technology under the background of Internet information, this paper studies the development roadmap planning mode of Internet information and artificial intelligence technology, and finds the basic model of neural network. The results show that the model is helpful to the planning of artificial intelligence technology development roadmap under the background of network information.

2 Method

2.1 Internet Information

(1) Internet information overview

Internet information technology is a kind of network rather than tree communication. Firstly, the high-speed networking of information sources has attracted many network users [4]. Low speed information sources will no longer necessarily lead to low-speed acceptance. The network speed of the receiver will be the superposition of the network speed of multiple information sources working at the same time, which will greatly improve the resource download speed and viewing fluency. At the same time, it also covers the major changes brought by the application and promotion of high technology to traditional economic industries. With the continuous expansion of the overall scale of China's Internet economy, the application of Internet e-commerce has also developed rapidly. In recent years, significant progress has been made in online payment, cloud computing and the Internet of things. For the intersection of traditional economy, its characteristics are more prominent, such as the convenience, efficiency, improvement of marginal benefits, high permeability and external economy of network economy [5].

(2) Static information acquisition technology

The basic information database mainly stores video data, etc.; The business database stores scenic spot information, passenger transport data and other data provided by each business department; The auxiliary information database stores maintenance, construction information and other information conducive to information service. Preprocess and fuse the basic traffic data and input it into the database; Static business data obtained from various business departments, such as scenic spot location information, toll station information, etc., are statistically classified and standardized in combination with basic information, and entered into the business database. Dynamic traffic information processing is to preprocess, classify and store the data obtained by each detector in the business database [6]. According to the characteristics of each business, integrate the basic data and business data, analyze in each data system, find out the data law and the correlation between the data, and generate the release information needed by the public.

2.2 Development Road-Map and Planning Mode of Artificial Intelligence Technology

(1) Artificial intelligence technology

Artificial intelligence technology is a technology that studies how to express and acquire knowledge and how to use knowledge in practice. Therefore, the analysis of the concept of artificial intelligence is also diverse. In essence, it is a simulation of human thinking. Thinking is the subjective reflection of objective reality, so thinking is both subjective and objective [7]. The basic idea of artificial intelligence is to take the machine as the carrier and use artificial intelligence technology to make the machine have the characteristics of human expression and thinking. With its unique adaptive learning ability and parallel computing ability, artificial intelligence technology can deal with the problem analysis and data modeling of complex systems, and obtain reliable calculation results more intelligently. At present, artificial intelligence technology is constantly combined with relevant technologies in different industries to achieve more perfect and intelligent problem modeling and solution, so as to promote the intelligent development of various industries. Artificial intelligence technology refers to classifying data through the internal relationship between data features in the training data set, with only features and no labels; The essence of reinforcement learning is to deal with the problems related to automatic decision-making and realize the process of continuous decision-making. The decision-making process is to try to make some behaviors, and then get a result without any label, and then use the feedback of the result to continuously adjust the previous behavior until the algorithm learns the best result corresponding to some behaviors in some cases.

(2) Neural network

In the training process, the weights of each neural network are continuously updated through the continuous connection of each neural network. After a period of time, the neural network can reach a relatively stable state [8]. The biggest advantage of this neural network is that each neuron is connected, which can make the training of neural network reach a better state. The reasoning of neural network is a nonlinear numerical operation based on network, and the reasoning conclusion is also numerical. Only by interpreting the input-output mode can we draw the corresponding logical conclusion. Neural network simulates the structure of human brain and maps the nonlinear relationship between input characteristics and output conclusions, but it does not need to establish any mathematical model. It only needs to estimate the required decision according to the input sampling data [9]. Therefore, based on the traditional BP neural network structure, the system adds a fuzzy layer before and after the input layer of the neural network to fuzzify the input information and defuzzify the output information, so as to realize the fuzzy BP neural network structure.

(3) RRT path planning

RRT path planning cannot provide the best path to achieve the goal. However, if there is a path, when the number of samples is close to infinity, the probability of finding the path is close to 1. RRT plans the path by building a tree from the source point. When nodes are randomly sampled in the workspace, it is necessary to detect the collision of random points [10]. If a node collides with an obstacle, the point will be discarded. If the path does not collide with an obstacle, a random point is added to the tree, and the node closest to the point is the parent node of the node. If the path causes collisions, the random points are discarded. Repeat the above process, add the randomly generated feasible nodes to the tree until one node is no more than the set threshold distance from the target point, and judge whether the target position can reach the formed path through the newly generated nodes. If it can be reached, the target location will be added to the existing tree, where the newly generated random point will become its parent node, indicating the end of the path planning process. If it cannot be accessed, it will continue to resample other nodes [11].

2.3 Basic Model of Neural Network

The input vector and output vector of neural network have the following relationship (1):

$$y = f(\sum_{i=1}^{m} w_i x_i - \theta) \tag{1}$$

As described above, θ is the threshold and f (x) is the excitation function; It can be a linear function or a nonlinear function.

Here, real number coding is adopted, and the following linear transformation formula (2) is used:

$$X(j) = a(j) + y(j)[b(j) - a(j)] \tag{2}$$

The j-th optimization variable x (J) whose initial variation interval is [a (J), B (J)] corresponds to the real number y (J) on the interval [0,1].

According to the proportional selection method, the selection probability PS (I) of parent individual y (J, I) is Eq. (3):

$$p_s(i) = F(i) \backslash \sum_{i=1}^{n} F(i) \tag{3}$$

Let P (I) be the sum of the previous I P. Generate N-5 random numbers, select P (I) according to this probability, select f (I) accordingly, and then select N-5 individuals in total [12].

3 Experience

3.1 Object Extraction

Epptrm compilation system adopts Web-based Distributed B/S architecture according to the characteristics of the compilation process of enterprise technology roadmap. Under the B/S architecture, users (administrators, team members, etc.) log in to the system through LAN or Internet, and exchange information with the background database through web server. Background database management extracts and transforms the original information database through data warehouse technology, so that the information can be reasonably reorganized and transformed into the corresponding database according to the needs. There are few times when a class can be separated.

3.2 Experimental Analysis

Although Chinese scholar Liu Chuanlin divided the preparation process of enterprise technology roadmap into four stages, he only divided the above second stage into two stages: roadmap analysis and roadmap drawing. Using the above development model, not only the complete separation of view, controller and model, but also the separation of business logic layer and persistence layer is realized. The road map resource guarantee is realized in the form of up-down linkage under the working mode. Before the overall planning of road map resources, a special working group shall be established to conduct docking review between the project team of major engineering projects and their key construction contents and the personnel of the main responsible units one by one, clarify the resource background of project construction and correct the problems existing in resource allocation in time. For the construction projects involving a wide range of fields, systems and differences, the personnel of each responsible unit shall be concentrated for coordination and consultation to jointly solve the key and difficult problems in the allocation of project resources. After forming unified review opinions, communicate and coordinate with all units, adjust and improve according to the feedback modification opinions, and finally determine the overall review results of road map resources. Of course, in the initial stage of the algorithm, in order to ensure the global solution and avoid obtaining the local optimal solution, the path selection of ant colony is not constrained by the corresponding conditions in a certain period of time. However, when a given time is reached, heuristic information can guide and accelerate the solution process.

4 Discussion

4.1 Pheromone Increment Dynamic Update Strategy

The new pheromone incremental update rule is more in line with the ant routing law. It can quickly reduce the initial value of the prime solution to a certain value. Then, with the increase of the number of iterations, the pheromone increment decreases gradually, which is convenient to expand the scope of ant routing and jump out of the local optimal solution. The adaptive change curve of dynamic pheromone increment is shown in Table 1.

Table 1. Dynamic pheromone increment adaptive change curve

type	X = Lk-Lbest
arccot(x)	0.54
L\ex	0.78

It can be seen from the above that the x = LK lbest value of arccot (x) is 0.54 and the x = LK lbest value of L\ex is 0.78. The specific presentation results are shown in Fig. 1.

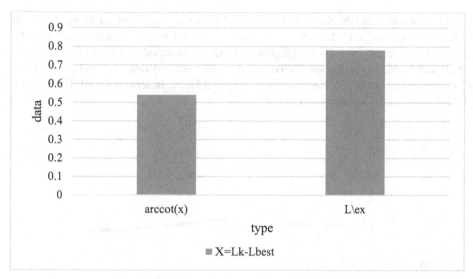

Fig. 1. Dynamic pheromone increment adaptive change curve

It can be seen from the above that when LK is less than lbest, the increase of the difference will sharply increase the pheromone increment on the path, which makes the algorithm easy to fall into local optimization. When the gap between the two is large, the result also has a critical value to control the maximum and minimum values, which will not increase indefinitely. This helps to avoid pheromones that are too large or close to 0 on a particular path. While ensuring the convergence speed, ensure that the pheromone will not be too concentrated to lead to stagnation, narrow the gap between the pheromone concentration of the optimization solution and other paths, and attract more ants to choose a better path.

4.2 Experimental Results and Analysis

In this experiment, there are three groups of service requests, one for each group. This paper will call these three groups of service requests on two scale service libraries, and compare the success rates of acsws PG, n-tiscf and a-tiscf in different scale service libraries. The experimental data and results are shown in Table 2.

Table 2. Comparison chart of service portfolio success rate

	10	20	30
ACSWS-PG	43.3	51.5	61.4
N-TISCF	45.3	53.7	60.6
A-TISCF	41.6	55.1	59.7

It can be seen from the above that the combination success rate of acsws-pg algorithm is 43.3% in service set 10, 51.5% in service set 20 and 61.4% in service set 30; The combination success rate of n-tiscf algorithm is 45.3% in service set 10, 53.7% in service set 20 and 60.6% in service set 30; The combination success rate of a-tiscf algorithm is 41.6% in service set 10, 55.1% in service set 20 and 59.7% in service set 30. The specific presentation results are shown in Fig. 2.

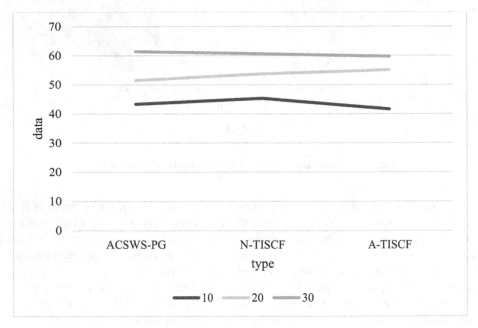

Fig. 2. Comparison chart of service portfolio success rate

It can be seen from the above that with the gradual completion of acsws PG, n-tiscf and a-tiscf service sets, the possibility of planning solutions gradually increases, so the combination success rate increases to varying degrees. Compared with the matching method based on semantic description, the keyword based matching method can not match the ontology concepts equivalent to each other, which limits the scope of service matching, so the success rate of service composition is relatively low.

5 Conclusion

Path planning is the process of generating a path from the source location to the target location. Path planning is to find an optimal path without collision in the presence of obstacles according to certain measurement standards (such as path length, running time, etc.), combined with its applicable objects and application scenarios. This paper tests the service composition success rate of acsws PG, n-tiscf and a-tiscf on different scale service libraries. The results show that with the gradual completion of the service set, the possibility of planning solutions gradually increases, and the success rate of the combination also increases to varying degrees.

References

1. Palade, V., Wolff, J.G.: A roadmap for the development of the 'SP Machine' for artificial intelligence. Comput. J. **62**(11), 1584–1604 (2019)
2. Elkawkagy, M., Heba, E.: Reduce artificial intelligence planning effort by using map-reduce paradigm. Int. J. Innovative Technol. Exploring Eng. **10**(7), 24–32 (2021)
3. Long, K.F.: A rapid study on the development of an interstellar roadmap and planning ahead for technology maturation. J. Br. Interplanet. Soc. **73**(1), 6–14 (2020)
4. Deepthi, K.C.: A novel artificial intelligence program testing service (ai-pts) model. J. Phys. Conf. Ser. **1228**(1), 12017–12017 (2019)
5. Fernández-Vigo, J., Fernández-Vigo, J.I., Kudsieh, B.: Artificial intelligence, robotics and cyborgs: the future of research and technological development in ophthalmology. Archivos de la Sociedad Española de Oftalmología (English Edition) **94**(7), 313–315 (2019)
6. Raknys, A.V., Gudelis, D., Guogis, A.: The analysis of opportunities of the application of big data and artificial intelligence technologies in public governance and social policy. Socialinė Teorija Empirija Politika ir Praktika **22**(6), 88–100 (2021)
7. Chen, J., Lin, C., Peng, D., et al.: Fault diagnosis of rotating machinery: a review and bibliometric analysis. IEEE Access **PP**(99),1–1 (2020)
8. Batarseh, F.A., Freeman, L., Huang, C.H.: A survey on artificial intelligence assurance. J. Big Data **8**(1), 1–30 (2021)
9. Sriram, V.P., Mathur, A., Aarthy, C.J., et al.: Model based using artificial intelligence to overcome the human resource problem in the healthcare industry. Ann. Rom. Soc. Cell Biol. **25**(4), 3980–3992 (2021)
10. Al-Fattah, S.M.: Artificial intelligence approach for modeling and forecasting oil-price volatility. SPE Reservoir Eval. Eng. **22**(3), 817–826 (2019)
11. Wassan, S., Gulati, K., Pallathadka, H., et al.: How artificial intelligence transforms the experience of employees. Turk. J. Comput. Math. Educ. (TURCOMAT) **12**(10), 7116–7135 (2021)
12. Reim, W., Eriksson, O.: Implementation of artificial intelligence (AI): a roadmap for business model innovation. AI **1**(2), 180–191 (2020)

Artificial Intelligence Technology in Computer Vision and Network Field

Zheqing Tang[✉] and Xiqiang Sun

School of Information Engineering, Heilongjiang Vocational College, Harbin 150001, China
347493701@qq.com

Abstract. In the era of rapid development of information, science and technology are constantly progressing, and artificial intelligence (AI) technology is also developing continuously. With the rapid growth of social economy, it has promoted the development of modern industries to a certain extent. The development of computer technology has also triggered a new revolution in AI technology. AI technology can use computers to recognize big data, image information and human movement. People's lives. The purpose of this book is to explore the application of AI techniques in computer vision and networking. This article explains the concepts of AI, computer vision. Analyze the development and prediction of AI, conduct appropriate analysis on the development of AI in the field of vision and computer networks, and conduct a number of basic technical research and model design around multiple technical issues in the computer and network fields, enhancing the field of computational vision The relevant AI research content has important scientific value and significance. Finally, a questionnaire is used to collect and analyze the application of AI in the two fields. Through experimental authentication, the image recognition accuracy of this paper is 99%, and it is more friendly to some middle-aged and elderly users.

Keywords: Artificial Intelligence · Computer Vision · Neural Network · Network Domain

1 Introduction

In recent years, with the advancement of science and technology and the improvement of human living standards, the penetration rate of the Internet is also increasing year by year, and the usage of smart phones is increasing. But while technology has made this article flexible, it has also brought in a lot of data. For example, in the world of the Internet, people continue to generate a large amount of data through searching, uploading, downloading, etc., including pictures, videos, texts and other formats. Today, computer vision and AI are closely related to human life, such as face recognition and tracking, traffic violation tracking, license plate recognition, mobile phone photo beauty, driverless technology, human war machines and so on. The birth and application of each product and the application of high technology are inseparable from the hard work and exploration of the scientific researchers behind it [1, 2].

In the application research of AI technology in the field of computer vision and network, many scholars have studied it and achieved good results, for example: Wang Q invented a hierarchical association method, which uses low-level feature information to construct Reliable short tracking trajectories, and then use the Hungarian algorithm to associate these short trajectory blocks to form longer tracking trajectories [3]. Li W proposes an algorithm using network flow and covering set techniques to associate short tracked trajectories with action features. The algorithm connects short tracked trajectory blocks by minimizing the energy function [4].

This article explains the concepts of AI, computer vision. Analyze the development and prediction of AI, conduct appropriate analysis on the development of AI in the field of vision and computer networks, and conduct a number of basic technical research and model design around multiple technical issues in the computer and network fields, enhancing the field of computational vision The relevant AI research content has important scientific value and significance. Finally, a questionnaire is used to collect and analyze the application of AI in the two fields.

2 Research on the Application of AI Technology in the Field of Computer Vision and Network

2.1 The Application of AI in Computer Vision

The role of computer vision is to recognize images well, while real-world images are dynamic and static. Among them, images also refer to still images, images, etc., as well as images with powerful multi-action and video capture capabilities. Computer vision makes it easier to detect still images and does not need to rely on many complex techniques. When looking for powerful images, the ability to recognize and manipulate can be enhanced by AI technology. First, computer vision can use sensors and other tools to capture a wide range of information and analyze, organize, and analyze all the information collected. Second, the collected data is processed by electronic equipment, which facilitates the processing of further information and ensures efficient image processing. In this process, computer performance is very important, so the next generation of computers will improve with the development of smart devices. Today, smart devices in the field of computer vision can recognize many complex image details, such as gestures, facial expressions, etc., and visual recognition capabilities also have great potential for development, which requires researchers in the field of computer technology to complete. Finish. Continue to explore exercises. In this regard, computer vision has the highest hardware value [5, 6].

Target tracking can be regarded as a target state estimation problem, because in a tracking video sequence, only the position and size information of the tracking target in the first frame is given, and then the algorithm needs to estimate the tracking target in all remaining video frames. Coordinates and size information. The tracking of a single target often brings great challenges, and the tracking of multiple targets is even more difficult. It can be said to be the limit of the tracking field, but in the actual target tracking application, many application scenarios need to be correct. Therefore, multi-target tracking is becoming more and more important in many practical applications in today's society, and sufficient technical support and scientific research need to be given. Many interference factors faced by the algorithm in single-target tracking also exist in multi-target tracking, such as frequent target occlusion, strong light interference, changes in the appearance of the tracking target, and complex interaction between multiple tracking targets [7, 8].

2.2 The Application of AI in the Network Field

Traditional AI technology covers computer technology, Internet technology, information technology, intelligence, psychology, ergonomics and many other fields. Therefore, AI is also a very advanced science. In the popular field of the Internet of Things, most AI applications must be based on the Internet platform, so the development of AI must be able to provide the best services for the Internet. Since then, the application of AI in the network has mainly focused on two points, one is network security, and the other is the evaluation of the system [9, 10].

The rapid development and popularization of the Internet, as well as the opening of the network itself, make the issue of network security a hot topic. In this case, in order to properly ensure the security of network information and expand the scope of the network, special technical support with architectural knowledge is required. Therefore, in the process of ensuring information security, computer users must first install scanning software to prevent various viruses and intrusions and prevent information leakage. And cause huge losses. A scanning software that operates based on a computer firewall that judges the security of multiple files transmitted over a network to determine whether to block them or not, and the process of this crisis is very similar to human thinking and justice and AI. By mimicking the capabilities of the human brain, technology can accomplish this task more efficiently.

2.3 AI Promotes the Industrialization of Computer Vision

The application of AI technology in computer vision also reflects the promotion of the development of computer vision. Since AI has played an important role in many fields in recent years and has been applied to industry and automation, computer vision can also be successfully developed with the help of AI and technology. The RGBD depth camera is based on a customized RGB camera with built-in information technology that not only transmits energy to the scene through passive capture and detection, but also analyzes and processes the information received from the human eye. The product has high expectations for applications in a wide range of visual identities and service areas. With the advent of smart technologies, there will be more technologies that can be applied to the effective development of computer vision and the computer vision industry [11, 12].

2.4 Algorithm Application

This paper collects data through questionnaires, and the data analysis is mainly carried out by Bayesian algorithm.

(1) Each data sample is represented by an n-dimensional feature vector $X = \{x_1, x_2, \cdots, x_n\}$, which describes the pairs of n attributes A1, A2,..., An respectively. n metrics for the sample.

(2) It is assumed that there are m classes, represented by C1, C2,..., Cm respectively. Given an unknown data sample (that is, without a class label), if the naive Bayesian classification method assigns the unknown sample to class C_i; the condition shown in formula (1) must be satisfied:

$$P(C_i|X_i) > P(C_j|X_i)1 \le j \le m, j \ne 1 \tag{1}$$

where $P(C_j|X_i)$ is the maximum posterior probability.

(3) In the case that the prior probability of class $P(C_1) = P(C_2) = \cdots = P(C_m)$ Ci is unknown, otherwise $P(C_i) = \frac{S_i}{S}$, where Si is the number of training samples in class C i, and S is the total number of training samples. According to the following Bayesian formula

$$P(C_i|X) = \frac{P(X|C_i)P(C_i)}{P(X)} \tag{2}$$

3 Application Design Experiment of AI Technology in Computer Visionand Network Field

3.1 Building a Computer Face Recognition System Based on AI

After the offline training process using the auxiliary big data image set, this paper successfully trains a stacked denoising autoencoder model, which can learn more robust generalized image features in response to more complex external interference factors. In order to better realize the face recognition task, this paper transfers the feature weights learned in the offline training process to the online face recognition process through knowledge transfer, which can also be called transfer learning. The AI recognition network in this paper includes a feature extraction network structure and a classification layer structure model for supervised learning. The former is based on the migration of the weight parameters learned by the encoder part during the offline feature learning process, while the latter classification layer is added to the previous feature extraction layer for supervised learning and fine-tuning of the overall network parameters. Therefore, in the online supervised face recognition process, the parameters in the entire deep face recognition model can be further fine-tuned and changed according to the corresponding face database.

3.2 Questionnaire on the Application of AI in the Network Field

In this paper, a questionnaire is designed to conduct a questionnaire survey on users. The questions of the questionnaire are: the status quo of AI in the network field, the future development of AI in the network field, and the satisfaction of experiencing AI. Each question adopts a 10-point scale. Score according to their own experience, and finally collect the questionnaire, and calculate the average score for each question.

4 Experimental Analysis of the Application of AI Technology in Computer Vision and Network Fields

4.1 Accurate Comparison of Face Recognition

In this paper, the face recognition algorithm constructed based on the application of AI in computer vision is compared with the traditional face recognition algorithm for face recognition accuracy. A total of 1000 faces are recognized, and the accuracy of the two algorithms is connected. The experimental data are shown in Table 1.

Table 1. Comparison of face recognition accuracy of two algorithms

	100	200	500	1000
traditional algorithm	96	93	92	89
AI algorithm	100	100	99	99

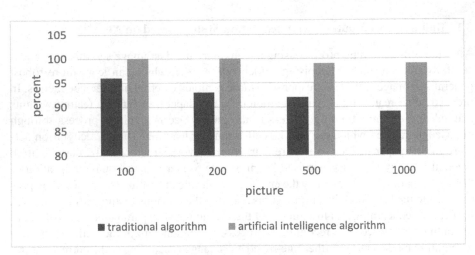

Fig. 1. Comparison of face recognition accuracy of two algorithms

From Fig. 1, we can clearly see that the accuracy of the algorithm optimized in this paper is higher than that of the traditional algorithm, and it is almost close to 100%.

Even in 1000 face recognition, the accuracy is as high as 99%. Accurate face recognition algorithm plays an important role in many computer vision applications, so the algorithm constructed in this paper has played a certain role in promoting computer vision.

4.2 Comparison of User Satisfaction

This paper, the designed questionnaire is distributed to two groups of users, and they are asked to rate the above questions according to their own ideas. Then, the questionnaires are collected, and the average score of each question is calculated. The experimental data is shown in Table 2.

Table 2. Views of users of different age groups on the application of AI in the network field

	1	2	3
young users	7	9	10
middle-aged user	6	7	6

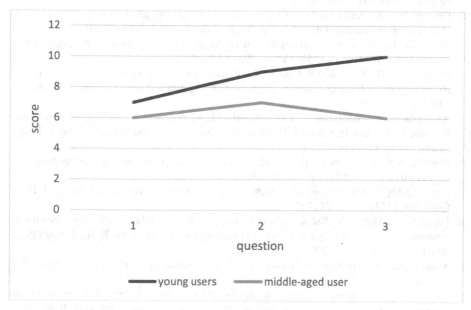

Fig. 2. Views of users of different age groups on the application of AI in the network field

As can be seen from Fig. 2, younger users are generally more satisfied with AI, and are more optimistic about the future development of AI. Therefore, in the future development of AI, it is necessary to pay attention to the use experience and operation teaching of some middle-aged and elderly customers.

5 Conclusions

In order to solve many technical problems in the field of vision and computer network, this book introduces the contribution to the development of computer vision and computer network technology through the research and exploration of many important AI technologies. In the field of computer assistance and networking, traditional mediation algorithms have been adapted to different generation problems, greatly reducing the difficulty of solving new generation problems. Creating a new system for visual arts combining direct-directed architecture and AI. AI technology is gradually applied in the fields of computer vision, network security technology, and administrators' management and evaluation of network systems, and has made significant contributions to the security of human information. At the same time, the gradual development of AI technology is also an inevitable trend.

References

1. Huszár, V.: Application possibilities of decentralization and blockchain technology using computer vision and AI in defense management, military and police organizations. Honvéd-ségi Szemle **148**(1), 4–14 (2020)
2. Concepcion, R.: Advancement in computer vision, AI and wireless technology: a crop phenotyping perspective. Int. J. Adv. Sci. Technol. **29**(6), 7050–7065 (2020)
3. Wang, Q., Lu, P.: Research on application of AI in computer network technology. Int. J. Pattern Recogn. AI **33**(5), 1959015.1–1959015.12 (2019)
4. Li, W., Jiang, B., Zhao, W.: Obstetric imaging diagnostic platform based on cloud computing technology under the background of smart medical big data and deep learning. IEEE Access **PP**(99), 1–1 (2020)
5. Alexopoulos, K., Nikolakis, N., Chryssolouris, G.: Digital twin-driven supervised machine learning for the development of AI applications in manufacturing. Int. J. Comput. Integr. Manuf. **33**(5), 429–439 (2020)
6. Postolit, A.V.: Prospects for the use of AI and computer vision in transport systems and connected cars. World Transp. Transp. **19**(1), 74–90 (2021)
7. Ren, Q.: Application analysis of AI technology in computer information security. J. Phys. Conf. Ser. **1744**(4), 042221 (2021)
8. Fomenko, I., Asieiev, V., Kulakovska, I.: Development of neural network and application of computer vision technology for diagnosis of skin injuries and diseases. Technol. Audit Prod. Reserves 2(2(58)), 6–11 (2021)
9. Yang, C., Liu, Z.: Application of computer vision in electronic commerce. J. Phys: Conf. Ser. **1992**(2), 022134 (2021)
10. Li, J., Wang, T.: Research on the application of AI technology in intelligent operation and maintenance of industrial equipment and system. J. Phys. Conf. Ser. **1992**(3), 032090 (2021)
11. Zhang, Y., Pei, Y.: Research on the application of AI technology in Island tourism. J. Phys. Conf. Ser. **1852**(3), 032015 (2021)
12. Liu, H., Li, Y., Liu, D.: Object detection and recognition system based on computer vision analysis. J. Phys: Conf. Ser. **1976**(1), 012024 (2021)

Research on Precise Ideological and Political Education in Colleges and Universities Based on the Analysis of Student Group Portraits

Min Lin[1($\boxtimes$)], Haiying Wu[2], and Hongwei Li[3]

[1] Institute of Surveying, Mapping and Remote Sensing Information, Guangdong Polytechnic of Industry and Commerce, Guangzhou 510510, China
linmin3000@163.com

[2] College of Economics and Trade, Guangdong Polytechnic of Industry and Commerce, Guangzhou 510510, China

[3] Guangzhou Huangpu Huiyuan School, Guangzhou 510555, China

Abstract. Relying on the education big data to build a student group portrait method that serves the precise ideological and political work of colleges and universities, this paper puts forward the data resource content, hierarchical label system and model building method of student group portrait. Exploring the application of cluster analysis method, outlier analysis method, and correlation analysis method in precision ideological and political work, the author proposed a portrait of college students' personality analysis, a portrait of fine ideological and political propaganda and education, a portrait of lonely behavior, a portrait of college students' academic early warning, a portrait of college students' comprehensive quality evaluation, a portrait of Internet addiction correction strategies, and a path to precision ideological and political work. Summarize the key links and technical ethics of the precise ideological and political work mode, and put forward four suggestions on data resource construction, in-depth portrait development, work practice path, and ideological and political technical ethics.

Keywords: Ideological and political education · Precise ideological and political thinking · Student group portrait · big data

1 Introduction

1.1 Preface

In the era of mobile Internet, big data is not only an information asset with unlimited potential, but also a disruptive technological change. Precise ideological and political education refers to the ideological and political work mode that accurately carries out ideological and political education activities under the guidance of precise thinking based on big data and other cutting-edge technologies. The big data user portrait, which analyzes the user's social attributes, consumption habits, preferences and other dimensional

A. Li et al. (Eds.): 6GN 2022, LNICST 505, pp. 221–229, 2023.
https://doi.org/10.1007/978-3-031-36014-5_19

data and labels the user's characteristics, has increasingly become a widely applicable working method to accurately judge the situation, predict the development direction, and build optimization strategies. This paper attempts to explore the application of the student portrait technology based on the big data user portrait technology in the precise ideological and political work of colleges and universities [1].

2 Constructing a Group Portrait Model of Precise Ideological and Political Students

2.1 Big Data Resources of Ideological and Political Education

Data collection is the first link in data utilization. The data resources in the above table are collected and stored in various business systems of secondary colleges and functional departments of colleges and universities. The university information work department can establish the university wide big data collection plan according to the university wide archiving scope table, and then integrate the university wide big data resources. The structured data can be stored in the structured database. For text, reports, pictures, audio Unstructured data such as videos can be captured, verified and stored in the unstructured database.

In general, the data in the archive scope table is from a wide range of sources, large in scale, and low in quality, and cannot be directly applied to the student group portrait model and algorithm. It often requires data pre-processing such as data cleaning to form common data table sets such as student attribute data table, student achievement data table, and book borrowing data table. These common data table sets are integrated according to the principle of student group portrait needs, Encapsulated in the student group portrait data resource library, a precise ideological and political entry data resource that can be directly read by the portrait model algorithm is formed. The scope, type and method of data collection in the specific student group portrait are related to both the existing big data resources and the entry data requirements of the portrait algorithm. Specific analysis should be made according to the specific algorithm requirements. For example, Zhang Jie and others listed the data collection scope into 10 categories according to the work experience of students and the BP algorithm requirements of student behavior, and then quantified them by sections。After processing, it is used as the entry data of BP algorithm. In the big data analysis mode, you can find out the data relationships hidden in the student group portrait data resource database, extract the internal connections and external characteristics of student behavior, describe the rules of student behavior, predict student behavior preferences, and accurately identify the commonalities of student group thinking, and accurately locate the differences in individual student thinking, Thus, it can provide students with refined ideological and political education services and precise ideological and political work assistance [2].

2.2 Portrait Function and Label System

User portraits, namely user information labeling, are used to label user characteristics by analyzing the user's social attributes, consumption habits, preferences and other dimensional data, so as to tap potential user information. It has prominent applications in police criminal investigation, information analysis, marketing and other aspects. Student group portrait is a user portrait method that is characterized and visualized by three types of tag systems that reflect the characteristics of students, behavior diagnosis and demand prediction attributes.

The establishment of portrait labels is the key work of student group portraits. The formulation of portrait labels should start from the analysis of ideological and political work scenarios, propose portrait requirements to describe the ideological and political objects in the scenarios, analyze the attributes of portrait requirements and respond to the requirements with corresponding function labels. A tag name is a semantic short text used to summarize the function or meaning of a tag. Labels are often multi-dimensional. For example, labels representing basic information functions are decomposed into five dimensions: name, gender, age, department and major. Labels are also often hierarchical. The hierarchical label system is a label tree, which is a hierarchical decomposition and subdivision of tree root labels. Each label has a hierarchy. The first level label is the tree root label, the second level label is a subdivision label subordinate to the first level label, and the third level label is a more subdivided label subordinate to the second level label. The higher the tag level, the more specialized the attribute functions. The highest level tag, also known as leaf tag, should be able to directly map to the image data resource table after data preprocessing.

If the weighted algorithm is used for portrait analysis, the tag is still weighted. The tag values at all levels are summarized to the tree root tag through the weighted algorithm to get the portrait tag values. This is the simplest student group portrait technology and the most common quantitative method for college ideological and political work. Portrait labels often assume a certain ideological and political work function, so whether the label selection is accurate and comprehensive directly affects the quality of student group portraits and the effect of ideological and political work. In general, the organization and design of the tag tree are also affected by ideological and political work experience, historical statistical conclusions, ideological and political data accumulation, and the selection of portrait algorithms. Therefore, the tag tree is not unique. For example, for the second level tag of learning attitude with behavior diagnosis function in Fig. 1, a four level tag tree of "learning attitude" can be established (see Table 2). When selecting and approving labels at all levels, portrait technicians should accurately select labels for each portrait function, reasonably arrange weights, respond to portrait algorithms, and scientifically organize the label tree grading system. After the hierarchical label system is established, the lowest level leaf label value can be directly collected from the student portrait data resource library through the mapping method, and other levels of label values up to the top level tree root label value can be calculated level by level according to the portrait algorithm. The advantage of student portraits is that they can use the tag values of various portraits obtained by special algorithms to make feature description and behavior diagnosis for students, which provides a more accurate way for the refined analysis of students ideological and political situation. For example, in Table 2, we collect the quantitative values (leaf tag values) of the students' "average ranking progress of overall evaluation scores" and "average ranking progress of usual scores" of each course, and obtain the course score progress tag value, score progress tag value, and learning attitude tag value level by level through statistical analysis algorithm. This is obviously a more refined quantitative method to describe the students' learning attitude, It also provides a precise object for ideological and political work of learning attitude correction. The head teacher and counselor can not only use the label value of the students' learning attitude portrait to analyze the overall learning appearance of the students in this class, but also extract students with different learning attitudes and give them advice and assistance.

3 Precise Ideological and Political Work Based on Student Group Portraits

3.1 Precision Ideological and Political Work Based on Cluster Analysis

Clustering analysis, also known as unsupervised learning, is a mathematical method to classify objects according to their closeness in nature. Because there is no classification information that represents the data category in clustering, cluster analysis can be used to divide the data into groups without preset classification, thus effectively avoiding the subjectivity and randomness of classification. The typical clustering analysis algorithms include K-means clustering algorithm, hierarchical clustering algorithm, SOM algorithm and FCM algorithm, each of which has its advantages and disadvantages. For example, K-means clustering algorithm has a good effect on low dimensional data sets, but because the initial clustering center of the algorithm is randomly selected, and the number of clusters needs to be preset, when processing a large number of clusters, it usually requires joint processing of several clustering algorithms to obtain satisfactory results. Therefore, it should combine the characteristics of tag data and specific ideological and political scenarios, Targeted selection of clustering algorithms for student portraits, and even use comprehensive analysis of multiple or multiple clustering algorithms to obtain portrait tag values.

3.2 Precision Ideological and Political Work Based on Outlier Analysis

Outlier analysis is also called outlier detection. Outliers are outliers that deviate from most of the data. Because they deviate too much from the group data, people suspect that these data outliers are not random factors, but come from completely different mechanisms. Outlier analysis is a data analysis method that discovers discrete objects that are significantly different from other data from the data set and analyzes their outliers. At present, it has been widely used in fraud detection Video surveillance, medical treatment, industrial damage detection and network intrusion detection.

3.3 Expand the Application Space of Information Technology with Continuous Influence

The outlier analysis includes distribution based outlier analysis, distance based outlier analysis, density based outlier analysis, clustering based outlier analysis, and depth based outlier analysis. Each type of outlier analysis method has its advantages and disadvantages. Therefore, in the accurate ideological and political student portrait, appropriate outlier analysis methods should be selected according to specific application scenarios and data characteristics.

In the ideological and political work of colleges and universities, by selecting appropriate outlier analysis algorithms, special outliers such as isolated behavior outliers and learning warning outliers can be accurately captured. Then, by analyzing outlier factors, we can build a map portrait of isolated behavior and a portrait of college students' academic warning, and carry out accurate ideological and political assistance for the outliers. Their portrait ideas and work paths are shown in Table 5. Association analysis is based on association rule mining algorithm. It analyzes the degree of association between tags to form an association degree list. The higher the tag in the list, the higher the degree of association. With the help of correlation analysis technology, the state of variables can often be predicted by other variables that are highly related to them. For example, through big data correlation analysis, it is known that the students who have been awarded excellent C language courses in a university also receive excellent ratings when learning data structure courses, which accounts for up to 80%.

3.4   Promote a Holistic Approach to the Application of IT

Then we can improve the teaching effect of the data structure course by improving the teaching goal of the C language course.

The commonly used association analysis algorithms are Apriori algorithm and FP growth algorithm. Apriori algorithm searches and iterates layer by layer through connection operation and pruning operation to find out the association relationship between data and establish association rules. FP growth algorithm based on frequent pattern tree directly generates frequent patterns by recursively calling FP growth algorithm, and there is no need to generate candidate patterns in the whole search and discovery process, so it is significantly better than Apriori algorithm in execution efficiency.

3.5   Regulating the Health Application of Information Technology with Benefit Evaluation

The ability of information technology, especially the ability of sustainable development of information technology, determines the benefit of information technology application. At present, the investment benefit of information technology in certain fields and some system is not high, especially under the premise that the resources occupied by vocational education is not enough, it needs to be regulated by benefit evaluation.

Health applications of information technology. The selection of benchmarking system for vocational education informatization needs to introduce the concept of benefit evaluation into vocational education informatization, and explore and form a shared, iterative and modular problem-solving concept in the process of informatization construction, so as to efficiently solve complex and diversified problems by using information technology.

4 Suggestions on Precise Ideological and Political Work Based on Student Group Portraits

From the perspective of big data, the new path of ideological and political work in colleges and universities linked by student group portrait technology is the only way to transform and upgrade from traditional ideological and political work to accurate ideological and political work. From the above, we can see that data resources, portrait technology, and practice path are the three key links of the new path, so we propose three suggestions to promote the integration and development of big data and accurate ideological and political work in colleges and universities. At the same time, student portrait technology is a powerful tool for ideological and political education, rather than a weapon for ideological and political management. Finally, some suggestions are made on the ethics of accurate ideological and political student portrait technology.

4.1 Combine Science and Comparability

Suggestions on the construction of accurate ideological and political portrait data resources (Table 1).

Table 1. Text analysis results of informationization research based on Nvivo

The serial number	The dimension	keywords
01	content	Rural education informatization; National education informatization; Special education inormatization; Educational technology; "InternetNet+"; Basic education; Regional planning; Regional education informatization;
02	function	Information leadership; Intelligent education; Big data; Targeted poverty alleviation through education; Smart campus; The beauty of morality, intelligence and physiquelaw; Rural education; Special education; Supply-side reform; Information literacy;
03	system	Evaluation index system; Educational governance; Intelligent education; Educational technology; Basic education; Information-based teaching; Education cloud; Learning society; Digital education resources;
04	standard	Technical standards; Curriculum standards; Quality standard; Competency standards; Policy orientation; Application; International experience; information. The source construction; Quality management;
05	value	Educational equity; Informationization of education management; Educational resources

Table 2. IPrecise ideological and political portrait data

The serial number	keywords	The serial number	keywords
01	The technical level	151	Information concept
02	Business covers	152	Standard interaction
03	Content to deepen	153	Talent cultivation
04	Strengthen cooperation	154	policy
05	Students analysis	155	Social influence
...	...	...	...
50	Way to change	194	Information ethics

4.2 Spindle Coding Combining the Two Methods

With the continuous deepening of college information construction, education big data resources are also increasingly rich. Big data technology has brought new historical opportunities for the innovative development of college ideological and political work in the new era. Ideological and political workers in colleges and universities often face the dilemma of accurately identifying students, accurately serving students, accurately predicting students, and accurately evaluating students. It is the technical advantage of big data. The precise ideological and political work model, which can respond to precise needs, provide precise services, and promote accurate policy implementation, is increasingly valued by ideological and political workers in colleges and universities. The student portrait method in ideological and political work in colleges and universities also has higher and higher research value, And gradually become a research hotspot. Based on these research backgrounds, this paper starts with student portraits and explores the practice path of deep integration of big data technology and ideological and political work in colleges and universities.

5 Evaluation Standard Optimization Based on Delphi Method

In the ideological and political work of colleges and universities, the clustering analysis algorithm can be used to classify variables such as cartel personality factor scale indicators, obtain various sub student groups under various clustering variable indicator values, and then wedge these sub student groups into specific ideological and political work scenarios, providing the implementation path for each sub group to carry out accurate ideological and political assistance and refined ideological and political education. Based on the cluster analysis method, propose two typical ideological and political scenes, student portraits and precise ideological and political work paths.

$$K = (TA - \sum_{n=1}^{\infty} EF) + (TU - \sum_{n=1}^{\infty} EF) \tag{1}$$

The precise ideological and political work in colleges and universities based on student portraits is a new mode of ideological and political work, in which student portraits are the core and link, and it includes three main functional modules: ideological and political demand module, data warehouse module, and portrait visualization module, which all assume special functions in student portraits. The realization of the student portrait system in the precise ideological and political work starts with the student portrait demand of the ideological and political demand module, obtains the export data of the portrait algorithm through the entrance data collection of the data warehouse module and the operation of the portrait algorithm, and finally presents it through the user-friendly design of the portrait visualization module. The contents and implementation methods of each module are shown in Table 3. The computer implementation of the student portrait system is usually based on the design of a three-tier data warehouse. The first tier is to collect data sources related to accurate ideological and political education from various data platforms in colleges and universities, and to index and summarize them; The second layer is to extract, filter, clean, convert and load the data source of the first layer, and then map to generate the leaf tag value in the student portrait tag tree, that is, the leaf form value; The third layer is to conduct word frequency statistics, data modeling and other data analysis and processing on the data of the second layer, generate the portrait hierarchical tag value, and then obtain the student portrait tag value through visualization processing. Its main workflow is shown in Fig. 1. In work practice, we can use Hadoop platform and MapReduce model to build various online systems for student behavior profiling analysis according to the workflow shown.

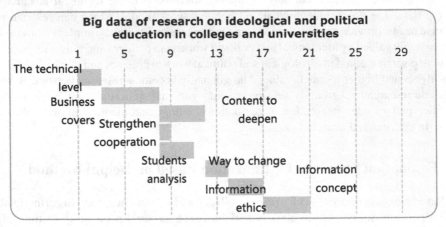

Fig. 1. Evaluation dimensions and observation indexes of vocational education informatization benchmarking system

Acknowledgement. This work was supported by grant of No. Pdjh2021b0744 from the special fund for science and technology innovation strategy of Guangdong Province in 2021; **and by grant of No. _2021GXSZ143_ from The** 2021 Guangdong Provincial Ideological and Political Education Project "Research on Accurate Ideological and Political Education in Colleges and Universities Based on Student Portrait Analysis"; **and by grant of No. (GDPIC)-2021-zx-18 from the** 2021 school level entrusted special project of Guangdong Polytechnic of Industry & Commerce; **and by grant of No. 202201011636 from the** 2022 basic and applied basic research project of Guangzhou basic research plan (general project) "Research on bonding mechanism of seawater and sand concrete based on thread characteristics of BFRP reinforcement". **And by grant of No.** *22GDZY0105* **from The** 2022 Higher Education Scientific Research Planning Project of the Chinese Association of Higher Education "Research on the Construction of the National Qualifications Framework and the Implementation of the 1+X Certificate System".

References

1. Lin, M.: Combined effects of expansive agents and glass fibres on the fracture performance of seawater and sea-sand concrete. J. Mater. Res. Technol. **20**, 1839–1859 (2022)
2. Min, L., Wu, H., Qiu, Y., Zheng, J.: Crack mechanism analysis of fiber seawater sea sand concrete based on deep learning. Build. Struct. **52**(S1), 1582–1586 (2022). https://doi.org/10.19701/j.jzjg.22S1426
3. Nouwen, W., Clycq, N., Struyf, A., Donche, V.: The role of work-based learning for student engagement in vocational education and training: an application of the self-system model of motivational development. Eur. J. Psychol. Educ. **2**(1), 1–24 (2021)
4. Du, J.: Exploration on the integration path of distance and open education and vocational education under the background of "Internet+", Open Access Libr. J. **8**(4), 1–15(2021)
5. The European Parliament and the Council. Recommendation on the establishment of the European qualification framework for lifelong learning. Official J. Eur. Union (6) (2008)

Heterogeneous Edge Network of Agricultural and Forestry Plant Protection UAV Research on Computing Offload and Resource Management

Ming Jiang[1]([⊠]), Zhenyu Xu[2], and Meng Wang[1]

[1] Harbin Institute of Technology, Harbin 150001, China
mjiang@hit.edu.cn
[2] Hui Zhou Engineering Vocational College, Huizhou 516023, China

Abstract. This paper is oriented to the research scenario of heterogeneous edge networks of agricultural and forestry plant protection UAVs. Based on the in-depth analysis of the heterogeneity of edge networks, the attributes of tasks and the performance of computing offload, this paper mainly studies the computing offload and resource management strategies applicable to heterogeneous edge networks. The goal is to reduce the energy consumption of users as much as possible by optimizing the offload decisions, radio resources and computing resources, under the premise of ensuring the completion delay of users' tasks so as to further improve the ability of heterogeneous edge computing networks to assist user computing. The research results are of great significance to improve user service experience, reduce the backhaul network pressure and the computing pressure of equipment with limited resources.

Keywords: Heterogeneous Edge Network · Computing Offload · Resource Management

1 Introduction

The hilly and mountainous areas in China account for nearly 70% of the land area. They are characterized by undulating terrain, complex and changeable landform and soil conditions, and large terrain drop, resulting in small agricultural production plots, mostly in the form of small sloping fields and terraces. Agricultural production still mainly depends on human and animal power. Modern surface agricultural machinery is difficult to operate, and the production efficiency is quite different from that in plain areas. In general, the level of mechanization in hilly and mountainous areas in China is obviously backward. There is a big gap between the mechanization scale and the operation speed and the plain areas. The low level of agricultural mechanization has become a bottleneck restricting the development of agricultural modernization in hilly and mountainous areas. During the 14th Five Year Plan period of agriculture, the development of agricultural mechanization in hilly and mountainous areas was listed as the key development

© ICST Institute for Computer Sciences, Social Informatics and Telecommunications Engineering 2023
Published by Springer Nature Switzerland AG 2023. All Rights Reserved
A. Li et al. (Eds.): 6GN 2022, LNICST 505, pp. 230–239, 2023.
https://doi.org/10.1007/978-3-031-36014-5_20

direction, and efforts were made to break through the bottleneck of various agricultural production and management.

As an important part of agricultural production management, plant protection plays a vital role in crop growth and yield assurance. The application of aerial pesticide by plant protection UAV has the advantages of fast operation flight speed, high spraying efficiency, strong ability to deal with sudden disasters, and can overcome the problem that ground agricultural machinery or manual work cannot enter the ground. In recent years, it has become more and more popular in agricultural production, and has become one of the research hotspots in the field of agricultural plant protection. The advantages of unmanned aerial vehicle (UAV) in plant protection such as high efficiency and low cost are becoming increasingly obvious, and the demand for agricultural aviation plant protection is increasing year by year. The application of UAV in the agricultural field indicates that the level of agricultural modernization in China has been greatly improved. With the national policy guidance, intensive and large-scale planting will become the new trend of agricultural development, and its demand for UAV plant protection operations will be growing.

At present, there are many studies on the application of agricultural aviation plant protection technology in areas with flat terrain and wide vision, such as large fields in plain areas. During plant protection operations, UAVs mainly fly manually and remotely. Operators remotely control UAVs for route flight operations or hover and target operations according to their own vision, experience and characteristics such as field boundaries or crop texture. The quality of plant protection operations depends on the proficiency of operators Experience, rows and rows of crops, surface texture and other environmental characteristics, manual operation of UAVs for plant protection operations are subject to double restrictions of equipment and operators, and the actual plant protection operations rely too much on operators. As the hilly and mountainous terrain fluctuates, the crop canopy is irregular, and the terrain is complex and the texture characteristics are not obvious compared with the field crops, which further increases the difficulty of UAV plant protection operation. Manual control cannot ensure that the UAV is consistent with the canopy area and the spacing is appropriate, resulting in poor uniformity of spraying between different regions, serious re spraying, leakage spraying and other phenomena, thus affecting the effect of plant protection operation, And then affect the yield and quality of crops.

The effect and efficiency of UAV plant protection operations are directly related to the cost of agricultural production and the yield and quality of crops, and affect the enthusiasm of farmers to use UAVs for production operations. Planning the flight path of UAV plant protection operation can effectively improve the efficiency of UAV plant protection operation. At the same time, combined with relevant UAV automatic control technology, it can further realize the automation and intelligent control of UAV plant protection operation, which will greatly improve the efficiency and effect of UAV plant protection operation in hilly and mountainous areas and other complex terrain areas. Therefore, path planning for UAV plant protection operation is very important, especially in hilly and mountainous areas where manual remote control is inconvenient.

2   Technical Requirements of the Industry, Products and Market for the Project

Path planning is one of the main research contents of motion planning. For path planning of UAV plant protection operation, it requires UAV to find an optimal path from the starting point to the end point of the target movement in its motion space according to certain optimization principles, such as the minimum energy consumption, the shortest walking route, the fastest walking time, etc. For plant protection UAV, its path planning should not only determine its operation direction and path according to the crop type and planting mode, but also consider the energy cost and operation efficiency to minimize the cost of its entire work process. Due to the undulation and changefulness of hilly terrain, the conventional path planning method cannot be directly used for crop plant protection in hilly and mountainous areas. Therefore, based on the analysis of the needs of UAV plant protection operations in hilly and mountainous areas, the research on the path planning of UAV plant protection operations in hilly and mountainous areas is carried out. The energy efficiency coefficient of UAV movement process is constructed as the constraint condition for the path planning of UAV plant protection operations, and intelligent algorithm is introduced to achieve the optimal path planning of energy consumption for plant protection operations. Exploring the optimal path planning method of UAV operation energy consumption based on energy efficiency constraints can improve the efficiency and effect of UAV plant protection operations in hilly and mountainous areas, which has important application value in promoting the process of agricultural mechanization in hilly and mountainous areas, expanding the scope of agricultural aviation plant protection operations, and realizing cost saving and efficiency increasing in agricultural industry.

With the rapid development of 5G, Internet of Things, big data, artificial intelligence, cloud computing and other information technologies, more and more devices are connected to the Internet. According to Cisco's data, the number of Internet of Things devices connected to the Internet has reached 50 billion by 2020. With the massive growth of access devices, users' requirements for quality of experience (QoE) are also getting higher and higher, which together lead to an exponential growth in the amount of data in the network. Massive big data gave birth to the technology of cloud computing. Due to the limited storage and processing capacity of devices, cloud computing has become the main way to solve the shortage of users' computing resources in the past decade. However, virtual reality, augmented reality, Internet of Vehicles, 4K live video and other emerging services under 5G network are sensitive to time delay. Specifically, Internet of Vehicles technology requires a delay of 5ms, virtual reality/augmented reality technology requires a delay of 7-15ms, online games require a delay of no more than 50ms, and high-definition live video requires an end-to-end delay of no more than 300ms. Under such delay requirements, cloud computing cannot meet the needs of users. Based on the above background, the European Telecommunications Standards Institute (ETSI) put forward the edge computing (MEC) architecture [1] in 2014. By deploying a platform with computing processing capability at the network edge to provide computing services for mobile users, Network Functions Virtualization (NFV) and Software defined Networks (SDN), as the enabling technologies of MEC, allow the deployment of MEC servers on the base station side. Users can upload delay sensitive tasks to the MEC server through the wireless link between the base station and the user, and download the results after processing. Figure 1 shows the implementation process of face recognition application combined with MEC. It can be seen from the figure that the user only performs the task of image acquisition, and the subsequent tasks are uploaded to the MEC server for execution. Finally, the user downloads the results.

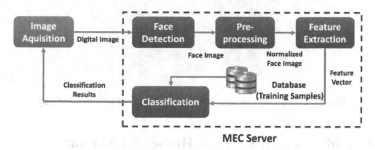

Fig. 1. Schematic diagram of MEC server performing face recognition task

In addition to base stations, UAVs are also considered to have the potential to serve as MEC servers. With the continuous maturity of technology, UAVs have the ability to provide users with communication support as aerial base stations and are considered to be an important part of the future network [2]. In June 2020, the Pterosaur I UAV, developed by the Chengdu Flight Design and Research Institute of China's aviation industry, carried a communication base station and continued to circle at an altitude of about 4000 m above sea level with a radius of more than 3000 m, with an effective coverage of more than 50 square kilometers and a single endurance of 35 h, effectively solving the problem of communication interruption in emergency situations. In July 2021, Yilong 2H UAV, equipped with communication relay equipment, will provide users with 5-h emergency communication service in the communication interruption area of Mihe Town, Henan Province, covering an area of 50 square kilometers and a relay transmission distance of 120 km. There are three main advantages of UAV as MEC server. First, when encountering natural disasters such as earthquakes, ground infrastructure such as base stations are often paralyzed. At this time, the UAV carries computing and communication modules that can provide communication and computing services for users in disaster areas. Second, under the scene of large-scale personnel gathering in concerts, tourist attractions and peak periods, UAV as MEC server can relieve the pressure of base station processing tasks, To improve users' QoE, Fig. 2 shows the hot spots of computing requests at different times of the day in the same place. The third is that the probability of Line of Sight (LoS) is high when UAV communicates with ground users, which can effectively reduce the time for users to calculate unloading. Therefore, by deploying computing power at the edge of the network, users with different performance requirements can selectively upload tasks with high computing resource requirements and delay sensitivity to the MEC server, and use communication resources to exchange computing resources to improve the service experience and reduce backhaul network pressure.

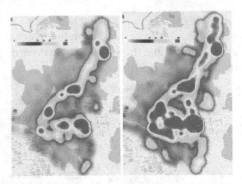

Fig. 2. Calculation request hotspots at different times of the day

3   Analysis of Research Status at Home and Abroad

3.1   Status and Analysis of Binary Computing Offload Strategies in Heterogeneous Edge Networks

In document [3], the concept and importance of workload allocation in edge computing are first pointed out, that is, the location and mode of task processing are determined by comprehensively considering the computing capacity and battery capacity of different edge devices. From the user's point of view, the definition of binary computing offload and partial computing offload is given, and the corresponding application of these two offloads is given. On the basis of literature [3], literature [4] gives a model of tasks in computing offload, modeling a task as a three-dimensional vector consisting of task size, CPU revolutions required by each bit of task and task completion deadline, giving a model of energy consumption for local computing, and further emphasizing the important influence of wireless links on computing offload strategy. Since the target problem established in the context of binary computing offload is an integer programming problem, which cannot be solved by convex optimization theory, firstly, the research status of binary offload strategy for edge computing in heterogeneous networks is analyzed.

3.2   Status and Analysis of Partial Computing Offload and Resource Management in Heterogeneous Edge Networks

Time delay and energy consumption are two core performance indicators in edge computing. The impact of the quality of the calculation offload strategy on the performance of the calculation offload is obvious and most important. However, on the basis of the correct calculation offload strategy, the overhead in the process of calculation offload can be further reduced by the management of radio resources, calculation resources and time resources. For example, on the premise of ensuring that the time delay meets the requirements, The minimum energy cost can be guaranteed by adjusting the transmission power and dynamic voltage frequency adjustment. Since the decision behavior of partial unloading can be represented by continuous variables within an interval, it is different from the integer programming problem in binary unloading. When tasks can be subdivided into unrelated subtasks (video compression, virus scanning) with small granularity, the partial unloading strategy and resource management method can be jointly optimized from the perspective of convex optimization. Further, when the equipment and the base station adopt different channel forms and different access methods for communication, the methods of resource management are also different.

3.3 Research Status of Computing Offload and Resource Management in Random Dynamic Heterogeneous Edge Networks

The predecessors have made in-depth research on the computing offload and resource management technologies of heterogeneous edge networks, but these works are based on two assumptions: one is that each user can obtain the channel state information (CSI) at the current time through the channel estimation at the base station before making the offload decision; the other is that each user generates a task at each time, The next task does not reach the user until the current task is processed, that is, the default condition for keeping the queue stable is always met. These two assumptions are reasonable in many application scenarios, but they are not applicable to all application scenarios. This is due to the randomness and dynamics of the actual network. The randomness is reflected in the CSI at the user end. When the base station communicates with multiple users at the same time, the high complexity of the channel estimation algorithm will cause errors in the channel estimation results and feedback delays, resulting in imperfect CSI at the user end. At this time, the first assumption is not true. Dynamism is not reflected in the mobility of users, but in the arrival rate of tasks. When computing requests are intensive, the time interval between each task arriving at the client is shortened, and whether the task is processed locally or unloaded to a remote server requires a certain amount of processing time, which leads to the possibility that tasks arriving at the user during the time period when computing requests are intensive may face queuing, At this point, it is necessary to design the calculation unloading strategy and resource management method on the premise of meeting the stability of the queue.

4 Literature Research Summary

In terms of the research on binary computing offload strategy of heterogeneous edge networks, the work done by the existing research can be summarized as solving the problem of "where is the best task to handle", which is mainly oriented to indivisible tasks, that is, the variable representing task decision is a binary variable, and the modeling problem is that integer programming problems often have NP Hard attributes. Starting from the simplest scenario of single cell single user, the scholars used dynamic programming, branch and bound, game theory and other methods to give the suboptimal solution of the NP Hard problem, with the goal of minimizing the delay or energy consumption as the optimization objective and the task decision as the optimization variable, and extended it to the network scenario of single cell multi-user and multi cell multi-user. Furthermore, combined with the high flexibility and controllability of UAV, UAV can play the role of MEC server in the scenario of UAV carrying computing resources. The existing research also considers the design of computing unloading strategy when only UAV provides computing services for users and base station and UAV jointly provide computing services for users. The research results show that compared with benchmark algorithms such as all tasks are locally computed and all tasks are computed on MEC server, the computation offload strategy designed by the existing work has greatly improved the performance of delay and energy consumption. The disadvantage is that although existing research has put forward many solutions for binary offloading in different scenarios, local optimal algorithms such as greedy algorithms and heuristic algorithms cannot adapt to the task attributes and channel states that change at each time, while for example, the complexity of branch and bound optimal algorithms increases exponentially when the network size is large, Because most of the tasks handled by the edge computing system are sensitive to time delay, it is difficult for algorithms with high computational complexity to be applied in the actual network even if they can obtain the optimal solution, and distributed solving methods such as game theory face the problem that convergence cannot be guaranteed, and there is less work considering UAV assisted edge computing in the existing work. Therefore, how to design a low complexity binary computing offload strategy for heterogeneous edge computing networks with time variability to effectively reduce the energy consumption and processing delay of users is a problem worth studying.

In terms of computing offload and resource management of heterogeneous edge networks, the work done by existing research can be summarized as solving the two problems of "where is the best task to handle" and "how is the best task to handle", which are mainly oriented to arbitrarily subdivided fine-grained tasks, that is, the variable representing task decision-making is a continuous variable. With the goal of minimizing energy consumption, the problem of "where to handle tasks best" is solved by optimizing task decision variables. Through the optimization of computing resources, radio resources and time resources, the problem of "how to best handle tasks" is solved. Since the optimization variables are all continuous variables, the problems after modeling can often be solved by convex optimization. Scholars mainly started from the most common scenario of single cell multi-user, different users accessing the base station using TDMA and FDMA, and using single antenna communication, and used block coordinate descent method, Lagrange multiplier method, continuous convex approximation and other methods to solve the problem. In recent work, some scholars have further explored the methods of computing offload and resource management in MIMO channel and NOMA access forms, and used positive semi definite relaxation method to optimize the transmission power covariance matrix and other resources. The research results show that the partial computation offload and resource management methods designed in the existing work can further reduce the energy consumption and processing delay of all users. The disadvantage is that although the existing research has achieved rich research results in the scenario of single antenna and multi-user orthogonal access, there is still less research in the miso and MIMO channels that are closer to the actual application scenario, and there is less work considering UAV assisted edge computing in the existing work. At the same time, considering the access scenario of ultra large scale IOT devices, the multi-user access mode will no longer be orthogonal access, but NOMA access. Whether it is MIMO channel or NOMA access, the form and solution of computing offload and resource allocation problems will be greatly changed. At present, the research in MIMO channel is mainly based on the semi positive definite relaxation method, and in NOMA access, the iterative optimization method is mainly used to solve the problem. Both methods are easy to converge to the local optimal solution, and there is still no work to consider the calculation unloading and resource allocation in multi-user MIMO-NOMA scenarios. Both MIMO technology and NOMA technology can greatly improve the spectrum efficiency of uplink communication and reduce energy consumption. Since the performance of computing offload is closely related to the uplink throughput, it is worth studying how to design energy-efficient computing offload strategies and resource allocation methods for MIMO-OMA scenarios from the perspective of optimization.

In terms of computing offload and resource management of random dynamic heterogeneous edge networks, the existing research work can be summarized as further considering the randomness and dynamic constraints of the actual network on the basis of solving "Where is the best task to handle "and" How to handle the best task ". Randomness is reflected in the CSI at the current time of the user. Existing work models the CSI at the current time as an estimated CSI plus feedback error, and models the problem as a random optimization problem for solution. The existing research has proposed heuristic algorithm, Markov decision process and other approximate solutions. The research results show that the existing research has lower energy consumption and task processing delay than the benchmark algorithm under the same channel model. The dynamic nature is reflected in the dynamic arrival of tasks. The existing work considers that users have local processing queues and remote unloading queues. The two queues are limited in length. On the basis of ensuring the stability of the queues, the calculation unloading and resource management methods are designed. By using Lyapunov optimization method, the global optimization problem is transformed into an optimization problem at each time, so that the stochastic optimization problem can be solved by convex optimization method. The research results show that by setting different control parameters, the user's energy consumption and processing delay present a compromise relationship. The disadvantage is that the existing research starts from randomness and dynamics respectively. When considering randomness, the CSI at the current time is modeled as the superposition of channel estimation and feedback error, and the problem is modeled as a random optimization problem for solution. When considering the dynamics, based on Lyapunov optimization theory, under the premise of guaranteeing the stability of the queue, the long-term average problem is transformed into the optimal problem at each time. However, at present, all Lyapunov based optimized computation offloading and resource management strategies are based on the premise of perfect CSI at the sending end at the current time, without considering the channel estimation error at the current time, which cannot always be true in heterogeneous edge networks where the channel state changes rapidly. Considering the imperfect CSI at the current moment, the deterministic optimization problem at each moment will be transformed into a stochastic optimization problem, which increases the difficulty of solving the problem. Therefore, how to design the computing offload and resource strategy to ensure the stability of the queue from a statistical point of view under the premise of considering the imperfect CSI is a valuable problem.

5 Conclusion

This paper studies the computing offload and resource management strategies applicable to the heterogeneous edge network. The goal is to reduce the energy consumption of users as much as possible by optimizing offload decisions, radio resources and computing resources on the premise of ensuring the completion delay of user tasks, so as to further improve the ability of heterogeneous edge computing networks to assist user computing. The research results in this paper are of great significance for improving user service experience, reducing backhaul network pressure and computing pressure of equipment with limited resources. At the same time, they can further promote the automation and intelligent control of UAV plant protection operations, and greatly improve the efficiency and effect of UAV plant protection operations in hilly and mountainous areas and other complex terrain areas.

References

1. Mobile-edge computing—Introductory technical white paper.
2. Zeng, Y., Zhang, R., Lim, T.J.: Wireless communications with unmanned aerial vehicles: opportunities and challenges. IEEE Commun. Mag. **54**(5), 36–42 (2016)
3. Shi, W., Cao, J., Zhang, Q., et al.: Edge Computing: Vision and Challenges. IEEE Internet Things J. **3**(5), 637–646 (2016)
4. Mao, Y., You, C., Zhang, J., et al.: A survey on mobile edge computing: the communication perspective. IEEE Commun. Surv. Tutorials **19**(4), 2322–2358 (2017)
5. Wang, F., Xu, J., Cui, S.: Optimal energy allocation and task offloading policy for wWireless powered mobile edge computing systems. IEEE Trans. Wireless Commun. **19**(4), 2443–2459 (2020)
6. Zhang, J., Hu, X., Ning, Z., et al.: Energy-latency tradeoff for energy-aware offloading in mobile edge computing networks. IEEE Internet Things J. **5**(4), 2633–2645 (2018)
7. Zhang, K., Gui, X., Ren, D., et al.: Energy-Latency Tradeoff for Computation Offloading in UAV-assisted Multi-Access Edge Computing System. IEEE Internet Things J.**8**, 6709–6719 (2020)
8. Zhang, L., Ansari, N.: Optimizing the operation cost for UAV-aided mobile edge computing. IEEE Trans. Veh. Technol. **70**(6), 6085–6093 (2021)
9. Wang, C., Yu, F.R., Liang, C., et al.: Joint computation offloading and interference management in wireless cellular networks with mobile edge computing. IEEE Trans. Veh. Technol. **66**(8), 7432–7445 (2017)
10. Wang, C.M., Liang, C.C., Yu, F.R., et al.: Computation offloading and resource allocation in wireless cellular networks with mobile edge computing. IEEE Trans. Wireless Commun. **16**(8), 4924–4938 (2017)
11. Liao, Z., Peng, J., Huang, J., et al.: Distributed probabilistic offloading in edge computing for 6G-enabled massive Internet of Things. IEEE Internet Things J. **8**, 5298–5308 (2020)
12. Feng, J., Pei, Q.Q., Yu, F.R., et al.: Dynamic network slicing and resource allocation in mobile edge computing systems. IEEE Trans. Veh. Technol. **69**(7), 7863–7878 (2020)
13. Zhou, W., Xing, L., Xia, J., et al.: Dynamic computation offloading for MIMO mobile edge computing systems with energy harvesting. IEEE Trans. Veh. Technol. **70**(5), 5172–5177 (2021)

14. Wang, H., Liu, C., Shi, Z., et al.: On the design of high power efficiency uplink MIMO-NOMA systems: a STBC and joint detection perspective. IEEE Trans. Veh. Technol. **70**(1), 627–638 (2021)
15. Song, Z., Liu, Y., Sun, X.: Joint task offloading and resource allocation for NOMA-enabled multi-access mobile edge computing. IEEE Trans. Commun. **69**(3), 1548–1564 (2021)

Unmanned Aerial Vehicle Communication for 6G Networks

Research on Anycast Scheduling Algorithm in Edge Computing Networks

Lin Wu[1], Xiao Lin[2], and Yao Shi[1(✉)]

[1] Harbin Institute of Technology, Harbin, China
shiyao@hit.edu.cn
[2] College of Physics and Information Engineering, Fuzhou University, Fuzhou, China

Abstract. In recent years, the development of edge computing technology has brought many conveniences to people's lives and many outstanding works have been proposed. However, these efforts do not focus on the selection and routing problem of computing nodes. In this paper, an algorithm is designed to integrate and downscale the link adjacency matrix and computing resource table of multiple moments to one dimension, changing the multi-layer topology into a single-layer topology. Based on this, a model of resource evaluation is proposed, which can evaluate the availability of link and node resources more accurately. Specifically, a bandwidth and computing resource fusion method based on network topology is proposed. On this basis, an anycast scheduling method is proposed, which features: 1) using a resource evaluation model evaluate computing and bandwidth resources; 2) introducing auxiliary points to achieve computing and bandwidth resource fusion, integrating resource availability evaluation values into the same topology and performing routing and resource scheduling; 3) updating the resource evaluation table in real time, thus achieving load balancing. Meanwhile the edge computing network scenario is established to realize the simulation of dynamic processes such as background flow and anycast service. On this basis, the performance of the traditional anycast scheduling method and the scheduling method proposed in this paper are compared. The experimental results show that the algorithm has excellent performance in terms of blocking rate and utilization, and has good practicality and superiority to meet the computing offloading tasks between nodes in edge computing networks.

Keywords: Edge Computing · Anycast

1 Introduction

Edge computing can be traced back to the Content Delivery Network (CDN) proposed by Akamai [1]. CDN is a caching file network based on Internet technology. It can direct the requests from customers to the terminal which has the shortest distance thereby reducing network latency and improving the response time and accuracy of user requests with the help of cache servers located in different locations and the load balancing, content distribution, scheduling modules of the management center service platform. CDNs

A. Li et al. (Eds.): 6GN 2022, LNICST 505, pp. 243–256, 2023.
https://doi.org/10.1007/978-3-031-36014-5_21

focus on backup data and cached files for content, while the basic idea of edge computing is functional caching. Later, Satyanarayanan et al. proposed the idea of Cloudlet [2]. Cloudlets are reliable and powerful computing servers that locate themselves at the edge of the network, connect to the Internet, and respond to mobile requests and provide computing resources to them. During this time, edge computing focuses on the downlink, and services from the cloud host are passed to the edge network host to reduce network congestion and latency. However, with the widespread adoption of the Internet of Things, the incremental data at the edge hit the Internet with an immeasurable trend. To better handle the computational load and data transfer bandwidth during data transmission, computation and storage, the focus is on adding computing resources and processing power around the user, i.e., the uplink of the Internet of Everything service function. This led to the advent of mobile edge computing (MEC).

In recent years, in the context of resource integration for edge computing, Pu has proposed a crowd-smart collaborative framework where each mobile client is described as a "potential provider" and the client can request computing services from the "potential provider" in necessary scenarios [3]. The "providers" are other endpoints in the network that are willing to offer computing services, and designs a common recruitment strategy to significantly increase the total amount of resources available. The group wisdom approach is a trend in the future, similar to P2P networks, which can greatly decentralize and improve the processing performance of servers. In [4], a multi-marketplace-based dynamic bi-directional auction mechanism, MobiAuc, is proposed to encourage endpoint cooperation and solve the problem of balanced allocation arising from transactions using dynamic bi-directional auctions in the context of complex networks with multiple endpoints.

In terms of improving the performance of edge computing, Li proposes a randomized combinatorial auction mechanism based on various parameter criteria of edge computing networks in order to reduce the collaboration overhead at the inter-node point of edge terminals [5]. This mechanism senses the client requests and includes an ellipsoidal approach to generate the set of requests and the weights possessed by each request by deriving the upper bound of the integrity gap. Also, Han designs a multidimensional space-based collaboration strategy that effectively reduces the cost of user terminals in performing resource collaboration [6].

In terms of task migration, Wang and Machen consider factors such as cost, network structure and mobile model heterogeneity in designing the task migration algorithm to predict the cost of running tasks on each mobile microcloud and the cost of task migration through the underlying prediction mechanism. The task migration framework is constructed using a hierarchical idea to minimize the total time for task migration [7, 8].

Furthermore, due to the development of some edge computing applications, cooperation between edge nodes and edge resource management bring new opportunities and challenges [9]. Based on the instability of the edge environment, the optimization of the edge computing architecture should be carried out by strengthening the cooperation between tasks. In this regard, several techniques are available [10].

However, these efforts pay more attention on the structure of edge computing, and do not focus on the selection and routing problem of computing nodes in edge computing.

This paper explores the routing problem for a multi-temporal layer bandwidth resource topology in an optical network-based edge computing system and proposes an evaluation algorithm that reduces the multi-layer topology into a single-layer topology for routing by measuring and evaluating the bandwidth characteristics of a single link over a number of times. This paper also proposes an engineering approach to incorporate two different levels of parameters, bandwidth resources and computing resources, into the same topology for routing. In Sect. 2, some relevant background information involved in this algorithm will be presented. In Sect. 3, the principle, steps and some implementation details of the algorithm and demonstrate the feasibility of the method will be specified. In Sect. 4, some experiments will be conducted to explore the best use scenarios of the algorithm and compare it with some other methods to demonstrate the superiority of the method designed in this paper.

2 Network Model

The network model considered in this paper is a time-shifted multilayer topology graph, in which the bandwidth resources of each link and the computing resources of each node are changed over time. The topologies are chosen as six-node topology, NSFNET topology and USNET topology, as shown in Fig. 1, Fig. 2 and Fig. 3.

The bandwidth resources can be controlled to maintain a specific occupancy rate to simulate the background flow in the existing network, setting the computing resources required per unit of bandwidth BW transmitted $M = BW * 1$. The time interval for each resource shift is 10 ms, and the multilayer topology model is shown in Fig. 4.

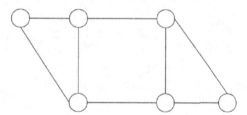

Fig. 1. Six-node network topology

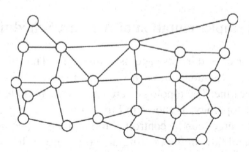

Fig. 2. USNET network topology

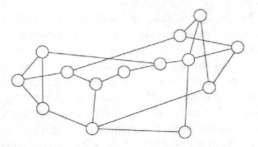

Fig. 3. NSFNET network topology

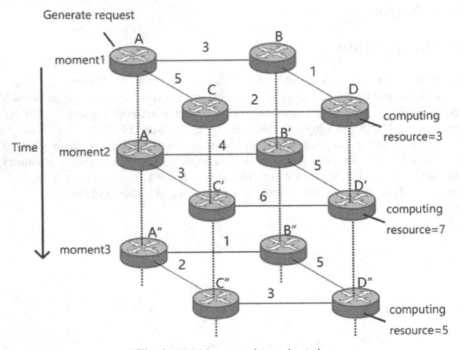

Fig. 4. Multi-layer topology schematic

3   Principle and Implementation of Anycast Scheduling Algorithm

The network model considered in this paper is a time-shifted multilayer topology graph, in which the bandwidth resources of each link and the computing resources of each node are changed over time. The topologies are chosen as six-node topology, NSFNET topology and USNET topology, as shown in Fig. 1, Fig. 2 and Fig. 3.

The bandwidth resources can be controlled to maintain a specific occupancy rate to simulate the background flow in the existing network, setting the computing resources required per unit of bandwidth BW transmitted $M = BW * 1$. The time interval for each resource shift is 10 ms, and the multilayer topology model is shown in Fig. 4.

Considering the bandwidth resources and computing resources at multiple moments, there is another time dimension in topology, so the traditional single-layer topology routing algorithm is clearly not applicable to this situation. In this paper, we propose an evaluation algorithm that integrates and evaluates the multi-moment resources into a single-layer topology graph where each link can reflect the overall situation of that link at multiple moments. In the single-layer topology, routing is performed by the typical Dijkstra [11] and KSP [12] algorithms, successfully reducing the complex routing work for multilayer graphs to routing work for single-layer topologies. The focus of the work is also changed from designing a multilayer graph routing algorithm to designing a mathematical model that can evaluate the resource situation well and is easy to work on.

Referring to the spectrum fragmentation evaluation formula proposed in paper [13], the following information in the topology is extracted for evaluation in this paper, considering the change of resources over time (where the evaluation method for link bandwidth is similar to the evaluation method for node computing resources, we will focus on bandwidth resources in the following): total average value of resources BW_{all}, and the average value of single link resources BW_{sin}, minimum value of single link resources BW_{min}, single link resource standard deviation BW_{std}.

Total average value BW_{sin}: Since the requirement of the proposed algorithm is to select the relatively optimal one from many links, the total average value is an important criterion to measure the quality of resources, and it can be well evaluated by comparing each value with the total average value.

Single-link resource average: the average of a set of data can be a good representation of their overall situation. Here, the average of a single link is introduced to compare with the total evaluation average, by introducing a Sigmoid-like function:

$$\phi_1(x, y) = \frac{1}{1 + e^{0.2 \times (x-y)}} \tag{1}$$

As shown in Fig. 5, input $\phi_1(BW_{all}, BW_{sin})$, the result is larger when the average is smaller than the total evaluation mean, which corresponds to a greater overhead in Dijkstra routing, and vice versa. The middle section of the function is a curve close to a straight line, which can play a good role in differentiation, but when the difference between the individual mean and the total mean is too large or too small the function result will converge to a constant, preventing too extreme results that affect the subsequent processing.

Single-link resource minimum BW_{min}: Although the average value can express where the situation of the link is relatively located in the overall network, considering that the average value cannot express the lower limit of this set of data, the efficiency of data transmission or computation is greatly reduced when the average value is very high but a very small value exists. The purpose of introducing a minimum value compared to the total mean is to exclude as much as possible the influence of extreme cases on the request. In a manner similar to the treatment of the mean, a Sigmoid-like function is introduced, but considering that the purpose is to exclude extreme cases, a high degree of differentiation is not required in the middle section of the function, and the two Sigmoid-like functions are combined into a new function as follows:

$$\phi_2(x, y) = \begin{cases} 2 - 1/(1 + e^{-0.35 \times (x-y/2)}) & (x<y) \\ 1 - 1/(1 + e^{-0.35 \times (x-y \times 3/2)}) & (x>y) \end{cases} \tag{2}$$

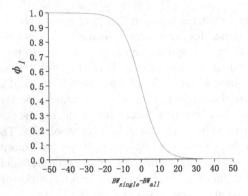

Fig. 5. Curve of ϕ_1

As in Fig. 6, set BW_{all}=50, input $\phi_2(BW_{min}, 50)$, x-axis for a single-link resource minimum BW_{min}, when the minimum value is much smaller than the average value of the function results will converge to a larger constant, and vice versa, to facilitate subsequent processing. The difference is located in the middle of the function, it can be understood as the minimum value of the resource will not have an excessive impact on the processing of the request, so the results of the function are similar. And the function of the front and back of the middle section are an approximation of a straight line, which can form a distinction between the results generated.

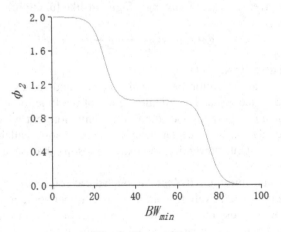

Fig. 6. Curve of ϕ_2

Standard deviation BW_{std}: The standard deviation can reflect the dispersion of a set of data, the standard deviation of the data is large corresponding to the degree of fluctuation, corresponding to the actual is the uncertainty of whether the request can be completed large. But consider a situation, if a set of functions has a large standard deviation at the same time the mean is also large, then it can be believed that the probability it can achieve the request is also relatively large. Set the final measurement results as follows:

$$result = \phi_1(BW_{all}, BW_{sin}) \times \phi_2(BW_{all}, BW_{sin}) \times BW_{sin} \div BW_{sin} \times \alpha \qquad (3)$$

After testing, set $\alpha = 10$, the final measured value of a relatively good set of links is 0–10, an average link is 10–25, and a worse link is 25 or more, which can better distinguish the resource availability of a set of links.

Since computing resources and bandwidth resources cannot be combined as the same class of overhead for computing, the shortest path selection for a class of overhead in the traditional routing method is invalid, and the destination of anycast is an arbitrary node, the shortest path algorithm such as Dijkstra cannot be applied for routing. However, since only one node needs to be selected for computing request processing, as shown in Fig. 7, the same virtual node can be connected to all computable nodes, and the overhead of this virtual node from each computing node is the evaluation value of available computing resources of this node, then the traditional shortest path selection method is introduced at this time, and the source node is set to this virtual node and the destination node is set to send the request to client terminal, then the program will first select the optimal compute node and then the optimal bandwidth path from that compute node to the client. This method well integrates bandwidth resources and computing resources into a single routing algorithm, and achieves the purpose of anycast scheduling algorithm to elect the request processing node in edge computing.

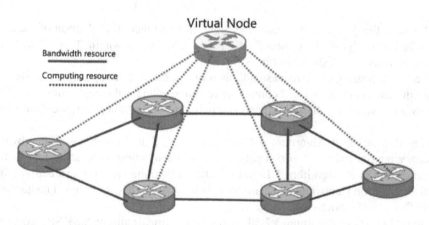

Fig. 7. Topology of computing resources connecting virtual nodes

The method for generating the evaluation matrix is presented below, and the pseudocode is shown in Table 1.

Step 1: Line ① of Algorithm 3.1 obtains the parameters of the entire topology to be evaluated.

Step 2: Lines ②–⑦ of Algorithm 3.1 evaluate the bandwidth resources of each link by Eq. 3.

Step 3: Lines ⑧–⑪of Algorithm 3.1 evaluates each node computing resources by Eq. 3.

Step 4: The two types of valuations are combined into one evaluation matrix E.

Table 1. Evaluation matrix generation method

Algorithm 3.1 Generate the evaluation matrix

Input: bandwidth table s, calculation resource table CS

Output: evaluation matrix E

① $[n,n,t]$=size(s) to obtain the number of nodes and layers, generate the $n*n$ matrix E, calculate the bandwidth and calculate the total average value of resources;

② **for** i =1:n **do**

③   **for** j = 1:n **do**

④   Obtain the mean, minimum, and variance of the links according to s;

⑤   Obtain the evaluation value result according to equation 3-3, $E(i,j)$=result;

⑥   **end for**

⑦ **end for**

⑧ **for** i = 1:n **do**

⑨   Obtain the mean, minimum, and variance of the node computed resources according to CS;

⑩   Obtain the evaluation value result according to equation 3-3, $E(n+1,i)$=result;

⑪ **end for**

⑫ Complement E to $n+1*n+1$ matrix;

⑬ return E.

Based on the design above, name the Sigmoid-like function evaluation of the anycast scheduling algorithm as SEAS, it's pseudocode is shown in Table 2 and it's implementation flow is shown in Fig. 8.

Step 1: According to the requested limited time t, the system inputs the n-node link bandwidth adjacency matrix and computing resource table for the next t moments. The expression of adjacency matrix[ai,j] and computing resource tablep[btn] are shown in 4 and 5.

Step 2: Line ② of Algorithm 3.2 first generates an n * n evaluation bandwidth adjacency matrix and a 1 * n computing resource evaluation table according to the evaluation model in Algorithm 3.1, and puts the computing resource evaluation table into the evaluation bandwidth adjacency matrix to obtain a (n + 1) * (n + 1) adjacency matrix E of n nodes with virtual nodes.

Step 3: Lines ③ of Algorithm 3.2 calculates the k optional paths by the KSP algorithm.

Step 4: Lines ④–⑩ of Algorithm 3.2 traverse each path to see if the demand is satisfied, if it is satisfied then stop the loop and output the path, if not then add the first calculated path to the Multipath table Multipath and perform the next round of calculation, a total of 5 rounds of calculation, if none of the demand can be satisfied then the request cannot be completed.

$$a_{i,j} = \begin{cases} 0, \; node \; i \; and \; j \; are \; not \; connected \\ 1, \; node \; i \; and \; j \; are \; connected \end{cases} \tag{4}$$

$$b_{tn} : \frac{n = 1, 2 \dots\dots k, k = node \; number}{t = 0, 1 \dots\dots t_{max}} \tag{5}$$

Table 2. SEAS algorithm implementation process

Algorithm 3.2 choose path

Input: Bandwidth table s, computed resource table CS, demanded bandwidth BWre-
quire, demanded computed resource CSrequire

Output: Final routing result Multipath

①   **for** i= 1:5 **do**

②   Generate an evaluation matrix E from Algorithm 3.1 based on bandwidth table s
    and   computing resource table CS;

③ $Path=KSP(E)$, n=Number of $Path$, $Multipath$=[],$finalpath$=0;

④   **for** j=1:n **do**

⑤   **if** the minimum sum of bandwidth on that link at each moment >= $BWrequire$
    & compute nodes >= $CSrequire$ **then**

⑥ $Multipath$=[$Multipath,Path$(j)],$fianlpath$=1;

⑦   **break**

⑧   **end**

⑨ $Multipath$=[$Multipath,Path$(1)], deduct according to the minimum bandwidth
    in $Path$(1) at   each moment and the computing resources table deducts the com-
    puting resources of the selected node at each moment;

⑩   **end for**

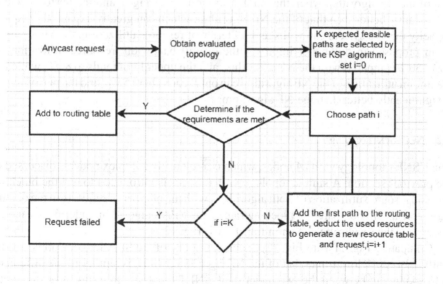

Fig. 8. Algorithm implementation flow

4 Model Simulation, Experiment and Comparison

Traditional anycast scheduling methods tend to simplify the scheduling process by using the nearly-first policy, the anycast scheduling algorithm (NF) is based on the nearly-first policy. The algorithm is designed to select only the neighboring nodes in the routing process. In the following of this paper, we will demonstrate the superiority of the SEAS algorithm by comparing it with the NF algorithm.

Experimental parameters:

(1) Link bandwidth: bandwidth resources of a single link at a single moment.

(2) Computing resources: The computing resources of a node at a single moment.

(3) Number of requests: The number of randomly generated requests.

Performance metrics:

(1) Blocking rate: the ratio of the number of failed requests to the total number of requests, used to reflect the effectiveness of the algorithm.

(2) Utilization: the ratio of the bandwidth resources used in the network to the total bandwidth resources after responding to all requests.

4.1 Number of Anycast Requests

This section explores the blocking rate and resource utilization of the SEAS algorithm with the number of requests under default and compares it with the NF algorithm, and the results are shown in Fig. 9 and Fig. 10.

By comparison, the blocking rate of the SEAS algorithm is 10%–20% lower than that of the NF algorithm when the number of requests changes, and the performance is significantly better than that of the NF algorithm, which can greatly expand the request capacity that the system can withstand. In terms of resource utilization, the SEAS algorithm proposed in this paper improves the overall bandwidth resource utilization by 30%–50% compared with the NF algorithm, and the upper limit tends to 80%, while the maximum utilization of the NF algorithm can only reach about 55%, and the performance is significantly better than the NF algorithm.

4.2 Network Topology

The USNET topology with 24 nodes, which is a relatively complex node, is discussed in the previous section. A simple topology with 6 nodes is introduced to test the blocking rate and resource utilization of both algorithms with the number of requests in the default case, and also to compare the blocking rate of the SEAS algorithm under 6, 14, and 24 nodes, and the results are shown in Fig. 11 and Fig. 12.

Comparing Fig. 11 with Fig. 12, the blocking rate of the SEAS algorithm is consistently 10%–20% lower than that of the NF algorithm, which is similar to the difference in blocking rate between the two under the USNET topology; in terms of resource utilization, the resource utilization of the NF algorithm keeps an upward trend with the increase in the number of requests and eventually stabilizes at about 55%, while the utilization of the SEAS algorithm eventually stabilizes at 85%, which is better than the performance under the USNET algorithm. Overall, the two algorithms each have similar

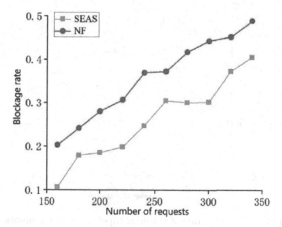

Fig. 9. Variation of blocking rate with the number of requests

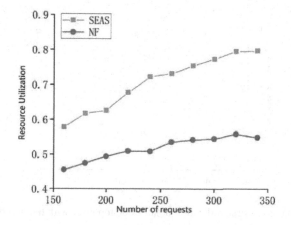

Fig. 10. Variation of resource utilization with the number of requests

characteristics and similar differences under different topologies, and it is also demonstrated that the performance of the SEAS algorithm proposed in this paper is constantly better than the NF algorithm by about 30%.

4.3 Algorithm Runtime

To explore the complexity of the algorithms, this section compares the computing speed of the SEAS algorithm and the NF algorithm by comparing their running times. The running software is Matlab 2020a, the system environment is AMD R5-5600X CPU, 16 GB 3600 RAM, and the computing topology is USNET, the results are shown in Fig. 13. This section also tests the computing time of the two algorithms under different topologies processing the number of 100 requests, and the results are shown in Fig. 14.

From Fig. 13, we can see that the complexity of SEAS algorithm in USNET is about twice as high as that of NF algorithm under different requests, and the change

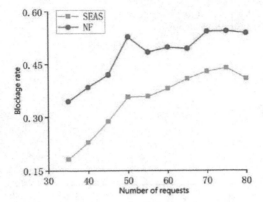

Fig. 11. Variation of blocking rate of six-node topology with the number of requests

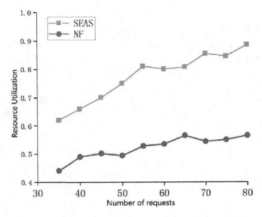

Fig. 12. Variation of resource utilization of six-node topology with the number of requests

of the operation time of SEAS algorithm shows that the complexity of its operation increases with the increase of the number of requests. SEAS looks for multiple paths when a request from the user side cannot be solved, and the complexity of the operation increases in this process, and the running time increases accordingly.

As can be seen from Fig. 14, with the simplification of the topology, the advantage of SEAS algorithm over NF algorithm becomes obvious, and only a small amount of extra computing time is required to obtain a good performance improvement in the 6node topology. Combining the previous experimental results, it can be concluded that the SEAS algorithm takes about less than twice the computing time compared to the NF algorithm, while having more than 30% performance improvement, and the simpler the topology, the better the performance improves.

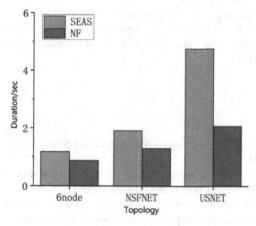

Fig. 13. Algorithm runtime

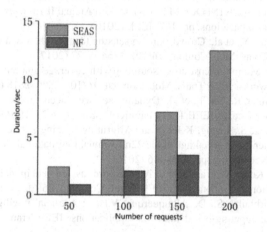

Fig. 14. Computing time of different topologies

5 Conclusion

In this paper, a SEAS algorithm is proposed to handle the node selection problem in edge computing networks. A comparison on the NF algorithm shows SEAS has an overall performance improvement of 20%–30%. By testing with different topologies, we find that the SEAS algorithm is universal in different topologies, and the simpler the topology, the less the complexity of the algorithm increases and the better the performance is. Overall, the SEAS algorithm proposed in this paper can well perform the functions of computing offloading and resource scheduling in edge computing networks, and has a large performance improvement over the existing traditional anycast scheduling methods.

Acknowledgement. This paper is supported by National Natural Science Foundation of China under grant No. 62201174, Guangdong Basic and Applied Based Research Foundation (2023A1515011886), Shenzhen Science and Technology Program (Grant No. RCBS20221008093131087).

References

1. Pallis, G., Vakali, A.: Insight and perspectives for content delivery networks. Commun. ACM **49**(1), 101–106 (2006)
2. Satyanarayanan, M., Bahl, P., Caceres, R., et al.: The case for VM-based cloudlets in mobile computing. IEEE Pervasive Comput. **8**(4), 14–23 (2009)
3. Pu, L., Chen, X., Xu, J., et al.: Crowd foraging: a QoS-oriented self-organized mobile crowdsourcing framework over opportunistic networks. IEEE J. Sel. Areas Commun. **35**(4), 848–862 (2017)
4. Zhang, H., Liu, B., Susanto, H., et al.: Incentive mechanism for proximity-based mobile crowd service systems. In: IEEE INFOCOM 2016-The 35th Annual IEEE International Conference on Computer Communications, pp. 1–9. IEEE (2016)
5. Li, J., Zhu, Y., Hua, Y., et al.: Crowdsourcing sensing to smartphones: a randomized auction approach. IEEE Trans. Mob. Comput. **16**(10), 2764–2777 (2017)
6. Han, Y., Wu, H.: Minimum-cost crowdsourcing with coverage guarantee in mobile opportunistic D2D networks. IEEE Trans. Mob. Comput. **16**(10), 2806–2818 (2017)
7. Wang, S., Urgaonkar, R., He, T., et al.: Dynamic service placement for mobile micro-clouds with predicted future costs. IEEE Trans. Parallel Distrib. Syst. **28**(4), 1002–1016 (2016)
8. Machen, A., Wang, S., Leung, K.K., et al.: Migrating running applications across mobile edge clouds: poster. In: Proceedings of the 22nd Annual International Conference on Mobile Computing and Networking, pp. 435–436 (2016)
9. Wan, L., Sun, L., Kong, X., et al.: Task-driven resource assignment in mobile edge computing exploiting evolutionary computation. IEEE Wirel. Commun. **26**(6), 94–101 (2019)
10. Sodhro, A.H., Pirbhulal, S., De Albuquerque, V.H.C.: Artificial intelligence-driven mechanism for edge computing-based industrial applications. IEEE Trans. Industr. Inf. **15**(7), 4235–4243 (2019)
11. Dijkstra, E.W.: A note on two problems in connexion with graphs. Numer. Math. **1**(1), 269–271 (1959)
12. Yen, J.Y.: Finding the K shortest loopless paths in a network. Manage. Sci. **17**(11), 712–716 (1971)
13. Peng, L., Park, K., Youn, C.-H.: Investigation on static routing and resource assignment of elastic all-optical switched intra-datacenter networks. Sci. China (Inf. Sci.) **59**(10), 60–75 (2016)

Research on UAV Communication Technology Based on 6G Network

Xinlu Li[✉], Zhenyu Xu, and Canquan Ling

Huizhou Engineering Vocational College, Huizhou 516000, China
49266692@qq.com

Abstract. The vigorous development of 5G makes human life more convenient and color-ful, but it also makes data transmission grow exponentially. Relevant research reports predict that mobile data traffic will reach by 2022 57eb/D, in addition to the requirements of the rising Internet of things related industries for ultra-high rate wireless data transmission and ultra-low delay, such as automatic driving, telemedicine, etc., the 5G related technologies currently widely developed can no longer meet the requirements of emerging services for existing communication performance. With the rapid development of wireless communication and un-manned aerial vehicle (UAV) technology, building a large-scale "unmanned aerial vehicle cloud" covering and connecting various wireless terminals in a vast area by taking advantage of the mobility, stability and wide coverage of UAV has become an important development direction of the future 6G wireless communication network. In recent years, with the development of scientific and techno-logical progress in China, UAVs have developed rapidly in the commercial and personal fields. The development of 6G network technology undoubtedly pro-vides new opportunities for the development of UAV industry. Firstly, this paper discusses and analyzes the application scenarios of UAV in 6G mobile communication; Then, the potential key technologies and challenges of UAV assisted 6G mobile communication are explored.

Keywords: 6G network · UAV · communications technology · Network architecture

1 Introduction

The Internet industry, industry and academia have all carried out research on the next generation mobile Internet. The vision of the future 6G technology is to "think about the world, and everything follows your heart" [1], as shown in Fig. 1. Specifically, it can be divided into intelligent connection, deep connection, holographic connection and ubiquitous connection [2].

Smart connection is the basic skeleton, on which the depth, holographic and ubiquitous connection can be realized. Although the 6G vision is beautiful, the existing 5G technology still cannot effectively support it. 6G will help fill the gap between the social and commercial needs after 2020 and the needs that 5G can support, as shown in Fig. 2.

© ICST Institute for Computer Sciences, Social Informatics and Telecommunications Engineering 2023
Published by Springer Nature Switzerland AG 2023. All Rights Reserved
A. Li et al. (Eds.): 6GN 2022, LNICST 505, pp. 257–271, 2023.
https://doi.org/10.1007/978-3-031-36014-5_22

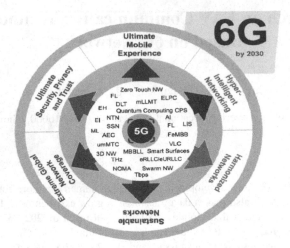

Fig. 1. The trend of 6G communication technology

Therefore, based on 5G technology and guided by the four connections of the 6G vision, the academic and industrial circles have carried out technological exploration and innovation on how to realize the ultra-low delay of the "one idea" of 6G, the deep coverage of "heaven and earth", the universal connection of "everything", and the beautiful demand of "follow your heart" intelligent interconnection. After previous research, the potential 6G key technologies widely recognized at present mainly include the application of terahertz frequency band [3], distributed super dimensional antenna technology [4], intelligent reflector [5], and embedded intelligence born in the network [6]. Therefore, the commercial use of 6G needs to make corresponding changes to the current ground base station and other infrastructure in the early stage, such as the increase of antenna arrays, the optimal configuration of the network inner layer processing system, etc.

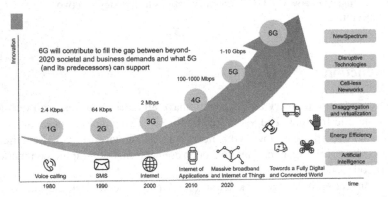

Fig. 2. 6G communication technology will effectively make up for the shortage of 5G

Although the basic communication facilities can basically meet the daily communication load, in case of special circumstances or unusual temporary scenarios, it is not enough to rely on ground wireless communication facilities alone, such as network reconstruction of major natural disasters, temporary communication deployment in remote areas, wireless resource allocation at major holiday gathering sites, etc. [7]. In order to effectively improve the quality of wireless communication in these scenarios, unmanned aerial vehicles (UAVs) can be deployed to assist communication [8]. As a small aircraft, unmanned aerial vehicle (UVA) belongs to the category of aircraft. It was first put into use in the last century and has a history of nearly a hundred years. Its principle is to realize semi autonomous or completely autonomous flight function through wireless remote control device or computer programming. With the development of technology, UAV has been upgraded continuously. After updating and iteration, it has become an important carrier in the fields of commerce, government and consumption, and its role has become increasingly prominent. Its own advantages (intelligence, low cost, and collaborative development towards multiple UAVs) can make 6G mobile communication more convenient. Therefore, UAV auxiliary communication is an indispensable potential technology in 6G mobile network [9].

As a small aircraft, UAV plays an important role in achieving the airspace coverage in the global three-dimensional depth coverage of 6G "air, space, earth and sea" [10]. Since its birth, UAVs have been used in military reconnaissance, surveillance, communication, etc. In recent years, with the development of technology, UAVs have formed an intelligent aircraft that combines flight control, network communication, power function and other technologies. After continuous exploration and technological upgrading, UAVs have been widely used in agriculture, forestry, transportation, meteorology and other civil fields. The main characteristics of UAVs include intelligence, low cost and the collaborative development towards multiple UAVs. In the past, UAVs usually performed tasks alone, but also faced the risk of failure and damage. The collaborative task execution of multiple UAVs can not only reduce the difficulty, but also facilitate re allocation in the event of failure. It is precisely because of this feature that UAVs can cooperate by sharing information. To improve the efficiency of task execution. Based on the advantages of UAV, UAV can be used as an airspace auxiliary communication platform. For example, under the scenario of high-density communication users, UAV can be deployed as a temporary base station or relay to assist wireless communication and increase user capacity. In addition, UAVs can also be used as highly mobile end users to collect data in environmental monitoring and other scenarios. Specifically, UAV assisted communication has the following advantages:

1) LOS channel [11]: Since UAV can hover or hover in the air, the channel between UAV and ground users is mainly a direct link. Because it can pass through the direct link without refraction or scattering, the channel condition between UAV and ground communication equipment is of high quality and low attenuation. With the help of UAV, the signal-to-noise ratio of the receiver can be effectively improved, thus achieving high-quality communication.
2) High mobility [12]: As a small aircraft, UAV can be controlled through remote control terminal. As there is no shelter in the air and its own position is not fixed, the deployment can be adjusted in real time to achieve emergency communication. In addition, for some non sudden but temporary application scenarios, UAV communication can also be deployed easily and quickly.

3) Low cost networking [13]: UAVs can be used in complex and changeable scenarios and environments. The bee colony composed of multiple UAVs can build a stable communication network in different application scenarios, and can be redeployed for many times. Therefore, UAVs can be used for low-cost temporary networking to meet different types of needs.

2 UAV Application Scenarios and Functions in 6G

China has carried out the construction of satellite Internet in 5G [14], which also brings convenience to the development of 6G communication technology. The current commercial 5G mobile communication is committed to realizing the interconnection between people, things and vehicles, and solving the problems of ultra-low delay, ultra large user bandwidth and ultra wide area coverage with high information concurrency. However, with the deepening of the application of the Internet of Things, the transmission delay, coverage, transmission rate and computing capacity provided by 5G still cannot meet the future needs. Therefore, 6G mobile communication will have lower transmission delay to ensure real-time information transmission, wider coverage to achieve "space, space, earth and sea" omni dimensional universal interconnection, faster transmission rate to achieve a smooth user experience, and evolve from external artificial intelligence to embedded endogenous intelligence. This section first introduces the deployment scheme of UAV in the satellite ground integration network architecture, and then discusses the role of UAV in the 6G mobile network in detail.

2.1 Application of UAV in Satellite Ground Fusion Network Architecture

The fundamental requirements of 6G mobile communication not only include the construction of a mobile communication network that integrates intelligence, perception and security based on communication functions, but also the seamless coverage of space, space, space and sea based on human centered and multi network integration [15]. Among them, the applicable scenarios of UAV include: space based network, joint satellite, ground facilities and maritime communication users to achieve multi-dimensional coverage, anytime access and secure connection in complex scenarios. The specific framework is shown in Fig. 3. The network is composed of space based network, air based network, sea based network and ground based network. Among them, the ground network mainly refers to the ground communication equipment, including the ground Internet and wireless equipment. The space-based network consists of satellites orbiting the earth that are relatively static with the ground. The space-based network is composed of temporarily deployed UAVs, airships, etc. These devices can provide relay services for ground-based or sea based users and forward information to space-based satellites. Sea based network refers to offshore platforms or ships, fishing vessels and other equipment operating at sea. Because it is far away from land, most offshore platforms are lost in the existing ground base station communication. Through the deployment of UAVs, the communication between sea based and land control centers can be realized.

UAV mainly plays the communication function at the air base network level in 6G mobile communication. By deploying UAVs in different scenarios, we can expand the

Fig. 3. Frame diagram of unmanned unit network

wireless communication network level from the basic communication of the ground-based network to the space based network, and then we can interconnect with the satellite or sea based network of the space based network to achieve the macro needs of 6G global coverage and scenario interconnection. In the air based network, UAVs have more flexible maneuverability than airships, balloons and other equipment. At the same time, UAVs in the space based network can also achieve more effective control of information transmission by configuring multiple antenna arrays, smart reflectors and other transceiver devices [16]. In addition, since the approximate rate of the air ground link is LOS communication link, the power attenuation at both ends of the transmitter and receiver will be smaller, and the signal-to-noise ratio at the receiver will be higher, which will significantly improve the transmission rate of users. In addition, due to the advantages of real-time and convenient deployment, UAVs can be used to achieve temporary deployment of base stations to meet the wireless communication needs of dense users in sudden or temporary situations.

2.2 Main Functions of UAV Assisted Ground Mobile Communication

UAV will play an important role in 6G mobile communication, because UAV has the characteristics of high mobility, easy deployment, LOS channel, etc. [17]. There are usually a large number of mobile devices in the ground-based network and the sea based network. In some special cases, only relying on the ground base station can not meet the communication needs of mobile devices. This section describes the importance of UAVs by introducing their potential applications in 6G scenarios. In the 6G mobile communication network, the specific application scenario of UAV is shown in Fig. 4.

(a)UAV base station swarm system

(b)Unmanned holographic projection system

(c)UAV Relay Network

(d)UAV data acquisition

Fig. 4. Specific application scenario of UAV

2.2.1 Drone Base Station Swarm System

In the future 6G mobile communication network, due to the application of terahertz, super large antenna array and other technologies, as well as the extensive demand for high-resolution video information and picture information, the communication data volume of end users will increase significantly. In addition, in the highly crowded convention and exhibition center, stadiums and gymnasiums where important events are held and other scenarios, the multiple data of IoT devices, massive images in the Internet of Vehicles and other sensing information need to be uploaded, analyzed and calculated, which will generate a large amount of data transmission. When the ground base station cannot bear the load, the UAV can be used for temporary base station deployment to share the user's data transmission needs.

2.2.2 UAV Holographic Projection System

As one of the 6G visions, "holographic communication" is an extended high fidelity reality based on virtual reality and augmented reality technology. As the holographic projection system needs to ensure that users can achieve the effect of high fidelity extended reality projection from all angles, the system needs to implement projection at multiple points, and each projection point cooperates with each other. In addition to sound effects and other sensory effects, users can experience the high fidelity extended effect of holographic projection. In this scene, using UAV to deploy each projection point can make the whole system more flexible, shorten the deployment time of holographic projection, and bring users a more multi-dimensional visual experience.

2.2.3 UAV Relay Network

A typical scenario in 6G mobile communication is "space, sky, earth and sea", with seamless three-dimensional coverage of global depth. At present, although 5G has been committed to the ubiquitous coverage of land mobile communication base stations, the sea users are still isolated from the outside world. Therefore, 6G needs to solve the problem of wireless coverage at sea level. The introduction of UAV into sea based network communication as a relay can ensure that the information between sea based communication users such as offshore platforms for oil operations, fishing vessels and ships for offshore operations is unblocked. In addition, due to the temporary location and range of activities of offshore platforms, fishing vessels and ships, it is also cost-effective to use efficient, low-cost, real-time deployable UAVs as relay nodes to achieve interconnection with the outside world.

2.2.4 UAV Data Acquisition

UAV has the advantage of flexible movement. It can fly into the unmanned area and realize remote control. In the large area of forests, basins, glaciers, plains and many other scenes that are not suitable for manual data collection and monitoring, flexible data collection can be achieved by deploying UAVs and optimizing their flight paths. At the same time, thanks to the large communication bandwidth and high transmission rate of the 6G mobile network, the UAV can achieve efficient data acquisition in a shorter time, which also overcomes the problem of insufficient acquisition time caused by the short endurance of the UAV.

3 Comparison of UAV Application in 5G and 6G Scenarios

3.1 The Most Obvious is that the Transmission Rate is Different

Theoretically, the download speed of 6G can reach 1TB per second. The transmission capacity of 6G network will be 100 times higher than that of 5G. 6G reduces the network delay from milliseconds to microseconds. This means that the control of unmanned vehicles and unmanned aerial vehicles will be very free, and users will not even feel any delay.

3.2 Different Technologies Applied

5G requires a large number of base stations for networking, while 6G is based on satellites and supported by the global satellite positioning system, telecommunications satellite system, earth image satellite system and 6G ground network. Compared with 5G, 6G will use more advanced radio equipment and a larger number of radio waves, including ultra-high frequency (EHF) spectrum, which can provide ultra-high speed and huge capacity in a short distance.

3.3 Different Coverage

The main goal of 5G network is to keep the end users connected all the time. In the future, 5G network will support not only smart phones, but also smart watches, smart home devices, and so on.On the basis of 5G and global satellites, 6G achieves seamless global coverage. Network signals can reach any remote village, enabling patients in mountain areas to receive telemedicine and children there to receive distance education. It can also help people predict the weather and quickly respond to natural disasters.

6G is the sixth generation mobile communication technology and also an extension after 5G. On the basis of 5G, 6G will further expand from serving people, people and things to supporting the efficient interconnection of agents, and realize the transition from the interconnection of everything to the intelligent interconnection of everything.

4 Key Technologies and Progress of 6G UAV Communication

On the basis of 5G, 6G expands its existing ultra-low latency, massive connections, ultra bandwidth and other scenarios to achieve higher peak transmission rate, faster user experience rate, lower transmission delay, more access users, greater mobile bearing capacity and higher spectral efficiency. The leap of these indicators needs comprehensive technological innovation. Currently, the 6G key technologies widely recognized by the industry mainly include terahertz, super large-scale antenna array, 6G network endogenous intelligence, intelligent reflector, intelligent edge computing, etc. Therefore, this section explores the application of 6G key technologies in UAV auxiliary communication.

4.1 Terahertz Communication

As the most breakthrough technology in 6G mobile communication, terahertz is rated as one of the key technologies that will change the future [18]. Between microwave and light waves, this interval is also called "THz gap". Its spectrum area provides higher available bandwidth, and extremely high frequencies make it possible for higher data transmission, as shown in Fig. 5.

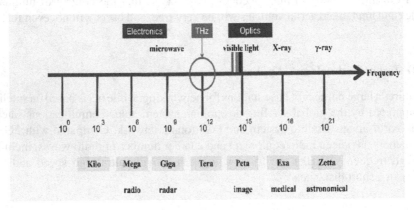

Fig. 5. Terahertz spectrogram

In order to meet the explosive growth of data, simply using existing frequency bands for wireless transmission has been unable to meet people's daily data needs. From millimeter wave at the present stage to terahertz in the future, the available frequency band of wireless communication has made a revolutionary breakthrough, and the transmission rate will also be significantly improved. The terahertz frequency band is 0.1–10 THz, with higher frequency and shorter wavelength, which makes the main lobe of the beam shaping narrower, increases the difficulty of eavesdropping, and has higher security, as shown in Fig. 6. However, terahertz signals have greater attenuation than the previous generation of low-frequency signals, and the air to ground LOS channel in UAV communication will greatly reduce the attenuation of terahertz signals, thus ensuring the communication quality. Large scale antenna array (MIMO) technology can greatly improve the spectral efficiency by reasonably allocating antennas. In addition, MIMO technology can also deal with the problem of large fading in the millimeter wave band, so that the communication quality and endurance of the terminal can be improved and extended to varying degrees.

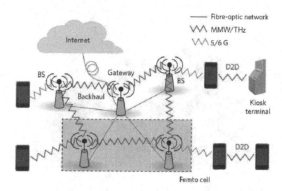

Fig. 6. Terahertz communication can improve information transmission rate

4.2 Large Scale Antenna Array

Wireless communication can use the channel properties to achieve the power gain of the user receiver through multi antenna technology [19]. In addition, the directivity of the antenna can also be used to effectively suppress eavesdropping through beam shaping and signal precoding to ensure communication security. 6G mobile communication will expand it on a larger scale based on 5G 256–1024 antenna array. It is estimated that a single base station will have more than 10000 antennas. As 6G mobile communication will use terahertz frequency band for transmission, even if the super large antenna array is very large in terms of the number of antennas, its volume will not be too large. For example, the nano antenna can embed 1024 array units working at 1 THz within 1 mm^2 [20], which is more conducive to its loading on the UAV platform with limited load for signal reception and transmission.

4.3 Intelligent Reflector

The intelligent reflector can control the amplitude and phase of signal reflection through software programming to realize the self reconstruction of wireless channel [21]. The intelligent reflector is composed of several low-power passive reflective components.

These reflective components can control the reflected signal through the external voltage and phase drive, thus realizing more comprehensive control of the beam shaping signal transmission. Because the intelligent reflector does not need RF forwarding and other functions, the energy consumption is low. At the same time, the intelligent reflector has a simple structure and is easy to install on other object surfaces, such as unmanned aerial platforms. The UAV communication platform equipped with an intelligent reflector is shown in Fig. 7. Through the aerial intelligent reflector, the received signal can be reflected to the shielded user terminal to improve the wireless communication quality. In addition, UAV equipped with intelligent reflector can also bring higher channel gain through superposition of direct and reflected signals.

Fig. 7. UAV communication platform equipped with intelligent reflector

4.4 Intelligent Edge Computing

Throughout the history of computing mode development, from the era of centralized mainframe computing, to the era of distributed personal terminal computing, to the era of big data cloud computing, central computing and distributed computing have developed alternately. In the future 6G mobile communication, as the network focuses more on the endogenous intelligent computing capability, the future network will adopt the method of integrating intelligent cloud computing and intelligent edge computing to make the computing system more flat. At the same time, blockchain distributed storage and other decentralized technologies will be used to realize the protection of user data privacy [22]. The technical core of mobile edge computing (MEC) technology is to disperse the cloud computing center platform into multiple edge clouds to optimize the user experience. On the one hand, the application of this technology in UAVs can reduce the energy consumption and improve the endurance of UAVs by transferring the complex computing services in UAVs, and on the other hand, it can reduce the communication delay of UAVs to facilitate better agile control. The UAV platform applying intelligent edge computing can perform real-time intelligent computing and control in combination with the surrounding environment without relying on the central control system. Its specific application scenario is shown in Fig. 8. The base station can allocate the computing tasks to the UAV, and the UAV can reasonably unload the computing tasks to each end user with computing capabilities, so as to realize intelligent edge computing.

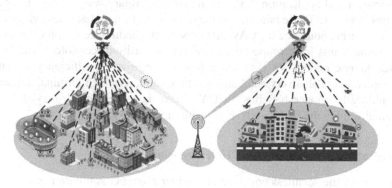

Fig. 8. Application scenarios of intelligent edge computing

4.5 Distributed Blockchain Network

In the 6G mobile communication network, the deployment of the Internet of Things and the Internet of Vehicles will generate massive data anytime and anywhere. However, due to the openness of wireless communication, the security of users in ultra dense networks is particularly important. Blockchain technology guarantees the validity of network data by storing user data distributed on each user terminal to ensure that data cannot be illegally tampered with. In the ultra dense heterogeneous network, UAV can be deployed as the node of the distributed blockchain network to realize the safe and efficient storage and transmission of user information. However, when the network scale increases to a certain extent, the data index will have a large delay and the storage of user data also needs more space, which is also a challenge that the future UAV distributed blockchain network will face.

5 Technical Challenge and Future Direction of 6G UAV Communication

UAV assisted mobile communication has a very broad prospect in 6G. However, because the development of UAV communication itself is still in the initial stage, and 6G has a new technological development compared with 5G, there are still many challenges to apply UAV to 6G mobile communication, which requires in-depth exploration and research. This section discusses the technical challenges and future research directions of 6G oriented UAV communication from the aspects of UAV's endurance time, integration of "air, space, earth and sea" full coverage heterogeneous networks, RF related antenna technology and terahertz technology, and security issues of mobile users.

5.1   Endurance Time of UAV

How to break through the endurance of UAV? It has always been a bottleneck limiting its development and application [23]. The majority of rotary wing UAVs are powered by batteries, and most of the batteries on the market are lithium batteries, which cannot provide long-term endurance for UAVs. At present, the endurance of rotorcraft is about 30 min. Some teams have proposed that energy acquisition technology can be used to provide kinetic energy for UAVs, and how to improve the efficiency of wireless energy acquisition is also very challenging. In addition, although terminal devices that can automatically replace batteries for UAVs have been developed, they still cannot fundamentally solve the problem of short endurance of UAVs.

5.2   Integration Between UAV and Heterogeneous Network

In order to meet the seamless coverage of a wider area, 6G is committed to realizing the full dimension communication of "space, space, earth and sea". Therefore, how to realize the high-speed, low latency and massive connection of data interaction between UAVs in the airspace network and other heterogeneous networks has become a technical problem to be solved urgently. The transmission protocols and network architectures of different networks are different. Data transmission across networks requires caching and forwarding, which will result in redundant processing steps. Therefore, in order to solve the interaction of data between different types of networks, it is necessary to redesign the network architecture and data distribution protocols and consider their compatibility, so as to ensure the accuracy of user data while achieving low latency and high bandwidth transmission.

5.3   Compatibility of Intelligent Reflector and Super Large Antenna Array with UAV

The intelligent reflector can actively adjust the incident signal through software definition, so as to change the phase and amplitude of the reflected signal, so as to achieve the goal of reconstructing the channel to improve the signal power of the receiver, and at the same time suppress interference. As the intelligent reflector is passive reflection and does not need to transmit signals through the receive amplify/decode forward mode, it is more energy-saving than the traditional relay. However, in the actual deployment, since the intelligent reflector needs to be assembled on the surface of the UAV, the size and weight of the intelligent reflector need to be effectively limited considering the size of the UAV and the limited endurance load capacity. In addition, since the 6G uses a very large antenna array, even if the terahertz frequency band will significantly reduce the unit size, the antenna array is huge, and its volume still needs to be considered in the design.

5.4   Terahertz Related Technology and Equipment Development

As one of the breakthrough technologies in 6G mobile communication, terahertz has wider bandwidth and can provide a transmission rate close to Tbit/s. On the one hand, because of its high frequency and short wavelength, it has narrower main lobe width and more accurate transmission direction in beam shaping, thus ensuring user information security. However, due to the limited volume and endurance, the search and alignment technology of terahertz beam is difficult to achieve. On the other hand, terahertz frequency is high and easy to be absorbed by molecules, so terahertz transmission attenuation increases, which also results in short transmission distance. In addition, the current semiconductor, metal materials and optical elements cannot meet the performance of terahertz communication. Therefore, we need to vigorously develop materials suitable for terahertz frequency band in the future.

5.5 Security of User Information

Due to the broadcast characteristics of wireless communication, the user's information exposure in the air has caused security risks. In addition, the operating range of UAV is in the air. Whether it is air to ground channel or air to air channel, it is closer to the LOS channel, so UAV communication is easier for eavesdroppers to estimate the channel, and then intercept and eavesdrop the user's private information. The terahertz channel will be used in 6G mobile communication. Although its channel model has not been fully established, the line of sight channel is more stable, so the channel characteristics are easier to be obtained by eavesdroppers, thus posing a threat to user information privacy. In addition, the eavesdropper may also transmit interference noise to attack the normal communication of the UAV. How to overcome the active interference attack is also an urgent problem to be solved.

5.6 Collision Avoidance in Swarm Network

The high mobility of UAV has attracted extensive attention. However, in the large-scale UAV cellular network, its mobility poses great challenges to the channel modeling, flight deployment and trajectory optimization of the cellular system. Although the air to ground wireless channel can be approximated to the LOS link, due to the complexity of the cellular network and the mutual interference between UAVs, there is still great uncertainty in the UAV channel, which will also affect the air to ground channel modeling, and further interfere with the trajectory planning of each UAV in the 6G mobile communication network, affect the formation flight of UAVs, and even cause conflicts. Therefore, how to effectively avoid conflicts with drone swarms is also a serious challenge for the future 6G UAV communication network.

5.7 Spectrum Scarcity of Massive Dense Access

In the 6G mobile communication network, the UAV needs to be used as a temporary air base station to support the ultra dense access of mass users. Although UAV can share part of the network load, the limited spectrum resources will still greatly limit the user's information transmission rate and cause high network delay. Although the introduction of terahertz band will alleviate the shortage of spectrum, the problem of low utilization of spectrum resources still needs to be solved. Therefore, it is extremely urgent to effectively introduce cognitive radio technology into the 6G UAV communication, sense the spectrum through the UAV and efficiently use the redundant frequency bands, so as to improve the scarcity of spectrum resources.

6 Summary

6G mobile communication will further enhance the network communication performance index on the basis of 5G's low delay, large access and high bandwidth. This paper focuses on the UAV communication in the space based network under the "air, space, earth and sea" seamless coverage network architecture of 6G communication technology; At the same time, the application scenarios of UAV in 6G are predicted according to its different responsibilities in the communication network architecture. In addition, the potential key technologies in 6G UAV communication, such as terahertz, super large antenna array, intelligent reflector, artificial intelligence computing, blockchain, are described. Finally, the technical challenges and future development trend of UAV communication facing 6G are prospected.

References

1. Wireless Management Research Institute of CCID think tank 6G concept and vision white paper. China Computer News (008) (2020). https://doi.org/10.28468/n.cnki.njsjb.2020. 000054
2. Zhang, P., Niu, K., Tian, H., et al.: Technology prospect of 6G mobile communications. J. Commun. **40**(1), 141–148 (2019). https://doi.org/10.11959/j.issn.1000-436x.2019022
3. Xie, S., Li, H., Li, L., et al.: A survey of terahertz communication technologies for 6G networks. Mob. Commun. **44**(6), 36–43 (2020). https://doi.org/10.3969/j.issn.1006-1010.2020. 06.006
4. Chen, S., Zhang, J., Jin, Y., et al.: Wireless powered IoE for 6G: Massive access meets scalable cell-free massive MIMO. China Commun. **17**(12), 92–109 (2020). https://doi.org/10.23919/ JCC.2020.12.007
5. Long, W., Chen, R., Marco, M., et al.: A promising technology for 6G wireless networks: intelligent reflecting surface. J. Commun. Inf. Netw. **6**(1), 1–16 (2021). https://doi.org/10. 23919/JCIN.2021.9387701
6. Letaief, K.B., Chen, W., Shi, Y., et al.: The roadmap to 6G: AI empowered wireless networks. IEEE Commun. Mag. **57**(8), 84–90 (2019). https://doi.org/10.1109/MCOM.2019.1900271
7. Zhao, N., Lu, W., Sheng, M., et al.: UAV-assisted emergency networks in disasters. IEEE Wirel. Commun. **26**(1), 45–51 (2019). https://doi.org/10.1109/MWC.2018.1800160
8. Chen, X., Li, D., Yang, Z., et al.: Securing aerial-ground transmission for NOMA-UAV networks. IEEE Netw. **34**(6), 171–177 (2020). https://doi.org/10.1109/MNET.011.2000101
9. Wang, J., Na, Z., Liu, X.: Collaborative design of multi-UAV trajectory and resource scheduling for 6G-enabled internet of things. IEEE Internet Things J. **8**(20), 15096–15106 (2021). https://doi.org/10.1109/JIOT.2020.3031622
10. Liu, C., Lu, L., Wang, S., et al.: Prospects for a multi-access air-space-terrestrial integrated 6G network architecture. Mob. Commun. **44**(6), 116–120 (2020). https://doi.org/10.3969/j. issn.1006-1010.2020.06.017
11. Khuwaja, A.A., Chen, Y., Zhao, N., et al.: A survey of channel modeling for UAV communications. IEEE Commun. Surv. Tutor. **20**(4), 2804–2821 (2018). https://doi.org/10.1109/ COMST.2018.2856587

12. Duo, B., Wu, Q., Yuan, X., et al.: Anti-jamming 3D trajectory design for UAV-enabled wireless sensor networks under probabilistic LoS channel. IEEE Trans. Veh. Technol. **69**(12), 16288–16293 (2020). https://doi.org/10.1109/TVT.2020.3040334
13. Costantino, D., Angelini, M.G., Vozza, G.: The engineering and assembly of a low cost UAV. In: Proceedings of 2015 IEEE Metrology for Aerospace (MetroAeroSpace), Benevento, Italy, pp. 351–355 (2015). https://doi.org/10.1109/MetroAeroSpace.2015.7180681
14. Dai, C., Zhang, M., Li, C., et al.: QoE-aware intelligent satellite constellation design in satellite internet of things. IEEE Internet Things J. **8**(6), 4855–4867 (2021). https://doi.org/10.1109/JIOT.2020.3030263
15. Zhu, X., Jiang, C., Kuang, L., et al.: Cooperative transmission in integrated terrestrial-satellite networks. IEEE Netw. **33**(3), 204–210 (2019). https://doi.org/10.1109/MNET.2018.1800164
16. Shafique, T., Tabassum, H., Hossain, E.: Optimization of wireless relaying with flexible UAV-borne reflecting surfaces. IEEE Trans. Commun. **69**(1), 309–325 (2021). https://doi.org/10.1109/TCOMM.2020.3032700
17. Jiang, X., Chen, X., Tang, J., et al.: Covert communication in UAV-assisted air-ground networks. IEEE Wirel. Commun. **28**(4), 190–197 (2021). https://doi.org/10.1109/MWC.001.2000454
18. Chen, Z., Ma, X., Zhang, B., et al.: A survey on terahertz communications. China Commun. **16**(2), 1–35 (2019). https://doi.org/10.12676/j.cc.2019.02.001
19. Zhang, S., Jin, S., Wen, C., et al.: Improving expectation propagation with lattice reduction for massive MIMO detection. China Commun. **15**(12), 49–54 (2018). https://doi.org/10.12676/j.cc.2018.12.003
20. Akyildiz, I.F., Jornet, J.M.: Realizing ultra-massive MIMO (1024×1024) communication in the (0.06–10) terahertz band. Nano Commun. Netw. **8**, 46–54 (2016). https://doi.org/10.1016/j.nancom.2016.02.001
21. Wang, H., Liu, C., Shi, Z., et al.: On power minimization for IRS-aided downlink NOMA systems. IEEE Wirel. Commun. Lett. **9**(11), 1808–1811 (2020). https://doi.org/10.1109/LWC.2020.2999097
22. Xie, Z., Liu, J., Sheng, M., et al.: Exploiting aerial computing for air-to-ground coverage enhancement. IEEE Wirel. Commun. **28**, 50–58 (2021)
23. Jiang, X., Sheng, M., Zhao, N., et al.: Green UAV communications for 6G: a survey. Chin. J. Aeron. **35**, 19–34 (2021). https://doi.org/10.1016/j.cja.2021.04.025

Synchronization Technology for Underwater Acoustic Mobile Communication

Xinyang Li, Wei Li, and Yao Shi$^{(\boxtimes)}$

Harbin Institute of Technology, Shenzhen 518000, Gaungdong, China
22S052014@stu.hit.edu.cn, shiyao@hit.edu.cn

Abstract. Synchronization, as the premise of high-quality communication, is a problem that cannot be underestimated. Underwater acoustic communication faces many problems that land communication does not have. For example, the large time delay expansion, the strong Doppler effect, and the time-varying channels. Therefore, this paper focuses on the synchronization technology for underwater acoustic mobile communication. In view of the serious influence of Doppler on underwater acoustic communication synchronization technology, Doppler factor block estimation methods of various preamble signals are analyzed. This article evaluates the Doppler estimated performance of two commonly used chirp signals LFM and HFM. Simulation results reveal that the estimation performance of both signals increases with sweep length, the performance of HFM signals is better than that of LFM signals. The maximum improvement of Doppler estimation error performance can reach about 50%. In order to solve the large error of Doppler estimation, this paper propose a Doppler compensation method using Q-learning in the case of blind estimation. Compared with the system without reinforcement learning, the bit error rate is reduced by two orders of magnitude, which verifies that Q-learning can significantly improve Doppler estimation and compensation.

Keywords: underwater acoustic communication · synchronization · chirp signal · Doppler estimation · Doppler compensation · Q-learning

1 Introduction

With the increase of the depth and breadth of ocean exploration and development, the demand for underwater communication of all kinds of underwater equipment has surged, and the requirements are getting higher and higher. As a kind of shear wave, when electromagnetic wave propagates in the conductor, the attenuation degree is proportional to the frequency, and the penetration depth is inversely proportional to the frequency. Therefore, electromagnetic waves in common frequency bands in terrestrial communications cannot be transmitted very far underwater. The frequency of sound wave is lower, and its attenuation in water is three orders of magnitude smaller than that of electromagnetic wave. It can be transmitted thousands of kilometers away. Therefore, underwater acoustic communication is the most reliable way in underwater communication at present [1].

© ICST Institute for Computer Sciences, Social Informatics and Telecommunications Engineering 2023
Published by Springer Nature Switzerland AG 2023. All Rights Reserved
A. Li et al. (Eds.): 6GN 2022, LNICST 505, pp. 272–289, 2023.
https://doi.org/10.1007/978-3-031-36014-5_23

Underwater acoustic communication refers to the communication mode adopted between underwater equipment and between surface mother ship and underwater equipment. Its basic principle is to convert various voice or digital image information into electrical signals, and then use digital processing devices to digitally process these electrical signals, and then convert them into acoustic signals through digital transducers. The receiving transducer converts the acoustic signals into electrical signals, and then digitally decodes them, so as to recover various information sent by the transmitters [2]. In addition, underwater acoustic communication plays an irreplaceable role in many fields, such as underwater rescue, underwater monitoring and marine scientific research. Therefore, underwater acoustic communication has become one of the indispensables supporting technologies for human underwater activities [3, 4].

However, underwater acoustic channels are very different from wireless channels. These characteristics can be summarized as follows: random time-space-frequency, sparse channels, narrow band width, serious Doppler effect, obvious multipath effect. Among them, multipath effect and Doppler effect have the greatest impact on underwater acoustic communication, so these two points have become the key problems that need to be studied and overcome in mobile underwater acoustic communication system.

2 Related Works

Underwater acoustic communication was first proposed by European and American countries to meet military needs during the World War Two. Nowadays, underwater acoustic telephone is still widely used in the communication equipment of submarines and underwater operators. But its shortcomings are also obvious, it has a single function and can only be used for voice transmission, while it can't do anything for the transmission of pictures and even videos with higher requirements for communication technology. Frequency shift keying technology, which appeared in the early 1980s, requires a high *SNR* to have a good *BER* performance, and the frequency band utilization of this kind of method is low, but the available bandwidth of underwater acoustic communication system is narrow. Underwater acoustic channel is a nonlinear system that changes at any time in time domain, frequency domain and space domain. In addition, the serious multipath effect has also become one of the most serious challenges of UWA communication.

Since 21*st* century, with the rapid development of hardware integration technology and cloud computing, the underwater acoustic communication technology has grown rapidly. Northeastern University and Massachusetts Institute of technology, have successively invested in the research of underwater acoustic communication, and achieved gratifying results. The *AM* communication system developed by *AQU* company in the United States adopted orthogonal frequency division multiplexing technology, which can communicate at a maximum rate of 9 kbps with a distance of 5 km between the receivers and transmitters; The *S2C* underwater acoustic communication equipment developed by *EVOL* company in Germany is characterized by the use of spread spectrum carrier. The system can communicate within 8 km at the rate of 31.2 kbps; In addition, some foreign research institutions have applied the network theory of wireless communication to underwater acoustic communication to realize the networking of underwater communication, so as to achieve the underwater space integrated communication. Table 1 shows some representative underwater acoustic communication research results.

Table 1. Underwater acoustic communication prototype [5]

Research institutions	Testing environment	Modulation mode	Equalizer	Carrier frequency
University of Birmingham	Shallow water	2-DPSK	nothing	50 kHz
University of Newcastle	Shallow water	4-DPSK	DFE	50 kHz
Northeastern University	Deep sea	M-PSK	MDFE	1 kHz

The underwater acoustic communicator test device developed by Zhu's team was tested in the pool environment and the marine environment respectively, with an error probability of 10–4; The research group led by Professor Xu et al. has successfully realized the clear transmission of underwater signals within 10 km. Harbin Engineering University has long been engaged in the fields of adaptive equalization technology, $OFDM$, $QPSK$ and vector sensors for underwater acoustic communication, and has successfully realized the underwater transmission of data and images.

Synchronization technology is the premise to ensure the reliable transmission of information. External synchronization method, also known as insertion pilot method, adds pilots for synchronization at the transmitter, and the receiver obtains synchronization signals according to pilots. The advantage of this method is the fast synchronization speed, but additional resources are needed to transmit pilot information; The main idea of this method proposed by Bayan is to use the block estimation method to estimate the Doppler factor [6], that is, add the known chirped signal [7] at the beginning and end of the transmitted data, then use the same chirped signal and the received signal as the matched filter at the receiver. From the output of the matched filter, the expansion or compression of the signal in time-domain affected by Doppler is calculated, so as to estimate the Doppler factor. Zhang et al. [8] proposes a method to achieve synchronization by using the good autocorrelation characteristics of UW sequences in data blocks. The existing research on Doppler factor estimation mainly focuses on the use of traditional methods for Doppler factor estimation and compensation. Although the algorithm is simple, the BER effect of the system is not ideal. Different from the previous research, this paper proposes a Doppler factor estimation compensation method using Q-learning, which can significantly improve the BER performance of the system.

The main contents of this paper are arranged as follows: Firstly, the main characteristics of underwater acoustic channel are analyzed, and a simple system model is built in Sect. 3; Then two common chirped signals and matched filter method are introduced, and the Doppler factor estimation performance of the two chirped signals under different conditions is compared and analyzed in Sect. 4; Finally, a Doppler factor estimation and compensation algorithm based on Q-Learning is proposed in Sect. 5, and it is verified that this method can greatly improve the BER performance of the system.

3 System Model

Underwater acoustic channel is always changing in time-space-frequency domain, so it is one of the most complex channels at present. Its characteristics can be summarized as follows: narrow available bandwidth, serious Doppler effect, large path loss, serious multipath effect, strong noise [9]. Compared with traditional wireless communication, the channel in shallow water environment is very different, which is mainly shown by the following five points: (a), seriously limited bandwidth; (b), serious inter symbol interference; (c), channel tracking and estimation are difficult; (d), serious Doppler effect; (e), channel sparsity;

3.1 Multipath Effect of Underwater Acoustic Channel

The multipath effect caused by the characteristics of underwater acoustic channel will seriously distort the signal. Multipath effect refers to the phenomenon that the same signal reaches the receiver through multiple paths. Suppose the transmitted signal is:

$$x(t) = \alpha \cos \omega_0 t \tag{1}$$

The signal at the receiver is represented by the superposition of many signals as follows:

$$y(t) = \sum_{i=1}^{n} \alpha_i(t) \cos \omega_0 [t - \tau_i(t)] \tag{2}$$

$\alpha_i(t)$ represents the amplitude of the signal on the i-th path, $\tau_i(t)$ is the time delay of the received signal on the ith path, both of which are closely related to the channel. After simple mathematical transformation, it can be changed into:

$$y(t) = \sum_{i=1}^{n} \alpha_i(t) \cos \omega_0 t \cos \tau_i(t) - \sum_{i=1}^{n} \alpha_i(t) \sin \omega_0 t \sin \tau_i(t) \tag{3}$$

Let $X_P(t) = \sum_{i=1}^{n} \alpha_i(t) \cos \tau_i(t)$, $X_Q(t) = \sum_{i=1}^{n} \alpha_i(t) \sin \tau_i(t)$, the formula becomes:

$$y(t) = X_p(t) \cos \tau_i(t) - X_q(t) \sin \tau_i(t) \tag{4}$$

$$y(t) = Q(t) \cos[\omega_0 t + \tau(t)] \tag{5}$$

$Q(t) = \sqrt{X^2 P(t) + X^2 Q(t)}$, $\tau(t)$ respectively represents the envelop and the phase of the received signal. Therefore, it can be seen that the signal at the receiver can be approximately regarded as a slowly varying narrow-band signal [10].

3.2 Doppler Effect of Underwater Acoustic Channel

Different from traditional land communication, the speed of sound in water is much smaller than that of electromagnetic wave propagation in vacuum, so even a small relative movement between the transmitter and the receiver will cause a very serious Doppler shift to the signal. The schematic diagram of Doppler effect is as follows (Fig. 1):

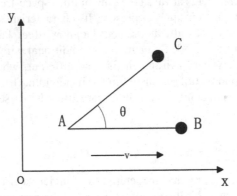

Fig. 1. Schematic diagram of Doppler effect

The transmitting end moves from A to B at speed v, and the Doppler frequency shift Δf is calculated as:

$$\Delta f = \frac{v}{c} f cos\varphi \tag{6}$$

where f refers to the frequency of the transmitted signal (Hz); c represents the speed of sound in water (m/s); v represents the speed of sound in water, φ indicates the angle (RAD) between the signal transmission direction and the relative moving speed of the transceiver.

3.3 Transmission Loss of Sound Wave in Water

When the sound wave propagates underwater, the diffusion effect and energy attenuation will cause the signal delay, attenuation and distortion, which is usually called transmission loss. When the frequency of sound wave is greater than 1 kHz, the dominant factor of sound wave attenuation loss is absorption loss. The formula of absorption coefficient of sea water for sound waves with different frequencies proposed in document [11] is as follows:

$$\alpha = 0.11 f^2/(1 + f^2) + 44 f^2/(4100 + f^2) \tag{7}$$

where f represents the frequency of sound wave (Hz), and dB/km represents the unit of absorption coefficient. The absorption effect is proportional to the frequency of the sound wave. It can be calculated that the absorption coefficient corresponding to the 30 kHz frequency is about 8 dB/km; When the frequency increases to 50 kHz, the absorption coefficient increases to 16.8 dB/km, that means, if the signal transmitted for 1 km at this frequency, the energy will be attenuated by 50-times.

3.4 Simple Model of Underwater Acoustic Channel

Ray model, as a classical physical model in underwater acoustics, regards the sound line as rays, starting from the source node and spreading outward to the receiving end. In underwater acoustic communication, there are many different paths from the sending end to the receiving end, which are called eigenpaths [12], and the corresponding signals are eigenpath signals. The eigenpath model is shown in (Fig. 2).

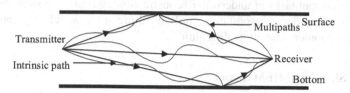

Fig. 2. Schematic diagram of eigenpath

There is a main signal component and many secondary components, of which the secondary component is a random component, which can be regarded as a random variable subject to Gaussian distribution. Together with the main signal components, the channel can be regarded as a rice fading model [13]. The probability density function of variables satisfying rice distribution is:

$$f(r) = \frac{r}{\sigma_n^2} e^{-(r^2 + \beta^2)/2\sigma_n^2} I_0(\frac{r\beta}{\sigma_n^2}), r \geq 0 \tag{8}$$

where, I_0 is the zero order Bessel function, $\sigma^2{}_n$ refers to the power of each component signal of the multipath signal, β represents the maximum value of the amplitude of the main component, $K = \beta^2/2\sigma^2{}_n$ denotes the rice factor. When the propagation distance is very long or the signal attenuation is serious, the main component in the signal is very small, and K tends to zero. At this time, the channel becomes Rayleigh model. Assuming that the signal at the sending end is s(t), through the impulse response $h(\tau, t)$ channel the noise is AWGN and the receiver signal expression is:

$$y(t) = \sum_{p=1}^{N} A_p s([1 + a_p]t - \tau_p) + n(t) \tag{9}$$

Receiving signal is the superposition of multiple signals, the influence of Doppler effect is embodied in time-domain compression or expansion. When the Doppler factor $a_P > 0$, time-domain is compressed; when $a_P < 0$, the time domain is expanded.

4 Doppler Estimation and Compensation for Underwater Acoustic Mobile Communication

As a crucial part of communication system, frame synchronization is the premise for each communication system to decode correctly. Only when the synchronization bit of the received signal is accurately found can the subsequent decoding and a series of information processing operations be carried out. The specific waveform of the preamble will greatly affect the synchronization quality, and different forms of preamble have different requirements for detection methods. Because the low speed of sound in the water, underwater acoustic communication is much more sensitive to the relative motion of the transmitter and the receiver than traditional radio communication, which is specifically affected by Doppler effect. Doppler effect will cause the frequency offset of the received signal, and the frequency offset of the broadband signal will change with the signal frequency. Therefore, how to accurately compensate the Doppler effect has become one of the important tasks of underwater acoustic communication system design. This section mainly introduces several commonly used preamble waveforms and some the time domain Doppler estimation algorithm.

4.1 LFM Signal and HFM Signal

The instantaneous frequency of LFM changes linearly with time. The biggest advantage of this signal is good Doppler invariance, which means that after a large frequency shift of LFM signal, a relatively obvious autocorrelation peak can still be obtained through the matched filter. LFM signal expression is:

$$s(t) = A exp\{j[2\pi(f_0 t + \frac{1}{2}kt^2)]\}$$ (10)

after differentiating the phase, the instantaneous frequency of LFM signal can be obtained as $f_1 = f_0 \pm \beta t/2\pi$, the instantaneous frequency changes linearly with time. When the positive sign is taken, it is positive frequency modulation, otherwise it is negative frequency modulation. HFM signal is strictly Doppler insensitive signal. The HFM signal expression is:

$$s(t) = \frac{1}{\sqrt{T}} exp\left\{j\left[\frac{2\pi}{K}\ln(1 + Kf_0 t) + \varphi_0\right]\right\}$$ (11)

where, the initial and cut-off frequency of HFM is respectively f_L and f_H, the time that the frequency changes from f_L to f_H is T, the initial phase $\varphi_0 = 0$, $K = \frac{-B}{T f_H f_L}$, $f_0 = \frac{f_l + f_h}{2}$ is the carrier frequency, the instantaneous frequency expression is:

$$f(t) = \frac{d}{dt}\left(\frac{1}{K}\ln(1 + Kf_0)t\right) = \frac{Kf_0}{K(1 + Kf_0 t)} = \frac{1}{Kt + f_0^{-1}}$$ (12)

The above formula is the upper swept HFM signal, which can be recorded as HFM+, and the lower swept signal is HFM-:

$$s(t) = \frac{1}{\sqrt{T}} exp\{j[\frac{2\pi}{K}\ln(1 - Kf_0 t) + \varphi_0]\}$$ (13)

the instantaneous frequency is:

$$f(t) = \frac{d}{dt}\left(\frac{1}{K}\ln(1 - Kf_0)t\right) = \frac{-Kf_0}{K(1 - Kf_0 t)} = \frac{1}{Kt - f_0^{-1}}$$ (14)

Different from LFM signal, the instantaneous frequency of HFM signal increases in the form of hyperbola rather than linear relationship, and the expression of instantaneous frequency is:

$$f(t) = \frac{f_L}{1 + f_L t} \tag{15}$$

4.2 Matched Filter Method

As a linear time-invariant filter, matched filter is the optimal detector in *AWGN* environment. If the time domain waveform of the preamble is $s(t)$, the frequency domain expression is $S(w)$, and the system function of the matched filter is $H(w)$:

$$S(w) = \int_{-\infty}^{\infty} s(t) e^{-jwt} dt \tag{16}$$

$$H(W) = CS^*(w) e^{-jw_0 t} \tag{17}$$

where C is the constant representing the signal gain; $S^*(w)$ represents the complex conjugate spectrum of the known preamble signal; $e^{-jw_0 t}$ indicates the linear phase factor; t_0 means the observation time of the matched filter, which is usually selected as the time when the signal ends. Finally, the unit impulse response of the matched filter can be obtained as:

$$h(t) = \frac{1}{2\pi} \int_{-\infty}^{\infty} H(w) e^{jwt} dw = \frac{1}{2\pi} \int_{-\infty}^{\infty} CS^* e^{jwt_0} e^{-jwt} dw = Cs(t - t_0) \tag{18}$$

The schematic diagram of matched filter is (Fig. 3):

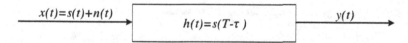

$$x(t) = s(t) + n(t) \quad \boxed{h(t) = s(T - \tau)} \quad y(t)$$

Fig. 3. Schematic diagram of matched filter

It can be seen that the purpose of matched filter is to calculate the correlation between signals. The expression of LFM signal after passing through matched filter is:

$$y_o(t) = s(t) * h(t) = s(t) * s^*(-t) \tag{19}$$

when $0 \leq t \leq T$, there are:

$$y_0(t) = e^{j2\pi f_0 t} \int_{t - \frac{T}{2}}^{\frac{T}{2}} e^{j2\pi k u^2} \cdot e^{j2\pi k(t-u)^2} du$$

$$= Te^{j2\pi f_0 t} \frac{\sin\left(\pi k T t \left(1 - \frac{t}{T}\right)\right)}{\pi k T t} \tag{20}$$

similarly, when $-T \le t \le 0$, there are:

$$y_o(t) = Te^{j2\pi f_0 t} \frac{\sin\left(\pi k T t \left(1 + \frac{t}{T}\right)\right)}{\pi k T t} \tag{21}$$

therefore, it can be expressed as:

$$y_o(t) = Te^{j2\pi f_0 t} \frac{\sin\left(\pi k T t \left(1 - \frac{|t|}{T}\right)\right)}{\pi k T t}, \quad -T \le t \le T \tag{22}$$

The ratio of the pulse width T before compression to the pulse width t after compression of the LFM signal is called the compression ratio $D = \frac{T}{\tau} = \frac{T}{1/B} = TB$, that is, the product of the time bandwidth. Therefore, when there is a large time bandwidth product, the LFM signal has good pulse compression characteristics. The simulation waveform of LFM signal after passing through matched filter is shown in the following (Fig. 4):

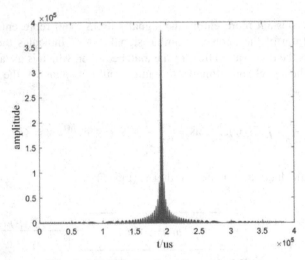

Fig. 4. LFM passing through matched filter

HFM signal, the same as LFM signal, has pulse compression characteristics. Therefore, after passing the HFM signal through MF, the waveform can be obtained as shown in the following (Fig. 5):

From the above analysis, it can be seen that both LFM and HFM have pulse compression characteristics, but by comparing their waveforms after passing through the matched filter, it can be seen that the correlation peak of HFM signal is narrower and more obvious, and has better pulse compression characteristics. Therefore, it is more suitable for synchronization as a preamble signal.

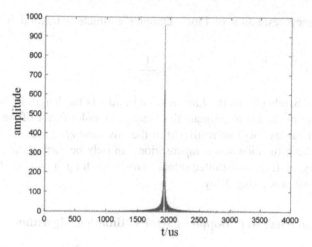

Fig. 5. HFM passing through the MF

4.3 Doppler Estimation Algorithm

As the most commonly used time domain estimation method, the main principle of block estimation method is that the Doppler effect is specifically manifested in the compression/expansion of the signal in the time domain. So, the prior information of the duration of a piece of data in the transmitted signal and the duration of the corresponding part of the received signal detected by the receiver can be used to estimate the Doppler factor of the signal. The specific implementation method is to add signals with specific parameters at the beginning and end of the transmitted signal of a frame. The resolution of this method depends on the bandwidth of the matched filter and the length of the data packet in the transmitted signal. The schematic diagram of block Doppler estimation method is shown as follows (Fig. 6):

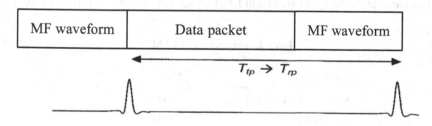

Fig. 6. Schematic diagram of block Doppler estimation method

Where, the length of the transmitted data frame is T_{tp}, and the length of the received data frame is T_{rp}. The estimated value of the Doppler factor can be calculated as follows:

$$\hat{a} = \frac{T_{rp}}{T_{tp}} - 1 \tag{23}$$

The frequency resolution of block Doppler estimation method is calculated as follows:

$$\delta \approx \frac{1}{BL} \tag{24}$$

where, B is the bandwidth of the known signal and l is the length of the transmitted data frame. This method is to estimate the average Doppler factor of the signal, so the estimation performance will be restricted in the environment of fast Doppler change. Because Doppler estimation and compensation can only be carried out after receiving the complete signal. If the transmitted signal frame is too long, it will lead to the problem of too long signal processing delay.

4.4 Simulation Analysis of Doppler Factor Estimation Algorithm

There are two correlation peaks at the beginning and end of the signal, which correspond to the end of the transmitted chirped signal respectively. The interval between the two chirped signals at the sending end is known, and the corresponding interval at the receiving end can be obtained through the output of the matched filter. The estimated value of the Doppler factor can be calculated from Eq. (23). The theoretical value is calculated by the theoretical calculation formula of Doppler factor, and compared with the estimated value, the estimation error of Doppler factor can be obtained. The frame structure used in the simulation is as follows (Fig. 7):

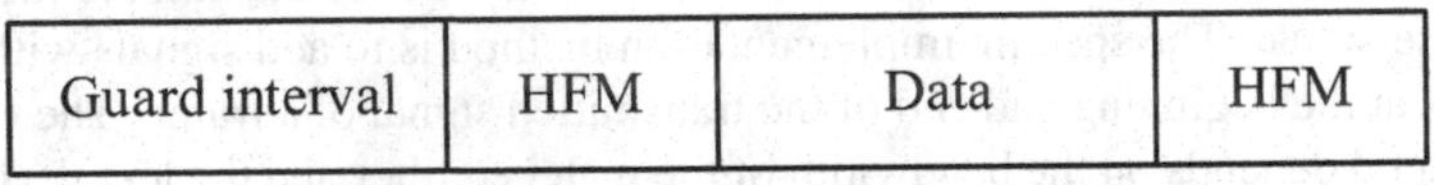

Guard interval	HFM	Data	HFM

Fig. 7. Data frame of the sending signal

The parameter settings of HFM and LFM signal are as follows (Tables 2 and 3):

Table 2. Parameters of HFM

Parameter	Value
Sampling frequency f_s	48 kHz
Bandwith B	4 kHz
Center frequency f_c	10 kHz

The transmitted data is modulated by BPSK, with 500 *bits* per frame, $snr = 10$ dB, and the number of multi-paths is 10. HFM signal and LFM signal are as synchronization signals respectively. The curve of Doppler estimation error of the transceiver with the length of Chirped signal at different relative moving speeds is as follows (Fig. 8):

Table 3. Parameters of LFM

Parameter	Value
Sampling frequency f_s	48 kHz
Bandwith B	4 kHz
Initial frequency f_0	8 kHz
Terminal frequency f_H	12 kHz

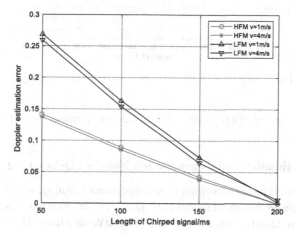

Fig. 8. Curve of Doppler estimation error with Chirped signal length

From the above curves, the Doppler estimation errors of the two Chirped signals decrease with the increase of the signal length and relative moving speed respectively. The estimation error of HFM signal is smaller than that of LFM signal.

Set the sweep length of the two chirped signals to 100 ms, then change the length of the transmitted data from 50 to 500 *bits*, and keep other parameters unchanged. We can get the following curve (Fig. 9):

We can draw the following conclusions:

(1) The Doppler estimation performance of HFM signal is better. With the increase of sweep time, the performance of the two methods is close and the error is at a low level. However, the disadvantage of this method is that the auxiliary synchronization data is introduced, which will lead to the inefficient transmission of the system. Therefore, the performance of Doppler estimation of HFM signal is better.

(2) The larger the relative moving speed, the more obvious the stretch/compression of the signal is. The theoretical Doppler factor itself is large, so the Doppler estimation errors of both signals decrease slightly with the increase of the moving speed.

(3) The Doppler estimation error decreases significantly as the increase of data length. Because the Doppler estimation resolution of this method is determined by Eq. (24). Therefore, when the data is short, the resolution is poor, resulting in a large estimation

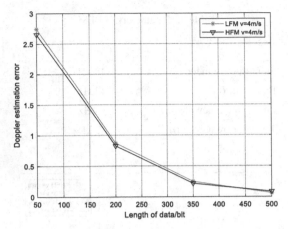

Fig. 9. Curve of Doppler estimation error with data length

error. As the data length increases, the resolution increases, so the estimation error decreases.

4.5 Doppler Estimation and Compensation Based on Q-Learning

Q-learning is a value-based algorithm in reinforcement learning, and it is an algorithm independent of the environment model [14]. $Q(s, a)$ refers to the maximum cumulative return value when taking action a in the state of s at a certain time. The environment will be rewarded by the action feedback of the agent; The table used to store the value of the state action value function is called the *Qtable*, and the values in the *Qtable* correspond to the maximum expected future reward value that can be obtained when taking different actions in each state. Through it, we can find out the corresponding optimal behavior in each state, and then find out the optimal action in each state to get the maximum expected reward. The main idea of this algorithm can be represented by the following Fig. 10 [15]:

Use the following equation to get the rewards:

$$NewQ(s, a) = Q(s, a) + \alpha[R(s, a) + \gamma \max Q'(s', a') - Q(s, a)] \qquad (25)$$

where $NewQ(s, a)$ refers to the updated *Qvalue* corresponding to the current state and action, $Q(s, a)$ corresponds to the current *Qvalue*, α is the learning-rate, $R(s, a)$ is the immediate reward that can be obtained by taking this action in this state, γ is the discount coefficient which represents the decay of future rewards, $maxQ'(s', a')$ refers to the maximum value of the expected reward corresponding to all possible actions in the new state. The reward function is set to:

$$r = \frac{1}{\delta + BER} \qquad (26)$$

where *BER* represents the bit error rate of the system. r is related to state s and action a. In order to avoid the case where the denominator of the reward function is zero, a constant delta is set so that the expression is always meaningful.

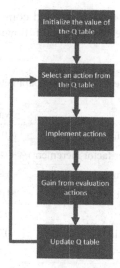

Fig. 10. Schematic diagram of Q-learning

The method to calculate the values of *Qtable* can be mainly divided into following steps:

(1) Initialize the *Qtable*;
(2) Select an action and execute it according to the *Qtable* and status at this time; Since the initial *Qtable* is full of 0, random selection is required first, and then the epsilon-greedy strategy is used for selection. Epsilon is a parameter used to indicate the randomness of the strategy (when epsilon = 0.9, it means that 90% of the cases choose the action according to the optimal value of the *Qtable*, and 10% of the time chooses the action randomly). Therefore, starting from a fairly random strategy and then slowly turning to deterministic means that epsilon is set to a large value at the beginning (usually 0.9 or 1), that is, the agent is allowed to explore the environment and select actions randomly; With the deepening of the agent's understanding of the environment, the value of epsilon is gradually reduced, so that the agent can make more choices by the experience.
(3) Use Eq. (25) to update the *Qtable* after taking actions and getting rewards;
(4) Judge whether the *Qtable* converges. If it converges, it ends; Otherwise, repeat steps (2) and (3).

Because the block Doppler estimation method is only suitable for the case of constant Doppler factor, the estimation performance will be seriously degraded when the channel conditions are changeable; The transmitted signal data frame length is large, so it is also seriously affected by time-varying characteristics. In the previous section, block estimation method is used for Doppler estimation and coarse synchronization. In this section, Q-learning method is used for accurate synchronization. The idea of this method is as follows:

(1) Use the known chirp signal, the first 200 published symbols and a small number of subsequent symbols to build a training environment;

(2) Q-learning algorithm is used to estimate and compensate the Doppler factor; The specific parameter settings are shown in the following Table 4:

Table 4. Q-learning parameters

Parameter	Value
State (Doppler factor)	[0.001, 0.003]
Action (Doppler factor increment)	0 or 0.0001
Reward function Eq. 26	$\delta = 0.01$
Training times Episodes	100
Learning rate α	0.5
Greedy probability ε	0.7
Discount factor γ	0.9

The algorithm process is shown in the following table:

Algorithm 1. Q-learning training Doppler factor algorithm process

---

For i $= 1:N\_episodes$

$s = 0.0021$ (Status initialization)

For Steps Ct $= 1:N\_steps$

$$\begin{cases} a = \arg\max_a Q(s,a), \quad \varepsilon \\ random \text{ choose}, \quad 1\text{-}\varepsilon \end{cases}$$ (Select actions based on greedy strategy)

Execute action to get reward r, and new status s'

if r≥85 (Judge whether to end this training)

break

end

$Q(s,a) = Q(s,a) + \alpha * (r + \gamma * \max(Q(s',a')) - Q(s,a))$ (Update Q table)

$s = s'$ (Update status)

End

End

4.6 Simulation Results

In order to compare the performance of the method without Q-learning, the method without Q-learning is first simulated. The data of Double-moon Lake test is used in the simulation. Since the linear frequency modulation signal with known parameters is added to the data, the same linear frequency modulation signal is used for matching filtering at the receiving end in order to find the synchronization head. The linear frequency modulation signal has the same parameters as those used in the simulation in the previous chapter. After finding the synchronization head, the block Doppler estimation method is used to estimate the Doppler factor, and then the spline interpolation is used to compensate the Doppler and synchronize again. After coherent demodulation, calculate the bit error rate; Then Doppler estimation and compensation are performed for the method using Q-learning. The simulation results are shown in the following Fig. 11:

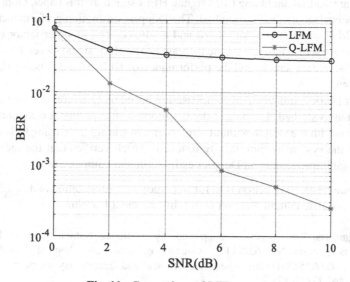

Fig. 11. Comparison of BER curves

It can be clearly seen from the above figure that Q-learning has significantly improved the synchronization performance. When the *SNR* is greater than 6 dB, the *BER* can reach below 10^{-3}. When the *SNR* is about 10 dB, the *BER* performance is very ideal; In contrast, the *BER* of synchronization performance without Q-learning is close to 10^{-1}, which is two orders of magnitude worse than that with Q-learning. Therefore, it can be seen that Q-learning greatly improves the performance of synchronization.

5   Conclusion

In this paper, the synchronization technology in underwater acoustic communication is studied. Through comparison and simulation, it is verified that the performance of synchronization of HFM signal is better than that of LFM signal; The Q-learning reinforcement method is used to estimate and compensate the Doppler factor, and the *BER* performance of the system is significantly improved. This paper mainly focuses on the following aspects:

(1) Analysis of underwater acoustic channel characteristics. Underwater acoustic communication is very different from terrestrial wireless communication. Therefore, this paper first studies the characteristics of acoustic wave propagation in water and the main characteristics of underwater acoustic channel.
(2) Chirp signal and Doppler estimation and compensation methods. In view of the fact that Doppler effect can cause the signal to expand and contract, two chirped signals are studied, including LFM signal, HFM signal. In this paper, Doppler-factor block estimation method are studied. The Doppler estimation performance of HFM and LFM as preambles is simulated and analyzed. The Doppler factor estimation performance will improve with the increase of the chirp signal sweep length and the transmission data length, and the performance of HFM signal is better than that of LFM signal;
(3) Doppler factor estimation and compensation based on Q-Learning. The principle of Q-learning is studied. The data of double-moon lake experiment were analyzed and compared with the system without reinforcement learning. By using Q-learning, the *BER* of the system is significantly reduced, which verifies that the method has a significant improvement on Doppler estimation and compensation.

The future research direction is to further study synchronization and equalization in underwater acoustic communication with reinforcement learning.

Acknowledgments. This paper is supported by National Natural Science Foundation of China under grant No. 62201174, Guangdong Basic and Applied Based Research Foundation (2023A1515011886), Shenzhen Science and Technology Program (Grant No. RCBS20221008093131087).

References

1. Wang, Zhou, Song, research on development of underwater wireless communication technology. Communication technology, **47**(06), 589–594 (2014)
2. Cai, L., et al.: Underwater acoustic communication and its research progress. Physics **35**(12):1038–1043 (2006)
3. Xie: Research on Channel Estimation and Equalization Algorithm for Mobile Node Underwater Acoustic Communication. Electronic Science and technology (2020)
4. Liu: Research on channel estimation for underwater acoustic OFDM communication systems. Huazhong University of Science and Technology (2020)
5. Xu: Research for underwater acoustic synchronous positioning based on single-carrier communication technology. South China University of Technology (2010)
6. Sharif, B.S., Neasham, J., Hinton, O.R., et al.: A computationally efficient Doppler compensation system for underwater acoustic communications. IEEE J. Oceanic Eng. **25**(1), 52–61 (2000)
7. Minh, D.L.: Wireless Communications Using Chirp Signals. Waseda University, Tokyo (2008)
8. Zhang, H.: Underwater acoustic communication system based on UW frame structure and its performance analysis. Comput. Eng. Appl. **44**(21), 85–88 (2008)

9. Harris, A.F., Zoris, M.: Modeling the Underwater Acoustic Channel in ns2. In: Nstools 2007 (2007)
10. André, M., van der Schaar, M., Zaugg, S., Houégnigan, L., Sánchez, A.M.: Sea observatories and acoustic events: towards a global monitoring of ocean noise. IEEE Underwater Technol., 1–3 (2015)
11. Thorp, W.H.: Deep ocean sound attenuation in the sub-and low-kilocycle-per-second region. Acoust. Soc. Am. (38), 648 (1965)
12. Geng, X., Zielinski, A.: An Eigenpath underwater acoustic communication channel model. In: OCEANS 95 MTS/IEEE Challenges of Our Changing Global Environment Conference, vol. 2, pp. 1189–1196 (1995)
13. Bao: Research on underwater acoustic cooperative detection technology based on single carrier frequency domain equalization. Harbin Institute of Technology (2016)
14. Yuan. Research on automatic generation method of piano fingering based on Q learning [D] South China University of technology, 2020.DOI:https://doi.org/10.27151/d.cnki.ghnlu. 2020.001936
15. Chen: Research on LTE/WLAN network access control algorithm based on Q learning. Harbin Institute of Technology (2013)

UAV Path Planning Based on APF-Q-Learning

Wenji Yuan and Yao Shi[✉]

Harbin Institute of Technology, Shenzhen 518000, Guangdong, China
180210315@stu.hit.edu.cn, shiyao@hit.edu.cn

Abstract. With the broadening of UAV application fields, the working environment of UAVs has become more and more complex. Intensive, dynamic and non-convex are the main characteristics of the obstacle environment under the new demand, and the complex obstacle environment brings great challenges to the working operation and flight of UAVs. This paper puts forward a reinforcement learning algorithm named APF-Q-learning algorithm, which is the combination of the artificial potential field (APF) method and the Q-Learning algorithm, and the reward function is designed to make the value function table converge faster. The simulation results also show that the proposed algorithm can better solve the problems of local optimum and slow convergence of the value function.

Keywords: route planning · artificial potential field method · reinforcement learning

1 Introduction

1.1 Subject Background

Unmanned aerial vehicle referred to as "UAV", is a kind of wireless remote control equipment collocation autonomous control program to realize autonomous operation of unmanned aircraft. UAVs are utilized in various fields due to their highly intelligence and flexible operation, UAV technology represents the development of high-tech industries in the field of science and technology in today's society.

With the expansion of UAV applications in various fields, the working environment of UAV becomes more and more complex. Dense, dynamic and non-convexity are the main characteristics of obstacle environment under new requirements. Various kinds of obstacle environment bring many challenges to the work of UAV. For example, on October 1, 2021, a UAV crash occurred in Zhengzhou High-tech Zone, Henan Province, China. During a UAV show, several UAVs collectively exploded, lost control and fell from a high altitude at the same time. The occurrence of these accidents reminds us that we need to treat UAV technology with higher requirements and high standards, and as one of the key technologies of the UAV control system—path planning technology is becoming more and more important.

Path planning algorithms require UAVs to find a safe, feasible and collision-free path from the starting state to the target state in the specified environment with different

© ICST Institute for Computer Sciences, Social Informatics and Telecommunications Engineering 2023
Published by Springer Nature Switzerland AG 2023. All Rights Reserved
A. Li et al. (Eds.): 6GN 2022, LNICST 505, pp. 290–300, 2023.
https://doi.org/10.1007/978-3-031-36014-5_24

obstacles based on the given evaluation criteria. According to the different principles of various path planning algorithms, path planning methods can be roughly divided into five categories: based on mathematical planning, potential field, landmark map, spatial decomposition and machine learning respectively. Among them, the first four categories have existed for a long time, and formed a relatively mature system composed of various improved optimization algorithms. The algorithms based on machine learning is relatively new, and compared with other types of algorithms, it has better real-time performance and can better handle dynamic problems. Therefore, it is very important to study the application of machine learning in the field of UAV path planning technology.

1.2 Research Status and Analysis

Research Status of Path Planning

Path planning has a wide range of applications in many fields, including cruise missiles, missile attack defense, civil GPS, urban road planning network, UAV obstacle avoidance flight, etc. According to different principles of path planning algorithms, traditional path planning algorithms can be divided into the four categories: based on mathematical programming, road marking map, spatial decomposition, and potential field.

Among them, Method based on potential field is to plan the environment by modeling it as a virtual potential field. O.khatib, an American scholar, first introduced the Artificial Potential Field (APF) into the field of path planning [1]. The artificial potential field APF algorithm has simple principle and simple structure [2], high execution efficiency, good real-time and dynamic performance, and is suitable for online planning. However, its principle simply models the environment as a gravitational repulsive force field, which leads to the removal of some other information in the environment, making it unable to plan the complex environment well. Moreover, the algorithm will fail to complete path planning due to the existence of local minimum points in the environment model [3].

Research Status of Reinforcement Learning

Reinforcement learning use a "trial and error" mechanism, which is the result of human and animal learning behavior, and the mechanism is not only related to learning body itself, is more important in the process of learning and the environment interaction [4]. Reinforcement learning regards the learning body as an "Agent", and the Agent will select an Action according to a certain policy under the environment State. After the Agent completes the Action, the environment will change, making the environment change to "State'", and at the same time, an immediate feedback signal, named the reward signal is fed back to the agent, and then the agent responds to the received reward signal and performs certain subsequent actions [5].

Reinforcement learning has great advantages and wide application prospects in solving complex optimization decision problems, and path planning problem is a typical optimization decision problem [6]. When the reinforcement learning agent is in a relatively complex environment, its path planning problem does not need to make global planning for the complex environment, which greatly improves the dynamic, portability and real-time performance of the algorithm, and has the advantages of other traditional path planning algorithms. Therefore, we explore reinforcement learning algorithms with better performance, instead of continuing to study traditional algorithms. At present, the types of reinforcement learning algorithms at home and abroad can be mainly divided into value-based algorithm, policy-based algorithm and Trust Region algorithm, among which the standard Q-learning algorithm is a representative algorithm [7]. This algorithm is a supervised learning method, which can learn the changing environment scene and plan the feasible collision-free path.

Reinforcement learning has shown broad application prospects in the field of path planning and has broad research prospects, but it is still a relatively new field. Some reinforcement learning algorithms are not perfect and have obvious shortcomings. For example, the standard Q-learning algorithm requires its environment State space and its Action space to be discrete, for which more and more researchers are joining this field and trying to enhance these classical algorithm systems [8, 9]. The field of path planning based on reinforcement learning is still in the stage of exploration and development.

2 UAV Path Planning Based on APF-Q-Learning

This section presents the basic principle and system implementation of UAV path planning based on APF-Q-learning algorithm. APF-Q-learning algorithm introduces the idea of virtual force field, the core of APF algorithm, into Q-learning algorithm, and optimizes the reward matrix with the concept of virtual force field, so as to improve the performance of UAV path planning based on Q-learning algorithm.

2.1 Basic Theory of APF-Q-Learning Algorithm

As an important part in reinforcement learning, the design of reward function is of great significance in the process of reinforcement learning. The essence of reinforcement learning is continuous learning in the interaction with the environment, and reward is the link between the agent and the environment, which guides the agent to continue learning and finally move towards the goal.

However, in path planning, the feedback function in reinforcement learning is often sparse. For example, in Q-learning algorithm, when reaching the abnormal termination state of "collision" and "exceeding the maximum number of steps", the UAV obtains a large negative reward (i.e. punishment); When the UAV reaches the correct termination state of "reaching the target point", the UAV obtains a large positive reward; But in other stages that occupy most of the steps, UAVs do not get any reward value, or they get the same small reward value for each step on average. In the whole algorithm process, there are only three state reward values. Such sparse reward values make the training of reinforcement learning algorithm have the following disadvantages:

(1) During the training of reinforcement learning algorithm, due to the sparsity of the reward function and the convergence of the surrounding reward functions, the value function will converge slowly, making the agent unable to find a better path quickly.
(2) When the reinforcement learning algorithm is being trained, the purpose of agent action decision is not obvious.

(3) Sparse reward function leads to low reliability of the training results of the algorithm, which is easy to produce wrong training results

For the sparse feedback function reward in reinforcement learning, we often needs to be designed by analyzing the specific path planning task manually, so as to optimize the feedback function reward to accelerate the convergence of the algorithm model.

This paper proposes to use the basic idea of virtual force field in APF algorithm to design the feedback function reward in path planning based on reinforcement learning algorithm. It uses the gravitational potential field of the target point and the repulsive potential field of the obstacle to carry out real-time calculation of the feedback function for each step of UAV motion.

In order to guide the UAV to continuously approach the target point, it is necessary to design a feedback function with a larger value when it approaches the target point. Therefore, at each time in the path planning, just like the gravitational potential field function in the APF algorithm, the feedback function reward is proportional to the square of the Euclidean distance between the current position and the target point position:

$$R_{target}(q) = -\frac{1}{2}\alpha d^2(q, q_{goal})$$

(1)

wherein, α is the feedback coefficient near the target point; $d(q, q_{goal})$ is the Euclidean distance between the current position and the target point position.

In addition to the reward for UAV by the "gravitational potential field" of the target point, the influence of the "repulsive potential field" of the obstacle on the UAV should also be considered. When the UAV approaches the obstacle and enters the distance threshold of its repulsion potential field, it will receive a negative reward, that is, punishment. The UAV changes the direction of action, as shown in the Eq. (2):

$$Reward_{obstruction}(q) = \begin{cases} \frac{1}{2}\beta\left(\frac{1}{d(q,q_{obs})} - \frac{1}{Q}\right)^2 , & d(q, q_{obs}) \leq Q \\ 0 , & d(q, q_{obs}) > Q \end{cases}$$

(2)

wherein, β is the feedback coefficient near the obstacle; $d(q, q_{goal})$ is the Euclidean distance between the current position and the obstacle position; Q is the distance threshold of the obstacle acting on the UAV. Beyond this distance, the obstacle has no impact on the UAV.

2.2 System Implementation of the APF-Q-Learning Algorithm

Through the previous analysis, combined with the two reward function feedback mechanisms in the Q-learning algorithm collision penalty mechanism and arrival reward mechanism, there are four reward function feedback mechanisms in the APF-Q-learning algorithm, which makes the sparse reward function in the original Q-learning more reasonable.

The specific reward function types are shown in Table 1 below:

Table 1. Reward function

Reward function type	Meaning of reward function
$Reward_{arrived}$ (r_1)	Reward for reaching the target point
$Reward_{knock}$ (r_2)	Penalty for collision with obstacles
$Reward_{target}$ (r_3)	Reward for approaching the target point
$Reward_{obstruction}$ (r_4)	Penalty for approaching obstacles

According to the reward function types described in the above table, the total reward of each step can be expressed as the weighted sum of the reward functions of each type, and the total reward function is recorded as r_{sum}, the calculation formula is shown below:

$$r_{sum} = \sum_{i=1}^{4} w_i r_i \tag{3}$$

r_i is the reward function of different types, w_i is the weight coefficient of different types of reward functions.

The specific algorithm process of path planning based on APF-Q-learning algorithm is shown in Table 2:

Table 2. APF-Q-Learning algorithm process

APF-Q-Learning algorithm process
1. Rasterize map and establish the state matrix S of N*N on the grid map;
2. Establish Q matrix and initialize;
3. Using the formula of APF algorithm to calculate $r_3 r_4$
4. The reward matrix R is obtained by the weighted summation of various types of r;
5. Cycle the specified number of times:
6. Initialization matrix S;
7. Cycle:
8. According to ε- greedy policy, execute an action in A(S);
9. Get the corresponding reward R and the state of the next time S';
10. $Q(S_t, A_t) \leftarrow Q(S_t, A_t) + \alpha \left(R_{t+1} + \gamma \max_a Q(S_{t+1}, a) - Q(S_t, A_t) \right)$
11. $S \leftarrow S'$
12. Until S terminates;

3 Analysis of Experimental Results of UAV Path Planning Algorithm

This section analyzes and compares the performance of APF algorithm, Q-learning algorithm and APF-Q-learning algorithm in path planning.

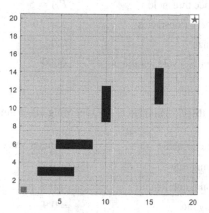

Fig. 1. Environment grid model

Table 3. Obstacle coordinates

Group	Specific coordinates
Group 1	(3, 3) (3, 4) (3, 5) (3, 6)
Group 2	(6, 5) (6, 6) (6, 7) (6, 8)
Group 3	(9, 10) (10, 10) (11, 10) (12, 10)
Group 4	(11, 16) (12, 16) (13, 16) (14, 16)

As shown in Fig. 1, the flight environment of UAV is modeled as a grid map and the grid size is 20 * 20 in this experiment. There are four groups of obstacles in the map, and a total of 16 grids are marked as obstacle points. The specific obstacle point coordinates are shown in Table 3. There are 382 passable grid points and two specially marked grid points. The red box icon in the lower left corner of the figure is the UAV starting point with coordinates of (1, 1), and the red pentagram icon in the upper right corner of the figure is the target point. Its coordinates are (20, 20).

The parameters of various algorithms in this experiment are shown in Table 4, 5 and 6, and the simulation results of various algorithms are shown in Fig. 2, 3, 4 and 5.

Figure 2 shows the simulation results of path planning based on APF algorithm. The built-in counter of the program shows that the number of steps of the simulation path is 1564. After combining steps size, the path length is 31.28. From the experimental results, it can be concluded that the path planning based on APF algorithm can give a better path without collision and reach the destination. Moreover, because it does not depend on the

Table 4. Parameters of APF algorithm

Parameter name	Parameter value
Attractive force gain coefficient	$k = 10$
Repulsive force gain coefficient	$m = 100$
Distance threshold	$P_O = 5$
Number of obstacles	$n = 16$
Step size	0.02
Maximum cycle iterations	6000

Table 5. Parameters of Q-learning algorithm

Parameter name	Parameter value
Learning rate	$\alpha = 0.2$
Discount coefficient	$\gamma = 0.9$
Greedy rate	$\varepsilon = 0.9$
Number of obstacles	$n = 16$
Maximum cycle iterations	300

Table 6. Parameters of APF-Q-Learning algorithm

Parameter name	Parameter value
Learning rate	$\alpha = 0.2$
Discount coefficient	$\gamma = 0.9$
Greedy rate	$\varepsilon = 0.9$
Number of obstacles	$n = 16$
Maximum cycle iterations	300
Attractive force gain coefficient	$k = 0.1$
Repulsive force gain coefficient	$m = 0.4/0.8$

grid map, and the movement direction calculated by the gravitational repulsion field is not limited by the grid, the UAV movement direction in the path planning based on APF algorithm is more flexible, which makes the obtained path smoother and more consistent with the actual flight path. However, it can still be seen that there are unreasonable decisions when the obtained path is close to the Group 4 of obstacles, which makes the obtained path deviate from the theoretical optimal path.

Figure 3 shows the simulation results of path planning based on Q-learning algorithm. The total number of steps is 22, of which the number of horizontal and vertical steps is 6

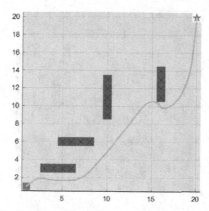

Fig. 2. Path planning based on APF algorithm

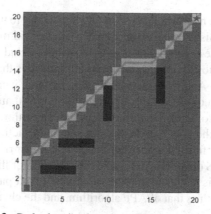

Fig. 3. Path planning based on Q-learning algorithm

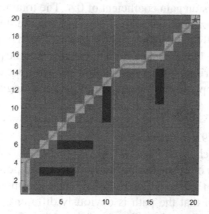

Fig. 4. Path planning based on APF-Q-learning algorithm (repulsion gain coefficient is 0.4)

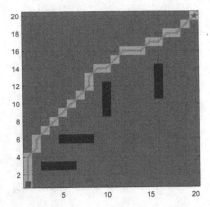

Fig. 5. Path planning based on APF-Q-learning algorithm (repulsion gain coefficient is 0.8)

and the step size is 1; The number of steps moving diagonally to the upper right is 16, and the step size is 1.414. This is because the map is a square grid map. Therefore, the path length is 28.624. From the experimental results, it can be concluded that the path given by the algorithm is not obviously unreasonable, which indicates that the processing effect of the algorithm is good. And from the path length obtained, it can be seen that the path planning simulation path of Q-learning algorithm is shorter than that of APF algorithm by about 8.5%. It can also be seen that the Q-learning algorithm requires limited action space and is affected by the grid map. In this simulation, the action space of UAV is only 8, which are up, down, left, right, upper left, lower left, upper right and lower right, that is, UAV can only select 8 directions to fly, and the selection of flight direction is far less than APF algorithm. This results in that the simulation result path based on Q-learning algorithm is not as smooth as that of APF algorithm, and the change of UAV flight angle is abrupt.

Figure 4 shows the simulation results of path planning based on APF-Q-learning algorithm, with the repulsion gain coefficient of 0.4. The total number of steps is 22, of which the number of horizontal and vertical steps is 6 and the step size is 1; The number of steps moving diagonally to the upper right is 16, and the step size is 1.414. Therefore, the path length is 28.624. It can be seen from the results that the path length is consistent with the Q-learning algorithm. Observing the specific path, we can find that the first 17 steps of the path are completely consistent with the Q-learning algorithm.

Its path is:

path[1]:1 → 21 → 41 → 61 → 82 → 103 → 124 → 145 → 166 → 187 → 208 → 229 → 250 → 271 → 292 → 293 → 294.

Only in step 18, it is changed from 294 → 295 to 295 → 315, so that the path is not close to the fourth group of obstacles, but away from a grid point.

Change the repulsion gain coefficient to 0.8, and the simulation results are shown in Fig. 5. It can be seen that the path is obviously different from the path shown in Fig. 3 and Fig. 4. The total number of steps of the path is 24, of which the number of

---

[1] The two-dimensional path is converted to one-dimensional linked list. The conversion formula is: 1D order number = (number of rows-1) * 20 + number of columns.

steps moving horizontally and vertically is 10 and the step size is 1; The number of steps moving diagonally to the upper right is 14, and the step size is 1.414. Therefore, the path length is 29.796. Although its path is about 3.9% longer than the result when Q-learning and APF-Q-learning repulsion gain coefficient are 0.4, it can be seen from the figure that due to the existence of the obstacle penalty reward function, the path is no longer close to the obstacle planning, and within the distance of one grid point around the four groups of obstacles, the planned paths all choose to detour. This makes the collision free target constraint of path planning better than that of the same algorithm when the repulsion gain coefficient is 0.4 and the Q-learning algorithm, and does not cause collision due to the path being too close to the obstacle. It can be seen that APF-Q-learning can adjust to multiple constraints of path planning by adjusting the gain coefficient, and set the appropriate gain coefficient. It can also optimize the path without collision constraint under the condition of ensuring the shortest path, and can optimize paths without collision constraint by sacrificing the path length of the part.

4 Conclusion

In this paper, aiming at the path planning technology of UAV, the grid environment model is used to describe the objective constraint, environmental obstacle avoidance constraint and path shortest constraint. Aiming at the slow convergence caused by sparse reward function in standard Q-learning algorithm based on reinforcement learning, an optimized Q-learning algorithm: APF-Q-learning algorithm is proposed by using the virtual force field theory of APF algorithm. By adding two new reward function types, the problem of sparse reward function in standard Q-learning algorithm is solved, and the iterative convergence efficiency is improved.

Acknowledgments. This paper is supported by National Natural Science Foundation of China under grant No. 62201174, Guangdong Basic and Applied Based Research Foundation (2023A1515011886), Shenzhen Science and Technology Program (Grant No. RCBS20221008093131087).

References

1. Khatib, O.: Real-time obstacle avoidance for manipulators and mobile robot. Int. J. Rob. Res. (1985)
2. Li, W.H.: An improved artificial potential field method based on chaos theory for UAV route planning. In: 2019 34rd Youth Academic Annual Conference of Chinese Association of Automation (YAC). IEEE Press, Piscataway (2019)
3. Aggarwal, S., Kumar, N.: Path planning techniques for unmanned aerial vehicles: a review, solutions, and challenges. Comput. Commun. (2020)
4. Sutton, R.S., Barto, A.G.: Reinforcement learning: an introduction. IEEE Trans. Neural Netw. (1998)
5. Claus, C.: The dynamics of reinforcement learning in cooperative multiagent systems. In: National Conference on Artificial Intelligence. American Association for Artificial Intelligence(1998)

6. Coutinho, W.P/, Battarra, M., Fliege, J.: The un-manned aerial vehicle routing and trajectory optimisation problem, a taxonomic review. Comput. Ind. Eng. (2018)
7. Watkins, C.J.C.H., Dayan, P.: Q-learning. Mach. Learn. (1992)
8. Qie, H., Shi, D., Shen, T., et al.: Joint optimization of multi-UAV target assignment and path planning based on multi-agent reinforcement learning. IEEE Access (2019)
9. Lu, L., Shao, X., Wei, Y., et al.: Intelligent land-vehicle model transfer trajectory planning method based on deep reinforcement learning. Sensors (2018)

Simulation Analysis of Inter-digital Electrodes Sensor Based on HFSS

Hanxiao Yuan and Yao Shi[⊠]

Harbin Institute of Technology, Shenzhen 51800, Guangdong, China
shiyao@hit.edu.cn

Abstract. In the past few decades, as people have become more and more concerned about physical health, a large number of studies have been used to measure physiological information (such as heart rate, respiration, and blood pressure), which provides great value for predicting diseases. As a component of sensors, interdigital electrodes have developed rapidly in the field of sensors and are widely used in the field of biological detection. Moreover, interdigital electrodes can be non-invasive, low-cost, reliable, and not affected by environmental conditions, making interdigital electrodes' performance more important. This paper proposes a method to simulate and optimize interdigital electrodes' performance through HFSS. Firstly, the equivalent circuit model of the interdigital electrode is studied and calculated, and the initialization sensor parameters are obtained. Then the effects of electrode length, electrode width, spacing, and substrate thickness on the performance of interdigital electrodes are analyzed by simulation, and the interdigital electrode model is optimized to better detect some physiological information about the human body. In addition, the detection of human physiological information is simulated, which can provide a reference for future research.

Keywords: Interdigital electrodes · Planar capacitance sensor · HFSS

1 Introduction

The last two decades have seen a growing trend toward the demand for real-time monitoring, interdigital microelectrodes have attracted more and more attention and have been widely used in various fields [1]. Interdigital electrodes have been used as the core components of sensors in recent years. They are developing rapidly in the field of sensors and are widely used in biological detection, chemical detection, and gas detection [2], and they have also shown good performance in the application of non-invasive detection of physiological information such as wrist pulse [3]. However, much uncertainty still exists in the effects of electrode parameters on the performance of detecting human body information including but not limited to heart rate, and blood pressure. This study aimed to develop a better design and optimization method of interdigital electrodes for detecting heart rate.

Inter-digital electrodes are planar capacitors, which are realized by electromagnetic coupling between coplanar electrodes. They are among the most commonly used periodic electrode structures [4]. They are widely employed as quasi-lumped elements in

A. Li et al. (Eds.): 6GN 2022, LNICST 505, pp. 301–312, 2023.
https://doi.org/10.1007/978-3-031-36014-5_25

microwave-integrated circuits and monolithic microwave-integrated circuits for wireless technology applications, due to their intrinsic low cost, construction simplicity, and repeatability [5]. They can also be used as an electrochemical sensors widely used in biological science, electronic communication, chemical testing, and other fields [2].

For interdigitated electrode resonator, the number of electrodes will change the capacitance value, and the length of electrodes will affect its working stability and capacitance density. If the length is too long, the resonance frequency may shift and the parasitic parameters may deteriorate, which will lead to unsatisfactory working stability of the interdigital electrode [6]. Studying the effects of these parameters on the performance of interdigital electrodes has a considerable impact on the design of the device.

This paper first described the effects of electrode length, width, spacing between electrodes, substrate thickness, and electrode shape on the performance of interdigital electrode resonators. The optimized model is obtained by HFSS simulation software. Secondly, considering the change in the performance of the interdigital electrode when the human body enters the fringing field range of the interdigital electrode [7], we simulate the change of the resonant frequency of the model when the blood vessel diameter changes periodically. Simulation results reveal the effect of pulse cycle variation on the model.

2 System Model

As a parallel plate capacitor, the overall structure of the interdigital electrodes can be divided into circular, rectangular, and trapezoidal. The design principle is following the rule of the planar integrated circuits. We need a brief overview of the theoretical model. As shown in Fig. 1, several common interdigital electrode structures are listed. And the specific shape is divided into rectangular, arc-shaped, or circular electrodes. The equivalent circuit is shown in Fig. 2. C and R are parasitic capacitance and parasitic resistance respectively, and C_s is substrate parasitic capacitance [8]. Figure 3 is a model of frequency response. The resonant frequency can be expressed as:

$$f_0 = \frac{1}{\sqrt{2\pi LC}} \tag{1}$$

The Q-value of the planar capacitance can be estimated by:

$$Q = \frac{1}{R\omega_0 C} \tag{2}$$

Because of the spatial electric field generated between different electrodes, the spatial electromagnetic coupling between coplanar electrodes results in the same frequency but a different amplitude of the AC signal produced by the electrodes. The capacitance can be calculated by calculating the amplitude ratio between electrodes with different amplitudes.

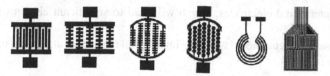

Fig. 1. Structure types of interdigital electrodes

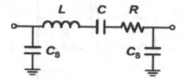

Fig. 2. Equivalent circuit

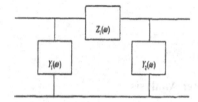

Fig. 3. Frequency response

The capacitance value of the rectangular interdigital sensor is calculated by the structural parameters. Such as electrode width, electrode thickness, substrate thickness, substrate dielectric constant, electrode length, and electrode number. The relationship between the mutual capacitance of the sensor and the structural parameters can be expressed as:

$$C = \varepsilon_0 \left[\frac{\varepsilon_m + \varepsilon_s}{2} \frac{K\left[\sqrt{\left\{1 - \left(\frac{a}{b}\right)^2\right\}}\right]}{K\left(\frac{a}{b}\right)} + \varepsilon_n \frac{h}{a} \right] * (N - 1) * L \qquad (3)$$

where ε_0 is the vacuum permittivity, ε_m is the permittivity of the sample, ε_s is the relative permittivity of the substrate, ε_n is the permittivity of the gap caused by the electrodes, h is the electrode thickness, a is the electrode spacing, s represents the electrode width, b represents the sum of the electrode spacing and electrode width, N represents the number of electrodes of the sensor, L represents the sensor electrode length, K represents the first-type complete elliptic integral.

If a human body is placed within the fringing-field range of the interdigital electrodes, the parasitic capacitance of the plane capacitance will be affected. The human body will generate additional displacement currents and conduction current channels between the electrodes, changing the original magnetic field characteristics and distorting the fringing field of the interdigital electrodes, which will lead to significant changes in electrode performance.

The equivalent circuit model when the interdigital electrodes are placed on the human wrist is show in Fig. 4.

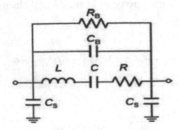

Fig. 4. Equivalent circuit around the human wrist

3 Simulation Model

3.1 Simulation Parameter Analysis

A sensitive layer of chemical or biological nature deposited over the electrodes can also interact with a gas or liquid environment, allowing monitoring of the concentration of chemicals in such materials as air, transformer oil, or the human body [9]. The interdigital electrodes can be used as a resonant circuit when the human body is the detection object. The resonant frequency and S parameters play a key role in evaluating system performance. This study investigates the relationship between system performance and design parameters to make optimization easier without repeating time-consuming finite element simulations.

Length Analysis. The effect on the resonant frequency of varying the length of the electrode is shown in Fig. 5. From Eqs. (1) and (2), it can be concluded that the electrode length is inversely proportional to the resonant frequency of the interdigital electrode. The simulation results are consistent with the theory. The S parameters have a slight effect on electrode length. When the electrode length is between 13 mm and 14 mm, the curve is the smoothest, the burr is the smallest, and the generated parasitic capacitance is also the smallest.

Width Analysis. The effect on the S paraments of varying electrode width is shown in Fig. 6. Experiments show that the return loss will be increased with the decrease of the electrode width. Greater return loss means better transmission performance. And it can be seen that when the electrode width is 0.1 mm, the parasitic capacitance will become larger and the performance will get worse.

Spacing Analysis. The effect of electrode spacing on interdigital electrodes is similar to the effect of width. It is shown in Fig. 7. As the electrode spacing increases, the return loss will be reduced. It means that the performance is gradually worsening. The reason is that the impedance of the resonant frequency point is closer to 50 ohms so its matching situation is better. But it should be noted that, when the width of the electrode is 0.1 mm, the shape of the curve starts to become uneven. It can be seen that the electrode spacing should not be too small.

Substrate Thickness analysis. As shown in Fig. 8, the effect on S-11 paraments of When the thickness is less than 0.7 mm, the S11 value becomes smaller as the thickness increases. But when the thickness is greater than 0.7 mm, the smoothness of the curve begins to deteriorate. At the same time, parasitic resonance and burrs also appear.

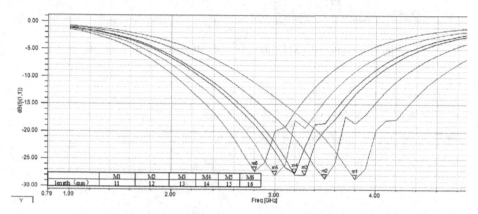

Fig. 5. Compare the S11 parameters of different electrode lengths

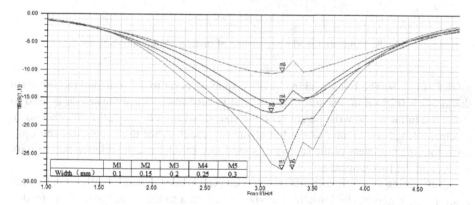

Fig. 6. Compare the S11 parameters of different electrode widths

3.2 Initialization and Optimized Models

The interdigital electrodes sensor has the same principle of operation as the more conventional parallel plate. According to the design principle, we get the Initialization design

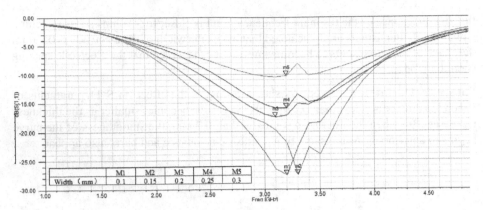

Fig. 7. Compare the S11 parameters of different electrode spacing

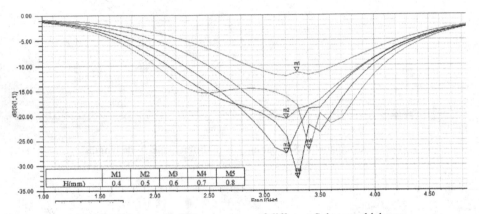

Fig. 8. Compare the S11 parameters of different Substrate thickness

model as Fig. 9. The Initialization electrode spacing is set to 0.1 mm, and the substrate thickness is 0.254 mm, the substrate material is FR4 plate. Since the sensor is used to study the influence of wrist parameters, the size should not be too large. We choose an electrode length of 11 mm as the Initialization model. After the simulation and optimization, the thickness of the substrate is modified to 0.6 mm, the relative permittivity is 4.6, and the loss tangent is 0.02.

Considering that it is difficult to buy a coaxial feeder that meets the Initialization design requirements, the Initialization size is adjusted to the actual size of the feeder. In addition, the distance between the feed points is too short to place the two coaxial feeders, which will make the connector very difficult to rotate and connect to the VNA. Therefore, the distance between the feed points should be enlarged. At the same time, the other parameters should be adjusted to ensure good performance. Finally, an optimized interdigitated electrode is obtained. The S-curve result is relatively smooth, and it has no obvious burr.

The design parameters, the simulation model of the Initialization model, and the optimized model are shown in Fig. 9, 10, 11 and 12. The result after optimization is shown in Fig. 14. It can be seen that the model resonance at 3.2 GHz, the reflection coefficient is less than −25 dB, and the transmission coefficient is −0.35 dB. Compared with the simulation result of the Initialization model, Fig. 13, the matching is much better and the return loss increased by 20 dB. The design goal is well accomplished.

Name	Value	Unit	Evaluated Va...	Type	Description	Read-only	Hidden
l1	11	mm	11mm	Design		□	□
l2	3.5	mm	3.5mm	Design		□	□
l3	2.5	mm	2.5mm	Design		□	□
l4	2.5	mm	2.5mm	Design		□	□
gap2	0.15	mm	0.15mm	Design		□	□
gap1	0.8	mm	0.8mm	Design		□	□
w1	0.2	mm	0.2mm	Design		□	□
w2	0.5	mm	0.5mm	Design		□	□
out_diameter	0.7	mm	0.7mm	Design		□	□
inter_diamet...	0.5	mm	0.5mm	Design		□	□

Fig. 9. Initialization model size

Name	Value	Unit	Evaluated Va...	Type	Description	Read-only	Hidden	∧
l1	13.3	mm	13.3mm	Design		□	□	
l2	2	mm	2mm	Design		□	□	
l4	1.7	mm	1.7mm	Design		□	□	
gap2	0.15	mm	0.15mm	Design		□	□	
gap1	0.8	mm	0.8mm	Design		□	□	
w1	0.15	mm	0.15mm	Design		□	□	
w2	0.55	mm	0.55mm	Design		□	□	
out_diameter	1.5	mm	1.5mm	Design		□	□	
inter_diamet...	1.2	mm	1.2mm	Design		□	□	

Fig. 10. Optimized model size

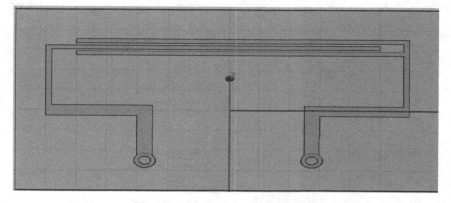

Fig. 11. Initialization model by HFSS

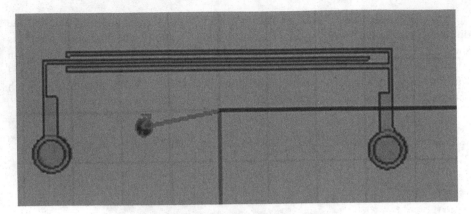

Fig. 12. Optimized model by HFSS

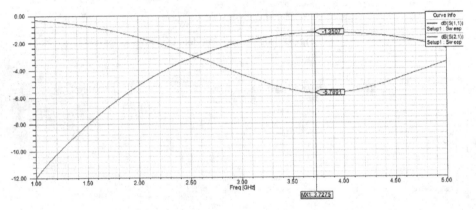

Fig. 13. Initialization simulation S parameter

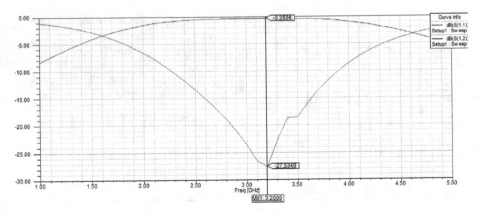

Fig. 14. Optimized simulation S parameter

3.3 Simulation Model of the Human Body

The permittivity and conductivity of the human body will alter the magnetic field around the electrodes. Therefore, when designing the interdigital electrode sensor, the influence of the edge effect on the human body should be considered. The parameters of the human wrist are shown in Table 1. The dielectric constant of skin is set to be 44.6 and the conductivity is 1.70; the dielectric constant of fat is to be set to 4.4 and the conductivity is 0.08; the dielectric constant of muscle is to be set to 54.0 and the conductivity is 2.20; The dielectric constant is 53.0 and the conductivity is 2.7. The model is shown in Fig. 15. The model includes interdigital electrodes, skin, fat, muscle, blood vessels, and muscle. The blood vessels are contained in muscles. It can simulate the situation of the human wrist over the interdigital electrodes.

The simulation result is shown in Fig. 16. Experiments show that the wrist model of the human body will cause the resonant frequency of the interdigital electrode from 3.2 GHz to 2.3 GHz, and the reflection coefficient will increase from −27 dB to −20 dB.

Table 1. Parameters of the human wrist

	Skin	Fat	Muscle	Blood vessel
permittivity	44.6	4.4	54	53
Conductivity(s/m)	1.7	0.08	2.2	2.7
Height	0.5	0.5	30	0.5–1
Length(mm)	200	200	200	200
Width(mm)	50	50	50	50

The sensor is designed as a wearable device and is placed around the human wrist to detect the physiological information in the wrist pulse, which can be expressed by the periodic changes in the diameter of the blood vessels. In the wrist model, the blood vessel diameter is changed from 0.5 mm to 1.0 mm, and the response of the interdigital electrode sensor is obtained as follows.

The result shows that when the blood vessel diameter changes from 5 mm to 10 mm, S11 changes from −20 dB to −22 dB. It can be seen from Fig. 17 that as the blood vessel diameter increases, the return loss decreases and the matching degree becomes better. In addition, as shown in Fig. 18, the s11 phase is also different. This characteristic makes the interdigital electrode sensor carry the physiological information of the wrist pulse.

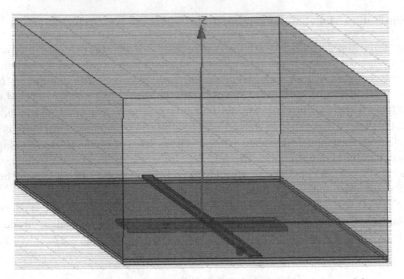

Fig. 15. HFSS model with interdigital electrode under wrist model

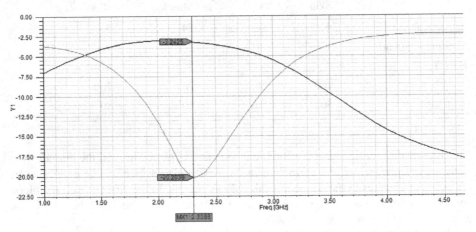

Fig. 16. S11 parameters of the interdigital electrode under the wrist model

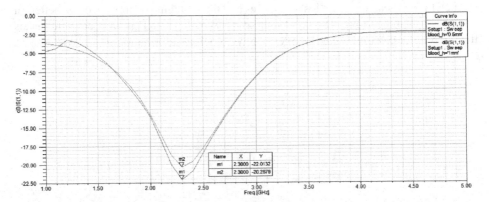

Fig. 17. Compare the S11 amplitude of models with different vessel diameter

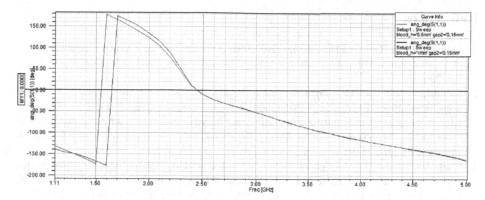

Fig. 18. Compare the S11 phase of models with different vessel diameter

4 Conclusion

This paper described the simulation design of interdigital electrodes based on HFSS software and evaluated the influence of the electrode parameters. This study has shown that the increase in the length of the electrode will lead to a decrease in the resonant frequency, and the increase in the electrode width and the spacing between the electrodes will lead to an increase in the reflected energy, and will also cause the deterioration of the performance. The increase in the thickness of the substrate will lead to larger return loss and better performance, but when the substrate thickness is too large, it will decrease the smoothness of the curve and the appearance of parasitic resonance points. In addition, we also studied the influence of the human wrist on the S-parameters of the interdigital electrode and concluded that: the human wrist model makes the resonant frequency of the sensor a significant decline of 0.9 GHz. At the same time, the study described the effect of changes in vessel diameter on its phase. Since the periodic change of the diameter of human blood vessels can reflect the human heart rate, interdigital electrodes can detect the human body's physiological information. These findings have significant implications for the optimization of interdigital electrode sensors. A key strength of the present study is the consideration of the actual product size so that it can be better produced and used.

The present study was subject to several potential methodological weaknesses. For instance, the dielectric constant of the human body is different due to individual differences, and the dielectric constant of the air is also different due to time and space reasons, so it is inevitable that the simulation results will deviate from the actual results. They need further development.

Acknowledgments. This paper is supported by National Natural Science Foundation of China under grant No. 62201174, Guangdong Basic and Applied Based Research Foundation (2023A1515011886), Shenzhen Science and Technology Program (Grant No. RCBS20221008093131087).

References

1. Mendelson, Y., Ochs, B.D.: Noninvasive pulse oximetry utilizing skin reflectance photoplethysmography. IEEE Trans. Biomed. Eng. **35**, 798–805 (1988). https://doi.org/10.1109/10.7286
2. Mamishev, A.V., Sundara-Rajan, K., Yang, F., Du, Y., Zahn, M.: Interdigital sensors and transducers. Proc. IEEE. **92**, 808–845 (2004). https://doi.org/10.1109/JPROC.2004.826603
3. Kim, B.-H., et al.: A proximity coupling RF sensor for wrist pulse detection based on injection-locked PLL. IEEE Trans. Microw. Theory Techn. **64**, 1667–1676 (2016). https://doi.org/10.1109/TMTT.2016.2549531
4. Chen, T., Bowler, N.: Design of interdigital spiral and concentric capacitive sensors for materials evaluation. In: Presented at the Review of Progress in Quantitative Nondestructive Evaluation, Denver, Colorado, USA, vol. 32 (2013). https://doi.org/10.1063/1.4789232
5. Caratelli, D., Cicchetti, R.: A full-wave analysis of interdigital capacitors for planar integrated circuits. IEEE Trans. Magn. **39**, 1598–1601 (2003). https://doi.org/10.1109/TMAG.2003.810410
6. Huang, Y., Zhan, Z., Bowler, N.: Optimization of the coplanar interdigital capacitive sensor. In: Presented at the 43rd Annual Review of Progress in Quantitative Nondestructive Evaluation, Atlanta, Georgia, USA, vol. 36 (2017). https://doi.org/10.1063/1.4974695
7. Cho, N., Roh, T., Bae, J., Yoo, H.-J.: A planar MICS band antenna combined with a body channel communication electrode for body sensor network. IEEE Trans. Microw. Theory Techn. **57**, 2515–2522 (2009). https://doi.org/10.1109/TMTT.2009.2029952
8. Bahl, I.J.: Lumped Elements for RF and Microwave Circuits. Artech House, Boston (2003)
9. Esfandiari, R., Maki, D.W., Siracusa, M.: Design of interdigitated capacitors and their application to gallium arsenide monolithic filters. IEEE Trans. Microw. Theory Techn. **31**, 57–64 (1983). https://doi.org/10.1109/TMTT.1983.1131429

6G Network Security Technology Based on Artificial Intelligence

Xinlu Li[✉], Canquan Ling, and Zhenyu Xu

Huizhou Engineering Vocational College, Huizhou 516000, China
49266692@qq.com

Abstract. In the future, human society will enter the era of intelligence, and 6G will also achieve cross integration with information technologies such as artificial intelligence (AI). 6G uses primitive artificial intelligence to continuously empower the whole society in the future and realize true universal intelligence. How to use 6G native AI to intelligently manage and control the future network resources and wireless resources, and how to use 6G network security technology are both hot research directions and key directions of future communication networks. Artificial intelligence technology has created new opportunities for innovation and business model driven by machine learning technology in 6G network. The end-to-end network automation of the future communication requires the system to actively discover dangers and threats, apply intelligent mitigation technology, and ensure the self sustainment of the 6G network. But in fact, the alliance between 6G and AI is also a double-edged sword. In most cases, AI technology can protect the security and privacy of the network, and may be used by criminals to violate information security and privacy. This paper analyzes the role of AI in 6G network security, analyzes the challenges that AI technology may encounter in 6G security, and proposes solutions.

Keywords: Artificial intelligence · 6G · Network security

1 Introduction

6G emerging technologies include terahertz band, artificial intelligence, optical wireless communication, 3D network, UAV, intelligent reflective surface IRS, wireless power transmission, etc. 6G communication will achieve various system functional characteristics by introducing the integration of these new technologies: ubiquitous mobile ultra wideband, ultra-high speed low delay communication, large-scale machine communication, ultra-high data density. The application scenario is shown in Fig. 1.

2019 is the first year of 5G. Since the construction of 5G, more than 700000 5G base stations have been commercialized globally. At the same time, operators and communication fields around the world also began to explore and study the 6G network technology. It is expected that by 2030, the 6G network will begin to realize commercial use, and the end-to-end intelligence of the Internet communication network in the

© ICST Institute for Computer Sciences, Social Informatics and Telecommunications Engineering 2023
Published by Springer Nature Switzerland AG 2023. All Rights Reserved
A. Li et al. (Eds.): 6GN 2022, LNICST 505, pp. 313–323, 2023.
https://doi.org/10.1007/978-3-031-36014-5_26

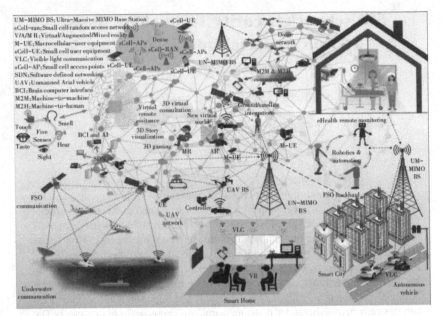

Fig. 1. Application architecture scenario of 6G communication

future will be developed into a technology that enables devices to independently detect hazards, automatically solve crises, and achieve self-protection. Therefore, it is not a traditional encryption method to realize the security design and handling of network sudden exceptions by artificial intelligence technology. Independent identification and response to potential hazards is an important and key link.

2 Basic Principles

Among the technical capabilities of 6G, the simultaneous wireless connectivity of the system will be 1000 times higher than that of the 5G system. Compared with the enhanced mobile broadband (eMBB) in 5G, 6G will provide ubiquitous network services uMUB. Ultra reliable low latency is a key feature of 5G communication, and it will also become a key factor in providing 6G communication of uHSLLC. The 6G communication system will provide large-scale connection equipment (up to 10 million/km^2), Gbit/s rate in any coverage area, and even new coverage environments such as sky (10000 km) and ocean (20 n miles). The 6G system will provide ultra long battery life and advanced battery technology for energy collection. Mobile devices in the 6G system do not need to be charged separately. For different 6G service types, the applicable 6G technologies under different characteristic services of uMUB, uHSLLC, mMTC and uHDD can be displayed. Each technology can enhance one or more services, as shown in Table 1.

With the gradual marginalization of the Internet, the virtualization of software makes the boundaries of information security more and more blurred, and the security problems brought by the Internet architecture are increasingly prominent; With the in-depth and extensive integration of edge computing, artificial intelligence technology and big data

Table 1. Characteristics of emerging technologies under different 6G services

key technology	uMUB	uHSLLC	mMTC	uHDD
artificial intelligence		√	√	√
Terahertz communication	√	√		
Optical wireless communication technology	√	√	√	√
Wireless optical communication front-end/return network	√	√		
Large scale MIMO	√	√	√	√
Blockchain		√		
3D Network		√		√
Quantum communication	√	√	√	
UAV		√	√	√
No cellular communication	√	√	√	√
Wireless information and energy transmission integration WIET	√			√
Perceptual communication integration	√			√
Access back network integration	√	√		
Dynamic network slice	√	√		
Holographic beam	√	√		
Big data analysis		√	√	√
Backscatter communication			√	
Smart reflector		√	√	√
Proactive caching		√	√	√
Mobile edge computing	√			

mining technology, the internal security of the edge Internet is facing unprecedented new challenges [1]. The future network communication needs to break the traditional conventional network security protection concept and create an information security cooperation system that can not only adapt to the evolution process of 6G transformative technology, but also promote the cross domain aggregation process of 6G network. The system adapts to green Internet technology and green terminal technology, and meets the lightweight network security protection requirements of low power consumption and low computing capacity, and the information security system is transformed from external to internal. On the 6G network, through the integration of information technology and service, it is the aggregation of various security protocols and security systems to realize the security management of the network system. The 6G is the initiative to take the security measures of the network system, which should form an independent driving force, respond to the network security changes, and generate a defense force against the stability of the network system [2].

The internal security structure of 6G network system includes connection side security and network side security, as shown in Fig. 2. The security of the connection side will adopt "cohesion and governance" to implement "gatekeeper type" security guarantee for the 6G endogenous security network system; The security of the Internet domain puts forward that the security stability force of the network system from the inside to the outside, which is the key aspect of "taking the initiative to live". The access side information security will include port security and base station security. From the perspective of interface side information security and network side information security, the potential security problems and challenges of network security in 6G are analyzed, and specific endogenous security protection contents are proposed [3].

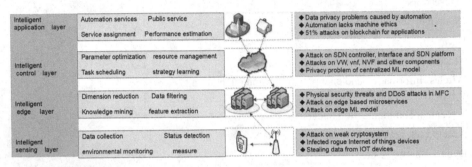

Fig. 2. Intelligent 6G architecture and 6G security and privacy issues

3   Relevant Progress and Standardization at Home and Abroad

The research and standardization work on artificial intelligence and intelligent wireless communication networks has become a research hotspot in the industry, including but not limited to the relevant policies issued by the state, the classification of network intelligence capabilities in the industry, and the standardization organization's formulation of the development goals of network evolution and the standards of application interfaces, services and data formats.

3.1   Artificial Intelligence Policies at Home and Abroad

China has put forward an important AI strategy from 2015, and issued a number of planning measures from 2016 to 2020, providing solutions in terms of industrial research, transformation and upgrading, landing operation, big data platform construction, and promoting the intelligent transformation of enterprises. The government work report in March 2019 upgraded AI to "Intelligence+", and promoted the transformation and upgrading of traditional industries relying on the industrial Internet platform. At present, some research results of the industry and university sessions have been achieved. Shanghai Jiaotong University uses intelligent agents based on artificial intelligence to solve the problem of automatic driving path planning through the establishment and derivation of a knowledge base. Baidu, Alibaba, Cambrian Company and other Internet companies have focused on the new intelligent ecology of the integration of Duanyun, and have created various kinds of intelligent cloud servers, intelligent terminals and core processor chips of intelligent robots.

Internationally, the United States: signed an agreement in February 2019 calling on the United States to lead the development of international artificial intelligence standards, and released the automatic driving 4.0 plan in January 2020 to speed up the implementation of the automatic driving industry; Nvidia's Tesla P100 system is equipped with a variety of deep learning algorithms, which can achieve high-performance computing and large-scale workloads, greatly improving throughput; Google DeepMind's algorithm is widely used in medical, gaming, e-commerce and other fields; Microsoft has changed the original technical framework of speech recognition by using deep convolutional neural network to achieve a fully automatic AI simultaneous interpretation system. UK: From 2018 to 2020, we will release the industrial strategy, establish an AI office, build the Alan Turing Institute, and work with Oxford University, Cambridge University and other universities to promote the transformation of technology into industry. Japan: In July 2018, the second strategic innovation promotion plan was released to promote the development of network space technology, auto drive system and intelligent logistics services based on big data and artificial intelligence. EU: The "Horizon 2020" project will be implemented in 2020 to create an AI ecosystem support platform and promote the effective convergence of theories, algorithms, data and other resources.

3.2 Progress of Standardization Organization

In March 2018, the Third Generation Partnership Program (3GPP) introduced the R15 standard of 5G new air port (NR), supported 5G non independent (NSA) networking and independent (SA) networking modes, and froze the R15 standard in June 2019. In September 2018, 3GPP formulated the R16 standard of 5G NR, focusing on the impact of intelligent transportation oriented vehicles on the outside world.

The R16 standard will be frozen on July 3, 2020 for information (V2X), positioning enhancement, MIMO enhancement, power consumption improvement, etc. 3GPP plans to release R17 version at the end of 2021, focusing on issues such as small data transmission optimization, frequency research above 52.6 GHz, and non terrestrial network NR, to adapt to SA mode in multiple application scenarios.

In November 2017, the International Telecommunication Union Telecommunications Standardization Department (ITU-T) established a machine learning working group for the future network to study network services and needs, machine learning technology, and machine learning based perceptual network architecture. In October 2019, ITU-T held a network 2030 seminar, reached consensus on the three application scenarios of 6G, and formulated standard proposals for 11 groups, including the application of artificial intelligence in network performance. In February 2020, the International Telecommunication Union - Radio Communication Department (ITU-R) started the research work on the 6G network in 2030. ITU plans to complete the Future Technology Outlook Proposal in the first half of 2021, including the overall objectives, application scenarios, system capabilities, etc. of the future communication system.

In February 2017, the European Telecommunications Standardization Institute (ETSI) established an experiential network intelligence working group to adaptively adjust network services with artificial intelligence to achieve intelligent operations such as policy control and business deployment. In January 2018, a zero contact network and service management working group was established with the goal of automatically implementing the process of network delivery, deployment, configuration, maintenance and optimization. In 2019, the white paper "Necessity and Benefits of Automating Network and Service Operations in the Next Generation Network" was released, summarizing the 5G network automation service management and operation objectives. On June 29, 2020, the white paper "Artificial Intelligence and Future Development Direction" was released to investigate the application of artificial intelligence in network optimization, privacy/security, data management and other fields.

4 Network Security Problems in 6G

4.1 Pre_6G Safety Issues

Software defined Networking (SDN), network function Virtualization (NFV), multi access edge computing (MEC), network slicing and other technologies in 5G are still applicable to 6G systems, so their security issues will also be inherited by 6G. Security issues related to SDN include attacks on SDN controllers, attacks on North and South interfaces, and attacks on inherent vulnerabilities of SDN controller platforms [2]. The security problems related to NFV are attacks against virtual machines (VM), virtual network functions (VNF), virtual machine hypervisors, VNF managers, and NFV choreographers [4]. Due to the large-scale distributed characteristics of 6G system, MECs in 6G are vulnerable to physical security attacks and distributed denial of service (DDoS) attacks. The attack on network software technology makes it difficult for 6G network to realize dynamic and full automation [5].

4.2 Security of 6G Architecture

The 6G cellular network will be reduced from a small cell to a micro cell, and more intensive cellular deployment, mesh network, multi connection and device to device (D2D) communication will become the normal. Distributed networks are more vulnerable to attacks by malicious parties because each device has a mesh connection, which increases the risk of being attacked [6]. The core convergence of radio access network (RAN) makes the functions of high-level ran more centralized and coexists with distributed core functions, such as user plane micro services (UPMS) and control plane micro services (CPMS) [7]. An attacker can target UPMS and CPMS to affect multiple radio units served by microservices.

4.3 Safety of 6G Technology

The 6G communication network will rely on artificial intelligence to achieve a fully autonomous network. Therefore, attacks on artificial intelligence systems, especially machine learning (ML) systems, will affect 6G [8]. Poisoning attacks, data injection, data manipulation, logic damage, model evasion, model inversion, model extraction and member inference attacks are common attacks against ml systems. Since users usually cannot see the data processing process, attacks on collected data and unintentional use of private data may lead to privacy problems. Blockchain technology is also the key technology of 6G system. Blockchain is applicable to decentralized resource management, spectrum sharing and service management in large-scale distributed 6G networks. Due to the public storage of data in the blockchain network, the current security mechanism based on asymmetric key encryption is vulnerable to attack by others, which increases the difficulty of privacy protection. Visible light communication (VLC) is also a technology suitable for indoor systems (such as positioning systems) and outdoor systems (such as vehicle to vehicle communication) [9]. Common attacks against VLC systems, such as eavesdropping, interference, and node leakage, will hinder the safe use of VLC.

5 Artificial Intelligence Provides Security and Privacy Protection in 6G

(1) Data information is poisoned. In this case, error prone tag information is embedded in the application of relevant information, or misleading machine learning algorithms appear for the corresponding modification targets and supporting objects; (2) Make changes to the distributed process of calculation for information about local upload or operation weight; (3) There is pattern poisoning, which is mainly caused by the malicious model replacing the deployed pattern. Among the three different types of threats, the data is poisoned, which is a primary challenge. Therefore, it is necessary to develop a supporting anti-virus application.

5.1 Safety Issues Before Using Artificial Intelligence to Identify/Optimize 6G

Among the application networks supporting SDNNFY, the multi-layer threat monitoring and prevention methods of deep reinforcement machine learning technology and corresponding neural networks can be adopted. Like some traditional schemes, they can also effectively resist IP attacks, as well as the attacks of flow table overload, DDoS and control plane saturation. In addition, the whole processing process of ML mode applied with the supply of server address has shorter duration and higher accuracy. Therefore, the corresponding test DDoS attacks in the SDN environment have been confirmed. By cooperating with 6G network technology, it can be expected to dynamically deploy virtualization application functions as required. In this way, by adopting the adaptive security technology of ML, the overall scheme can more effectively resist the SDNNFY threat.

Due to the limitation of equipment resources, large-scale heterogeneous intelligence security and privacy protection are still components of the important role of artificial intelligence in 6G information systems. For artificial intelligence in pre_The security of the 6G system and the information application of the structure, including technical security, as well as the application of larger-scale equipment in the 6G information application to solve the problem of key management in the Internet, thus generating a large amount of data information, It is easy to make the traditional "authentication / authorization" system unable to provide more adequate security in the large-scale Internet of things. The sub network in 6G can also be regarded as the extension of the local 5G network outside the vertical area, and learning based security technology is more available in the sub network and among different sub networks. The calculation method for deploying the peripheral application ml can also better capture the activities of some subnets, so as to effectively monitor the malicious traffic information. In order to better improve the network efficiency, it is necessary to ensure the application security of different sub networks, so as to fully obtain more secure information, ensure that it can be timely injected into the ML model, confirm whether there is malicious supply, and use dynamic countermeasures [10].

5.2   Using Artificial Intelligence to Optimize the Security of 6G Architecture

Like all current artificial intelligence systems, 6G network has the same system application. For the distributed features, we mainly use the edge joint learning mode to further improve the network security in large-scale equipment and data information environment, so as to more effectively ensure the security and effectiveness of the entire communication. The 6G architecture mainly envisages the Internet intelligence technology, which is applied to artificial intelligence through different network hierarchies, and prevents service attacks on the micro unit cloud server from the lowest layer. In combination with the corresponding equipment in the current mesh network, most of the connectivity will allow the multi base station to evaluate the behavior of the equipment through the artificial intelligence classification algorithm and adopt the weighted average mode to jointly judge the authenticity. Frequent conversions often occur between microcells and multiple access technologies. Therefore, by using the behavior-based mode, the cost caused by frequent key exchange can be better reduced. By applying association learning, different levels of authorization can be realized between the sub network layer and the wide area network layer [11].

5.3   AI Enabled Network Intelligent Maintenance

The type and number of equipment supporting the construction of 6G network will increase sharply, posing a severe challenge to network operation and maintenance. At the same time, with the evolution of network intelligence, the capability of network automatic maintenance has been greatly improved. The existing personnel are still configured according to the traditional maintenance plan. The situation of excessive staffing and low maintenance efficiency is becoming increasingly prominent. A set of maintenance models that meet the needs of network technology development is urgently needed. The 6G network needs efficient and simple operation and maintenance, and ultimately achieves the zero touch operation and maintenance mode. In this process, we need to use AI capabilities to tap the potential of operation and maintenance data in the network, and ultimately minimize the operation and maintenance costs, while improving the network utility as much as possible. Adopt innovative means such as big data analysis and AI intelligent algorithm to build a multi-dimensional three-dimensional network maintenance efficiency benchmarking model based on network resources, business income, user size and geographical distribution, establish a scientific quantitative evaluation system of network maintenance efficiency, and reconstruct and enhance the network line team capacity.

6 Technical Problems and Countermeasures of 6G Network Security Based on Artificial Intelligence

Although AI is very important in 6G system, AI has its security, privacy and moral problems [12]. For example, in a driverless application scenario, an attacker uses a UAV to project a manipulated traffic light image on a road banner to mislead the driving control based on artificial intelligence in an autonomous vehicle. Artificial intelligence can be a tool for launching intelligent attacks, as shown in Fig. 3.

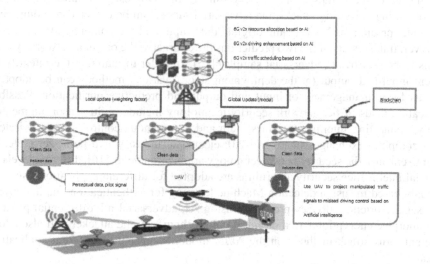

Fig. 3. Schematic diagram of AI launching intelligent attack

6.1 Privacy in Artificial Intelligence

Because the AI operating system has the ability of large-scale data mining, coupled with the processing speed of the future computer and the high intelligent requirements of the future Internet, the AI operating system is easy to disclose secrets. 6G must use billions of devices to obtain large-scale user data analysis, but users cannot understand how external information systems manage their personal data analysis. Therefore, the established smart application system relies on physical data attributes, and can also use private data analysis of large-scale users. IOT devices that submit large-scale personality data analysis to AI operating systems are also potential targets for data information theft, such as low-power sensor devices. The retrieval training data information of model reverse attack on ml can also be the source of secret violation [13]. Methods: edge joint learning was used to maintain personal data closer to users through physical control, and to ensure data information security. 4.2 foothold of artificial intelligence in 6G application.

The application of artificial intelligence technology in 6G should focus on how to use artificial intelligence to analyze channel characteristics rather than source characteristics. 5G is a function added to the original artificial intelligence. It is hoped that 6G will be the original artificial intelligence in the future. The foothold of artificial intelligence application in 6G should mainly be on channel processing rather than source processing. It is suggested that the main focus of attack should be on the lower layer of layer 1 to layer 3 and the control surface, rather than on the application layer [14]. 4.3 attack 6G with artificial intelligence.

The solution of attackers using intelligent technology of artificial intelligence is usually to adopt a more intelligent defense system, and can also use the distributed intelligence of the computer itself. According to the simplest prevention technology for computing poisoning attacks, the adversarial model can be detected by comparing the model predictions between the original data input and the compressed data input. However, if the results of the two predictions differ greatly, the original network system seems to be destroyed (adversarial sample) [15]. In order to maintain the integrity of system input and output (at the deployment stage), various methods can be adopted, such as fuzzy management of input and output and predictive purification. Possible application fields of 6G network security technology include multi-sensor augmented reality, connecting intelligent robot system and autonomous control system, wireless brain computer exchange, smart grid 2.0, electronic industry five point zero, etc. in order to enhance the security of 6G technology application fields [16], different levels of artificial intelligence security algorithms are adopted for different applications, such as anomaly based intrusion detection Machine learning for authentication and authorization, service-oriented privacy protection using AI, adversarial ml, differential privacy, homomorphic encryption based on ml, AI blockchain, etc. the attacker will also adopt different virus attack methods on the Al/ml model according to different application scenarios.

7 Summary

Artificial intelligence is the key technology in the next generation 6G mobile network, and ensuring security is the key factor to achieve the goal of 6G. 6G supporting artificial intelligence must provide intelligent and robust security solutions for system security. This paper outlines the numerous opportunities and challenges faced by intelligent security and privacy protection as part of the role of artificial intelligence in 6G systems. In addition, it also discusses the challenges of security and privacy protection based on artificial intelligence to determine the future research direction and propose feasible solutions.

References

1. Shu, J., Peng, C.: Analysis of China's network security technology landscape. Mod. Comput. (6), 68–73 (2021)

2. Sun, H.: Research on network security technology based on blockchain. Changjiang Inf. Commun. **35**(1), 167–169 (2022)
3. Swim the river application of network security technology in computer maintenance. Sci. Technol. Innov. Appl. **12**(13), 189–192 (2022)
4. Xu, S.: CTF competition based on network security technology. Radio Television Inf. (z1), 50–52 (2021)
5. Sheng, Y.: Research on computer network security technology based on network security maintenance. Wirel. Internet Technol. **18**(20), 100–101 (2021)
6. Li, Y.: Research on network security technology of computer laboratory under big data technology. Shihezi Sci. Technol. (6), 21–22 (2021)
7. Yu, Y.: Research on network security technology of computer laboratory under cloud computing technology. Electron. Manuf. (2), 95–97 (2021)
8. Huang, X.L., Cheng, S., Cao, K., et al.: A survey of deployment solutions and optimization strategies for hybrid SDN networks. IEEE Commun. Surv. Tutor. **21**(2), 1483–1507 (2019)
9. Nencioni, G., Garroppo, R.G., Gonzalez, A.J., et al.: Orchestration and control in software-defined 5Gnetworks: research challenges. Wirel. Commun. Mob. Comput. **2018**, 1–18 (2018)
10. Ziegler, V., Viswanathan, H., Flinck, H., et al.: 6Garchitecture to connect the worlds. IEEE Access **8**, 173508–173520 (2020)
11. Wang, T., Wang, S.W., Zhou, Z.H.: Machine learning for5G and beyond: From model-based to data-driven mobile wireless networks. China Commun. **16**(1), 165–175 (2019)
12. Blinowski, G.: Security of visible light communication systems—a survey. Phys. Commun. **34**, 246–260 (2019)
13. Samuel, N., Diskin, T., Wiesel, A.: Deep MIMO detection. In: 2017 IEEE 18th International Workshop on Signal Processing Advances in Wireless Communications (SPAWC), 3–6 July 2017, pp. 1–5. IEEE, Sapporo (2017)
14. Afolabi, I., Taleb, T., Samdanis, K., et al.: Network slicing and softwarization: a survey on principles, enabling technologies, and solutions. IEEE Commun. Surv. Tutor. **20**(3), 2429–2453 (2018)
15. Ma, X., Gao, J.N., Yang, F., et al.: Integrated power line and visible light communication system compatible with multi-service transmission. IET Commun. **11**(1), 104–111 (2017)
16. You, X.H., Wang, C.X., Huang, J., et al.: Towards 6G wireless communication networks: vision, enabling technologies, and new paradigm shifts. Sci. China Inf. Sci. **64**(1), 1–74 (2020)

Research on Key Technologies of Agricultural and Forestry Plant Protection UAV

XiuLian Lin, Zhenyu Xu[✉], and YeTong Wu

Huizhou Engineering Vocational College, Huizhou, China
hitusa@126.com

Abstract. With the rapid development of artificial intelligence and other technologies, intelligent agriculture has become the focus of the application and research of Internet of things technology in the field of modern agriculture. Intelligently processing the information and flight situation captured by UAVs in real time to assist flight decision-making and provide feasible solutions for unmanned, automated and intelligent management is an indispensable and important link in the construction of intelligent agriculture. Pear, citrus and longan are important fruit crops in Guangdong Province. They are vulnerable to wood lice. Among them, pear and citrus are the most severely affected. When wood lice are rampant, they can destroy the whole orchard. UAV agriculture, forestry and plant protection is one of the guarantees for the sustainable development of agricultural production in Guangdong Province, and is also a hot research direction at present. The plant protection light rotorcraft using unmanned ultra-low altitude operation has the characteristics of small chemical liquid consumption, high operation efficiency, flexible movement, good terrain adaptability, hovering and no need for fixed takeoff and landing airports. This paper introduces the energy efficiency optimization algorithm of information collection based on multi-objective and multi constraint conditions in UAV path planning for agriculture, forestry and plant protection.

Keywords: Agricultural and Forestry Plant Protection · UAV Energy Efficiency Optimization Algorithm

1 Background

Crop diseases and insect pests are an important factor affecting grain production. They have many kinds, wide range of influence, fast diffusion speed and difficult control, and have brought huge economic losses to agricultural production [1, 2]. China is one of the countries with high incidence of diseases and insect pests, and the types and coverage of diseases and insect pests are increasing year by year. All growth stages of crops may be threatened by diseases and insect pests [3]. In general, the affected seedlings are weak and shed leaves in the early stage, affecting flower bud differentiation and causing serious decline in yield and quality.

There are many technical studies on the control of wood lice in various fruit producing areas in China, but chemical control is the main one. At present, there are several methods for disease and pest control: agricultural control method, biological control method, chemical control method and physical control method [4]. Among them, although the chemical control method is inferior to the physical and biological control methods in terms of green environmental protection and has direct harm to human body, the chemical control method is still the main means for controlling pests and diseases because of its high efficiency, obvious effect and no environmental constraints [5, 6]. Generally speaking, the research on integrated pest management technology is not deep enough. Therefore, we should study various comprehensive prevention and control technologies and constantly improve the problems existing in the production process (Fig. 1).

Fig. 1. UAV plant protection

At present, the developed countries have widely adopted aerial plant protection as a chemical control method for pests and diseases [7]. The United States mainly uses manned fixed wing aircraft due to the large amount and area of plain cultivated land. The annual spray area is up to 32 million hectares, accounting for 50% of the cultivated land area, and the market share of aviation plant protection is 65% [8]; Due to the complex terrain, Japan mostly has a large degree of steepness and gentleness of the surface unit. Small UAVs are widely used in Japan, and it has a relatively complete sales and after-sales service system, with a market share as high as 60% [9]. China's terrain is relatively complex, including large concentrated fields, small scattered fields and irregular farmland [10]. For the latter, it is often difficult to achieve the expected plant protection effect when spraying with drones, and it will also cause pesticide waste and chemical pollution. Therefore, it is very necessary to vigorously develop agricultural plant protection drones in China.

The plant protection UAV started relatively late in China, and it is only in recent years that the research and application of plant protection UAV have been formally launched. As early as the late 1990s, China first introduced the plant protection UAV from Japan, but it has not been widely used. In 2005, China officially launched the research and development of plant protection UAV; In 2006, driven by the Nanjing Institute of agricultural mechanization of the Ministry of agriculture, China began to try to use drones to carry out agricultural operation pilot projects, which promoted the development of plant protection drone scientific research in China. In 2008, China's first plant protection UAV was born in Hanhe, and systematic research on the spray technology of plant protection UAV was started. Since then, the plant protection UAV industry has entered a rapid development stage in China; In 2010, China's first plant protection UAV was delivered for use. Since then, the plant protection UAV has been gradually applied to China's agricultural plant protection work. In the "12th Five Year" scientific research plan, the Ministry of science and technology and the Ministry of agriculture both regard agricultural aviation application as an important investment direction, and put forward an initiative to develop relevant technologies of plant protection UAVs. By 2020, the number of UAVs for agriculture, forestry and plant protection in China has reached 70779, with a year-on-year increase of 77.52%. Since 2017, the Ministry of agriculture and rural areas has started to implement the purchase of agricultural machinery and the guidance of plant protection drones. The annual number of agricultural and forestry plant protection drones has increased from less than 10 in 2017 to 15300 in 2020. The market size has reached 2.5 billion yuan, a year-on-year increase of 44.5%, and the annual operation volume is nearly 300 million mu.

The plant protection UAV can perform remote control operation, which avoids the danger of operators exposed to spray environment, and reduces the labor intensity compared with the backpack manual operation, and has shown significant advantages in the prevention and control of diseases and pests among crops such as rice. In addition, the UAV can also capture the crop situation in real time at all links, and carry out the whole process and all-round pest monitoring on crops such as fruit trees. After finding abnormal and rapid positioning, the UAV can deal with it immediately to avoid greater economic losses. In addition, with the development of digital transmission, remote sensing technology and video real-time transmission technology, UAV has gradually become the main monitoring measure for forest fire prevention, which has effectively made up for the defects in forest fire prevention, greatly improved the speed and accuracy of forest fire prevention information acquisition, greatly shortened the fire extinguishing time, and saved human, material and financial resources.

Although agricultural UAV as an important part of agricultural aircraft has been gradually practiced and promoted in the market, the environmental factors of farmland are complex and uncontrollable. During this period, natural factors such as temperature, humidity and unstructured farmland as well as non natural factors such as field obstacles such as power poles, trees and power grid facilities need to be considered, In the process of operation, the plant protection UAV can usually change the controllable operating parameters to reduce the limitations brought by natural factors. However, the changeable obstacle types make it more difficult for the plant protection UAV to avoid obstacles in the field. At the same time, the disadvantages of the plant protection UAV in the initial stage are also very obvious. First of all, the price of UAV is relatively high, which is about 50000–150000 yuan, which is difficult for large farmers and ordinary farmers to accept; Secondly, the endurance of UAV is not strong. Generally, a flight can only last for 10 min–15 min. When large-scale prevention and control is needed, it is necessary to carry multiple batteries or assign multiple UAV groups to complete the operation.

Therefore, how to achieve autonomous operation with low energy consumption and high efficiency is also the main research direction of the current plant protection UAV. Trajectory planning is an important part of the autonomous operation UAV system. The so-called trajectory planning is to plan the operation route with the best or suboptimal energy consumption according to certain work requirements and under various constraints. At present, most of the plant protection UAVs are based on remote control, which is too dependent on human factors, and the implementation effect is not ideal. Peng Xiaodong et al. Obtained the operation route of the UAV under visual remote control through the GPS coordinate acquisition system, and pointed out the serious deviation between the artificial real-time planned route and the theoretical route, and the high operation omission rate and repetition rate of the UAV. Ding Tuanjie et al. also pointed out that in the case of remote control, the driver's control load is large, the control time is delayed, and the data link performance is required to be high, and there are many technical difficulties. Therefore, before the UAV carries out the monitoring work, if a reasonable route can be planned according to the operating area and surrounding facilities, so that the UAV can fly autonomously along this route at a fixed altitude and speed, the requirements on the flight technology of the operator and the difficulty of variable control technology can be greatly reduced, and the effect of accurate operation can be achieved. At the same time, with the rapid development of agricultural informatization, information collection is also faced with difficulties such as redundancy and heterogeneity. For the plant protection UAV, how to achieve more efficient information collection through reasonable trajectory planning has become one of the challenges to be addressed. The author mainly studies the energy efficiency optimization algorithm of information collection based on multi-objective and multi constraint conditions.

2 Establishment of Energy Efficiency Collection Model for Information Collection

Since the performance of UAV is restricted by the battery capacity, we consider designing a multi UAV signal energy interaction network system based on the distributed energy carrying transmission information collection technology, and using the fanet network composed of UAV clusters to conduct wireless energy transmission and information collection to the ground sensor nodes. Considering the characteristics of wide distribution and large number of agricultural and forestry sensors, the UAV network is equivalent to a large-scale many to many communication scenario when conducting signal energy interaction, with high computational complexity and difficulty in solving the problem. Therefore, we first use k-means algorithm to cluster the sensor nodes, transform the large-scale network into multiple small-scale networks, and solve the signal energy interaction problem of the UAV network in a distributed manner.

K-means is a distance based clustering algorithm. The algorithm steps are:

Step 1: select k initial clustering centers.

Step 2: calculate the distance between the node and each cluster center, and divide it into the class corresponding to the nearest center.

Step3: recalculate the centroid of each class as the new cluster center.

Step 4: repeat step 2 and step 3 until a certain stop condition (number of iterations, minimum error) is reached.

The distributed UAV signal energy interaction network model after clustering is shown in the figure. The sensor network is divided into (Fig. 2):

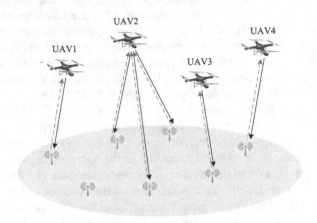

Fig. 2. UAV signal energy network system model

At present, most of the energy collection circuits are in half duplex mode, so we generally use TDMA (time division multiple access) to design the communication protocol of the UAV signal energy interaction network in the drawing, that is, the downlink energy transmission and uplink information acquisition occur in two time periods. We divide the total duration of the whole task into several time slots with small intervals, and assume that the duration of each time slot is t, and define the number of UAVs in the air UAV group as m, where the i-th UAV is marked as M_i, $1 \leq M_i \leq M$, the number of sensor nodes is n, and the j-th sensor node is marked as N_j. $1 \leq N_j \leq N$. For the UAV M_i, we define the duration allocated to energy collection as $\mu_i T$, the duration allocated to information collection as $(1 - \mu_i)T$, and $0 \leq \mu_i \leq 1$. Since the total time is fixed, if the time allocated for energy collection is too long, although the energy collected by the node can be increased to increase the transmission power and improve the total throughput, the time for UAV information collection will be compressed at the same time, thus reducing the system throughput. Therefore, there is a trade-off between the energy collection time and the information collection time, and we need to reasonably allocate the division ratio μ_i (Fig. 3).

The connection factor between the UAV M_i and the sensor node N_j is defined as λ_{ij}, $\lambda_{ij} = 1$ which means that M_i and N_j are connected, and vice versa. It is specified that a sensor node can only be connected to one UAV, but a UAV can communicate with multiple nodes through TDMA or FDMA. Therefore:

$$\sum_{i=1}^{M} \lambda_{ij} = 1 \qquad (2.1)$$

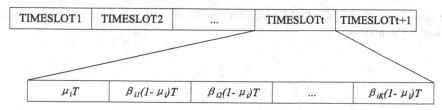

Fig. 3. Communication protocol when the sensor node adopts FDMA mode for data transmission

$$\sum_{i=1}^{M}\sum_{j=1}^{N}\lambda_{ij} = N \tag{2.2}$$

And we record the number of nodes connected to the UAV as K_i, and

$$K_i = \sum_{j=1}^{N}\lambda_{ij} \tag{2.3}$$

Therefore, in each instantaneous time slot, if the UAV and the node adopt TDMA for data collection, the information collection time of several sensor nodes connected to M_i is $\beta_{ik}(1 - \mu_i)T$, $1 \le k \le K_i$ and there are:

$$\sum_{k=1}^{K_i}\beta_{ik} = 1 \tag{2.4}$$

In each instantaneous time slot, if the UAV and the node adopt FDMA mode for data collection, the node connected to the UAV can send data to the target UAV at the same time. Therefore, the information collection time with several connected sensor nodes is $(1 - \mu_i)T$.

Since we divide the time slots into very small ones, it can be considered that the UAV position does not change in each time slot T. assuming that the coordinates of the UAV are $q_i(t) = (x_i(t), x_i(t))$ and the coordinates of the sensor nodes are $w_j = (x_j, y_j)$, the distance between them can be expressed as:

$$d_{ij} = \sqrt{H^2 + \|q_i(t) - w_j\|^2} \tag{2.5}$$

where H is the flight height of UAV, assuming the transmission power of UAV M_i is P_i, the energy collected by the node N_j in the downlink phase can be expressed as:

$$E_{ij} = \lambda_{ij}\mu_i TP_i h_{ij} d_{ij}^{-\alpha} \tag{2.6}$$

where, h_{ij} is the channel gain between the UAV M_i and the node N_j, and α is the large-scale fading factor.

Since the UAV M is not necessarily the target UAV of the node N, the energy actually collected by the node N is $\sum E_{ij}$. After the node collects energy, it is assumed that the node uses all the energy for uplink data transmission. When multiple sensor nodes with the same target UAV use FDMA mode for information transmission, the transmission power of the node is:

$$p_j^F = \frac{\sum_{i=1}^{M} E_{ij}}{(1 - \mu_i)T} \tag{2.7}$$

Accordingly, the transmission power of the sensor node communicating with the same UAV in TDMA mode in the time slot is:

$$p_j^T = \frac{\sum_{i=1}^{M} E_{ij}}{\beta_{ik}(1 - \mu_i)T} \tag{2.8}$$

Therefore, we can get the corresponding throughput of the sensor node in FDMA and TDMA communication modes within the unit bandwidth as follows:

$$R_j^F = \lambda_{ij}(1 - \mu_i)T \log\left(1 + \frac{p_j^F}{\sigma^2}\right) \tag{2.9}$$

$$R_j^F = \lambda_{ij}(1 - \mu_i)T \log\left(1 + \frac{p_j^F}{\sigma^2}\right) \tag{2.10}$$

From the above expression, we can analyze that in FDMA mode, although the information transmission time shared by each node is increased compared with TDMA mode, the corresponding transmission power is reduced; In TDMA mode, although the time of information transmission is shortened, the transmission power is also improved. Therefore, we need to pay attention to the comparison between the two schemes.

The energy consumption of UAV is divided into flight energy consumption and communication energy consumption. The expression of flight energy consumption power with respect to flight speed V is:

$$P(V) = P_{blade}\left(1 + \frac{3V^2}{U_{tip}^2}\right) + P_{induced}\left(\sqrt{1 + \frac{V^4}{4v_0^4}} - \frac{V^2}{4v_0^2}\right)^{1/2} + \frac{1}{2}d\rho sAV^3 \tag{2.11}$$

where, P_{blade} is the blade profile power in hovering state, U_{tip} is the blade tip speed, $P_{induced}$ is the induced power in hovering state, v_0 is the average rotor induced speed in forward state, d represents the fuselage drag factor, ρ is the air density, $s\rho$ is the rotor real size, A and is the rotor disc area.

In a time slot T, the total flight energy consumption of M UAVs is:

$$E_{pro} = MTP(V) \tag{2.12}$$

In a time slot T, the communication energy consumption of M UAVs is:

$$E_{com} = \sum_{i=1}^{M} \mu_i TP_i \tag{2.13}$$

Increasing the transmission power of the UAV can make the sensor nodes collect more energy to improve the system throughput, but it also faces the cost of increased energy consumption. Therefore, we take energy efficiency as the objective function of the optimization problem, aiming to consider how much bit information gain can be brought by energy consumption per joule. When several sensor nodes connected to the same UAV use FDMA for uplink information transmission, our research problem is expressed as:

$$\max_{\mu_i, \lambda_{ij}, q_i(t), P_i} \frac{\sum_{j=1}^{N} R_j^F}{E_{pro} + E_{com}}$$

$$s.\,t.\ C1: R_j^F \geq R,\ 1 \leq j \leq N$$

$$C2: 0 \leq \mu_i \leq 1,\ 1 \leq i \leq M \tag{2.14}$$

$$C3: \lambda_{ij} = 0 \vec{\boxtimes} 1,\ 1 \leq j \leq N,\ 1 \leq i \leq M$$

$$C4: \left\| q_i(t) - q_j(t) \right\|^2 \geq D,\ 1 \leq i \leq M$$

$$C5: 0 \leq P_i \leq P_{peak},\ 1 \leq i \leq M$$

We plan to obtain the optimal time allocation ratio when maximizing energy efficiency, solve the tradeoff between energy collection time and information collection time, the connection factor between UAV and sensor nodes, determine which sensor nodes each UAV is responsible for at this moment, and the position of each UAV at this moment, so as to determine the optimal motion trajectory of UAV and the transmission power of each UAV, and solve the tradeoff between transmission power and throughput. R in the constraint condition C1 represents the lowest expected throughput of each node and ensures that each node can transmit a certain amount of data. C2 and C3 are mentioned above, so they are not repeated here. D in C4 refers to the safe distance between two UAVs. By defining the safe distance, we can avoid the collision of UAV motion trajectory at a certain time. C5 refers to the maximum transmission power of UAV antenna, and C5 gives the power limit of UAV.

The optimization problem when a node sends data through TDMA corresponds to:

$$\max_{\mu_i, \lambda_{ij}, \beta_{ik}, q_i(t), P_i} \frac{\sum_{j=1}^{N} R_j^T}{E_{pro} + E_{com}}$$

$$s.\,t.\ C1: R_j^T \geq R,\ 1 \leq j \leq N$$

$$C2: 0 \leq \mu_i \leq 1,\ 1 \leq i \leq M$$

$$C3: \lambda_{ij} = 0 \vec{\boxtimes} 1,\ 1 \leq j \leq N,\ 1 \leq i \leq M \tag{2.15}$$

$$C4: 0 \leq \beta_{ik} \leq 1,\ 1 \leq i \leq M,\ 1 \leq k \leq K_i$$

$$C5: \sum_{k=1}^{K_i} \beta_{ik} = 1$$

$$C6: \left\| q_i(t) - q_j(t) \right\|^2 \geq D,\ 1 \leq i \leq M$$

$$C7: 0 \leq P_i \leq P_{peak},\ 1 \leq i \leq M$$

Compared with the FDMA mode, the TDMA mode adds optimization variables β_{ik}, that is, in addition to optimizing the uplink and downlink time ratio, the uplink data transmission time is planned to be allocated to each sensor node connected to the UAV at the moment.

3 Conclusion

The energy efficiency optimization problem of multiple UAVs is very complex, which contains shaping variables, non convex objective functions and constraints, and it is difficult to solve, so it is necessary to design efficient algorithms with low complexity to solve them. First, for energy efficiency optimization, the idea of fractional planning can be used. For multivariable optimization problems, we can use the method of alternating optimization to "fix" some variables first, convert the problem into a single variable optimization problem, and finally reach the approximate global optimal solution through continuous iteration. In this process, special attention should be paid to the selection of initial values of variables, especially the position coordinates of UAV. In order to better solve the problem, we can use the Hungarian matching algorithm in graph theory to give the initial values of the position coordinates of UAV. In addition, for non convex optimization problems that need to be solved, such as the optimization of UAV coordinates, SCA (continuous convex approximation) technology can be used to take the Taylor expansion form of the original problem as a new optimization target, and then CVX related tools can be used to obtain approximate solutions. When optimizing the connection factor, because its value can only be 0 or 1, it needs to be solved by integer programming.

References

1. Ding, G., Wu, Q., Zhang, L., Lin, Y., Tsiftsis, T.A., Yao, Y.D.: An amateur drone surveillance system based on the cognitive internet of things. IEEE Commun. Mag. 56(1), 29–35 (2018)
2. Motlagh, N.H., Taleb, T., Arouk, O.: Low-altitude unmanned aerial vehiclesbased internet of things services: comprehensive survey and future perspectives. IEEE Internet Things J. 3(6), 899–922 (2016)
3. Yong, Z., Rui, Z.: Energy-efficient uav communication with trajectory optimization. IEEE Trans. Wirel. Commun. 16(99), 3747–3760 (2016)
4. Wu, Q., Zeng, Y., Zhang, R.: Joint trajectory and communication design for multiuav enabled wireless networks. IEEE Trans. Wirel. Commun. 17(3), 2109–2121 (2018)
5. Franco, C.D., Buttazzo, G. 'Energy-aware coverage path planning of uavs'. In: 2015 IEEE International Conference on Autonomous Robot Systems and Competitions, pp. 111–117 (2015)
6. Wang, H., Ding, G., Gao, F., Chen, J., Wang, J., Wang, L.: Power control in uavsupported ultra dense networks: communications, caching, and energy transfer. IEEE Commun. Mag. 56(6), 28–34 (2018)
7. Lyu, J., Yong, Z., Rui, Z.: Cyclical multiple access in uav-aided communications: a throughput-delay tradeoff. IEEE Wirel. Commun. Lett. 5(6), 600–603 (2016)
8. Zhang, C., Zhang, W.: Spectrum sharing for drone networks. IEEE J. Sel. Areas Commun. 35(1), 136–144 (2017)
9. Zhan, P., Yu, K., Swindlehurst, A.L.: Wireless relay communications using ann unmanned aerial vehicle'. In: 2006 IEEE 7th Workshop on Signal Processing Advances in Wireless Communications, pp. 1–5. IEEE (2006)
10. Orfanus, D., Freitas, E.P.D., Eliassen, F.: Self-organization as a supporting paradigm for military uav relay networks. IEEE Commun. Lett. 20(4), 804–807 (2016)

The Development Demand and Application Prospect of Intellectualization in the Logistics Industry for 6G Technology

Liudan Zhu⬤, Zhiguo Li, Kaipeng Deng, Yinteng Huang, and Naifeng Liang(✉) ⬤

City College of Huizhou, Huizhou 516025, China
17043692@qq.com

Abstract. The modern logistics industry is one of the most inextricably linked to communication technology. The extensive integration of the logistics sector with communication technology has accelerated the growth of intellectualization. The advantages of 6G technology, such as bigger information capacity, higher transmission rate, more equipment connections, faster transmission speed, etc., play a significant role in improving logistics and intellectualization. This thesis mainly analyzes the integrated application of 6G technology in the logistics industry and looks ahead to the logistics information system, intelligent warehousing, smart transportation and distribution, smart handling, smart tracking and tracing, and the construction of intelligent supply chain system based on 6G technology.

Keywords: 6G technology · Logistics Industry · Intellectualization · Application

1 Introduction

6G refers to the sixth-generation mobile communication technology. Six Chinese ministries, including the Ministry of Science and Technology, held a kick-off meeting for 6G technology research and development in November 2019, announcing the formation of the National 6G Technology R&D Promotion Group and Overall Expert Group, signaling the official start of China's 6G development. With the ultimate performance of sub-millisecond air interface transmission delay, integrated mobile communication technology services with comprehensive capabilities such as connectivity, computing, and artificial intelligence, 6G technology will build out an integrated green and low-carbon network from the sky to the land of inherent intelligence and security.

Intelligent Logistics is the comprehensive utilization of cloud computing, big data, artificial intelligence, intelligent logistics equipment, and other technologies based on the extensive application of modern communication technology and IoT. Through comprehensive perception, information integration, and big data processing, a real-time, effective, and environmentally friendly logistics operation system organically combines and optimizes logistics resources, services, information, and specifications. It can effectively boost an organization's ability to compete while providing customers with timely,

A. Li et al. (Eds.): 6GN 2022, LNICST 505, pp. 333–341, 2023.
https://doi.org/10.1007/978-3-031-36014-5_28

accurate, quick, and easy services. Intelligent logistics is directly related to the growth of emerging technologies such as mobile Internet, cloud computing, big data, and IoT. The primary goal of intelligent logistics is to achieve complete command and control over the entire process, as well as each node of logistics operations and management, such as raw material procurement, warehousing, loading and unloading, transportation, and distribution, through the use of modern information technology, intelligent equipment, and other related technical means. As a result, it improves the logistics system's capability of intelligent analysis, decision-making, and automatic operation execution, thereby improving logistics management and operation efficiency. Logistics operations and management links are also improved in terms of information, sophistication, dynamism, and systematicity. Intelligent logistics captures a large amount of online production business data from the real world, constantly improving the research quality of data collection. By combining logistics with technologies such as IoT, cloud computing, and big data, it is now possible to create an intelligent warehouse capable of managing goods and products thoroughly while also highlighting the issues that have arisen as logistics has grown, thereby providing a more comprehensive practice-led procedure for the logistics sector, resulting in ongoing increases in production efficiency.

2   Intellectualization of the Logistics Industry in China

After years of development, China's logistics sector has transformed, shifting from a traditional mode of development based heavily on manual, decentralized, and inefficient labor to a modern one based on digitalization, intelligence, systematization, and efficiency. Big data and mobile internet connections are at the core of modern information technology, which has become the driving force behind new developments in the logistics sector. With the deep integration of modern communication, IoT, big data, cloud computing, and other technologies, the current logistics sector will enter a new era of intelligence. The intelligent development of the logistics industry has a more solid foundation and greater imagination as a result of the ongoing development, maturity, and enhancement of 6G technology from ideal to reality.

The logistics industry has grown to play a significant role in the country's economic system, as evidenced by the fact that in 2021, China's total social logistics amounted to 335.2 trillion yuan, an increase of 9.2% year over year, and the total annual revenue of the logistics industry was 11.9 trillion yuan. Among them is the development of intelligent logistics. As shown in Fig. 1, the size of China's smart logistics market is expected to grow significantly over the five-year period from 2017 to 2021 at an average annual rate of 18.5%.The size of China's smart logistics market exceeded 640 billion yuan in 2021, maintaining a growth rate of more than 10%, despite the COVID-19 pandemic and other negative issues. The future market for intelligent logistics is massive and exciting.

Intelligent logistics can efficiently address several issues in China's commodity circulation and international trade, including a low level of informatization, high cost of circulation, and clumsy logistics procedures. The majority of the inefficiency issues with traditional logistics can be resolved based on the examination of the fundamental theory of intelligent logistics application. China is currently actively promoting the development of intelligent logistics, using new information technology as the fundamental platform.

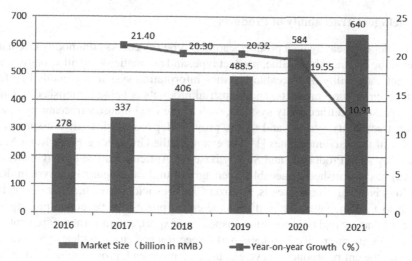

Fig. 1. China's Intelligent Logistics Market Size and Growth Rate, 2016–2021

The country is working to realize the operation of information technology for logistics procurement, transportation, warehousing, distribution, and other logistics operations and management links, as well as the information sharing and efficient operation of the entire supply chain from upstream suppliers to midstream manufacturers. The following aspects are currently the main emphasis of China's growth in the field of intelligent logistics.

2.1 Automation of Warehouse Operation Management

An automated warehousing system includes logistics management software, automatic stackers, an automatic conveyor system, and an automatic three-dimensional racking system. Through automatic information exchange, the entire autonomous operation of products, including entrance, stocking, storage, and delivery, can be realized. Recently, several domestic companies, including JD Logistics and SF Express, have developed automated, unmanned warehouses. The automated warehousing system based on modern communication and IoT technology offers the following advantages in logistics management: First, the intelligent identification accuracy of the automated warehousing system is significantly improved, reducing the time and error rate of goods identification and increasing the effectiveness of entering and leaving items in the warehouse. Second, coordination and synergy between the operation subsystems in the warehouse are stronger, and information is transferred between the operation linkages faster and more accurately. Third, the automated warehousing system may continuously check the stock for products that are about to expire in order to avoid defective inventory and raise management standards. The computer may implement online control of the equipment to handle the products swiftly and precisely according to the first-in-first-out principle, allowing the automated warehousing system to make full use of the storage space.

2.2 Intelligent Traceability of Products

Logistics depend heavily on a product's ability to be traced. As commodity circulation broadens, the origin, safety, value, product type, and authenticity are all strongly linked to product traceability. A traceable logistics information system for goods like food, medicine, agricultural products, and industrial products is being established in China. These sophisticated traceability systems, such as the food industry traceability system, the drug traceability system, and so on, provide dependable logistical assurance for the safety of food and medicines [1]. For example, the Guangdong-Hong Kong-Macao Greater Bay Area Production and Supply Base for Agricultural Products (Guangdong-Huizhou) has established a traceable green agricultural safety guarantee system. RFID technology is used to control seeds, fertilizers, and pesticides from the start of vegetable planting to field management, and then the entire process of vegetable picking, processing, packaging and transportation, inspection, export, and the other aforementioned processes. Furthermore, it expedites export inspection and customs clearance while also replicating the entire production cycle at the consumer end, providing quick and accurate certification of vegetable source, safety, and production process. IoT, which is based on modern communication technology, RFID technology, and databases, can improve the efficiency of automatic identification, inspection, and supervision of vegetables. The product traceability system currently plays a significant role in item tracking, identifying, enquiring, estimating, and so on. in the pharmaceutical business, agricultural sector, and manufacturing industry [2]. Intelligent product traceability is crucial for bettering the real-time information exchange between people and things, enhancing the dynamic management of the logistics process, and efficiently gaining access to cargo data.

2.3 Visualization in the Logistics Process

Using modern communication technology, RFID, barcode, sensor, satellite positioning, video, and other technologies, the logistics process can automatically gather data and information to achieve a comprehensive perception of logistics and provide a database for intelligent logistics management. An intelligent logistics information network connects various logistics information systems to determine all events that occur throughout the logistics process, including the target's identity (who/which), location (where), time (when), state (what), and action (how). This enables visualization of the entire logistics process as well as the resolution of logistic tracking, tracing, and monitoring issues. Vehicle placement, monitoring, online scheduling, distribution, and visual management are all made possible by logistics technologies such as satellite navigation, RFID, sensors, and others [3]. There is not an intelligent visual network now, although certain fundamental uses are more widespread. Some logistics companies, for instance, have installed a GPS-based intelligent logistics management system, while others have real-time vehicle positioning and cold chain temperature monitoring for seafood. These companies first recognized the importance of transparency and visual management of logistics operations [4]. Comprehensive logistics visualization is the best example of complete and deep integration of logistics management and modern information technology, which will further improve the level of logistics management and actually achieve effective tracking and control of the logistical process.

2.4 Intellectualization of Logistics Distribution Center

Because of the rapid development of new business forms and e-commerce models, logistics distribution centers must handle a higher volume of more dispersed customer orders every day, and multi-variety and low-volume have become the logistics norm. The traditional manual-based distribution center operations have found it challenging to meet the New Retail's logistics and distribution requirements. The development of a fully automated logistics distribution center, intelligent logistics operations control, an automated operation network, and other systems based on modern communication technology, intelligent sensing technology, RFID, mobile computing, and other technologies can successfully achieve comprehensive commercial flow, product flow, information flow, and fund flow. The efficiency of distribution is significantly increased by coordinated management.

Some cutting-edge automated logistics distribution centers, for example, use robots for loading and stacking, automatic guided vehicles (AGV) for material handling, automated transport sorting lines for picking operations, auto-mated stackers to complete inbound and outbound operations automatically, seamlessly integrated logistics center information and ERP systems, and full automation of the entire logistics distribution center and all aspects of manufacturing, which also forms elementary IoT applications [5]. Intelligent logistics facilities and equipment based on modern information technology have laid a solid foundation for increasing logistics effectiveness. Intelligent sorting systems that automatically transfer goods and packages to the appropriate operation links based on parcel numbers are another example. This improves transfer speed, lowers the cost of manual operations, and increases efficiency, which adapts to the evolving trend of new commercial forms. Electronic label-assisted picking systems can also reduce manual recognition errors and increase picking efficiency significantly.

2.5 Intelligent Supply Chain

The term "supply chain" refers to a comprehensive logistics system that connects the entire logistics process, beginning with raw material procurement and ending with product manufacturing, storage and transportation, sales, and waste recycling. Modern businesses have developed sophisticated supply chain systems as a result of the ongoing advancement of current information technology. It primarily employs information and communications technology, sensor technology, RFID, barcode technology, video surveillance technology, wireless network transmission technology, IoT, and other modern information technologies to construct a comprehensive set of systems, including a procurement demand system, bill of material (BOM) system, distribution management system, warehouse management system, and the ability to trace the entire production process [6]. Moreover, the intelligent supply chain can establish a data exchange platform, logistics information sharing platform, financial management settlement system, and decision support analysis system to support the informatization of logistics enterprises and the overall supply chain.

Despite the rapid development of intelligence in China's logistics industry, many small and medium-sized businesses with fragmented business models lack adequate infrastructure for logistics equipment and information technology due to a lack of laws and technical standards in related industries. There are also some issues with the intelligent growth of the logistics sector, specifically low levels of application adoption for logistics information technology; insufficient intelligence in the logistics supply chain; and low levels of intelligence in logistics information tracking, logistics warehousing management, transportation, distribution, and logistics handling equipment. As information and communications technology and intelligent equipment technology advance, the logistics sector will usher in a new era of rapid intellectualization.

3   Characteristics of 6G and Advantages in Logistics Application

Among other things, 6G has significant characteristics such as higher data rate, higher capacity, shorter latency, more device connections, higher spectrum and energy efficiency, and support for higher mobile speed applications. It has potential application benefits in the development of the logistics industry.

3.1   Fast Transmission Speed and Strong Network Ubiquity

In terms of network access, 6G will include a variety of network access methods, including mobile cellular, satellite communication, unmanned aerial vehicle (UAV) communication, hydroacoustic communication, visible light communications, and others. In comparison to 4G and 5G, 6G has higher network speed requirements. Currently, 5G base stations have a maximum bandwidth of more than 20 Gb/s, whereas 6G will use "spatial multiplexing technology," which means its base stations will be able to access hundreds or even thousands of wireless connections at the same time, and its capacity will be up to 1000 times that of 5G base stations to ensure that every device accessing the base station can enjoy a faster network speed. The 6G network successfully combines the 5G network with the deep-ocean network, satellite communication network, and other networks. The satellite communication network, which spans a variety of disciplines such as civil communication, navigation, remote sensing, and telemetry, enables global integration of air, sea, and earth. The goal of 6G is to achieve true global coverage by integrating an "air-sea-earth" network that spans regions, airspace, and marine areas, thus adapting to more complex application scenarios. The development of intelligent logistics can better guarantee the information transmission of logistics equipment and facilities under a variety of circumstances thanks to the significant improvement in network ubiquitous capability enabled by 6G technology.

For instance, 6G technology can be used to track and monitor logistical data and facilities in a variety of situations, such as when a ship is sailing across the ocean, a train is speeding down a mountainous railroad, an airplane is flying overhead, and so on.

3.2   Lower Power Consumption and Shorter Transmission Latency

Greater connection density, higher transmission bandwidth, lower end-to-end delay, higher reliability and certainty, and more intelligent network characteristics are essential for the rapid promotion and long-term development of mobile communication networks and vertical industry convergence applications, according to the network performance requirements of industrial applications. The current 5G network speed is adequate, but 6G has the potential to be ten times or even a hundred times faster than 5G, and network latency can be reduced from milliseconds to sub-milliseconds or even microseconds, significantly improving communication performance. With 6G, network performance will improve significantly in terms of transmission rate, end-to-end delay, reliability, connection density, spectrum efficiency, and network energy efficiency, allowing it to meet the diverse network requirements of various vertical industries. Consider smart factories as an example. 6G can lower latency to sub-second (1ms) or even microsecond (us) levels, which can gradually replace wired transmission between factory machines and realize the wireless and resilience of manufacturing at a higher level. Logistics automation and unmanned vehicles have relatively high standards and requirements for network communication rates. According to current technical calculations, 6G will eventually achieve a minimum latency of 0.1ms or less, allowing for rapid response and establishing the technical framework for human and autonomous distribution in the logistics sector in the future [7].

3.3 Large Terminal Accesses and High Transmission Security

The adoption of mobile terminals will be supported even further by 6G after multiple iterations of mobile communication technology. The enhanced connectivity of mobile terminals and equipment facilities via a 6G network in the fields of intelligent warehousing, transportation, and distribution would contribute to the development of the intelligence of the logistics industry. With the aid of 6G technology, every logistics node can be tracked and identified, and every application network system can be connected to the logistics system in accordance with actual needs, greatly boosting the efficiency and standard of logistical services [8]. IOE in 6G era demands higher network security standards. In terms of network security management and protection, 6G will shift from traditional external security to embedded security [9]. 6G will further evolve the network security model in the direction of endogenous, autonomous, and collaborative in response to new services, new technologies, and changes to meet the security needs of complex services and flexible networks through the two-way development of network architecture and protocols. If 5G is thought of as patch-type security, 6G is endogenous security.

4 Prospect of Intelligent Application of Logistics Industry Based on 6G Technology

With the advent of new technologies like Internet+, IoT, cloud computing, big data, artificial intelligence, and blockchain, the modern logistics sector has entered an era of information-driven, technology-driven, and intelligent-driven logistics. The upgrading of the manufacturing sector and the transformation of commercial formats have jointly supported the intelligent development of the logistics industry to a new stage as China's e-commerce and New Retail continue to sustain rapid growth. It has become a societal consensus to reduce labor costs and replace workers with machines. All of these factors have aided the advancement of logistics mechanization, automation, and intelligence, as well as the rapid rise in demand for intelligent logistics equipment. 6G has paved the way for communication technology to advance to higher levels of intellectualization in the logistics industry.

4.1 Logistics Technology Towards Digitalization and IoT

Smart logistics, which serves as a vital link between manufacturing and consumption, supply and procurement, is the foundation of today's social production and circulation system. Industry 4.0 is the most effective way to improve the efficiency of modern logistics and reduce logistical costs. It is based on intelligent logistics that utilize modern communication technologies and IoT. The integration and growth of the logistics equipment sector and intelligent manufacturing systems will be aided further by the development of 6G technology, and the logistics field will rapidly move toward digitalization and IoT. The ongoing development of 6G technology allows for the effective and intelligent collection and transmission of logistics data. Furthermore, the advancement of IoT and 6G technology will encourage the interconnection of logistics facilities and equipment, enable remote equipment monitoring and maintenance, and improve intelligent transmission, all of which will increase intelligence utilization and operation and maintenance efficiency. IoT enabled by 6G will soon play a significant role in effective supply chain management by providing the connections and data required for smart supply chains, such as smart production, smart storage management, and smart distribution and transportation. Future logistical technological advancements will primarily focus on digital and IoT technologies that can improve the automation, operational effectiveness, and accuracy of intelligent supply chain management.

4.2 Logistics Equipment Towards Standardization and Intelligence

The basis and key step toward achieving intellectualization is standardization. Equipment and facilities for logistics are digitalized and standardized for production in accordance with the requirements of logistics application scenarios and the logistics operation mode. To achieve the overall function of intelligent logistics, the essence of which is to actualize the virtualization of hardware resources and programmable management control, the objective is to command, dispatch, and manage virtual hardware using software based on contemporary communication technology. Logistics equipment is the hardware basis for the realization of intelligent logistics. Intelligent logistics equipment integrates sound, light, electricity, machinery, electronics, control, and information technologies, including acquisition systems, storage systems, transmitting and sorting systems, machine vision recognition systems, human-machine collaboration in many technical fields and hardware fields, such as interactive systems, information management systems, etc. Under the 6G technology, new technologies like intelligent technology, robotics, wireless communication technology, big data cloud platform, humanoid simulation technology, sensing technology, and micro-control technology are continuously developing and making strides. These technologies are gradually being applied to warehousing, transportation, distribution, etc.

4.3 Logistics Operations and Management Towards Unmanned Operations

As automation control technology advances, there are fewer and fewer situations in intelligent logistics that require operator intervention, and it is becoming clear that cross-border integration of intelligent logistics equipment is on the rise. New technologies like intelligent technology, robotics, wireless communication technology, big data cloud platform, humanoid simulation technology, sensing technology, and micro-control technology are constantly developing and making strides under 6G technology. These technologies are gradually finding their way into warehousing, transportation, and distribution. Picking, distribution, and other logistics links provide a strong technological guarantee for the manufacturing industry to achieve automation, digitalization, and intelligence. The future warehouse distribution center and distribution center will be entirely unmanned because of advances in automatic loading and unloading technology, automatic multi-piece separation technology, automatic bagging technology, six-sided high-speed item information automatic identification technology, supercapacitor technology, and other technologies.

5 Conclusion

The logistics sector is a vital artery for the national economy, serving as a fundamental, strategic, and leading industry to support national economic development. A high-level, high-quality domestic and international "dual circulation" will be built on the basis of 6G technology by encouraging the development of an intelligent logistics information system, intelligent logistics supply chain, intelligent logistics traceability system, intelligent warehousing center, and intelligent transportation and distribution system.

References

1. Sundmaeker, H., Guillemin, P., Friess, P., Woelffle, S.: Vision and Challenges for Realising the Internet of Things. Publications Office of the European Union, Luxembourg (2010)
2. Tajima, M.: Strategic value of RFID in supply chain management. J. Purch. Supply Manag. 13(4), 261–273 (2007)
3. Baoyun, W.: Review on internet of things. J. Electron. Meas. Inst. 23(12), 1–7 (2009)
4. Asif, Z., Mandviwalla, M.: Integrating the supply chain with RFID: a technical and business analysis. Commun. Assoc. Inf. Syst. 15(24), 393–426 (2005)
5. Aldin, N., Stahre, F.: Electronic commerce, marketing channels and logistics platforms-a wholesaler perspective. Eur. J. Oper. Res. 14(2), 270–279 (2013)
6. Schuster, E.W., Allen, S.J., Brock, D.L.: Global RFID: The Value of the EPC Global Network for Supply Chain Management. Springer, New York (2007). https://doi.org/10.1007/978-3-540-35655-4
7. Luan, N., Xiong, K., Zhang, Y., et al.: 6G: typical applications, key technologies and challenges. Chin. J. Internet Things 6(1), 29–42 (2022)
8. Wang, Q.: Intelligent transformation of logistics industry based on 5G technology. J. Commer. Econ. 8, 136–139 (2020)
9. Liu, S., Huang, R., Wang, Y.: Overview of global 6G research and development. Des. Tech. Posts Telecommun. (3), 16–20 (2021)

Challenges and Reflections on Vocational Education in 6G Era

Yinteng Huang, Yanjie Zhao, Liudan Zhu, Bingshuang Han, and Zhiguo Li[✉]

Ctiy College of Huizhou, Huizhou 516025, China
lizhiguo@tm.hzc.edu.cn

Abstract. Based on 5G, 6G expands from serving people, people and things to supporting efficient connections among intelligent agents, shifting from IOE to all things intelligent, and contributing to the creation of a bright vision of intelligent IOE and digital twin. This thesis discusses the trends of education metaverse development, considers the challenges and reflections on vocational education in the future, and reviews the drift of vocational education development in 6G era in accordance with the current situation of 6G development and Chinese vocational education. It also makes recommendations for improving top-level design and strategic planning in the hope of providing a support system for establishing high-quality 6G vocational education, thereby cultivating healthy development of modern vocational education and its practice in the 6G era.

Keywords: 6G · Vocational Education · Metaverse · Education Metaverse

1 Introduction

Since the rapid commercialization of 5G in 2019, the research and development on 6G have gradually been put on the agenda. Some of these 6G technologies, stored for years by then, are accelerating 5G commercialization, which has an enormous impact on development worldwide [1]. Applications of 5G have empowered all trades and professions, like medical health [2], internet of things [3], education [4], and more. Yet, 5G is unable to meet these growing demands, so it is imperative to develop 6G to match them [5, 6]. The wireless network was put into use in the 1980s, forming the first generation of wireless communication. Thereafter, each generation of mobile communication technology is trying to solve the existing problems in the industrial development of that moment, meanwhile pushing itself to a new height [7]. 1G communication technology is monopolized, resulting in poor user experience and high cost. 2G brings high-quality secure mobile voice communications and messages. 3G combines wireless communication, internet, and multimedia communication, and though not very successfully, it lays the foundation for the rapid prosperity of 4G mobile internet. 4G enables IoT applications via wireless networks, and 5G network hopes to open the gate for the Internet of Everything (IOE). Based on 5G from serving people, people and things, 6G communication technology expands to support the highly efficient interconnection of intelligent agents,

A. Li et al. (Eds.): 6GN 2022, LNICST 505, pp. 342–353, 2023.
https://doi.org/10.1007/978-3-031-36014-5_29

making a giant leap from IOE to Intelligent IOE, eventually, helping human society to implement a better vision: Intelligent IOE and Digital Twin [8]. A report from GSMA says China has built the world's largest 5G network. In January 2022, China's State Council rolled out a plan to facilitate development of the digital economy in the 14th Five-Year Plan period (2021–2025). According to the document, China will strengthen its support of 6G research and development, like prospectively storing technologies and propelling 6G network building.

To adapt to the new situation, promote higher quality development of vocational education, expect to further improvement of labor quality and technical skills, and promote employment and entrepreneurship, China revised and adopted the Vocational Education Law in April 2022 [9]. With the promulgation and implementation of this law, vocational education will surely gain scale and systematic development and highlight its status. Also, the General Office of the CPC Central Committee and the General Office of the State Council unveiled Modernization of Chinese education 2035 and the government plan to accelerate the Modernization of Chinese Education 2018–2022 [10, 11], which put forward "to promote services in the whole process of teaching and education with information means, to accelerate innovation and development of smart education, and to construct "Internet + Education" service platform. On the way from 5G to 6G, the constant technology creation is of necessity to bring education upgrades and reform, and permeate all taches of vocational education, all of which derive a better vision of the education metaverse. Overall, higher vocational education will meet challenges and opportunities in 6G era.

2   6G

2.1   An Overview of 6G

The 6th generation of mobile communication, or 6G, is a theoretical wireless network mobile communication technology with the capability to transmit data at a microsecond level over the air (OTA) [12]. Additionally, it combines artificial intelligence, mobile communication technologies, and the ability to connect and calculate. Technically, 6G makes it possible for the physical and digital worlds to interact. In the future, people may be able to use a mobile device to access the digital world and manage the real environment, or perhaps create digital twin.

2.2   Vision of 6G

As depicted in Fig. 1, 1G wireless communication technology enables voice communication, 2G adds message functionality, 3G ushers in the mobile internet era, 4G fosters a thriving internet economy, 5G nurtures the golden age of information communication with big data and artificial intelligence, but 6G may bring about a global revolution. Mobile communication has so far reached 6% of the world's population. In comparison to 5G's characteristics of high data rate, high capacity, and low latency, 6G has the capabilities of super-speed rate, super-capacity, and zero latency. 6G is approximately 50–100 times faster than 5G in terms of speed. While 6G can hit the microsecond level of latency, 5G is at the millisecond level. Using spatial multiplexing technology, a 6G base station may connect hundreds to thousands of wireless devices at once, 1000 times more than a 5G base station. With the addition of satellite base stations, the 6G network can reach everyone, eliminating the blind zone and providing complete worldwide coverage. By doing so, it can bridge the gap between the real and virtual worlds and transcend their respective boundaries. In addition to offering a wealth of connections and services for industrial upgrading, social governance, and smart living, 6G can offer strong support for connecting virtual space with the perception of people, things, and conditions. It can also pave the way for a world with extensive coverage and intelligent IOE. Future 6G technology will be immersive, intelligent, and all-encompassing, supporting 8 primary categories of corporate applications. They are sensory connectivity, intelligence interaction, communication perception, inclusive intelligence, immersive cloud XR, holographic communication, digital twin, and comprehensive coverage. Intelligent business applications, such as communication perception, inclusive intelligence, and digital twin, can assist the 6G communication system to perform better, contribute to the digitalization of the real world, and ultimately entice people to enter the digital twin's virtualized environment [8].

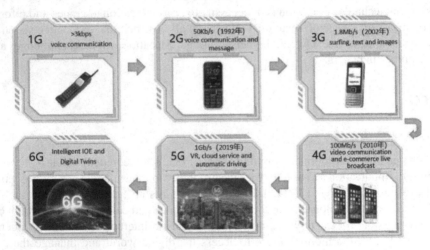

Fig. 1. Communication technology and its applications

2.3 The Current Development of 6G at Home and Abroad

Since the first global 6G wireless summit took place in Finland in March 2019 [13], key nations and regions have released a number of white papers, including roadmaps and plans for R&D. Despite being in the early stages, significant progress has been made, including the development of TeraCom [14], block-chain [15], and Intelligent Reflecting Surfaces (IRSs) for 6G [16]. Table 1 shows that certain institutes' ideas for 6G also call for greater technological standards for 6G conversely. Strategic planning for 6G research and development is currently in full swing. 25 businesses and academic research organizations joined together to officially begin the research project Hexa-X under the auspices of the 6G Smart Networks and Services Industry Association(6G-IA). It has completed the 6G industry-university-research framework and presented a clearer path map. In order to advance the worldwide unified 6G standard and industrial ecology, 6G-IA and China IMT-2030(6G) have endorsed a 6G collaboration agreement to carry out significant cooperation in 6G vision, essential technologies, standard research, and experimental verification [17]. Korea was the first to implement the "government guidance + enterprise leading" collaborative development strategy, which is intended to spur 6G innovation and development. Additionally, it is declared that they will "lead 6G business application" and competes to be the first to implement 6G worldwide business application in 2028. Finland published a white paper on 6G-Drivers and Main Research Challenges for 6G Ubiquitous Wireless Intelligence, in which they carefully projected future developments in 6G visions and technical applications [18]. In order to increase the competitiveness of the communication sector globally and to finish basic technical research by 2025, the Ministry of Internal Affairs and Communications of Japan has released a 6G Holistic Strategy and set research goals for key technologies. The US government places a high priority on 6G research and collaborates with its allies to examine 6G standards and technology. The 6G Road Map was released in February 2022 by the alliance Next G to outline the long-term goals, technological direction, and growth path for 6G. They emphasize that the government should promote 6G research through legislation, funding, and the creation of research initiatives [19]. China's State Council unveiled a strategy in January 2022 to promote the growth of the digital economy during the 14th Five-Year Plan period (2021–2025). The agreement states that China will increase its support for 6G research and development, improve the storage of 6G technology, and take part in the promotion of 6G international standardization [20]. In an effort to achieve this, China established two offices, the 6G general Expert Group 6G and the Technology R&D Promotion Working Group (IMT-2030 (6G)). These offices work to advance fundamental theories, key technologies, and 6G standards.

Table 1. 6G visions from main white papers

Time	Publishing Agencies	Name of White Paper	Visions
2019.9	Oulu University 6G Flagship	Key drivers and research challenges for 6G ubiquitous wireless intelligence	Ubiquitous wireless intelligence
2020.3	CCID	White paper on 6G and visions	Depth intelligent IOE
2020.8	Purple Mountain Laboratories	6G wireless network: vision, Enabling technologies, and new application paradigm	Full coverage, full spectrum, all-service and more secure

(continued)

Table 1. (*continued*)

Time	Publishing Agencies	Name of White Paper	Visions
2020.12	DT mobile	Overall Coverage and Intelligent scene: White paper on 6G vision and technology development	To build close-link cyberspace between human society and physical world
2021.5	6GANA	From cloud AI to network AI	AI inference benefit human beings and things
2021.6	IMT-2030(6G) Promotion Group	White paper on 6G vision and candidate technologies	Intelligent connection of everything, digital twin
2021.8	Huawei Technologies CO., LTD	6G: The next horizon	From IOE to intelligent IOE

3 Current Situation of Vocational Education Informatization

As more input has been poured in, the construction and development of vocational education information have entered a new and quick growth period. Although vocational colleges have carried out a great amount of exploration and practice and achieved notable results, yet, there are still some problems in the field of informatization construction due to the influences of subjective and objective factors.

3.1 Imperfections of Teaching Management Informatization

Education management informatization refers to the use of information technology in the teaching process with the goal of providing students with an authentic learning environment. The majority of vocational colleges' teaching management is still mostly in the traditional mode, the construction of informatization is still in the early stages, and the teaching management informatization is still insufficient and lagging behind. These flaws are listed below. First, there is a lack of unified coordination in practice. Furthermore, the development and application of network resources has not matured; for example, it is still impossible to share or use information resources, and vocational colleges are untrained in internet use. Last but not least, the level of construction and management of informatization must be cultivated and improved. Because of traditional and backward teaching management, teachers rely on the traditional management mode to solve existing issues. However, it is urged that education concepts, teaching methodologies, and teaching management be renewed and iterated upon. In this situation, the government requires vocational colleges across the country to establish digital campuses by upgrading campus networks, multimedia classrooms, and digital simulation training systems, establishing uniform and standard data centers, and improving the state of information technology. As a result, it contributes to the high-quality informatization development of vocational education.

3.2 Inadequacy of Sharing and Using Information Resources

As is well known, sharing and using information resources between network platforms and network devices, such as a computer, smart screen, mobile phone, and so on, is a critical component of informatization. The extent to which information is shared has a significant impact on education informatization and even teaching quality. However, at the moment, the overall level of information sharing in vocational education is low. Initially, most vocational colleges are in the early stages of development, with no fully formed mechanisms for information sharing and application. Due to a lack of channels, information communication is insufficient or cannot be connected. As a result, information sharing is inefficient and ineffective. Furthermore, there are several limitations to using information technology in some vocational colleges. Some teachers are not paying enough attention to modern teaching, and their teaching methods are inadequate to meet the demands of the new era. Some students lack motivation to study or learning abilities. In teaching or learning, neither the teacher's nor the students' primary roles are played. All of the aforementioned factors impede the advancement of vocational education informatization.

3.3 Shortage in Creating Information Teaching Applications

Vocational education, with its high technical content, aims to cultivate highly qualified talent with professional skills. However, students are usually in a passive study mode because they lack learning autonomy, and few teachers can create a positive classroom environment. The information means teachers adopt may not be able to meet the information resource demand in teacher-student and student-student communication in class. Aside from the epidemic's impact, online courses are widely used in most colleges and have become the norm in teaching. There are numerous issues that arise when using online courses in vocational education. For one thing, most teachers' traditional single-way teaching mode has now been added to unshareable information resources, which has an unfavorable effect on teacher-student communication, causing students to take a passive role in class. Even if students communicate via the network, they may not achieve the desired effect due to device, site, or other factors. All of the aforementioned factors contribute to students' lack of enthusiasm for learning, active exploration, and creation. In this case, using the "Internet+" teaching mode is critical in order to increase students' learning autonomy. If 5G or 6G can support virtual simulation systems, creating more virtual career scenes, particularly in the fields of high technology and sophistication, or high consumables, it can greatly cultivate students' interest and improve teaching efficiency, thereby improving the quality of professional talent training.

Many vocational colleges are now converting their 14th Five Year Plan informatization project to digital teaching. Many innovative 5G applications are being developed for vocational education informatization. However, the existing network service and qualified education resources do not have the desired effect on both educators and students. Some educational resources, such as HD video classrooms, video teaching, and virtual reality classrooms, continue to be of lower quality. It is much more expensive to build, operate, and maintain than previous mobile communication systems. Despite significant progress, it is still not possible to achieve zero-delay interaction and data feedback. The aforementioned pain points and difficulties are hoped to be addressed in "6G+ education" in the future.

4 6G Communication Technology and Education Metaverse

4.1 6G Communication Technology and Metaverse

Since its inception, the community has been deeply concerned about the metaverse. However, different people have different ideas about what the metaverse is. The metaverse, according to Chen G, is a virtual world linked and created through science and technology, mapped and interacted with the real world, and has a digital living space of a novel social system [21]. According to Ning HS, the general cyberspace (metaverse) is a unified description of traditional cyberspace and cyber-enabled physical, social, and thinking spaces formed by ubiquitous connections between things and deep convergence of spaces [22]. Wang and his colleagues proposed a widely accepted idea that the metaverse is essentially a combination of physical space, social space, cyberspace, and thinking space, by combining network, software, hardware, and users into a virtual reality system, and that virtuality is mapping but independent of the real world [23]. To put it another way, it can transport virtual space from the human imagination into physical space in the metaverse. At the moment, the metaverse is primarily focused on the field of immersive cultural tourism, which is referred to as the cultural tourism metaverse. It usually appears to be some kind of consumer application, such as a digital game or digital culture with high interaction and strong sensory experiences, as a fusion of multidisciplinary productions. Unfortunately, 5G is not capable of completely satisfying the metaverse consumers' experience on these applications. 6G can help metaverse development by providing high-bandwidth, low-latency data access, and is also known as the metaverse's spring. Wu hequan, a member of the Chinese Academy of Engineering, stated at a conference that the business mode in the metaverse is still in the minority and does not currently bring significant changes to social media, AR, or VR. The metaverse is not a rigid demand for 6G; rather, 6G is.

4.2 Education Metaverse

The education metaverse, a metaverse application direction, assists in the creation of digital identities for teachers, students, and education administrators, as well as the construction of teaching scenes in virtual spaces. In these scenes, teaching activities and interaction can take place in order to solve existing problems in vocational education. According to Fig. 2, the education metaverse is a virtual reality fusion education environment built by emerging information technologies such as 5G+, 6G, VR, AR, MR, digital twin, AI, blockchain, and so on. It connects virtuality and reality, combines the digital and physical worlds, and is also an advanced and intelligent educational environment that promotes learning and social interaction. In terms of satisfying human living and production needs with current technologies, the digital world is still far ahead of the physical world. It is widely agreed that a new world should be created that connects the physical and virtual worlds, allowing people to pursue more immersive and factual experiences. The global continuous COVID-19 outbreaks are driving the internet to develop

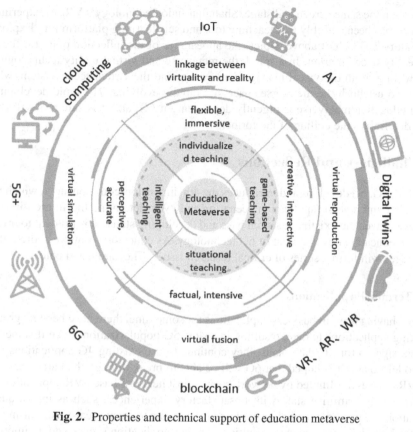

Fig. 2. Properties and technical support of education metaverse

the digital world in depth and to build a new parallel universe from the physical world, which opens up a large space for the exploitation of 5G+/6G communication foundation and terminal products. In vocational education, metaverse-based courses can not only endow teaching with realistic, visible, and participatory features, inspire students' study interest, but also improve existing experience in intelligent class and significantly reduce the cost of experiments and outing investigation. Furthermore, the course's immersive experience has the potential to help break the high marginal cost of vocational education, alleviate the scarcity of educational resources, and create new development space for vocational education and the learning service industry.

The United States established the world's first online virtual high school. The hospital of Seoul National University attempted real-time surgery sharing via VR/AR, symbolizing the education metaverse's first foray into medical education. During the "Challenge Cup" China University Student Entrepreneurship Plan Competition, Beijing Institute of Technology released a large-scale immersive digital interaction space. It is the first time that super-large-scale online activities have been hosted through digital space, the first time that an achievement library about college students' innovation and entrepreneurship has been presented, and the first time that digital humans have competed with college students on the same screen and stage. Shanghai Judo Technology's VR/3D experimental series has been a highly free teaching tool and self-learning platform for "Exploring Laboratory." The chart above depicts the appearance of the inflection point for the virtual reality C-end market. In a spiral, the metaverse and virtual reality technology are intertwining. Both the visual management system and the virtual scene system, which help to co-establish the metaverse space, are rapidly evolving. The rapid development of the education metaverse is urgently dependent on 6G, and it is safe to say that the latter determines the ceiling of the former.

5 Challenges and Reflections

Based on 5G, 6G develops and introduces the 4th dimension-consciousness, which may bring rich and diverse application scenarios and even determine the future direction. However, given the existing research base and developing status, it is prudent to investigate the education development of 6G technology. As educators, how we address these challenges will form a series of critical research issues. They are listed below.

5.1 Terminal Applications

Despite having been in business applications for some time, there have been no groundbreaking applications to date, resulting in a slow 5G popularization. Even if some consumers sign up for 5G data plans, they continue to use existing 4G applications. This is also left to 6G; it is hoped that 6G will be able to break through the barrier. Because AR/VR devices are limited by network speed, most network-based VR applications are in a relatively primitive state with unsatisfactory experiences, such as image quality resolution. 6G provides a much faster transmission rate to ensure real-time transmission of ultra-high-definition images, resulting in richer application scenes and an improved consumer experience. Users in the future metaverse or large-scale virtual social systems, such as Ready Player One, will be able to connect to the virtual world at any time and from any location. With increased data rate, capacity, and short latency, the network can not only meet the real-time demand of the virtual world, guarantee HD image, but also make immersive learning in vocational education possible in the 6G era, which was not possible in the 5G era.

5.2 Multi-directions and Endurance Capacity

6G technology is still in the conceptualization and vision stages. Meanwhile, some preliminary alternate education experiments, such as the education metaverse, are being conducted, but no repeatable experimental conclusion has been reached. However, the multidimensionality resulting from the multilateral-coordination condition, knowledge-sharing system, and students' high-level thinking and cognitive ability may be overlooked. Furthermore, when 6G technology is used in a mobile device, the power dissipation will undoubtedly increase. The current 5G technology has caused a number of facilities to have limited endurance. If there is no revolutionary breakthrough in lithium battery technology, it will be extremely difficult to achieve lower power consumption and solve heat dissipation.

5.3 System Construction

The development of 6G and the demands for education modernization in China necessitate the establishment and improvement of a set of intellectual property protection systems, as well as a new education service supervision system. As a result, original content's intellectual property rights can be protected, the reward of knowledge payment can be guaranteed, and content distribution and promotion can be clearer and more effective. Only in this environment can the mode of content co-creation flourish. It can also significantly increase educators' interest and confidence in creating education metaverse content. In this case, the original content resources in vocational education can be greatly expanded. However, constructing a set of significant systems for sharing digital education resources and benefit distribution is a significant challenge.

5.4 Inadequacy of Education Research in 6G

According to current research, academic circles are focusing the majority of their efforts on the field of 6G key technologies and development directions. However, studies on how the 6G educational revolution affects teachers, students, and education administrators are scarce. Furthermore, the education management department has yet to develop long-term strategical top-level design and planning; all of these issues must be resolved and detailed into practical measures. Teachers must not only understand traditional information literacy, data literacy, network literacy, media literacy, and meta-literacy, but also master how to endow these with content. So, before heavily promoting 6G in vocational education, educators must be trained to improve the aforementioned literacies, acceptance analysis capabilities, and technology application abilities.

5.5 Ethical Issues in 6G Era

Based on 5G, 6G is endowed with "consciousness," the ability to efficiently connect "People-Things-Scenes," analyze learners' conditions with AI, and formulate individualized services for learners. Nonetheless, when we enjoy the convenience of technology, we are also taking significant risks. For example, whether the educator can respect students' growth laws; whether information disclosure in collected data, such as physiological data-face recognition and brain wave detection; and whether the collected data may misjudge learners. There is also the question of whether learners will become addicted to the 6G immersive education metaverse, and how to address this issue. As a result, when 6G is implemented in vocational education in the future, technical ethics must be taken into account.

6 Conclusion

It is undoubted that 6G will have a significant impact on vocational education, but not always directly. In many circumstances, it acts as a mediator or moderator. As a result, the 6G effect on vocational education cannot be treated as a technical factor alone, but must be considered in the context of integrating social change. When 6G progresses toward multidimensional development, the negative consequences must be considered. According to 6G visions and the metaverse trend, the education metaverse and immersive learning method would be one of the main directions of vocational education. The intersection of 6G and a specific subject would be another mode leading vocational education. It is possible that the education metaverse training location contributes to the cultivation of targeted individualized education. In the 6G era, vocational education is undoubtedly a new presentation that is highly integrated with communication technology; therefore, vocational colleges must thoroughly examine the trend of vocational education, emphasize top-level design and strategic planning, provide support foundation and support system, and continuously improve the quality of personnel cultivation in vocational education.

China's Education Modernization 2035 policy emphasizes the importance of general planning and regional promotion on the path to education modernization. However, more emphasis should be placed on specifying objects, building incrementally, implementing precise policy, and promoting coordination. More specific and experimental studies on exploring 6G to solve difficult issues in education are expected to be conducted in the future, and more activeness and creativity will be infused into vocational education, ushering in a new chapter of education reform in the 6G era.

Acknowledgment. Partially Funded by Educational Science Research Project of Guangdong province (2021GXJK576), and Partially Funded by Ideological Education Project of Guangdong province (2020GXSZ177), Partially Funded by Scientific Research on Education in Vocational Colleges of Huizhou (2022hzzjkt05).

References

1. Liu, S., Huang, R., Wang, Y.: Overview of global 6G research and development. Design. Tech. Posts Telecommun. **3**, 16–20 (2021)
2. Li, S., Sun, N.: Analysis and research on 5G medical and health technology user adoption behavior and influencing factors. In: ICEMME, Chongqing, China, pp. 226–230 (2020)
3. Chettri, L., Bera, R.: A comprehensive survey on internet of things (IoT) toward 5G wireless systems. IEEE Internet Things J. **7**(1), 16–32 (2020)
4. Yang, D., Sui, B.: "5G+XR" supported practical teaching reform: modes, challenges and suggestions. Vocat. Tech. Educ. **42**(17), 43–47 (2021)
5. Strinati, E.C., Barbarossa, S., Gonzalez-Jimenez, J.L., et al.: 6G: the next frontier: from holographic messaging to artificial intelligence using subterahertz and visible light communication. IEEE Veh. Technol. Mag. **14**(3), 42–58 (2019)
6. Elmeadawy, S., Shubair, R.M.: 6G wireless communications: future technologies and research challenges. In: 2019 International Conference on Electrical and Computing Technologies and Applications, ICECTA, pp. 2–7. Ras Al Khaimah, United Arab Emerites (2019)
7. Liu, G., Wang, Y., Wang, A.: 6G latest progress and future development. Radio Commun. Technol. **47**(6), 668–678 (2021)
8. Liu, G., Jin, J., Wang, Q., et al.: Vision and requirements of 6G: digital twin and ubiquitous intelligence. China Internet **44**(6), 3–9 (2020)
9. Jin, X., Shi, W.: Renewal of the social status of vocational education—an interppretation of the genral provisions section of the revised vocational education law of the People's Republic of China. High. Vocat. Educ. Explor. **21**(3), 1–6 (2022)

10. P.R. China, The State Council: China's Education Modernization 2035 Plan. (in Chinese). http://www.gov.cn/xinwen/2019-02/23/content_5367987.htm. Accessed 15 Sept 2022
11. P.R. China, The State Council: Implementation plan for accelerating the modernization of education (2018–2022). http://www.gov.cn/zhengce/2019-02/23/content_5367988.htm. Accessed 15 Sept 2022
12. Yu, L.: 6G may not be far away from us. East China Sci. Technol. **9**, 10–11 (2022)
13. P.R. Finland, White Paper on 6G Drivers and the UN SDGs. https://www.6gflagship.com/white-paper-on-6g-drivers-and-the-un-sdgs/. Accessed 20 Aug 2022
14. Boulogeorgos, A.A.A., Jornet, J.M., Alexiou, A.: Directional terahertz communication systems for 6G: fact check: a quantitative look. IEEE Veh. Technol. Mag. **16**(4), 68–77 (2021)
15. Gupta, R., Nair, A., Kumar, N.: Blockchain-assisted secure UAV communication in 6G environment: architecture, opportunities, and challenges. IET Commun. **15**(10), 1352–1367 (2021)
16. Sejan, M.A.S., Rahman, M.H., Shin, B.S., et al.: Machine learning for intelligent-reflecting-surface-based wireless communication towards 6G: a review. Sensors **22**(14), 1–21 (2022)
17. P.R. China, IMT-2030 (6G) Promotion Group: IMT-2030 (6G) Promotion Group and 6G-IA Signed 6G Cooperation Memorandum to Jointly Promote 6G Innovative Development and Global Unified Ecology. https://www.imt2030.org.cn/html/default/zhongwen/xinwendongtai/1532538678008631297.html?index=4&language=zh. Accessed 12 July 2022
18. Gao, F., Li, M.: White paper released by the University of Oulu, Finland preliminary 6G vision and challenges. Scitech China **12**, 94–97 (2019)
19. Lin, Z., You, Y., Wei, W.: Research and trend analysis on the global development and competition state of 6G. J. Inf. Secur. Res. **8**(11), 1135–1140 (2022)
20. P.R. China, The State Council: Development of the Digital Economy in the 14th Five-Year Plan Period (2021–2025). http://www.gov.cn/zhengce/zhengceku/2022-01/12/content_5667817.htm. Accessed 15 Sept 2022
21. Tu, Y., Zhang, L.: Understanding the metaverse: culture, society and the future of mankind. Explor. Free Views **4**, 65–94 (2022)
22. Ning, H.S., Ye, X.Z., Bouras, M.A., Wei, D.W., Daneshmand, M.: General cyberspace: cyberspace and cyber-enabled spaces. IEEE Internet Things J. **5**(3), 1843–1856 (2018)
23. Wang, W., Zhou, F., Wan, Y., et al.: A survey of metaverse technology. Chin. J. Eng. **44**(4), 744–756 (2022)

Author Index

Printed in the United States
by Baker & Taylor Publisher Services